GOING OFF THE
BEATEN PATH

GOING OFF THE BEATEN PATH:

An Untraditional Travel Guide to the U.S.

Mary Dymond Davis

The Noble Press, Inc.

CHICAGO

Publisher's Note: The author and the publisher have attempted to provide current and accurate information, but they cannot be held responsible for any changes or discrepancies. We suggest that you contact the organizations listed here to verify the information.

Printed in the United States of America

Library of Congress Cataloging-in-Publication Data

Davis, Mary D.
    Going off the beaten path : an untraditional travel guide to the U.S. / Mary Dymond Davis.
        p. cm.
    Includes indexes.
    ISBN 1-879360-01-2 : $15.95
    1. Human ecology–United States–Directories. 2. Environmental protection–United States–Directories. 3. Appropriate technology–United States–Directories.
    4. United States–Description and travel–1981–-Guide-books. I. Title.
    GF503.D39 1991
    363.7'00973–dc20   90–63428
                                                                            CIP

10 9 8 7 6 5 4 3 2

Previously published as *From Walden Pond to Muir Woods: Alternative Ways Across America*, ASPI Publications, 1990.

Noble Press books are available in bulk at discount prices. Single copies are available prepaid direct from the publisher:

Marketing Director
The Noble Press, Inc.
213 W. Institute Place, Suite 508
Chicago, IL 60610

To my mother

Contents

Appendix

Index

Foreword

A lot of people talk about getting in better touch with the earth and its landscapes, but Mary Davis has actually done something about it. In this wonderfully original book she gives traveling a new point: to see and understand how human beings inhabit the land. She tells us how we can find the California wind farms where thousands of wind machines of fanciful, varied designs carry out their stately danse with the air. She tells us how to find and hike over Storm King Mountain on the Hudson, focal point of a titanic environmental legal clash. Her book overflows with the information we need to plan and enjoy new and more meaningful kinds of trips—whether in our own regions or in distant reaches of the country.

But the book is far more than an environmentalist's sightseeing guide; it also tells you how to find people and organizations who are working hard to make modern life more genuinely pleasureful—through new and fun ways of being ecologically responsible, through new modes of conviviality, through new technologies, and through new ways of organizing work and community. Networking through electronic conferences or just by phone and mail can be wonderful; but there's also the even more important level of learning by experience and sharing. So Mary Davis leads you to places where you can find out about sustainable, organic agriculture or the latest in cogeneration technology, not to mention reforestation, wilderness survival skills, or the art of tracking. These are exciting trips, even if you take them only in the process of reading.

The addresses are often remote, whether rural or urban; you won't find these folks next to the McDonald's at a highway interchange. They're tucked away out there in the real world, trying to bring some sense and sensitivity to it. Some of them are accessible only by mail or phone. Others encourage visits, and looking for them will often take you into new territories—where the beginnings of enlightenment are traditionally found. Mary Davis has assembled here a generous, far-reaching collection of ingenious people carrying on important, mostly delightfully small-scale enterprises—the salt of the earth, the hope of the planet.

And she has provided guidance to a rich assortment of unusual places. Some will soothe the spirit or astonish the senses; others will inspire last-ditch defense by all who love them. All are part of the web of new meanings that Mary Davis casts across our continent. If you tend to read newspapers and get depressed about humankind, the book should prove a good antidote; it's local news about survival, about the new world slowly rising from the compost-pile of industrialism, about the seeds of the future germinating in our beloved but troubled country.

ERNEST CALLENBACH
SAN FRANCISCO

Preface

From Walden Pond to Muir Woods: Alternative Ways Across America [the title under which *Going Off The Beaten Path* was first published] treats the environmental movement as an unfolding process. It tells much about the history of the movement, provides information on current activities of environmentalists, and, through putting people in touch with one another, will, we hope, help to strengthen efforts to create a sustainable society. As the word "Ways" in our title suggests, we designed the book to serve both as a guide for travelers and as a reference tool for concerned citizens to use where they live.

Our conception of a sustainable society is that of ecologists, in the general rather than the scientific sense of the word. It includes peace, social justice, cultural diversity, self-sufficient local communities, and a harmonious relationship between humans and the ecosystem of which we are a part. We concentrate here on the last of these elements, both to give the guide focus and to reflect our belief that unless we preserve the environment our other efforts will be in vain. *From Walden Pond to Muir Woods* describes projects that point the way to an America that uses natural resources without depleting them, maintains the diversity of species, and enjoys the benefits of pure food, clean air, clean water, and wilderness.

In addition to explicit environmental concerns, we treat a few topics not generally addressed by environmental groups but essential to environmental preservation in the long term: an alternative economic system, an alternative defense system, and the creative arts, which help to keep alive our imaginations and our sympathies with nature. Other social issues enter indirectly through descriptions of associations with broad interests and through references to the nonviolent movement, which has influenced environmentalists. Two areas that we would like to have covered but that we felt needed a more thorough treatment than we could afford are environmental education for young people and health care. These are treated only indirectly.

The guide opens with a chapter of tribute to past environmentalists and ecologists. It then presents concrete examples of ways in which people can meet their basic needs while making only a minimal impact on the natural world. In the third part we describe a variety of natural areas, as we outline the roles that government agencies and private organizations play or should play in protecting them. Part IV introduces readers to programs and projects through which they can learn about and become involved in caring for the environment; and describe, and tell how to meet members of, three contemporary movements putting into action fresh approaches to preserving the planet.

Turning to the lighter side of outdoor activities, the fifth part describes opportunities for participating in sports that are kind to the environment. Moving Around, Part VI gives suggestions on transportation, organic food, restaurants, lodgings, and other centers where environmentalists can meet one another, and means of finding environmental jobs. The book closes with supplementary resources, including a generous sampling of national and local environmental organizations not previously treated.

For each subject to which we devote a chapter or section we present a sampling of places to visit and tell readers how to locate other such places. The guide only introduces each topic. Given the size of the United States and the broad subject coverage, attempting a comprehensive treatment would have been folly. By contacting staff at the places listed and by using the resources in the descriptive sections and in the final chapter, readers can create their own networks.

The places we describe are good examples of the topics they represent, but not necessarily the best possible examples. Evaluating all businesses, associations, and institutions working for a sustainable society is beyond our capabilities.

Any selection of a few places from the entire United States will omit favorite spots of individual readers. Reasons for omissions include the following: we did not know about the site; the staff did not respond to our query; the staff was not equipped to handle visitors and requested to be left out; for reasons of space we had to make an arbitrary choice among numerous appropriate places. If we failed to include a site that you believe we should have mentioned, or included a place that you believe should not have been listed, write to the author in care of The Noble Press. We shall not be able to answer correspondence, but we shall consider all suggestions carefully in future editions.

Within subject categories we have included a variety of types of projects. We believe that simple living is a key to environmental preservation, and we have indicated so in the text; but we have deliberately avoided making every entry conform to narrow guidelines. Some of the entries, in fact, present points of view that are incompatible with one another. For example, we emphasize vegetarian restaurants, but include some farms where animals are raised for meat. The Earth needs all its defenders. By presenting many facets of the environmental and ecology movements, we hope to further cooperation among them. If a sustainable society is to be realized, it will be created by people of many different backgrounds, working in many places, in diverse ways, but supporting one another.

The admission prices stated are the cost for a single adult. Most places have special rates for groups and children. As to days of opening, we do not include exceptions to the regular pattern for national holidays. The prices of books and periodicals are those charged to individuals. (For periodicals they refer to a one year subscription.) The cost to institutions and businesses may be much higher.

To avoid repetition we have generally omitted the word "nonprofit" from descriptions of sites and projects. Most work directed toward an alternative America is nonprofit. Since the guide is intended for a broad audience, we have used few technical terms. Two that appear are "riparian": along river banks, and "endemic": limited to a specific locality.

As a general rule, we have listed the sites under each heading in geographical order. We start in the Northeast, move south through the East, north through the central states, and south again in the West.

With few exceptions we describe each site or organization only once, however varied its program. We have used cross references to link sections of the guide. We list each item in the general index under the subjects to which it pertains. To find all references to a given subject, even one that is the title of a chapter section, use the general index. Use the geographic index to locate sites in a particular state.

Before visiting an individual or association, phone or write to arrange a mutually agreeable time. Many of the places listed have specified that they cannot welcome unexpected visitors. All sites should be contacted ahead of time to verify location and hours. We have made every effort to ensure the accuracy of the information in this guide, but typographical errors can occur and organizations do change.

PREFACE TO THE SECOND EDITION

Since I began to write the first edition of this book, numerous introductions to the environmental and ecological movements in the United States have been published, but, to the best of my knowledge, no other environmental travel guide to the country as a whole has appeared. Therefore to continue to fill a gap, I have increased the number of sites to visit and given less information of a general nature than I did previously. Since the people likely to use the book on their travels are also likely to want to learn more about the environmental movement, I have, however, retained the concluding resource section, though in somewhat shortened form.

I carried on much of the revision of the book during the 1991 Gulf War. As I was struck by the fact that during the past year many new ecological initiatives had arisen and many old projects had been strengthened, I realized that the Americans who were finding their entertainment in the media's reports of the war were missing what is truly exciting about the United States today. Preparing for and waging war against other countries is unfortunately standard procedure. What is new is that we are now developing ways of meeting human needs, including maintaining social relationships, without engaging in activities that destroy the environment. The people who are discovering and putting into effect creative alternatives, and the wildlife and the lands that they are restoring are the real story. Positive change is afoot. This guide is designed to help readers to see it.

Acknowledgments

This book is the product of the willingness of hundreds of individuals and organizations to provide information on their own activities and on related projects. Among those to whom I owe a special debt for their numerous suggestions are Lois Arkin, David Albert, Ernest Callenbach, Paul Gallimore, David Haenke, Greg Kahoe, Susan Meeker-Lowry, Matthew Miles, T. Montgomery, Brian Tokar, and David N. Zurick.

John Davis and George Rector played key roles in putting together the first edition of the book. John Davis advised on the contents, particularly for the chapter on natural areas, and edited the entire text of the original version of the manuscript. George Rector conducted a major portion of the research on agriculture, energy, intentional communities, and arts and crafts, and drafted the sections of the text on Thomas Jefferson, historic farms, seed saving, and earthworks. For the revised edition, John Davis served informally as a consultant.

To all of these people and organizations I am deeply grateful. The guide would not have been possible without their help.

PART I

Places for Remembering

CHAPTER ONE

Places Associated with Noted Environmentalists

Though the people named below represent a variety of careers, all helped lay a foundation for or contributed to what are now the environmental and ecology movements. I present them at the beginning of the guide to honor them as representatives of the many who have helped preserve the natural world and to illustrate ways that individuals can work for the Earth. The emphasis is on the most basic method, living simply, without wasting natural resources.

The individuals are described in terms of places where they lived, traveled, or worked. Seeing these places can increase our understanding of the relationship between the environmentalists and their surroundings. Many of the sites are natural areas that remain much as they were when the people we celebrate were alive. Outdoor places that are not subjected to harmful human activities remain fresh, while the artifacts that were associated with a life crumble and fade.

The chapter is not a roster of the most important environmentalists, although many of the people cited would unquestionably belong on such a list. Numerous other men and women of importance to the environmental and ecology movements are referred to later in the book.

MONTICELLO (Charlottesville, VA)
THOMAS JEFFERSON (1743–1826)

Jefferson's correspondence and journals describe in detail native plants and animals, the weather, and agricultural experiments. Through them we learn that the natural world was a constant source of pleasure, renewal, and wonder to a man facing overwhelming public responsibilities.

Jefferson felt closest to nature at Monticello, his Virginia estate. Construction of the house and grounds, both of which he himself designed, began in 1770 and continued through his years as governor of Virginia and president of the United States. A working farm, Monticello reflected Jefferson's belief that an ideal society would be an agrarian democracy made up of small landholders.

In Jefferson's time, the grounds contained both ornamental and vegetable gardens, two orchards, a vineyard, and an 18-acre ornamental forest. The vegetable garden, measuring 1,000 feet by 80 feet, was Jefferson's pride and joy. With over 250 varieties of vegetables and herbs, it showed his strong interest in horticultural experiments. Because of his many tests of new or unusual plant varieties and his many observations and notes, Monticello served in an unofficial sense as one of the country's earliest agricultural experiment stations. The gardens also provided food for Jefferson, his family, and his many guests. For his personal diet, Jefferson chose to avoid meat and rely on his harvest.

He was sensitive to what he perceived as abuses to the land, and warned other farmers about the harmful effect that crops like tobacco had on the soil. To assure a sustainable agriculture, he cautioned against the loss of topsoil and recommended that the soil's fertility be maintained by returning plant and animal wastes to cultivated fields. He reasoned that the land needed protection and, sometimes, restoration.

Five years after Jefferson's death, Monticello was sold outside the family. It passed through numerous hands until, occupying a much smaller site than in Jefferson's time, it was purchased in 1923 by the Jefferson Memorial Foundation, which restored it. Monticello may now be visited daily, 9:00 A.M.-4:30 P.M. Admission is $7. For further information, contact the Public Affairs Department, Monticello, Box 316, Charlottesville, Virginia 22902 (804-295-8181).

The Thomas Jefferson Center for Historic Plants documents, collects, and distributes heirloom plants. Varieties grown by Jefferson form the nucleus of the collection. The plant shop, located in the Monticello Shuttle Station, is open to the public from April through October. The plant nursery at Jefferson's Tufton Farm, two miles east of Monticello, is open to interested groups by appointment. Contact the Thomas Jefferson Center for Historic Plants, Monticello, P.O. Box 316, Charlottesville, Virginia 22902 (804-979-5283).

WALDEN POND (Concord, MA)
HENRY DAVID THOREAU (1817–1862)

Thoreau moved into a ten-by-fifteen-foot cabin he had built on Walden Pond south of Concord, Massachusetts, 4 July 1845. Though he lived there for only two years, two months, and two days, his account *Walden: or, Life in the Woods* (1984) has exerted and continues to exert an enormous influence on philosophers and preservationists.

An environmentalist reading Thoreau today is struck by the extent to which his concerns parallel ours. He advocated and exemplified simple living: his average weekly expenditure at Walden Pond was 27 cents, a trifle even in the nineteenth century. As far as possible he made, raised, or bartered for what he needed. Nothing was to be wasted: the boards for his cabin came from a shack he bought from an Irish laborer. The natural world was a source of refreshment, delight, and instruction to Thoreau, and he spent hours watching, listening to, and learning from his surroundings at the pond. He admired Indians for their closeness to the earth and for the simplicity of their lives. He traveled to Maine and to Cape Cod and once even as far as Minnesota, and he wrote about his journeys; but he turned down opportunities for trips to Europe. It was better to know one's immediate neighborhood as thoroughly as possible than to rush across the globe.

Underlying his stay in the woods and his views was a belief in being an individual. He was convinced that the actions of one person matter. While living at Walden Pond, he spent a night in jail for refusing to pay a poll tax that would support slavery. For him it was more important to follow the dictates of conscience than the laws of the state.

He built his cabin on land that Ralph Waldo Emerson had bought to prevent its being logged. In 1922 Emerson's heirs gave the land to the state. The pond is now on the 330-acre Walden Pond State Reservation, just off Route 126.

At one end of the pond is a popular bathing beach. The reservation is heavily used, even in winter when cross-country skiers follow its trails. Anyone seeking solitude is advised to come in the middle of the week in the early morning or late afternoon.

A replica of Thoreau's cabin stands near an entrance to the reservation; an inscribed fieldstone marks Thoreau's actual hearthsite. (Thoreau and Emerson agreed that the cabin would not remain on the land after Thoreau left.) The plants in the reservation are similar to those of Thoreau's day, but most of the trees—White pine, Pitch pine, oak, maple, hickory, birch, etc., – are only sixty to eighty years old. The 400 pines that Thoreau planted in his bean field when he left the pond succumbed to the 1938 hurricane or to fire and only the stumps remain. The trail around the pond is 1.7 miles long. Other trails wind through the reservation and connect with the trail system of the extensive Lincoln and Concord Conservation Lands.

The reservation can be reached by a train ride to Concord from Boston's North Station and a half hour's walk. For information contact Walden Pond State Reservation, 915 Walden Street, Concord, Massachusetts 01742 (508-369-3254).

Developers have threatened to build condominiums within a half mile of the pond and an office park about 700 yards from it. The Walden Woods Project (18 Tremont Street, Suite 630, Boston, Massachusetts 02108; 617-367-3787) bought the condominium site, with the help of massive loans from the developer and banks, and is negotiating for the office site. Walden Forever Wild (P.O. Box 275, Concord, Massachusetts 01742; 203-429-2839) is working on another aspect of preservation by promoting legislation to change the reservation into Walden State Sanctuary, which would eliminate the bathing beach though not close the area to walkers. J. Parker Huber's *The Wildest Country: A Guide to Thoreau's Maine* (Appalachian Mountain Club, 1982) enables readers to follow in the path of Thoreau in Maine.

CENTRAL PARK (New York, NY)
FREDERICK LAW OLMSTED (1822–1903)

By the mid-nineteenth century the large American cities, particularly those along the Atlantic coast, were extremely crowded. Few had any public open spaces; and, with rare exceptions, the spaces that did exist were totally inadequate for the surrounding population. Olmsted was one of the first Americans to understand the need for urban parks, and he was responsible, above anyone else, for the creation of urban parks in this country. Today he is considered the father of American landscape architecture.

His first commission as a landscape architect was Central Park in New York. He and Calvert Vaux, a former pupil of Andrew Jackson Downing, who early advocated green space in cities, won a contest for a new design for the park. The design took advantage of the natural terrain: "The time will come when New York will be built up . . . and the picturesquely-varied, rocky formation of the Island will have been converted into formations for rows of monotonous straight streets, and piles of erect buildings. There will be no suggestion left of its present varied surface, with the single exception of the few acres contained in the Park. . . . It therefore seems desirable to interfere with its easy, undulating outlines, and picturesque, rocky scenery as little as possible. . . ." They sunk the four transverse roads, required by the terms of the contest, below the level of the park so that they are not seen by people in the park.

A map of Manhattan may show the park as a large open space. It is far from that. Walking in the park, one passes through a wide variety of spaces, including wooded areas. Unfortunately this feature of the 843-acre park can make it dangerous to be alone there today. The park is fifty-one blocks long, though relatively narrow. The north end, in particular, is unsafe for people not thoroughly familiar with the city.

A more pleasant aspect of the park in our time is its continuing use as a site for demonstrations. In 1982, 550,000 to 800,000 people marched from the United Nations to the park's eighteen-acre Great Lawn, in what was probably the largest peace demonstration ever in the United States. The march was in conjunction with the United Nations's second special session on disarmament. In 1988 for the third such special session approximately 60,000 people walked from the United Nations to the park.

Olmsted himself had a social conscience that was evident in his advocacy of racial justice, his serving as general secretary of the U.S. Sanitary Commission during the Civil War, and his attitude to green space. In 1865 the Governor of California appointed him to head a commission to make recommendations on the management of Yosemite, at that time in the hands of the state. His report set forth the individual's right to enjoy public scenery and the government's responsibility to protect that right. Later he assisted John Muir in his attempt to stop the flooding of Hetch Hetchey.

Central Park was so successful as a site for rest and refreshment from the urban rush that many U.S. cities imitated it, often with the help of Olmsted. Prospect Park in Brooklyn, Belle Isle Park in Detroit, Franklin Park and the Arnold Arboretum in Boston, and the park system of Louisville, Kentucky, are among his many achievements. Towards the end of his life he spent much time working on the Biltmore Estate in Asheville, North Carolina, today preserved as he designed it. The estate is open to visitors daily: 9:00 A.M.-5:00 P.M.; admission, $19.95 (704-255-1776).

POWELL PLATEAU (Grand Canyon National Park, AZ)
JOHN WESLEY POWELL (1834–1902)

The mile-deep Grand Canyon of the Colorado River, with rocks as old as two billion years, draws 3.5 million visitors a year. Most of them go to the south rim. In contrast to it, the north rim offers relative peace, a wide choice of trails, plus coolness in summer. The Forest Service is promoting heavy logging of the Kaibab Plateau in the Kaibab National Forest, an edge of which occupies most of the north rim of the canyon. The service, however, has not been able to harvest trees on the subsidiary Powell Plateau, because it belongs to the National Park Service. Powell Plateau served as temporary habitation for Anasazi Indians between 1050 and 1150 A.D., and numerous Anasazi sites have been identified there.

Powell Plateau is named after the explorer John Wesley Powell, the first white man to travel through the Grand Canyon. This trip took place in 1869. His description of the adventure, *Exploration of the Colorado River of the West and Its Tributaries* (1875), though a government document, has been widely read and admired. His next major publication, *Report on the Arid Regions of the United States, with a More Detailed Account of the Lands of Utah* (1879), set forth far-sighted principles for handling government-owned land. Powell advocated surveying and then classifying land according to type: timberland, irrigable land, mineral land, and pasture land; and opening it to settlement only according to strict rules for proper management of each type. Had his ideas been followed, land in the West would not be as overgrazed, overdeveloped, and short of water as it is now.

The northern third of Powell Plateau, which has an elevation of 7,000 feet, is covered with stands of virgin Ponderosa pine, intermixed with oak, and is reputed to be one of the few areas in the West that has been subject to neither logging nor grazing. Thus the plateau is a fitting memorial to the explorer.

SLABSIDES (Esopus, NY)
JOHN BURROUGHS (1837–1921)

In the middle decades of the twentieth century visitors streamed to the homesteads of Helen and Scott Nearing (the first near Pikes Falls, Vermont, and the second at Harborside, Maine) to learn how to live "the good life." The mecca for thousands of travelers in the late nineteenth and early twentieth centuries was Slabsides and other retreats of nature writer and philosopher John Burroughs.

Burroughs was a man with a strong and innate sense of place. Long-time friend Walt Whitman wrote of him, "He is a child of the woods, fields, hills—native to them in a rare sense (in a sense almost of miracle)." Born and raised on a farm near Roxbury, New York, in the heart of the Catskills, he made the state his base for most of his life. During a nine-year period he worked for the U.S. Treasury Department in Washington in order to support his family, but he "chafed in cities." While in Washington, he published his first nature book, *Wake-Robin* (1871), named for the White Trillium that he remembered from the Catskills.

After resigning from his Washington post, he bought land near West Park, along the Hudson River, where he built a house and planted vineyards. Near this estate, called Riverside, he constructed a rustic, bark-covered cabin—Slabsides—in 1895. He spent his last summers in an old farmhouse he restored on his family homestead near Roxbury. "You see I am a real authochthon. These hills fathered and mothered me. I am blood of their blood and bone of their bone, and why should I not go back to them in my last years?" He died on a train carrying him back from a winter in California and was buried on the farm on his eighty-fourth birthday.

To his era Burroughs was a symbol of the simple life, living close to the natural world. His many essays and books drew attention to the "calm, slow radiance of the woods in autumn," a weasel chasing a chipmunk, "a silver-gray cocoon" attached to a twig. His friendship with Walt Whitman enlarged his perspective; he helped Whitman to see details.

Burroughs' writings are still fresh for those who would explore them. A fine introduction is *Harvest of a Quiet Eye: The Natural World of John Burroughs* with photographs and text selections by Charles F. Davis (Tamarack Press, 1976).

Just beneath the rock summit of Slide Mountain in the heart of the Catskills is a tablet in memory of John Burroughs, "Who in his early writings introduced Slide Mountain to the world. He made many visits to this peak. . . ." Burroughs used to climb up from Woodland Valley, along the west branch of Cornell Brook. *The New York New Jersey Trail Conference's New York Walk Book* (Anchor Press/Doubleday, 1984) tells how to reach the spot today.

The John Burroughs Association owns and maintains Burroughs' cabin Slabsides, now through the association's efforts, surrounded by the 180-acre John Burroughs Sanctuary. The sanctuary grounds, in West Park, New York, are open daily throughout the year. Slabsides, still essentially the same as during Burroughs' lifetime, is open the third Saturday in May and the first Saturday in October from 11:00 A.M.-4:00 P.M., when a Burroughs' lecture is given.

For information write to Ms. Lisa Breslof, the John Burroughs Association, 15 West 77th Street, New York, NY 10024.

JOHN MUIR NATIONAL HISTORIC SITE (Martinez, CA)
JOHN MUIR (1838-1914)

Although Muir is a towering figure in the U.S. environmental movement, he was not a native American. Born in Dunbar, Scotland, he came to this country with his family to live in Wisconsin when he was ten. After studying briefly at the University of Wisconsin and surviving a variety of mishaps and adventures, he made his way to southern California in 1868. California was his base for the rest of his life, although he traveled as far away as Australia.

His physical endurance and skill were astounding. On mountain climbing expeditions he took with him blankets, bread or crackers, oatmeal, and tea. These would be his only supplies for weeks on end. He made many first ascents in Yosemite, with a well-fitting pair of shoes as his only equipment. Yet he never sought recognition as a climber. His intense desire was to experience and learn about the natural world and to share his enthusiasm and knowledge.

Writing books and articles in leading national periodicals, he acquainted the American public with the beauty of their country and with the need to take steps to preserve it. Wilderness was to him a necessity. To further his teaching, he became a cofounder and first president of the Sierra Club in 1892. In conservation battles of the late nineteenth and early twentieth centuries, he symbolized as well as spoke for the forces that fought to preserve the natural world as opposed to those, represented by Gifford Pinchot of the National Forest Service, who would manipulate it for human benefit.

For environmentalists Yosemite is indissolubly associated with John Muir. Muir fought successfully to have the area declared a National Park in 1890; he explored it, discovered its glacial origin, and wrote passionately of it. His disappointment at the failure of attempts to stop the damming of the Tuolumne and the flooding of Hetch Hetchy Valley contributed to his death a year after the congressional decision.

Because of Muir's fame and his journeys, numerous places, including Alaska's Muir Glacier, bear his name. The following two sites are units of the National Park System.

The fruit farm in Martinez, California that had belonged to the parents of his wife, Louie Strentzel, is now a National Historic Site. Muir made the farm his base after his marriage in 1880. Visitors can see the study where he wrote most of his books, and sample fruit from the trees on a portion of the farm land that he helped to care for. He is buried in a family graveyard in an orchard down the road from the house. For information contact John Muir National Historic Site, 4202 Alhambra Avenue, Martinez, California 94553.

Muir Woods National Monument is a forest dominated by old-growth Coast redwoods, twelve miles north of the Golden Gate Bridge. Congressman William Kent and his wife Elizabeth Thacher Kent donated the core of the 553-acre tract to the federal government in 1908, and asked that it be named after Muir. Muir wrote to Kent to thank him. Kent had done "in many ways the most notable service to God and man I've heard of since my forest wanderings began. . . . That so fine divine a thing should have come out of money-mad Chicago! Wha wad'a' thocht it!"

Growing among the redwoods are Douglas fir, Big-Leaf maple, Tanbark oak, and Bay laurel. As is usual in redwood forests, the floor is covered with ferns (here Sword fern, Ladyfern, California polypody, and Bracken fern), Redwood sorrel, and, after rains, mushrooms. Lichen and moss grow on the trees and rocks.

In the fall of 1963, when Rachel Carson visited San Francisco, David Brower, then executive director of the Sierra Club, took her on a tour of Muir Woods.

For information write to Muir Woods National Monument, Mill Valley, California 94941 (415-388-2595).

SAGAMORE HILL NATIONAL HISTORIC SITE
(Sagamore Hill, NY)
THEODORE ROOSEVELT (1858–1919)

As a conservationist Theodore Roosevelt set records. During his years as president (1901–09), he signed bills enlarging Yosemite National Park and creating five other national parks, set aside the first wildlife refuge and fifty-four subsequent refuges, signed the act making possible the establishment of national monuments and created eighteen such monuments. Furthermore, he expanded the forest reserve system from 34 million to 166 million acres.

In the last years of his presidency he came under the influence of Gifford Pinchot and others who wanted to use rather than to preserve natural resources. To Muir's dismay Roosevelt made no move to prevent the flooding of Hetch Hetchy Valley in Yosemite National Park, for example. Nevertheless, he can be credited with helping alert the American people to the need to preserve their natural heritage as well as with setting aside for conservation more than 234 million acres.

Roosevelt developed a passion for observing and also for hunting birds and other animals, as a boy in New York state. He gained his insight into the need to act to protect our natural heritage in the Badlands of what was then the Dakota Territory, where he learned that hunters like himself were exterminating the wildlife, and that cattle, including his own, were destroying the prairie.

The Theodore Roosevelt National Park now occupies the site of Roosevelt's awakening. The park consists of two widely separated, developed units and the undeveloped site of Elkhorn Ranch, which Roosevelt purchased in 1884. He apparently abandoned the ranch after 1890, and the buildings no longer exist. The cabin that he used on the Maltese Cross Ranch, in which he was a partner, has been restored and is behind the visitor center on the south unit. Among the animals inhabiting the park are American bison, Bighorn sheep, and elk, all reintroduced. The park's campgrounds are open all year, but services are reduced between October and April. For information contact Theodore Roosevelt National Park, Medora, North Dakota 58645 (701-623-4466).

Roosevelt's permanent home in the East, Sagamore Hill, New York, is now a national historic site. He had it built in 1884 and 1885 on land where he had roamed as a boy during vacations at his family's summer residence. The chief of visitor services writes that the hunting trophies on display often stimulate discussion of Roosevelt's conservationist activities and views. The site is open daily, 9:30 A.M.-5:00 P.M. Admission is $1. For further information contact the Sagamore Hill National Historic Site, Cove Neck Road, Box 304, Oyster Bay, New York 11771-1899.

Nearby is a 12-acre environmental education center and wildlife preserve, the Theodore Roosevelt Memorial Bird Sanctuary. Surrounding

Roosevelt's grave, it was donated to the National Audubon Society by W. Emlen Roosevelt, Theodore Roosevelt's cousin, in 1923. The sanctuary is at 134 Cove Road, Oyster Bay, New York 11771 (516-922-3200). Grounds are open daily, 9:00 A.M.-5:00 P.M.; the visitor center is open Mon.- Thurs. 8:00 A.M.-4:30 P.M.; Fri. 8:00 A.M.-2:00 P.M.; Sat. and Sun. 1:00-4:30 P.M. A donation of $1.50 is suggested.

BOK TOWER GARDENS (Lake Wales, FL)
EDWARD WILLIAM BOK (1863–1930)

From 1889–1919 as the editor of *Ladies' Home Journal* Edward Bok was the most persistent American advocate of simple living for the middle classes. In the Journal he started a department "How Much Can be Done with Little" with practical suggestions, and pioneered the "how to" journalistic style with instructions on how to live simply. Also through the magazine, he worked for pure food and drug legislation, city beautification, and wilderness preservation, and helped to save Niagara Falls. A practical Christian, he introduced serious articles and crusades to a medium previously devoted to light entertainment.

Bok retired at the age of fifty-five in order to devote himself to philanthropy. Among his many gifts was the establishment in 1923 of a $100,000 American Peace Award for the best practical plan by which the United States could cooperate with other nations to achieve and maintain world peace. He also created the "sanctuary for humans and birds" now known as Bok Tower Gardens at Lake Wales, Florida.

The gardens are on Iron Mountain, at 295 feet above sea level, the highest point in the state. A Singing Tower of pink and gray Georgia marble and tan Florida coquina rock houses a celebrated carillon. The tower is decorated with carvings of plants and birds and is set in a serenely beautiful garden of native and exotic plants, designed by landscape architect Frederick Law Olmsted, Jr. In the north and east sections of the 128-acre tract is the Pine Ridge Nature Reserve, a Longleaf Pine/Wire Grass community maintained in its natural state. Such communities are in danger of disappearing. The vegetation is adapted to fire. Therefore, the horticulturist at the garden worked with the Nature Conservancy to establish a burn program. The preserve is home to two endangered plants, a flowering annual and a dwarf plum that are fire adapted and liable to being shaded out by invading oaks and dense grass.

Bok Tower Gardens is open 8:00 A.M.-5:00 P.M. daily. Admission is $3. For information contact Visitor Services, Bok Tower Gardens, P.O. Box 3810, Lake Wales, Florida 33859-3810 (813-676-1408).

CARVER BIRTHPLACE (Diamond, MO)
GEORGE WASHINGTON CARVER (1864–1943)

Early in his career, George Washington Carver left a position at the Iowa State University to teach agriculture at Tuskegee Institute in Alabama, where he could help small farmers directly. He showed them how to diversify their crops; found multiple uses for the staples they grew such as peanuts; taught composting as a natural means of increasing soil fertility; and developed new ways of using waste—peanut shells could serve as mulch or as an absorbent, for example. He spread his ideas by writing and distributing pamphlets that the farmers could understand and by taking a "school on wheels" to communities, as well as through his classes at the Institute.

Despite his increasing fame and influence, he repeatedly refused to accept an increase in his salary of $125 a month. His records show that the only money he spent on himself was for the doctor and the dentist. He found no need to spend more, as the institute gave him room and board, and he wore his clothes until they were ragged and then often replaced them with gifts. During his last years and at his death he contributed some $60,000, the result of his frugality, to the Carver Museum and the George Washington Carver Foundation to support young blacks engaged in scientific research.

The site of the slave cabin in which Carver was born, in Diamond, Missouri, is now a national monument. A 3/4 mile nature trail winds through the monument, and prairie is being restored in two areas near the trail. (Diamond Grove Prairie, also in Diamond, is one of the biggest remnant prairies in the Ozarks.) There is a museum in the visitor center, open Wed.-Sun. 8:30 A.M.-5:00 P.M.

For information write to the superintendent or to the Carver Birthplace District Association, both at P.O. Box 38, Diamond, Missouri 64840 (417-325-4151).

Tuskegee Institute itself now includes a national historic site, where visitors can walk around the buildings constructed in the time of Booker T. Washington and George Washington Carver. Many of them were built from bricks made on campus by students.

The George Washington Carver Museum, established in Carver's lifetime, contains the historic site's visitor center. The structure was damaged in a fire in 1947. It has since been renovated twice and now displays both a history of the Institute and a survey of Carver's career. Objects in the latter display include artifacts that Carver made from farm products.

For information contact Tuskegee Institute National Historic Site, P.O. Drawer 10, Tuskegee Institute, Alabama 36088-0010 (205-727-3200). The site is open daily 9:00 A.M.-5:00 P.M.

FALLINGWATER (Bear Run, PA)
FRANK LLOYD WRIGHT (1869-1959)

Wright is today recruiting for the environmental movement *in absentia*. The Western Pennsylvania Conservancy owns Fallingwater, a house he designed in 1936. The conservancy, which is a land trust, has opened the house to the public. There it shows conservation exhibits and recruits members. The brochure on the house tantalizingly invites all visitors to combine a "Fallingwater tour with a visit to the Conservancy's lovely Bear Run Nature Reserve, a 4,000-acre expanse of wild mountain land . . . just 1/2 mile north."

Fallingwater, Wright's most famous creation, is well-suited to its new role. Dramatically cantilevered over a waterfall, it appears to be an integral part of the wooded slope on which it is constructed. Wright had it built of sandstone quarried on the property and laid up by local craftsmen. Edgar Kaufmann, Jr. described it eloquently when he presented it to the Conservancy in 1963, "House and site together form the very image of man's desire to be at one with nature, equal and wedded to nature . . . ."

Wright was and is a controversial figure. Nevertheless, at what we may consider his best he embodied in architecture a belief that people should live in close contact with the natural world. The natural features of a site mattered to him and should, he thought, matter to other architects. In his finest works he blended into a harmonious whole not only the interior and the exterior of a building but also the building and the surrounding land. He wrote in *An American Architecture* (Horizon Press, 1955), "Man takes a positive hand in creation whenever he puts a building upon the earth beneath the sun. If he has birthright at all, it must consist in this; that he too, is not less a feature of the landscape than the rocks, trees, bears or bees of that nature to which he owes his being."

Fallingwater, located half-way between the villages of Mill Run and

Ohiopyle on Pennsylvania Route 381, is open from 10:00 A.M.-4:00 P.M. every day except Mon., April-mid-Nov. Admission is $6 weekdays, $8 weekends. From Nov. 15-April 1 it is open for weekend tours. For information contact Fallingwater, P.O. Box R, Mill Run, Pennsylvania 15464 (412-329-8501).

Examples of Frank Lloyd Wright's Prairie-style architecture, low, earth-hugging buildings built between 1889 and 1909, can be seen in Oak Park, Illinois, ten miles west of downtown Chicago and near public transit lines. The buildings open to the public include Wright's newly restored Oak Park home ($4 Nov.-Feb.; $5 Mar.-Oct.). For information contact the Oak Park Visitors Center, 158 Forest Avenue, Oak Park, IL 60302 (708-848-1500).

Taliesin West, which Wright designed in 1938 for himself and his students, in the Paradise Valley at Scottsdale, Arizona (now at the intersection of Cactus and 108th Street), is in many respects an example of adaptation to environmental conditions. From the perspective of current water shortages, Wright's irrigation and pools seem reckless, but the structure is made of native stone and canvas and landscaped with local vegetation, nestles close to the ground, and employs facades that can be moved as breezes and sunlight shift. Tours are conducted Mon.-Thur. 1:00–4:00 P.M., Fri., Sat, Sun. 9:00 A.M.-4:00 P.M.; a ticket is $10. For information call 602-860-8810.

HAWK MOUNTAIN SANCTUARY (Kempton, PA)
ROSALIE EDGE (1877?–1962)

A contemporary of Rosalie Edge characterized her as "the only honest, unselfish, indomitable hellcat in the history of conservation." She began her public service as a suffragette, and carried the drive and tactics of the suffragettes into her environmental campaigns. The Emergency Conservation Committee, which she founded and controlled, attacked the National Association of Audubon Societies, state game departments, and the Bureau of Biological Survey, in particular because of their tendency to protect only selected species, notably game birds. She was a major force in bringing about sweeping reforms in the Biological Survey, which even underwent a name change to Fish and Wildlife Service; she helped to establish the Olympic and Kings Canyon National Parks; and, before her death, the National Audubon Society (another name change) began following a path acceptable to her.

Her favorite project was Hawk Mountain Sanctuary in Pennsylvania. She raised the money for the purchase of Hawk Mountain and was president of the Sanctuary Association from its founding in 1937 to her death. Each fall an average of 24,000 raptors of fourteen species pass over the sanctuary. For many years, before Rosalie Edge protected the mountain, hunters had used it as a vantage point from which to shoot thousands of birds annually. Since then, the mountain has been a center of research, education, and bird watching.

Located a few miles east of Drehersville, the sanctuary is open all year. Non-members must purchase a pass ($3) at the visitor center, open 8:00 A.M.-5:00 P.M. daily. Binoculars are recommended, although close observation from the North Lookout, reached by a 3/4 mile trail, is often possible. Whether or not raptors will appear depends on the weather and time of year. September is best for Bald eagles, ospreys, and Broad-Winged hawks; October for Sharp-Shinned and Cooper's hawks; November for Red-Tailed hawks and Golden eagles.

The sanctuary is on Route 2, Kempton, Pennsylvania 19529 (215-756-6961).

UNIVERSITY OF WISCONSIN'S ARBORETUM
(Madison, WI)
ALDO LEOPOLD (1886–1948)

Leopold had a distinguished career in forestry and wildlife management, and his book *Game Management* established that field as a new science. He is most often remembered, however, as the author of *A Sand County Almanac* (1949), which Stephen Fox characterizes as "the most admired, most quoted, most influential book in modern conservation." The book describes the passage of the seasons at a worn-out farm Leopold acquired in Wisconsin's Sand counties, thirty miles west of Muir's Fountain Lake home. It also sets forth in clear prose a land use ethic. Leopold had arrived at this ethic only gradually. In his early years he had favored manipulation of the environment to achieve human goals, notably a maximum number of game animals. The essay has the weight of considered thought: "A thing is right when it tends to preserve the integrity, stability, and beauty of the biotic community. It is wrong when it tends otherwise."

The farm with its "shack" is now part of the Leopold Memorial Reserve. Established in 1968, the reserve is a unique venture in private cooperative land management. Land owners adjacent to Leopold's farm agreed to put their "back forties," together with the farm itself, under a common management program designed to turn unproductive farm-land into productive wild land. Charles and Nina Leopold Bradley have been Directors of Research for the reserve since 1976. To protect the land the reserve is not open to the public, but the association offers fellowships to researchers for study on the property.

An example of Leopold's work and influence that is open to visitors is the University of Wisconsin-Madison's Arboretum. In 1933 the university created a chair in wildlife management for Leopold. Through this position he became a member of the interdisciplinary committee for the development of the arboretum in its formative years. Unlike most arboreta even today, the university property is not simply a collection of plants but a collection of plant and animal communities partially representing all the major communities native to Wisconsin and the upper Midwest. The existence of these communities has enabled the arboretum to pioneer the restoration of ecosystems. One of the communities in the arboretum, a 59-acre conifer forest, has been named the Aldo Leopold Pines. Also at the arboretum is the 60-acre Curtis Prairie, the world's first tallgrass prairie restoration project, and the 45-acre Greene Prairie, the handiwork of botanist Henry Greene.

The public can visit the arboretum at will. For information call or write the University of Wisconsin-Madison Arboretum, 1207 Seminole Highway, Madison, Wisconsin 53711 (608-263-7888).

TOR HOUSE (Carmel, CA)
ROBINSON JEFFERS (1887–1962)

In our era of nuclear weapons and the greenhouse effect, the poetry of Robinson Jeffers is oddly comforting. He wrote that we should not delude ourselves with "dreams of universal justice or happiness," because they will not come true. He believed, nevertheless, that even if life were completely destroyed, something of value would remain. He wrote in 1934, "I believe that the universe is one being. . . . The parts change and pass, or die, people and races and rocks and stars; none of them seems to me important in itself, but only the whole." His poem, "The Answer" closes with the statement that man must love that whole in order not to "drown in despair when his days darken."

His poetry of hawks and gulls, the sea and rivers, rocks and mountains reflects the rugged beauty of Big Sur on the California coast, where life was "purged of its ephemeral accretions." He and his wife lived from 1919 in Tor House on Carmel Point. Jeffers assisted local stonemasons in constructing the walls of granite boulders, brought up by horses from the beach below. Later, remembering the tower of the Irish poet Yeats, he built a granite tower next to the house. He and his wife called it Hawk Tower, in honor of a sparrowhawk that perched every day on his scaffolding.

Tor House still stands, now on Ocean View Avenue, Carmel, California, as other buildings have crowded around it. The Robinson Jeffers Tor House Foundation conducts tours of the house, tower, and garden every Friday and Saturday, 10:00 A.M.-3:00 P.M. Reservations should be made in advance with the foundation at P.O. Box 1887, Carmel, California 93921 (408-624-1813).The basic charge is $5.

The grandeur of Big Sur is awesome today. Away from Carmel, its appearance is much the same as in the poet's time. The protection afforded a portion of Big Sur by the Ventana Wilderness is one reason why Jeffers would be able to recognize the region today. Another is the Big Sur Land Trust (P.O. Box 221864, Carmel, California 93922; 408-625-5523) which, since its founding in 1977, has facilitated the protection of 10% of the private land on Big Sur.

C & O CANAL (Sharpsburg, MD)
WILLIAM O. DOUGLAS (1898–1980)

In the 1960s the Cumberland Chapter of the Sierra Club wanted to publicize a campaign to prevent the construction of a dam that would flood Red River Gorge in Kentucky's Daniel Boone National Forest. Supreme Court Justice William O. Douglas, "the most prominent conservationist in public life," was the man they needed, but how to attract his attention? The chapter sent him a postcard on the theory that even people too busy to open their mail read their postcards. Back came another postcard—Douglas would come. Come he did, to hike the gorge, with a following of journalists. The dam was not built.

Douglas was an avid walker. In his early sixties, for example, he hiked the entire Appalachian Trail; and he used his feet to participate in numerous campaigns in various parts of the country. The first and the best known was the campaign to set aside for recreational use the path of the Chesapeake and Ohio Canal, which ran 189 miles from Washington, DC, to Cumberland, Maryland.

Merlo Pusey, the editor of the *Washington Post*, supported a move to change the canal, no longer used for shipping, into a highway. Douglas wrote a letter to the editor in January 1954, asking him to hike the length of the canal's towpath in order to learn why it should not become a road. The two of them with twenty-four others started out from Cumberland, Maryland, on a rainy March day. Pusey changed his mind about the canal, without walking the entire length himself. The national media found the march entertaining. Today the canal is an historical park open to the public along its entire length.

The park winds from the mouth of Rock Creek in the Georgetown area of Washington, DC, through the Piedmont, past the Great Falls of the Potomac, and then through the ridge and valley section of the Appalachian Mountains. The path is nearly flat, but in places is rough and, in wet weather, has distinctly muddy sections. Hikers and especially bikers are advised to let the trail dry for two days after rain before using it. Water has been restored to some sections of the canal bed, providing opportunities for canoeists and boaters. Approximately every 6 miles along the towpath are primitive hiker/biker campgrounds, open year around.

The C & O Canal National Historical Park, P.O. Box 4, Sharpsburg, Maryland 21782 (301-739-4200), furnishes maps and other visitor information free of charge.

RACHEL CARSON HOMESTEAD (Springdale, PA)
RACHEL CARSON (1907–1964)

Silent Spring (Houghton Mifflin, 1962), Rachel Carson's last book, played the key role in launching the modern environmental movement. Carson caught the attention of a broad audience by examining in terms laymen could understand one particular environmental problem, the pesticide DDT. Through calling attention to this specific case, she opened up the entire question of environmental degradation; and people paid attention. Many disagreed vociferously with Carson, but half a million hard-cover copies of the book were sold, and it remained on the best-seller list of the *New York Times* for thirty-one weeks.

Carson had worked as a marine zoologist. In fact, she was one of the first two women to hold a professional position with the Fish and Wildlife Service. In her three earlier books, all on the ocean, she had expressed a deep understanding of the delicate relationships between the various elements of ecosystems and her fear of the damage that humans were causing by tampering with them.

Because the ocean was central in Rachel Carson's life, the Fish and Wildlife Service, after her death, renamed the Coastal Maine Refuge the Rachel Carson National Wildlife Refuge. The refuge is a series of nine salt marshes between Kittery and Portland, Maine. Carson had built a one-story summer cottage in West Southport overlooking Sheepscot Bay, to which she returned annually, and she conducted some of her research for *The Sea around Us* (1951) and *The Edge of the Sea* (1955) on land that belongs to the refuge. The refuge is at RR2, Box 751, Route 9 East, Wells, Maine 04090.

All preserves of the Maine chapter of the Nature Conservancy that touch salt water are designated parts of the Rachel Carson Seacoast in recognition of a legacy she left to the chapter for their continued care and protection. They include some thirty-five islands and a dozen coastal preserves. A small preserve in New Harbor on Muscongus Bay, where Rachel Carson conducted scientific studies, is named the Rachel Carson Salt Pond. *Maine Forever: A Guide to Nature Conservancy Preserves in the State of Maine* gives descriptions of over fifty of the properties owned and managed by the Maine chapter, along with maps and directions to those open to the public ($17.95, plus $2 postage, from the chapter at 122 Main Street, P.O. Box 338, Topsham, Maine 04086; 207-729-5181).

She spent the first twenty years of her life away from the ocean, in Springdale, Pennsylvania. The farmhouse where she was born, along with an acre of land, has been preserved as a memorial. On the acre is a garden of native wildflowers. Two rooms of the house are furnished as they were in 1907. The homestead is open Sat. and Sun. from May-Oct. from 1:00–4:00 P.M., and by appointment. The Rachel Carson Homestead Association manages it. Letters can be written to the association at the house, 613 Marion Ave., Springdale, Pennsylvania 15144. For an appointment phone 412-274-5459.

PART II

Places in Harmony With the Natural World

In this section I present ways in which people can fill their basic needs while making only a minimal impact on the environment. I move from examples of benign methods of raising food, constructing shelter, obtaining energy, and handling waste to alternative approaches to economics, to living with others in intentional communities and in cities, and to creating a peaceful world. I close with a section illustrating the importance of the creative arts to environmentalists.

CHAPTER TWO

Sustainable Farming and Gardening Projects

Agribusiness relies on large-scale cultivation of single strains of plants and animals that are susceptible to adverse weather conditions and disease, and on massive inputs of energy, water, pesticides, herbicides, and inorganic fertilizers.

The alternative is sustainable gardening and farming carried out near points of consumption. This type of agriculture, often called by the related terms "organic" and "low-input," relies on such practices as recycling nutrients through composting and growing together plants that benefit one another.

Organic gardeners and farmers may use one or more special approaches. Intensive practices (often called French intensive because of their use by French market gardeners) allow producers to get four to six times the vegetables per unit of land as in conventional gardening. A key is planting in raised beds dug to the depth of two spades and separated by paths on which the gardener walks. Biodynamic techniques, pioneered by Rudolf Steiner, are based on the belief that all parts of the planet are interrelated and that applications to plants and animals of specific compounds allows the power of the elements that the compounds represent to influence the growing process. Permaculture, which originated in Australia with Bill Mollison, involves complex, functional design of land and housing so that plants, animals, and people interrelate in a stable, fruitful way.

Below I list a sampling of gardens and farms demonstrating sustainable techniques, but a more complete listing can be found in two books: *Healthy Harvest III: A Directory of Sustainable Agriculture and Horticulture Organizations 1989*–1990 (Potomac Valley Press, Suite 105, 1424 16th Street NW, Washington, DC 20036, 1989), $16.95 plus $2 postage. *1988 International Green Front Report* (Friends of the Trees,

P.O. Box 1064, Tonasket, Washington 98855), $7 (of which twenty-five cents goes to the planting of trees) plus $1.05 shipping. Michael Pilarsky has crammed this book with valuable information relating to tree planting throughout the world. Friends of the Trees hopes to bring out a new edition by 1992. *The Freshwater Aquaculture Book: A Handbook for Small Scale Fish Culture in North America*, rev. ed., by William McLarney (Point Roberts, Washington: Hartley and Marks, 1988) provides means of locating aquaculture projects, as it lists national, state, and provincial aquaculture organizations and institutions offering programs in the field.

Organizations that arrange farm visits include:

FARMHANDS/CITYHANDS
c/o Wendy Dubit, Starr Ridge Road, RR 1
Brewster, New York 10509
914-279-5744

This organization takes city people to the country on one-day or overnight trips to engage in such rural activities as planting and harvesting crops, enjoying folk music, and trying their hand at crafts. Call or write for information.

BIO-DYNAMIC FARMING AND GARDENING ASSOCIATION
P.O. Box 550
Kimberton, Pennsylvania 19442
215-935-7797

To visit a biodynamic farm, contact either the above office or the association's offices in the Midwest or West (c/o Michael Fields Agricultural Institute, 3293 Main St., East Troy, Wisconsin 53120 [414-642-9665]; or Alan York, 11600 Anderson Valley Way, Boonville, California 95415).

ALTERNATIVE ENERGY RESOURCES ORGANIZATION
44 North Last Chance Gulch, #9
Helena, Montana 59601
406-443-7272

AERO will direct people to demonstration farms in Montana, Idaho, Wyoming, the western Dakotas and eastern Washington and Oregon. It publishes a guide listing some two hundred producers along with information about their farms and practices ($7, including postage.) Their quarterly *Sun Times* once a year lists organic farms in Montana and North Dakota.

State or regional organizations of organic farmers may also arrange farm visits. The Maine Organic Farmers and Gardeners Association, for instance, offers farm visits each summer. Farms listed in the May/June issue of the organization's newspaper hold "open houses." The Ohio Ecological Food and Farm Association also presents farm and garden open houses. The address of MOFGA is 283 Water St., P.O. Box 2176, Augusta, Maine 04330 (207-622-3118); OEFFA is at 65 Plymouth St., Plymouth, Ohio 44865 (419-687-7665).

THE FARMS AND GARDENS

GAP MOUNTAIN PERMACULTURE
9 Old County Road
Jaffrey, New Hampshire 03452
603-532-7321, 532-6877

GAP Mountain Permaculture is a community of three households, each on a leasehold in the Land Trust at Gap Mountain, incorporated in 1987. These leaseholds and 85 acres held in common, are in varying stages of permaculture design. Features include an orchard, chicken forage, a woodchip composting/graywater system, composting toilets of local design, greenhouses, systems for collecting roof water, and a constructed wetland for treating graywater. Most of the land will never be developed.

The community was founded to further sustainable agriculture and culture through the study, discussion, explication, and practice of permaculture, taking into account both environmental and social factors. It now gives courses and workshops in permaculture and runs a small internship program. There are limited facilities for camping. Visitors must call ahead.

GREENPOWER FARM
P.O. Box 624
Weston, Massachusetts 02193
617-893-7320

Run by the town of Weston through a conservation commission, Greenpower is a 15-acre organic farm that raises produce for soup kitchens and homeless shelters in Boston. The farm needs volunteer workers during the growing season. Nonworkers are welcome to visit. Contact Ward Cheney at the above address for information.

NEW ENGLAND SMALL FARM INSTITUTE
Jepson House, Jackson Street (P.O. Box 937)
Belchertown, Massachusetts 01007
413-323-4531

Promoting the increased and sustainable use of New England's agricultural resources, the institute manages 400 acres of public fields, wetlands, and woods. A Sustained Forest Management Demonstration Program is being carried out on 274 acres. The 2.5 acre Jepson Hill Fruition Park, one of four fruition demonstration sites in the state, displays low-maintenance fruit and nut trees and shrubs. The 3 acres around Jepson House, a typical rural farmhouse that now houses the institute, demonstrate small-scale self-sufficiency projects suited to rural homeowners. The institute is also the site of the White Oak Apprenticeship Farm.

If arrangements are made in advance, the staff will meet with individuals or small groups to discuss the institute's work and give a brief tour of the land. Hikers, picnickers, and campers are welcome to use the grounds, but campers are expected to participate in a Farm Workday, to do two hours of farm work, or to pay $10 in return for each night's stay. The institute has a library on alternative agriculture and related topics, where the public may read Mon.-Fri. 9:30 A.M.-3:00 P.M. Anyone wishing to use the library or grounds should call ahead.

STONEYBROOK MILLSTONE WATERSHED ASSOCIATION
31 Titus Mill Road
Pennington, New Jersey 08534
609-737-3735

The Watershed Association was created in 1951 to protect the water and land resources of the 285-square-mile Millstone River basin in central New Jersey. Since, it has worked with local farmers to halt soil erosion and pollution of surface and ground water. It acquired the farm in order to demonstrate the feasibility of sustainable agriculture techniques.

The farm produces vegetables, strawberries, herbs, flowers, eggs, and honey, and raises sheep. Products are sold to area stores and restaurants and at a stand at the farm. The farm also has a crafts shop selling goods made from farm products. Volunteer programs train people in organic methods. Visitors are welcome Mon., Wed., Thur., Sat. 9:00 A.M.–6:00 P.M. The farm organizes tours and festivals throughout the year, as described in the association's newsletter.

The association holds and maintains a 585-acre wildlife reserve with 8 miles of trails open to the public. In addition, it has a nature center with displays and environmental education programs for children and adults, and a 4-acre pond for fishing. Fees are charged only for programs. The newsletter can be picked up at the center.

RODALE RESEARCH CENTER
611 Siegfriedale Road
Kutztown, Pennsylvania 19530
215-683-6383

The Rodale Research Center, a division of Rodale Institute, conducts research and disseminates information on such topics as horticulture (both home garden and field scale production), field crop production (emphasizing reduced input and reduced tillage), composting, reduced input apple production, perennial cropping systems, legume selection for soil improvement, international agriculture, and issues related to farming at the rural/urban interface. A national network of cooperating farmers tests practices being developed at Rodale and presents results at workshops and field days.

Visitors can take a self-guided tour throughout the year, and guided tours from May through October. The center offers educational workshops and, in July and August, schedules field days. A bookstore is open from May through October. Write or call the center for additional information, including dates and maps.

URBAN FARMS, INC.
7214 Blair Road NW
Washington, DC 20012
202-882-6664; office 202-462-8800

The National Institute for Science, Law, and Public Policy owns this 10,000-square-foot farm in the Takoma Park neighborhood of northwest Washington. The institute is using it to demonstrate that it is possible to run an economically viable, ecologically sound farm in an urban setting. A staff of three raises vegetables, herbs, and flowers by the French intensive method, for sale through commercial markets. Visitors are welcome, mid-Feb.-mid-Dec.

SPRINGTREE COMMUNITY FARM
Rte. 2, Box 89
Scottsville, Virginia 24590
804-286-3466

Springtree is a small community on 118 acres of rolling pasture and woods. Members support themselves with income from outside work, but grow as much of their own food as possible. They have organic orchards and gardens and a variety of traditional and experimental small fruits, plus animals.

The most unusual aspect of the farm may be the use of trees to feed animals as well as people. Members have planted food trees along contour lines in the pastures and the hay fields as well as along perimeter fence lines. The fruit of persimmons and honeylocusts feed sheep and cattle; while mulberries, Siberian peashrubs, and persimmons sustain free-ranging chickens.

Springtree welcomes visitors, but asks that they write or phone ahead. They prefer people to stay for one or two weeks rather than for shorter periods. The regular visitor fee is $5 per day for adults and $2 for children; and is negotiable.

EDUCATIONAL CONCERNS FOR HUNGER ORGANIZATION (ECHO)
17430 Durrance Road
North Fort Myers, Florida 33917
813-543-3246

On a 5-acre farm visitors can see rooftop gardens, integrated aquaculture systems, and both common and underexploited tropical food plants. The underexploited plants are important food sources in one or two locations, but elsewhere are not known or used. They are the main concern of ECHO, a Christian organization that gives technical help to missionaries and to organizations such as the Peace Corps. ECHO obtains seed, grows the crop to produce more seed, and makes the seed available to farmers around the world, who themselves then grow and increase the seed. ECHO sends a newsletter to ninety-seven countries to announce the availability of seed and most importantly to network information.

A tour of the farm is given Friday at 10:00 A.M. If you cannot go Friday, call a week in advance to arrange an appointment.

CEDAR/NEW AGE COMMUNITY LAND TRUST (NACLT)
590 Pleasant Ridge Church Road
Edmonton, Kentucky 42129
502-378-5725

New Age Community Land Trust currently owns 42.5 acres of land in south central Kentucky. An intentional community is stewarding the trust's pilot plot of land and helping to develop a homesteading center, the Center for Ecological Design and Restoration (CEDAR). Trust members hope to acquire other parcels of land to be stewarded by interested individuals or groups.

So far CEDAR has developed a quarter acre of raised bed gardens on the contour and started a small goat dairy. They are experimenting with no-till, small grain production, harvestable by hand. They have also used organic, no-till methods to restore eroded bottomlands to pasture, and are introducing perennial herbs, fruits, and nuts.

Visitors stay in a small guest home without electricity. Members would appreciate notice two weeks before a visit. Pets are welcome but must be kept under control.

MEADOWCREEK PROJECT
Fox, Arkansas 72051
501-363-4500

Meadowcreek Project is an environmental education organization serving college students, faculty, and the general public. Its land in the Boston Mountains of the Ozarks is divided between a 1200-acre forest and a 300-acre farm, emphasizing livestock and perennial crops. Demonstrations include passive and active solar systems and resource-conserving manufacturing operations as well as sustainable agriculture.

Interns concentrate on Sustainable Agriculture/Horticulture, Applied Ecology, and Alternative Energy. All study the implications of sustainability, carry out a personal project, attend practical workshops, and participate in the work of Meadowcreek.

In addition to the internships, the center offers apprenticeships and a variety of workshops and courses. Contact the program coordinator for information about tours and programs.

LAREDO "BLUEPRINT" DEMONSTRATION FARM
c/o Laredo Junior College
West End Washington Street
Laredo, Texas 78040
512-724-7567

Israel and Texas set up this 40-acre farm as a joint venture to develop crops and agricultural technology, because the two areas have similar dry climates. Examples of other alternative technologies have been since been added with an eye to forming an integrated system. The many special features of the farm include buildings constructed from bales of straw; drip irrigation; wind-generated electricity; aquatic plants for water treatment; large- and small-scale shade systems for temperature, wind, and frost control; and cold, heat, and drought tolerant, and insect and disease resistant crops. The Center for Maximum Potential Building Systems (8604 F.M. 969, Austin, Texas 78724; 512-928-4786) helped to develop the farm, which it hopes will be a catalyst for change in the area. The farm is open Mon.-Fri. 8:00 A.M.-5:00 P.M.; weekends by appointment. For information or an appointment contact Project Manager Tony Ramirez at the Laredo address.

THE KERR CENTER FOR SUSTAINABLE AGRICULTURE
P.O. Box 588, Highway 271-S
Poteau, Oklahoma 74953
918-647-9123

Although the Kerr Center is situated on a 4,150 acre ranch that belonged to the late Senator Robert Kerr, it offers more than demonstrations of sustainable ranching. Sites on a tour include the Poteau Mountain U-Pik blueberry farm; the Rock Creek demonstration farm which includes a laying hen project with composting poultry barn floor; and a twelve-pond aquaculture facility where research is conducted on integrating aquaculture into a diversified farming system combining horticulture, poultry, and cover cropping.

The first stop is the visitor center in the Education Building, which includes a library. Tour leaders are available. Visiting hours are Mon.-Fri. 8:00 A.M.-5:00 P.M., but arrangements can be made in advance for a weekend visit. Appointments for tours are not necessary but appreciated. The center offers internships, apprenticeships, and a volunteer program.

THE LAND INSTITUTE
2440 East Water Well Road
Salina, Kansas 67401
913-823-5376

The Land Institute is a private, education and research organization directed by Dana Jackson and Wes Jackson, author of *New Roots for Agriculture* (Friends of the Earth, 1980) among other works. They believe that people living on land that was prairie should learn to farm by studying the prairie. Their goal is "to create prairielike grain fields."

The ongoing research at the institute is preparing the way for successful polyculture of perennial seed crops. Such an agriculture will reduce soil erosion, biologically control pests and weeds, provide fertility internally, and produce plant species that complement each other in time and space.

Visitors are welcome, but should contact the staff a few days ahead of time. The institute offers ten-month internships for college graduates or upper-level undergraduates.

PALMER ORGANIC FARM
HCO2 Box 7471-C
Palmer, Alaska 99645
907-745-0758

Ellen Van DeVisse welcomes visitors to her organic vegetable farm, in a section of Alaska famed for its giant produce. The farm will be closed to visitors during the summer of 1991, because of the absence of the owner, but will reopen early in September. The growing season extends from the end of May to around the end of October. Phone or write to Ms. Van DeVisse for an appointment.

ORGANIC FARM, EVERGREEN STATE COLLEGE
2712 Lewis Road
Olympia, Washington 98505
206-866-6000, extension 6161 or 6160

The college offers a year-long interdisciplinary program in ecological agriculture intended for undergraduates at the sophomore-junior level. The organic farm was started by students during the college's first year in order to inspire involvement in agriculture. A wide array of crops adapted to the Northwest is grown to demonstrate which do well in the region. Information on organic agriculture is available to callers and visitors to the farm.

The farm's 13 acres include a 2-acre demonstration and market garden with raised beds; small fruit and nut orchards; a poultry yard; solar greenhouses and other season-extending devices; an 8-acre woodlot/forest; a farmhouse constructed by students with materials largely milled on the farm; and community garden sites.

Visitors are welcome to stroll through the garden and greenhouses, ask questions, and purchase produce.

APROVECHO RESEARCH CENTER
80574 Hazelton Road
Cottage Grove, Oregon 97424
503-942-9434

Set among spectacular mountains and forests, Aprovecho uses its 40 acres of mostly wooded land for experiments with the use of non-commercial tree species, with harvesting wild plants, and with rebuilding soil. Aprovecho has three stands of Asiatic semi-timber bamboo, part of a long-term experiment in cultivating and using the plant for construction and erosion control.

In a 1.25-acre garden the center raises vegetables to feed residents of the land and to sell as part of a program to inform the public about a wide range of locally-grown produce. Experimental work revolves around trials of varieties not normally grown in the Northwest and production for winter harvesting.

Aprovecho wants to help people make the best use of their skills and resources, especially in the Third World. The institute teaches and researches innovative technologies for small-scale food production, heating, cooking, and housing; answers questions on alternative technology from all over the world; and publishes *News from Aprovecho* and an appealing children's magazine, *Skipping Stones: a Multi-ethnic Children's Forum* ($15 per year).

Members of End of the Road, a community of supporters that steward Aprovecho's land, look after guests. First visits should be either for an hour or so, or for a week during which guests work at the center. All visits must be arranged in advance. The center offers internships. Contact Linda Smiley.

GREEN GULCH FARM, ZEN CENTER
Star Route
Sausalito, California 94965
415-383-3134

A Buddhist practice center in the Japanese Soto Zen Tradition, Green Gulch is one of three centers that make up the San Francisco Zen Center. Located just north of San Francisco, it is in a beautiful valley that opens out onto the Pacific Ocean. At Green Gulch is a 1.5-acre hand-cultivated garden inspired by Alan Chadwick, whose intensive methods are still practiced there; and a 15-acre organic truck farm where the center grows produce for sale in San Francisco and Marin Counties. Green Gulch is open to visitors. For classes in gardening and flower and herb craft, preregistration and payment are required. Overnight accommodations are available at a cost of $35 and up for a single room.

CENTRAL ROCKY MOUNTAIN PERMACULTURE INSTITUTE
P.O. Box 631
Basalt, Colorado 81621
303-927-4158

Led by Jerome Osentowski, the institute manages 8 acres, one of which it farms intensively, at an elevation of 7,200 feet in a forest of Pinyon Pine and juniper, above the Roaring Fork Valley. Osentowski established the institute to demonstrate that "year-round regenerative and sustainable agriculture" can be carried on high in the mountains. He grows fruit, vegetables, and chickens organically, outdoors on terraces from June to October. During the winter he farms in a 2,300 square-foot greenhouse with an integrated heating system obtaining heat from solar energy, compost, and chickens. As a result he is able to sell fresh produce year round to restaurants and individuals and to feed the institute's staff.

From time to time the institute offers workshops and classes in permaculture. Osentowski employs interns, and he opens the farm to visitors by appointment. The charge for a tour is a $10 donation to the institute.

MALACHITE SCHOOL AND SMALL FARM
A.S.R. Box 21, Pass Creek Road
Gardner, Colorado 81040
719-746-2412

The Farm School began as a project to restore an abandoned 1880s homestead in semi-arid plateau country of the Sangre de Cristo range. It offers an informal educational program. College students can enroll in a variety of internships; and students and the public can take classes and weekend workshops, or participate in theme weekends, Elderhostels, and retreats. Topics presented include sustainable agriculture, alternative building techniques, and alternative energy.

The farm consists of 260 acres of pasture, hay and grain fields, and a kitchen garden. Only organic methods are employed, and most of the farming is done with draft horses. The original adobe farmhouse is the center of student and staff activities. Staff, students, and volunteers constructed a 3,500 square foot solar adobe addition out of bricks that they made themselves.

Visitors are welcome. Tours are given, and visitors have the opportunity to observe farm activities. Call ahead to make arrangements. Overnight accommodations are available. The standard adult price is $15; camping is half price. Breakfast is included; other meals can be purchased.

TELLURIDE INSTITUTE
P.O. Box 1770
Telluride, Colorado 81435
303-728-4981

Telluride is the coordinating agency for the Sustainable Mountain Agricultural Alliance (SMALL) and is conducting a survey of sustainable producers in the Four Corners Region. Its own agricultural project is an experimental food crop, botanical, and formal garden situated at a 9,400-foot elevation. It is the site of work on specialized growing techniques, food self-sufficiency, and plant varieties and seed exchanges appropriate to mountain regions. Visitors to the garden are welcome.

Projects of the institute may be theoretical rather than practical. In addition to agriculture, the institute is concerned with the exploratory arts, citizen diplomacy, local economic development, and humane use of new information and communications technologies. A schedule of events is available.

AGROECOLOGY PROGRAM, UNIVERSITY OF CALIFORNIA
Santa Cruz, California 95064
408-459-4140

Alan Chadwick, who developed and popularized French intensive organic gardening in the United States, first gained attention for the method in this country by establishing a garden on a steep hillside on the Santa Cruz campus in the late sixties. In 1972 students of Chadwick created a 25-acre farm to experiment with his techniques on a large scale. Today the original 4-acre garden includes ornamentals, food crops, and native California plants. The farm has raised-bed gardens, row crops, orchards, and research plots. The farm and garden are open daily for self-guided tours with an informative booklet. Tours with a docent are offered at 2:00 P.M. Sundays.

The university Agroecology Program is an educational and research group working toward the development of ecologically, economically, and socially sustainable agricultural systems. The program is open to undergraduates majoring in environmental studies and to graduate students. It also offers six-month apprenticeships in Ecological Horticulture.

LANDSCAPES SOUTHERN CALIFORNIA STYLE
450 Alessandro Boulevard
Riverside, California 92517
714-780-4170

Developed by the Western Municipal Water District of Riverside and the University of California Cooperative Extension of Riverside, this one-acre garden demonstrates that a good design, careful plant selection, and appropriate planting and maintenance techniques can result in an attractive, low-maintenance garden that uses little water or energy. Native ground covers as an alternative to lawns are shown, as are drip irrigation systems, and colorful dry climate plants.

The garden is open daily 10:00 A.M.-4:00 P.M., free of charge. For tour information call the office. Special events include water-efficient plant sales, monthly garden walks with the director, and seminars. Call for a schedule.

The Water District and Extension office publish cooperatively an annotated list of plants suitable for southern California, most of which can be seen in the garden.

HARMONIOUS EARTH RESEARCH (HER)
45 Kahele Street
Kihei, Hawaii 96753

An institute researching organic gardening and permaculture strategies in the tropics, Harmonious Earth Research has created several sites in Hawaii. The chief site, at the above address, is a quarter acre with a small house in a residential area. Located on the dry side of the island of Maui with a rainfall of five inches a year, the site has poor soil and temperatures in the eighties year round. The design aims to conserve water and create a micro-climate using edible species and on-site natural fertilizers. The institute is glad to receive visitors, especially from abroad.

HISTORIC FARMS

By raising historically authentic crops and livestock, historic farms help to maintain the genetic diversity of our food supply as well as function as museums. Stemgas (Box 328, Lancaster, Pennsylvania 17603) sells the *Farm Museum Directory*, describing over 140 farm and agricultural museums (2nd. ed., 1988, $3.50 postpaid).

HANS HERR HOUSE
1849 Hans Herr Drive, Willow Street
Lancaster County, Pennsylvania 17584
717-464-4438

Built by a Mennonite family in 1719, the Hans Herr House is the oldest structure in Lancaster County, Pennsylvania. Although the site no longer maintains an heirloom garden, it has an orchard of historic apple varieties. An exhibition on Mennonite rural life examines the religious group's impact on the agriculture of Lancaster County. As a result of the good stewardship practiced by the Mennonites since the early 1700s – the use of manures, crop rotation, general care of the land – the soil of the surrounding area remains fertile and productive.

The Hans Herr House is open 1 April-31 Dec., Mon.-Sat. 9:00 A.M.-4:00 P.M. Admission is $3.

CLAUDE MOORE COLONIAL FARM AT TURKEY RUN
6310 Georgetown Pike
McLean, Virginia 22101
703-442-7557

This farm represents a small-scale, low-income homestead in northern Virginia during the late colonial period. Twelve of a hundred acres of land are planted with corn, tobacco, and wheat and used for an orchard and kitchen garden. The staff tills, plants, and cultivates by hand. Split-rail and pile fencing protect the crops from the livestock which otherwise roams freely. The vegetables are those common during the eighteenth century.

The farm is open to the public from early April-late Dec., Wed.-Sun. 10:00 A.M.-4:30 P.M. It is closed during inclement weather. Admission is $2.

OLD WORLD WISCONSIN
S103 W37890 Highway 67
Eagle, Wisconsin 53119
414-594-2116

Situated on 576 acres in the Kettle Moraine state forest, Old World Wisconsin contains fifty historic structures, about 20 acres of farmed land, and twelve heirloom gardens. The lives of five ethnic groups that immigrated to Wisconsin between 1845 and 1915 are represented: Yankee, German, Norwegian, Finnish, and Danish. Gardeners can obtain seeds grown at the museum, and ideally, return some of the produce for display in the garden fair, held at the end of August.

Old World Wisconsin is open daily 1 May-31 Oct., 10:00 A.M.-5:00 P.M., except 9:00 A.M.-4:00 P.M. weekdays in May, June, Sept., and Oct. Admission is $7.

SUNWATCH
2301 West River Road
Dayton, Ohio 45418
513-268-8199

This twelfth-century Fort Ancient Village illustrates the closeness of an Indian community to the cycles of nature. The Fort Ancient Indians flourished in Ohio from 900 A.D. to the historic period. Scholars believe that the layout of the village, the scheduling of the planting season, and "Green Corn Rituals" and other cyclical celebrations were determined by the position of the rising and setting sun.

At the center of the village is a plaza containing a large red cedar pole, surrounded by four poles arranged in a parallelogram. Around them are concentric rings of houses, storage/trash pits, and burial places. At the Equinoxes anyone observing the rising sun through the central parallelogram would see the sun aligned with certain other village markers. Other alignments apparently marked the Solstices.

When excavation of the site began, the City of Dayton was planning to use the land as a sludge treatment pond. With the assistance of volunteers, the village has been partially restored. The site includes a garden representative of those tended by Fort Ancient Indians. The village is open year round, Mon.-Sat. 9:00 A.M.-5:00 P.M.; Sun. 12:00 noon-5:00 P.M. Admission is $4.

Cahokia Mounds State Historical Site a few miles west of Collinsville, Illinois, includes Woodhenge, four or five circular sun calendars, which once consisted of evenly spaced wooden posts. The calendars appear to have also been used to determine the changing seasons and cyclical ceremonial periods. Seen from the center, the alignment of the rising sun with the posts indicated the time of the year. The site is open daily 9:00 A.M.-5:00 P.M. No admission is charged. For further information contact Cahokia Mounds State Historic Site, P.O. Box 681, Collinsville, Illinois 62234 (6128-346-5160).

Three membership organizations devoted to preserving heirloom plant varieties receive visitors:

NATIVE SEEDS/SEARCH
2150 North Alvernon Way
Tucson, Arizona 85712
602-327-9123

Native seeds/SEARCH collects, increases, distributes, and researches traditional native crops and their wild relatives from the American Southwest and Northwest Mexico. The organization maintains a demonstration garden on the grounds of Tucson Botanical Gardens at the above address, open to the public daily 9:00 A.M.-4:00 P.M. A catalog describing collected varieties is available for $1 from the organization at the address: 2509 North Campbell Ave. #325, Tucson, Arizona 85719.

SEED SAVERS EXCHANGE
RR 3, Box 239
Decorah, Iowa 52101

Members of the Exchange save old-fashioned food crops from extinction by locating gardeners who are keeping seeds that are family heirlooms, traditional American Indian crops, garden varieties of the Amish or Mennonites, varieties dropped from seed catalogs, or outstanding foreign vegetables. They distribute and grow these seeds.

In 1986 the Exchange purchased 140-acre Heritage Farm, a conference center and campground surrounded by gardens and fields, where it maintains 6,000 rare vegetables, old-time apple varieties, and rare White Park cattle. Visitors are welcome June 1-Sept. 30 9:00 A.M.-5:00 P.M. Brochures for self-guided tours are available in the visitors' parking lot. The farm holds seasonal celebrations, open only to members and their families, and occasional workshops.

Publications of the Exchange include the *Seed Savers Yearbook*, which lists members and the seeds that they are offering to other gardeners (free to members), and the *Garden Seed Inventory*, which describes more than 5,000 standard vegetables and lists the companies that offer their seeds ($17.50 softcover postpaid).

TALAVAYA CENTER
Box 2, Tesuque Drive
Espanola, New Mexico 87532

Since 1983 Talavaya has collected more than 1,300 strains of nonhybrid native seeds traditional to the agriculture of the native populations of the Southwest of North America and the Andean Altiplano of South America. The center is helping to revive indigenous agriculture through instructing local farmers in indigenous growing techniques and through paying them to grow seed crops for the center. On the national level Talavaya supplies seed, research, and instruction in native low-cost farming techniques. Its ultimate goal is to foster grassroots education and widespread use of proven native seeds to help alleviate hunger.

The center welcomes visitors to its 10-acre facility, but requests that they write ahead for an appointment.

URBAN COMMUNITY GARDENS

Community gardens make the advantages of gardening available to people who do not own land. To find out whether there are such gardens near you contact the American Community Gardening Association, c/o Philadelphia Green—Penn State Urban Program, 325 Walnut Street, Philadelphia, Pennsylvania 19106.

BOSTON, Massachusetts

Boston has approximately 130 community gardens, and 8,000 vacant lots on which additional gardens could be developed. Since the late 1970s Boston Urban Gardeners and the Southwest Community Farm have enabled more than 5,000 families to grow flowers and vegetables on unused land. The two organizations are now combined as Boston Urban Gardeners at the Community Farm (46 Chestnut Avenue, Jamaica Plain, Massachusetts 02130; 617-522-1259). Every year the organization surveys the city's existing gardens to assess their needs, which it meets in part through a sponsorship program linking caring individuals, groups, and businesses with gardens in economically depressed areas.

According to Boston Urban Gardeners, the following six gardens are among the most accessible, beautiful, and productive: Fenway Victory Gardens (Northwest corner of the Back Bay Fens); Gardens for Charlestown (Sullivan Square in Charlestown, a neighborhood north of downtown Boston that is reached by the Charlestown Bridge over the Charles River); Boston State Hospital [Community Garden Project] (on the grounds of the Boston State Hospital in Mattapan, a neighborhood south of the city; the site is flanked by Franklin Park and Mount Hope Cemetery and can be entered via Morton Road); Lenox-Kendall Community Garden (at the juncture of Lenox, Kendall, and Tremont Streets in Boston's South End/Lower Roxbury neighborhood); Berkeley Gardeners' Association (on Berkeley Street between Shawmut and Tremont Streets in the South End neighborhood); and the farm at the association's office.

The first of these sites, the Victory Garden, is the only community garden formed in Boston in World War II that is still existing. In the late 1950s the community fought to prevent its being turned into a parking lot. The Fens, where it is located, are part of Boston's Emerald Necklace of green space designed by Frederick Law Olmsted.

NEW YORK, New York

New York City has more than six hundred community gardens, many on city-owned land leased to community groups for $1 a year through the Department of General Services' GreenThumb program. Most of the leases are for a year at a time, and the status of gardens on the Lower East Side is in question because of planned urban renewal programs.

There have been casualties in the past. Between 1980 and 1983 Manhattan lost to development 3 acres of open space, including 10% of its community gardens; and Adam Purple's legendary Garden of Eden on Eldridge Street has been paved over.

There was also a celebrated victory, the Clinton Community Garden at 413 West 48th Street. In 1984 when development threatened, the Trust for Public Land and Green Guerillas, an organization to assist in the formation and maintenance of community gardens, helped citizens to raise $100,000 to buy the land inch by inch. The support convinced Mayor Koch to transfer the lot to the Department of Parks and Recreation. The Green Guerillas now have a contract from the city to garden on the site.

The oldest of the Green Guerillas gardens and the project that started the community gardening movement in New York is the Liz Christy Memorial Garden, created in 1973 on the corner of Houston and Bowery Streets in the now threatened area. The Green Guerillas are working to secure the integration of this and other gardens into redevelopment plans. Though bordered by roads with heavy traffic, the Liz Christy Garden is a place of beauty and tranquility. Here are a pool with bullfrogs, bee hives, trees, flowers, vegetables, birds, butterflies, and a small summer house. The garden is open from May Day through Labor Day, except when raining, 6:30–8:30 P.M. Tue. and Sat. and whenever a gardener is there working.

In return for a stamped envelope, Green Guerillas will send a map showing numerous Lower East Side community gardens. Write to the Green Guerillas, 625 Broadway, New York, New York 10012 (212-674-8124). Some of the gardens are in rough neighborhoods. Visitors should know exactly where they are going before they start out and, if possible, walk with a resident of New York.

The director of Operation GreenThumb, Jane Weissman, offers to give people who call the GreenThumb office directions to community gardens. The office is at 49 Chambers Street, Room 1020, New York,

New York 10007 (212-233-2926). Ask for her, Gina Townsend, or Stuart Lowrie.

The La Guardia Corner [Community] Gardens, at the corner of Houston and La Guardia Streets on the edge of Greenwich Village, has the advantages of being readily accessible and next to Time Landscape, Alan Sonfist's recreation of a pre-colonial mixed oak forest.

PHILADELPHIA, Pennsylvania

Sponsored by the Philadelphia Horticultural Society, Philadelphia Green was created in 1978 with funding from the city's Office of Housing and Community Development. The Society had planted its first garden in 1974. Today the Society has some 1300 active projects, including community flower and vegetable gardens, celebration and neighborhood focal sites, garden blocks, street tree blocks, and educational programs and services. Money raised at the society's prestigious Philadelphia flower show, the oldest in the country, helps to support the projects.

As a four-year program, funded by the William Penn Foundation, Philadelphia Green is planting more than 3,000 trees, 80% of them in North Philadelphia. The organization planted the first of the trees, a cedar of Lebanon, September 1989, at the corner of 20th and Diamond. The site is a flourishing community garden, near a mural depicting Kenya.

For information on seeing other community gardens in Philadelphia, contact the Director's Office, Philadelphia Green, 325 Walnut Street, Philadelphia, Pennsylvania 19106-2777 (215-625-8280).

CHICAGO, Illinois

In Chicago the Open Lands Project, the Chicago Botanic Garden, and residents have worked together to create Grenshaw Goody Community Garden (3936 W Grenshaw) as a model for developing vacant lots into small-scale gardens and parks. The lot was donated by a private party to a local block club. Chicago has about fifty community gardens, not counting gardens on Chicago Housing Authority property. Grenshaw Goody is among the first (and few) gardens to be owned by the neighborhood residents who maintain it. The Open Lands Project, which includes a land trust, is at 220 S. State Street, Chicago, Illinois 60604 (312-427-4256).

CHEYENNE, Wyoming

The city of Cheyenne, Wyoming, has a city gardening project with a difference: the Cheyenne Botanic Gardens, with social service as its main goal. The Botanic Gardens is a solar greenhouse with 3,600 square feet of floor space. The west section is primarily for food production. In the diversified central section paths wind among herbs, flowering plants, and tropical fruit trees. The east section is devoted to the growing of trees, shrubs, and flowers for the city.

The greenhouse, built by the city with a Community Development Block Grant, has only two paid staff, but uses over 1300 hours a month of volunteer labor. The garden provides food, therapy, and education to senior citizens, the handicapped, and troubled youths; and these groups comprise the bulk of the volunteer force.

Located at 710 S. Lions Park Drive, Cheyenne, Wyoming 82001 (307-637-6548), the garden is generally open Mon. through Fri. 8:30 A.M.-4:30 P.M.; Sat. and Sun. 11:00 A.M.-3:30 P.M.

SAN FRANCISCO, California

In San Francisco the San Francisco League of Urban Gardeners (SLUG) works with some sixty community gardens and thirty school gardens and offers support to individual gardeners. SLUG's office at 2540 Newhall Street, San Francisco, California 94124 (415-468-0110) is glad to tell inquirers where in San Francisco they can see community gardens.

LOS ANGELES, California

The Common Ground Gardening Program in Los Angeles is one of twenty-one urban garden programs nationwide that is run by a university extension service, in this case that of the University of California. The program, which receives funding from the federal Department of Agriculture, has been in existence for twelve years. The basic purpose is providing a food source for low income people. Residents are furnished with land and instruction in gardening. The Common Ground Gardening Program now operates some fifteen gardens and has six in the planning stage, all on surplus public land or on private land leased to the program for $1 a month. For addresses of gardens to visit contact Common Ground (213-744-4341). The program operates a Master Food Preserver hot line that answers questions on all methods of food preservation (213-744-4348).

CHAPTER THREE

Resource-Conserving Buildings and Structures

From the point of view of the environment, the most suitable shelter is energy efficient, compact, and built of natural materials found on or near the site. Buildings with these characteristics can also be affordable.

CLIFF DWELLINGS

Native Americans of the Southwest knew centuries ago how to build energy efficient structures out of materials at hand. Their skill can still be seen in the remains of cliff dwellings and in pueblos. Among them are:

ACOMA PUEBLO (SKY CITY)
Western New Mexico
505-552-6606

Dating from the twelfth century, though located on what is believed to be the oldest continuously inhabited site in North America, Acoma Pueblo is an example of solar architecture. Three rows of adobe dwellings run east and west across a high plateau. Most doors and windows are on the south wall, which receives sun more directly in winter than in summer. Flat roofs of straw and adobe covered with pine timbers and branches insulate the homes from the summer heat. Acoma pueblo receives visitors almost daily, but requires them to phone to arrange a time. Admission is $6.

MESA VERDE NATIONAL PARK
Mesa Verde, Colorado 81330

Longhouse Pueblo at Mesa Verde, built around 1200 A.D., has adobe rooms and kivas or ceremonial chambers built across a wide, south-facing cave. During winter the adobe and the rock of the cliff absorb the warmth of the sun each day and slowly release it at night. In summer the cave shades the dwellings.

NINETEENTH-CENTURY STRUCTURES

White settlers took climate and site into consideration in planning their homes. In fact, until the era of cheap petroleum and electricity, even Americans living in towns and cities tended to build for energy efficiency. The "salt box" houses typical of New England, for example, had two stories facing south toward the sun, and one story, protected by an overhanging roof, facing north toward winter winds. On the south side there was often a pergola—lattice work covered in the summer with shading vines. Two specific nineteenth-century structures illustrate totally different approaches to energy efficiency:

SOD HOUSE MUSEUM
P.O. Box 28
Aline, Oklahoma 73716
405-463-2441

The museum contains one of the few remaining "soddies," built by homesteaders on the Great Plains. In the 1890s the owner of the structure plowed up a half acre of Buffalo Grass, cut it into strips, and divided them into eighteen-inch long blocks that he laid like brick in double rows. The museum is open Tue.-Fri. 9:00 A.M.-5:00 P.M., Sat. Sun. 2:00–5:00 P.M. There is no charge.

NATIONAL BUILDING MUSEUM
Judiciary Square, NW, F Street between 4th and 5th
Washington, DC 20001
202-272-2448

Constructed in 1882–1887, this masonry structure was designed by Montgomery Meigs to house the Pension Bureau. It is built around an inner courtyard, the Great Hall, which brings light into the interior of the building. Windows are eight feet in height. Fresh air entered the perimeter offices through vents below the windows and through the windows when they were open. Stale air flowed through open archways, into the Great Hall, and out through windows high above. Meigs said that the windows were "double glazed to prevent loss of heat in winter." Since the building has been renovated, the vents under the windows are indicated only by missing bricks.

The National Building Museum is a joint federal/private institution presenting exhibitions, educational programs, and publications on the history of American architecture. "An ultimate objective . . . is to encourage the public to take part in the on-going debate over what relationship our society should establish between the built and natural environments." The exhibitions are open Mon.-Sat. 10:00 A.M.-4:00 P.M.; Sun. noon-4:00 P.M. Admission is free.

PASSIVE SOLAR AND SUPERINSULATED STRUCTURES

The period between 1940 and 1970 saw the construction of buildings with extremely poor energy efficiency in the United States. Since the oil crises of the seventies, the nation has been slowly turning back to energy conservation. Among energy-efficient construction methods currently in use in this country are passive solar, superinsulation, earth sheltering, adobe, and cordwood. In the future, bioshelters may serve as homes.

Passive solar features are elements of building design that directly utilize sun and shade to achieve heating, cooling, or lighting. Such passive elements include a southern orientation, overhangs, deciduous trees to shut out sun in the summer and admit it in the winter, thick walls and floors, and attached solar greenhouses. Most can be incorporated into buildings during their siting and construction at no cost or at a modest cost that is recoverable through energy savings.

A particularly promising energy-saving technique is superinsulation: doubling the normal insulation and adding an airtight barrier. Superinsulation may be combined with passive solar features. Usually, superinsulated homes use window glazing that admits light, but prevents heat loss. Ventilation is provided by air-to-air heat exchangers.

Passive solar features and superinsulation are found in many of the centers and buildings described elsewhere in this book. In this subsection we present two striking examples not previously described and a school that teaches construction of energy-efficient frame buildings. In separate subsections, we then describe three types of buildings that normally exhibit passive solar features and/or effective insulation. Additional schools and resource centers that help people build energy efficient homes or conserve energy in their existing homes are presented later, under Energy Efficiency in the section on Energy.

LA CASA DEL SOL
Sisters of Charity
5820 Bender Road
Mount St. Joseph, Ohio 45061
513-922-1468

Under the leadership of Sister Paula Gonzalez, some thirty-five volunteers converted the frame of one end of an old farm building into a superinsulated, passive-solar home. They used only materials that had been recycled, bought with money made by recycling, or donated. Thus the creation of the new 1,500- square-foot structure cost less than $10 per square foot.

The south face of the building is made up of approximately 250 square feet of quadruple-insulated glass. A loft contributes to the flow of warm air through the building.

Sister Gonzalez is often on lecture tours rather than at La Casa del Sol, her home; but she shows the house by appointment as her schedule permits. Phone to make arrangements.

EMERALD PEOPLE'S UTILITY DISTRICT
33733 Seavey Loop Road
Eugene, Oregon 97405
503-746-1583

This consumer-owned utility bought transmission and distribution facilities in 1983 from Pacific Power and Light, an investor-owned utility. Conscious of its service mission, it has built a headquarters that consumes only 7.59 kilowatt hours of energy per square foot. Heavy insulation and window glazing keep in the heat. The windows, "T" shaped and with reflective light shelves below the bar of the "T," send light far into the building's interior and diminish the need for artificial light. In summer the concrete walls and ceilings absorb heat that is blown out at night by fans (an active solar feature) that drive cool air through the building.

To see the building, make an appointment in advance with the Public Affairs Department.

HEARTWOOD OWNER-BUILDER SCHOOL
Johnson Hill Road
Washington, Massachusetts 01235
413-623-6677

Established in the Berkshires in 1978 to teach the skills and knowledge required to build an energy-efficient house, Heartwood offers three-week house-building courses and one-week and weekend workshops, including Carpentry for Women and Renovation. Students in the three-week course join in on the construction of a custom house involving timber framing and conventional framing. Tuition for a three-week house-building course is $800. Visitors who make appointments are welcome.

UNDERGROUND STRUCTURES

Underground structures benefit from the fact that below the frost line the earth remains at a relatively stable fifty-four degrees Fahrenheit. They also offer such advantages as low maintenance, protection from natural and manmade disasters, and conservation of above ground space. Architect Malcolm Wells advocates building underground in order to preserve wilderness.

A few examples of institutional underground buildings follow. A selection of other underground structures is described in John Carmody's and Raymond Sterling's *Underground Building Design: Commercial and Institutional Structures* (Van Nostrand Reinhold, 1983) and *Earth-Sheltered Housing Design*, 2nd edition (Van Nostrand Reinhold, 1985). However, many of the structures described by Carmody and Sterling, in particular the private houses of the second book, are not open to visitors. The Underground Space Center at the University of Minnesota (790 Civil and Engineering Building, 500 Pillsbury Drive SE, Minneapolis, Minnesota 55455; 612-624-0066) provides an information and referral service for builders and the general public.

One of the most striking underground complexes built in this country is the ten acres of rooms, passages, and gardens at Fresno, California, that Baldasare Forestiere (1879–1946) dug out alone, using only hand tools over forty years. Unfortunately, the complex is at this writing closed to the public.

TERRASET ELEMENTARY SCHOOL
1411 Ridge Heights Road
Reston, Virginia 22090

Built in 1977, Terraset was one of the first buildings to be constructed underground primarily to save energy. A secondary benefit was maintenance of the appearance of the rolling, wooded countryside. Before the one-story school was built, the top of a knoll was cut off. Afterwards, earth was placed on the roof of the structure to imitate the shape of the original knoll. The most striking interior space is the media center with a high ceiling in pyramidal form and a skylight. Originally, evacuated tube solar collectors provided high temperature water for heating and, indirectly, for cooling; but the solar system is no longer in use. The school is open to visitors by appointment.

YATES FIELDHOUSE
Georgetown University
Washington, D.C. 20057

The 142,275-square-foot building, which is almost completely below ground, includes a four-lane, 200-meter track; twenty courts for various types of games; a swimming pool; exercise and dance space; and offices. The floor is 30 feet below ground. Because of the slope of the land, walls on the east and south are partly visible above ground, and the main entry is through a sunken courtyard on the southeast corner of the building. The flat roof is covered with artificial turf and serves as a playing field and track.

VISITOR CENTER
Jefferson National Expansion Memorial Gateway Arch
11 North 4th Street
Saint Louis, Missouri 63102

Missouri uses for storage more underground space left empty by mines than does any other state. Kansas City has more than 44 million square feet of warehouses, factories, and offices in abandoned mines, 90 to 210 feet below the surface, in limestone rock. Limestone was the material mined.

CIVIL AND MINERAL ENGINEERING BUILDING
500 Pillsbury Drive SE
Minneapolis, Minnesota 55455
612-624-0066

The 150,000-square-foot building on the Minneapolis campus of the University of Minnesota is 95% below ground, in two different types of space. Three levels are placed in soil that extends fifty feet below the surface. Under the soil is thirty feet of limestone. Beneath the limestone is softer sandstone that was mined to provide space for two additional stories. The lower of the two is 110 feet below grade. The upper and lower spaces are linked by two shafts containing elevators and stairs.

Active and passive solar optical systems collect sunlight and direct it through the building by means of lenses and mirrors. An ectascope, based on the principle of a periscope, allows people at the lowest level to view the surface.

The offices of the Underground Space Center are on the lowest level of the building. In addition to providing information and referrals, the Center conducts research and serves as a focal point for the planning of underground space use and as a base for international cooperation. The Center can be visited, Mon.-Fri. 8:00 A.M.-4:30 P.M.

Williamson Hall, also located on the University of Minnesota's Minneapolis campus, is 95% percent underground. It houses the campus bookstore and university admissions and records offices. A row of clerestory windows in the bookstore lets light into the store, and allows pedestrians above ground to see into it.

MOSCONE CONVENTION CENTER
747 Howard Street
San Francisco, California 94103
415-974-4000

The size of the Moscone Center, 840' x 525' (a large city block) and the center's role in increasing tourism may dismay ecologists; but better that the center be below ground than above. The only above-grade part of the complex is a glass-enclosed pavilion at the entry (30,000 square feet). The main exhibit hall (275,000 square feet) is the largest column-free exhibit space in the United States. The natural groundwater table is 10 feet above the lower floor of the center. A bentonite-based mixture is used for waterproofing. (Bentonite is a clay that expands when wet.)

To allow thousands of people to exit rapidly in an emergency, the building has 100,000 square feet of stairways and exit ramps.

STATE EMPLOYMENT DEVELOPMENT DEPARTMENT BUILDING
O Street, between 7th and 8th Streets
Sacramento, California

Designed by the Benham Group as a result of a nationwide competition, this California state office building occupies a block and a half divided by a street. A six-story structure with concentrating solar collectors on the south end of each of the top five floors is built on the northern half block. The floors are stepped back at a 45-degree angle on the southern wall to maximize collector efficiency. In the block to the south is a below-ground, one-level building topped by a park. A passage beneath the street ties the two together. A sunken walkway and courtyards help provide light to office windows in the southern building.

EARTHEN STRUCTURES

Building with earth rather than in earth shows great promise for low-cost housing.

PEOPLE'S ALTERNATIVE ENERGY SERVICE
Route 1, Box 3A
San Luis, Colorado 81152
719-672-3678

Costilla County, where San Luis is located, is a high-elevation, Hispanic area, where all the land is privately owned. Residents heat mostly with wood, which causes pollution and the cutting of forests. Since 1975 Maria and Arnie Valdez have been promoting alternatives to wood. They particularly encourage the use of adobe (sun-dried blocks consisting chiefly of clay and sand), and they emphasize the preservation of the passive solar adobe structures that are common in the area. Any adobe structure, without solar devices, is 30% percent solar efficient, Maria Valdez says; but government subsidized programs encourage people to move into less energy efficient buildings. The Valdezes work with low-income Hispanics for the most part and with other members of the community. Call for further information.

RAMMED EARTH WORKS
1350 Elm Street
Napa, California 94559
707-224-2532

David Easton, owner of Rammed Earth Works, builds walls from a mixture of sand (70%), soil (30%) and a little cement, sprinkled with water and compressed to half the original size by a pneumatic tamper. The walls, which are fourteen inches thick, insulate and are fire and termite proof. Rammed earth structures cost 10% to 20% more to build than conventional buildings, but energy savings gradually compensate for the extra cost. To visit a rammed earth building, contact Rammed Earth Works.

GELTAFTAN FOUNDATION
P.O. Box 145
Claremont, California 91711
714-624-5251

Iranian-born Nadar Khalili is perfecting a technique he has named Geltaftan: the creation of structures of adobe that, when built, are glazed like pottery and fired from within like a kiln, using a portable burner. The result is hardened buildings resistant to earthquakes, rain, and snow.

A small house that Khalili built can be seen at Future City Villages International in New Cuyama, California, between Bakersfield and Santa Maria. Call the project office, 805-969-5431, to arrange a visit.

Khalili offers workshops and programs in earth architecture; and the foundation is establishing an Institute of Earth Arts and Architecture in Hesperia, California. For information contact the foundation.

CORDWOOD MASONRY BUILDINGS

For a northern location, cordwood masonry dwellings are appropriate. Their walls are constructed of short logs (called "log-ends") laid widthwise in the wall with a special mortar matrix. The houses have outstanding insulation and thermal mass and are low in construction and maintenance costs.

EARTHWOOD BUILDING SCHOOL
RR 1, Box 105
West Chazy, New York 12992
518-493-7744

Earthwood conducts workshops in cordwood masonry and low-cost earth-sheltered house construction Memorial Day and Labor Day weekends.

Rob Roy, who with Jaki Roy runs the school, has written valuable books on low-cost, energy efficient structures, including *Cordwood Masonry Houses: A Practical Guide for the Owner-Builder* (Sterling, 1980). The center sells these books plus plans for cordwood houses.

The school is housed in Earthwood, a two-story, cordwood masonry structure that the Roys built. Earthwood can be visited on a consultation basis ($24 per hour). Write or phone ahead for an appointment.

JOHN RYLANDER
Route 1
Grey Eagle, Minnesota 56336
612-285-4456

John Rylander and his wife built a cordwood masonry, earth-sheltered home primarily with their own labor and materials. Walls are twenty inches thick and have poured cellulose insulation about five inches thick in the middle. The result is a wall with an R factor (insulation rating) of about 20. About ten inches of earth on the roof are planted with a grass/wildflower mix. The Rylanders burn an average of 2.5 cords of wood per heating season.

They have also built four composting toilets of their own design, one of which is inside their guest cabin. They garden organically, make maple syrup, and do other "earthy" things.

They are glad to show their buildings to visitors and for a modest sum will provide overnight sleeping accommodations.

YURTS

Based on the circular felt tents of the nomadic tribes of Mongolia, yurts are not energy efficient, but they can be an economical, handy form of shelter. Portable yurts made of such fabrics as poly-cotton canvas or vinyl-coated nylon, and a supporting lattice of wooden poles are used for winter camping and sometimes, at least in Montana and Wyoming, for year-round living. Nationwide, yurts with solid wooden walls have become quite popular, as they can be quickly built even by people without experience in carpentry. Like more traditional yurts, the wooden yurts can be used as family homes, but they more often serve as three-season, auxiliary buildings.

THE YURT FOUNDATION
Bucks Harbor, Maine 04618

Five or six yurts, including a four-story structure, can be viewed at the Yurt Foundation; but be prepared to walk 1.5 miles from the road to reach them. The foundation was created for the purpose of collecting traditional folk wisdom and combining it with modern knowledge to encourage simple living in contact with nature. The yurt symbolizes the blend of new and old. The foundation sells plans for yurts of three sizes and conducts yurt workshops.

The following two organizations each display permanent yurts plus a variety of other low cost, and/or energy efficient structures:

APPALACHIA – SCIENCE IN THE PUBLIC INTEREST (ASPI)
Route 5, Box 423
Livingston, Kentucky 40445
606-453-2105

Known nationally for its Simple Lifestyle Calendar, ASPI is an educational center for the Appalachians. It has constructed a cordwood house with a solar breadbox hot water heater, cistern, and composting toilet; a frame house with attached solar greenhouse, photovoltaic panels, and a wood-burning hot water heater; a yurt; a geodesic dome; a workshop with modified post and beam structure; and a classic pole structure. It has also overseen the building of an inexpensive two-bedroom superinsulated house on one of two land trusts for low-income people that it has spawned. Like the other buildings, this house can be visited by appointment.

ASPI created a nature trail on its property and maintains an organic, intensive vegetable garden. It is encouraging citizen monitoring of the environment and to that end has produced videotapes on monitoring water quality and strip mine reclamation sites.

The center offers environmental retreats, during which people can live in its bunkhouse and hermitages and enjoy the surrounding woods and neighboring river; or, instead, hike along the 257-mile Sheltowee Trace National Recreation Trail that passes nearby. The staff can furnish consulting, design, guiding, transportation of gear and food, and resource and liturgical services, as needed. Cost varies with the services rendered, but may be around $5 per person for people bringing their own gear and food.

WOODLANDS MOUNTAIN INSTITUTE
Main and Dogwood Streets, P.O. Box 907
Franklin, West Virginia 26807
304-358-2401
Teaching Campus: Spruce Knob, Cherry Grove, West Virginia

Woodlands is an educational and scientific organization dedicated to advancing mountain cultures and preserving mountain environments in the Appalachians and around the world.

The institute operates an appropriate technology demonstration project on its Spruce Knob campus. A self-guided tour includes earth-sheltered buildings, an inexpensive lightweight concrete house, a superinsulated octagonal house, a farmhouse renovated to make it energy efficient, yurts (among them, the largest free-span yurt in the country), and various energy-related equipment, including a 4000-watt wind generator, and a photovoltaic audio unit. Phone or write to arrange to take the tour.

The campus is located on 400 acres that were once a sacred hunting ground for the Seneca Indians. The Nature Conservancy and the Claude Worthington Benedum Foundation assisted in purchase of the land. Students and adults participate in Woodlands' programs on Appalachian ecology, geology, and history.

BIOSHELTERS

Bioshelters—greenhouses designed to be self-sufficient ecosystems—may serve as housing in the future, although at present no bioshelters with sufficiently well controlled temperatures to allow year-round human habitation are on the market, J. Baldwin points out in a survey of bioshelters for *Whole Earth Ecolog* (Harmony Books, 1990). Bioshelters are not constructed of all-natural materials. A demonstration model at New Alchemy Institute is made, for instance, from aluminum tubing developed for airplanes and argon-filled pillows of a Dupont fabric.

Nevertheless, these shelters have the planet-assisting advantages of obtaining their energy directly from the sun, providing for the recycling of wastes, and producing food out of season. One of their means of achieving these goals are fish tanks. The water and dark algae in the tanks absorb and store solar energy; water from the tanks irrigates and fertilizes land plants.

The following sites include biospheres that the public can view.

NEW ALCHEMY INSTITUTE
237 Hatchville Road
East Falmouth, Massachusetts 02536
508-564-6301

For more than twenty years, New Alchemy has been working towards an ecological future. Located on a twelve-acre farm, the institute promotes sustainable agricultural systems that restore ecological balance and help neighborhoods feed themselves.

Its research, education, and networking programs serve students, teachers, gardeners, small-scale farmers, and communities. Current research projects focus on biological pest control, cover crops and composting for soil fertility, greenhouse horticulture and organic market gardening.

Visitors to the Cape Cod farm can see an organic market garden and herb and flower gardens; an auditorium in an old barn that demonstrates resource conservation techniques such as superinsulation and air-to-air heat exchangers; and three greenhouses of advanced design, including a thirty-one-foot-in-diameter Pillowdome.

The institute is open for self-guided tours any day of the week between 10:00 A.M. and 6:00 P.M. The admission fee is $3. In addition to tours, New Alchemy's education programs include workshops, short courses, publications and internships.

THE WINDSTAR FOUNDATION
2317 Snowmass Creek Road
Snowmass, Colorado 81654
303-927-4777

Founded in 1976 by John Denver and Thomas Crum, the Windstar Foundation emphasizes service through research, communication, and education. Its offices are located in the Rocky Mountains on 1,000 acres of land, for which the Foundation serves as steward.

The EarthPulse Program is the Foundation's research and education program, providing publications, informational presentations, and recommendations for action.

Perhaps the best known of the Foundation's research projects is the Biodome Project. Windstar has a fifty-foot-in-diameter biodome in which fruit and vegetables are grown year round, despite frigid outdoor temperatures in winter. No fossil fuels are used for heating and cooling or through pesticides and fertilizer. Photovoltaic panels and a small water turbine produce electricity. Windstar is exploring a family of designs to adapt the biodome to different climates. Call for tour information.

BIOSPHERE 2
Highway 77, Mile Marker 96.5
Oracle, Arizona 85623

Biosphere 2 is a 3-acre miniature planet earth. (Its creators consider the earth to be Biosphere 1). An airtight structure as large as an airplane hangar, Biosphere 2 contains areas representative of seven biomes, including rainforest, desert, and urban human habitat. Eight human volunteers along with various other animals will be sealed into the structure for two years. They will grow all their food and recycle all wastes. Some people working on the project believe that the experiment will help us to live better on earth; others believe that it will prepare us to live in space.

The public can tour the site of Biosphere 2 daily, even after the shelter has been sealed. Tours include a slide show, exploration of a model of Biosphere 2, and a walk through the project's research and development center with its tropical garden, rainforest, savannah, desert, and animal bays. The price of a ticket is $9.50. For tour information call 900-737-5700 at a cost of $1.95 and for reservations, which are mandatory, call 602-896-2108.

Environmental Research Laboratory of the University of Arizona, which has worked on Biosphere 2, has designed a Solar Oasis for Phoenix that covers 2 acres. It will not be enclosed. Canopies that catch and towers that evaporate water will be parts of an integrated cooling system. At this writing, the opening date has not been set. For information, contact Environmental Research Laboratory, 2601 West Airport Drive, Tucson, Arizona 85706; 602-741-1990.

CHAPTER FOUR

Alternative Energy Sites

Currently renewable energy sources account for about 8% of energy use in the United States. Energy efficiency measures save at least 29 quads of energy a year, equal to more than 25% of the energy actually expended and to five times the annual production of the nation's nuclear plants (5.7 quads).

Below are listed examples of places to visit to see renewable energy technologies and energy-efficiency measures in effect. To find other such places contact the relevant state energy office or Energy Extension Service (EES). The *Energy Information Directory* published by the federal Energy Information Administration gives addresses and phone numbers for state offices, along with a variety of other sources of information. It is revised periodically and is available free from the National Energy Information Center, EI-231, Energy Information Administration, Forrestal Building, Washington, D.C. 20585 (202-586-8800). The organizations listed in Critical Mass Energy Project's *National Directory of Safe Energy Organizations* are another potential source of information. The 1991 edition costs activists $5. Order from the project at 215 Pennsylvania Ave. SE, Washington, D.C. 20003 (202-546-4996).

Many renewable energy technologies and certain energy-efficiency measures entail some environmental damage. Eliminating energy consumption, although often not feasible, is the most ecologically sound alternative. Even the manufacture of photovoltaic cells involves toxic chemicals. Selecting an appropriate source of energy therefore tends to be a matter of complex trade-offs. In general, ecologists favor decentralized over centralized energy production, not only for the sake of the environment but also for reasons of economics and stability; but I describe here some large plants in order to give a relatively complete overview.

Despite the drawbacks of the larger facilities, they do not, like nuclear power, produce nuclear waste or nuclear bomb material.

An example of the nuclear power plants that energy efficiency and renewable energy are replacing is Marble Hill in Madison, Indiana. It was canceled by Public Service Company of Indiana in 1984 when its first unit was 60% complete and its second unit 30% complete. In the essay "The Reactor and the Garden" Wendell Berry describes committing civil disobedience by trespassing at Marble Hill, across the river from Kentucky. The plant can be seen from Kentucky Route 42 between Carrollton and Bedford.

SOLAR APPLICATIONS

Solar energy has a long history that includes more than the passive solar architecture already noted. The first practical solar hot water heater was patented in 1891, as Ken Butti and John Perlin point out in *A Golden Thread* (Van Nostrand Reinhold, 1980). The first solar collector for house heating was installed at the Peabody Museum in Salem, Massachusetts, in 1882; a solar-powered generator was in use in St. Louis in 1904 and in Needles, California, a few years later. A Pennsylvania resident, Frank Shuman, even created a low temperature solar-powered engine that, attached to a pump, could raise 3,000 gallons of water 33 feet per minute; Shuman put it into operation in Egypt in 1913.

Because of a general lack of interest in solar technology in periods of abundant energy supplies, institutions and communities have not, as a general rule, attempted to preserve, or if preserved, call attention to early solar equipment and the sites connected with it. Edward S. Morse's solar heaters are no longer in existence, although Peabody Museum has a mock-up—in storage. Apparently nothing remains of Shuman's solar experiments. Those interested in solar history may have to content themselves with thinking of Samuel Pierpont Langley while climbing Mount Whitney, which at 14,494 feet remains the highest mountain in the lower forty-eight. Langley, an astrophysicist who became head of the Smithsonian, experimented on the mountain in 1881 with a box that captured and held heat under two layers of glass.

Readers can find modern applications of solar energy to visit, but fewer examples of renewable forms of energy are open to the public now than they were in the late 1970s and early 1980s, when the shock of the oil crises and the influence of former President Carter were strong. Some of the major demonstration facilities have closed, and numerous organizations that specialized in energy issues no longer exist or work primarily on other subjects. Many firms and utilities cite insurance regulations as a reason for not receiving visitors.

Solar technologies are of two main types: thermal and photovoltaic. Thermal designs convert the sun's energy into heat. The two major classifications of thermal applications are (a) basic collector technology, in which the heat is trapped and then transferred to air or water for storage or immediate use and (b) methods that concentrate the heat to produce high temperatures that may be used to generate electricity or carry out specialized tasks. Various types of passive systems in buildings are also thermal.

Collectors that heat water and space are often part of what are called "active solar" systems: pumps or fans transfer trapped heat from the collector to the points of use. (Passive systems rely on convection to distribute the heat.) As of 1987 the United States had 800,000 active solar domestic hot water heaters and 100,000 active solar space heating systems.

The nation has eight thermal electricity-generating stations in commercial operation. All are at Daggett and Kramer Junction and at Harper Lake in the Mojave Desert, owned and operated by California-based Luz International. The plants, called Solar Energy Generating Systems (SEGS) together produce almost 280 megawatts of electricity for Southern California Edison (an average-size nuclear reactor generates 1,000 megawatts). The plants are not open to the public.

Photovoltaic technology employs cells made of material that converts sunlight directly into electricity. These cells are commonly used to supply power to equipment, houses, and villages not linked to central utilities. The United States Coast Guard, for instance, uses more than 11,000 photovoltaic systems in navigational aids; and photovoltaic panels may be seen lighting signals along railroad tracks. More than 10,000 residences in this country draw on photovoltaics for part or all of their electricity.

Several photovoltaic electricity-generating plants are in operation, including a 6.5 megawatt station built by Arco Solar on Carissa Plain in central California and a plant run by the Sacramento (California) Municipal Utility District (SMUD). SMUD operates two units, each of which generates 1 megawatt and occupies 9 acres on the grounds of the Rancho Seco Nuclear Power Plant, 25 miles southeast of Sacramento, the first United States nuclear plant to be shut down as the result of a referendum.

Below we first list displays of thermal applications and then facilities with photovoltaic equipment, sometimes in combination with other renewable energy applications.

OFFICE BUILDING ANNEX 2, HOUSE OF REPRESENTATIVES
Washington, D.C. 20515

Authorized in 1978, this project consists of two different types of collectors. An array of 1190 square feet of low temperature flat plate collectors on the penthouse roof heats 70% of the water used in lavatories and in a cafeteria. Higher-temperature, concentrating evacuated tube collectors on the south half of the main roof power an absorption chiller for air-conditioning the House Information Systems computer center in the building. The solar panels are visible from the ground, including the Southwest Freeway running parallel to the Capitol.

CENTRAL UTILITY PLANT
Dallas-Fort Worth Airport, Texas 75261
214-574-8564

A Fresnel lens concentrator system produces both thermal and electrical energy, the latter by focusing light on solar cells. The photovoltaic component provides twenty-seven kilowatts of electrical power for the airport, and the thermal component heats water to fifty-seven degrees centigrade to supply half the energy needs of the 840-room East Amfac Hotel. To maximize output, the 110 collector modules track the sun. In operation since 1982, the system was created by ENTECH, headquartered at the airport. To arrange a visit, contact the utility plant.

AURORA PUBLIC SCHOOLS
1085 Peoria Street
Aurora, Colorado 80011–6297
303-344-8060

Of the forty-two schools in the Aurora Public School District, ten have flat plate solar collectors for heating water and space. In warming the buildings, the sun heats a glycol mix in the solar collectors. The liquid is pumped through heat exchangers over which air from the building is blown. The liquid in the exchangers gives up its heat to the air. Natural gas is used in the schools for conventional heating. A typical solar-equipped elementary school pays one-third of the natural gas bill it would pay if it had no solar collectors.

To arrange to visit one or more schools contact the District's Communications Services, 303-344-8060, extension 307.

ZOMEWORKS CORPORATION
1011A Sawmill Road, NW
Albuquerque, New Mexico 87104
505-242-5354

Zomeworks manufactures equipment for using the sun: solar water heaters, racks for mounting solar equipment, as well as architectural products. They are glad to show them to visitors. In front of their new factory is a "tracker garden," where various models of trackers can be seen moving like metal sunflowers. The factory grounds are landscaped with native plants.

SUNNYSIDE SOLAR
RD 4, Box 808, Green River Road
West Brattleboro, Vermont 05301
802-257-1482

A participant in the Clearwater Festival and other environmental programs, Sunnyside helps people to acquire and maintain alternate energy systems. The firm supplies parts for photovoltaic systems and complete systems and offers a one-day workshop every six weeks on photovoltaics, with training in theory and in practice. The owner's home, office, and workshop receive their electricity from an eight-panel Arco system. In addition to photovoltaic equipment, the firm handles hydroelectric, wind systems, and gas appliances. Visitors are welcome, but call ahead to be sure someone is there. A free catalog is available to those interested in ordering by mail.

PHOTOVOLTAIC PROGRAM, UNIVERSITY OF LOWELL
1 University Avenue
Lowell, Massachusetts 01854
508-453-0020

The program has several interactive displays on solar energy. Visitors may also see solar equipment being tested. A library of materials on renewable energy is available for consultation. Phone ahead to arrange a visit.

FLORIDA SOLAR ENERGY CENTER
300 State Road 401
Cape Canaveral, Florida 32920
407-783-0300

At the Florida center visitors can see research underway on a variety of solar hot water heaters and photovoltaic systems. The photovoltaic equipment is being tested on four structures, including a four-family, tract-type house. The center is open Mon.-Fri. 8:00 A.M.-5:00 P.M. Visitors take tours guided by a booklet and audio cassette.

The center offers courses for engineers, builders, homeowners, and teachers, and allows the public to use its extensive research library.

BACKWOODS SOLAR ELECTRIC SYSTEMS
8530 Rapid Lightning Creek Road
Sandpoint, Idaho 83864
208-263-4290

The owners of this company are glad to show to visitors who contact them in advance their mountain-top home, with its photovoltaic system and wind generator. The wind generator, originally their basic source of power, now supplements their solar equipment, which supplies 85% of their needs. Usually when the sun is not shining, the wind blows, they report. According to their mail-order catalog, they are "Quakers, vegetarians, peaceworkers, and amateur radio operators (KC7BX, WB7VAD)."

SOLAR ELECTRIC
116 4th Street
Santa Rosa, California 95401
707-542-1990

Solar Electric, a publicly owned corporation, has working solar electric systems and an electric car at its corporate offices. Visitors are welcome. Gary Starr, the president, is the author of *The Solar Electric Book: How to Save $$$ through Clean Solar Power: A Practical Guide*. The firm publishes the book ($11.95) and a mail order catalog, describing a variety of solar equipment.

ENERGY CENTER, SONOMA STATE UNIVERSITY
1801 East Cotati Avenue
Rohnert Park, California 94928
707-664-2577

The Energy Center is a private, non-profit organization, serving the campus and surrounding communities through programs in energy management and renewable energy education, professional training, consulting and information referral, demonstration projects, and scientific research. Displays at their campus facility include photovoltaic electrical generation, window insulation and shading devices, direct-gain passive solar heating, passive solar domestic water heating, convective loop solar space heating and cooling, and wind-powered electrical generation. Call ahead before visiting as hours change each semester.

GILDEA RESOURCE CENTER
930 Miramonte Drive
Santa Barbara, California 93109
805-963-0583

As a response to a major oil spill in the Santa Barbara Channel in 1969, Santa Barbara citizens founded the Community Environmental Council (CEC). The Gildea Resource Center was established in 1984 to house the CEC's operations and, at the same time, to exemplify designs suitable for a sustainable city.

The CEC held a design contest for the building, with energy efficiency the primary criteria. Solar features include a trombe wall, recessed skylights, photovoltaic solar panels, and siting to receive the maximum light and warmth in the morning and to be shielded from direct sunlight in the afternoon.

The center's 10,000 square-foot garden, which is both organic and drought resistant, demonstrates French intensive and Chinese gardening methods. Two local projects that have spun off the garden are a Community Gardens Program and a Safe Food Project, which is organizing a county-wide consortium of growers, grocers, and consumers with the aim of converting 20% of the county's agriculture to organic by 1990.

In the garden is a demonstration of various methods of backyard composting. The CEC has developed a comprehensive recycling program for Santa Barbara that includes buyback centers, curbside pickup, and a school newspaper collection program. The Council also tries to find ways of reducing the amount of waste generated.

Self-guided tours of the house and garden may be taken Mon.- Fri. 9:00 A.M.-5:00 P.M.

FLOWLIGHT SOLAR POWER
P.O. Box 548 (Sombrillo Road)
Santa Cruz, New Mexico 87567
505-753-9699

Since 1978 this firm, which specializes in supplying power systems for homes in remote locations and in water well pumping, has been running its shop tools using power generated by the wind and the sun. Its system also powers office computers, lights, a deep well pump, and home appliances. All can be seen by visitors.

WIND ENERGY SITES

In 1989 wind generators produced over two billion kilowatt hours of electricity in the United States, enough to meet the needs of a city larger than San Francisco. Most of these wind generators are in Hawaii and in three mountain passes in California: Altamont Pass flanking Interstate 580 just before its junction with Interstate 205 east of San Francisco; San Gorgonio Pass on either side of Interstate 10, north of Palm Springs; and Tehachapi Pass on State Route 58 between Bakersfield and Mojave.

Below is an introduction to Tehachapi Pass and to a few places in the eastern United States with wind generators. Several of the sites described elsewhere in the book employ small wind generators along with other sources of renewable energy.

For further information on wind energy, contact the American Wind Energy Association, 777 North Capitol Street NE, Suite 805, Washington, D.C. 20002 (202-408-8988) or its West Coast office, P.O. Box 277, Tehachapi, California 93581 (805-822-7956).

WINDFARM MUSEUM
RFD #2, Box 86
Vineyard Haven, Massachusetts 02568
508-693-3658

The "museum" displays wind machines ranging from eighteenth-century water-pumping windmills to state-of-the-art induction electrical generating machines. It also offers a lived-in passive solar home, farm animals, and energy exhibits with which visitors interact. Visitors are invited only for scheduled programs: July 1-Oct. 15, 2:30 P.M. daily. Admission is $5.

HULL HIGH SCHOOL
180 Main Street
Hull, Massachusetts 02045

At Hull High School, an Enertech 44 wind machine, manufactured in Norwich, Vermont, generates 400 kilowatt hours of electricity a day. Rather than using the electricity itself, the school sells it to the electricity utility. In return the school receives credits that reduce the amount it must pay for electricity by about $1,000 a month. The wind machine, which was bought in the mid-1980s with a grant, can be seen from the road.

ENVIRONMENTAL CENTER, INSTITUTE FOR ENVIRONMENTAL STUDIES
School of Theoretical & Applied Science, Ramapo College
505 Ramapo Valley Road, Mahwah, New Jersey 07430–1680
201-529-7742, 529-7747

A water windmill is among the alternative energy projects on display at Ramapo College's Environmental Center. Others include a passive solar classroom, raised bed intensive organic gardens, and a passive solar greenhouse. The center is supervised by the Institute for Environmental Studies, created for research and education by the environmental faculty as part of its commitment to helping solve environmental problems. The Institute has organized conferences on such topics as water problems in New Jersey and the state's rare and endangered wildlife.

Individuals and groups may tour the Environmental Center. Contact Patricia McConnell, Coordinator, at the above address for information and an appointment.

TEHACHAPI PASS
Northeast of Los Angeles, California

California has more than 14,000 wind turbines, with some 1,350 megawatts of generating capacity. Some 29% of these generators are in Tehachapi Pass, northeast of Los Angeles.

To see the windmills, follow Route 58 from Mojave towards Bakersfield. Take the first Tehachapi exit, turn right when you leave the ramp, and then right again onto Tehachapi-Willow Springs Road. This road goes over Oak Creek Pass and, at the summit, has an observation area for viewing the wind machines. At the junction of Tehachapi-Willow Springs Road and Cameron Road, park on the right. If you are a walker, cross the road and take the Pacific Crest Trail, which winds for several miles along Cameron Ridge among windmills and, in the spring, wildflowers.

The windmills near the Pacific Crest Trail are of two basic types: conventional style (like a stick bearing a propeller) and oval-shaped eggbeaters. The majority of the latter are three-bladed machines from Denmark. The wind turbines operate most efficiently, when the wind is between 20 and 40 mph. With the aid of computers, most turn themselves to face the wind and shut themselves down if the wind is too low or too high.

Calwind Resources, Inc. will allow people with a serious interest in wind energy to visit sites in Tehachapi Pass, at which the firm operates wind power plants. To arrange a visit, contact the firm's chief executive, Douglas Levitt, Calwind Resources, Inc., 23241 Ventura Blvd. #216, Woodland Hills, California 91364 (818-702-0249).

BIOMASS SITES

In 1989 biomass—organic matter that can be burned directly or used to create liquid fuel and methane (essentially, natural gas)—produced 4% to 5% of the energy consumed in the United States (some 3.5 quads), mostly from wood. Two-thirds of the wood burned for energy is consumed by industry, commerce, and utilities. (Clearcutting to obtain wood for the generation of electricity is becoming a major environmental problem in New England.) The remaining one third accounts for 10% of home heating. Ethanol (ethyl alcohol) mixed into gasoline to create gasohol is a major use of biomass. In 1988 more than 8% of the "gasoline" burned in this country was gasohol, in a 1:9 mixture. The production of gas from farm or municipal waste is an additional way of obtaining energy with biomass. This gas is burned directly or used to generate electricity. Some sixty landfill gas plants produced a total of approximately 139 megawatts of electricity in 1988. The burning of methane releases carbon dioxide, but less than the burning of oil.

"Waste to energy" systems that burn municipal waste are also in use but emit dangerous pollutants.

Biomass facilities in the Midwest are described in "Biomass Energy Facilities: 1988 Directory of the Great Lakes Region," prepared by and available free of charge from the Great Lakes Regional Biomass Energy Program, Council of Great Lakes Governors, 35 East Wacker Drive, Chicago, Illinois 60601 (312-427-0092). Most of the descriptions include a name, address, and contact person.

JOSEPH C. McNEIL GENERATING STATION
Burlington Electric Department
585 Pine Street, Burlington, Vermont 05401
802-658-0300

The Burlington Electric Department is operator and 50% owner of a wood-fired electricity generating station that at full load produces 50 megawatts of electricity. The McNeil Station, which began commercial operations in 1984, burns matchbook-sized woodchips (80%) and sawmill residues (20%), except when burning natural gas is more economical. The woodchips, made by chipping low-quality trees and harvest residues on the site where they grew, mostly come from privately owned woodlots. When the plant is operating at full load, it consumes eighty-five tons of material per hour. The station is equipped with filters that cut stack emissions to 1/100 of the allowable federal level, the department reports. A private contractor markets the ashes of the burned chips mixed with limestone as a soil conditioner. The plant draws water from wells. The water that is not lost in stack emissions is monitored, treated to balance the pH, allowed to cool, and then pumped into the Winooski River.

Tours of the plant are available, usually Mon.-Fri. 8:00 A.M.-4:00 P.M. Call the Customer Relations Specialist at extension 362 to arrange a visit.

SMALL FARM PROJECT
Heifer Project International
Route 2, Box 33
Perryville, Arkansas 72126
501-889-5124

The Heifer Project's emphasis on farming with livestock is controversial, but the basic aim of its Small Farm Project is praiseworthy: experimenting with traditional farming methods from the Third World to find means of assisting farmers in the United States and elsewhere. Along a portion of their Learning Trail, the staff transformed 2.5 acres of steep, eroded hillside by erosion control methods from the Philippines, Haiti, and Central America and created a small farm with a simple family house. One of the alternatives with which they are working at the farm is a biogas fuel system built by a former Peace Corps worker following a design created by an organization in the Philippines. Visitors can tour the Project seven days a week by appointment.

GEOTHERMAL SITES

Putting to work geothermal energy, heat stored below the earth's surface, provides more than 7% of California's electricity. In 1989 installed capacity nationwide was 2,700 megawatts. Geothermal sources are of two basic types: high temperature (over 150 degrees centigrade) used for generating electricity, and low (below 90 degrees centigrade) and moderate (90–150 degrees centigrade) temperature, usually employed for heating.

In generating electricity with a high-temperature resource, a company brings from the ground a) steam, or b) water so hot that it flashes into steam when it reaches the surface, or c) hot water that can be run through heat exchangers to heat a hydrocarbon and, in the process, change it into gas. In each case, the steam or gas runs a turbine. The highest quality sources are those in the first category; but harnessing geothermal energy causes problems.

The Geysers geothermal field in California illustrates the positive and the negative aspects of high-temperature geothermal sources. The field, which steadily delivers dry steam at about 340 degrees Fahrenheit and 100 pounds per square inch of pressure, generates 2,000 megawatts of electricity, enough to meet the needs of 1,500,000 people. However, the numerous generating plants degrade forty square miles of land and, because of dissolved chemicals and particles in the steam, cause air and water pollution. Most of the plants are owned by Pacific Gas and Electric, which has decided the field's potential is being depleted too fast to make additional plants feasible. The field, moreover, is expected to yield 2,000 megawatts for only about thirty years. (Strictly speaking geothermal energy is not a renewable resource.)

The Geysers field is northeast of Geyserville, itself about forty miles north of San Francisco. Passersby can see an impressive display of steam, and the seventeen-mile drive back into the hills to reach the plants is attractive.

Low or moderate temperature geothermal fluid is a far more benign energy source. Normally it is used directly to furnish heat, although small electric power generation applications are possible. For direct heat applications, geothermal fluid may be brought to the surface and piped through the area to be warmed or through heat exchangers that transfer the heat to another fluid that circulates through the area being heated. The geothermal fluid may also be left in the ground and heat exchangers lowered into it.

GEO-HEAT CENTER, OREGON INSTITUTE OF TECHNOLOGY
3201 Campus Drive
Klamath Falls, Oregon 97601
503-882-3583

The Oregon Institute of Technology campus is heated and partially cooled by water at 192 degrees Fahrenheit from three hot water wells, which range in depth from 1,300 feet to 1,800 feet. The Geo-Heat Center acts as a clearinghouse on all aspects of low- and moderate-temperature geothermal energy. It provides technical information by meeting groups and by answering inquiries, and it maintains a geothermal library for lay and technical readers. To individuals and groups the center offers tours of campus facilities and of geothermal applications in the area, including a district heating system in Klamath Falls and local greenhouses. To arrange a tour contact the center's director, Paul J. Lienau.

CITY OF OURAY
P.O. Box 468
Ouray, Colorado 81427
303-325-4323

Hot water presents itself gratis to the town of Ouray. The geothermal source here is hot springs. The spring water moves, mostly by gravity, to three motels and to city buildings. There, through radiators, it heats space and, through heat exchangers, water. It also warms the municipal swimming pool. Contact the city hall, if you wish to tour the system.

HYDROPOWER

With 88,000 megawatts of capacity, hydropower provides 10%-14% of the electricity used in the United States, depending on the weather. In 1987, 90% of the energy produced by hydropower came from 300 large dams. Large-scale hydropower is so damaging to the environment that construction of big new dams to generate electricity is grinding to a halt in this country. Smaller-scale, less harmful plants, are still being built — most in streams that nevertheless ought to be left unfettered.

BREITENBUSH HOT SPRINGS
P.O. Box 578
Detroit, Oregon 97342
503-371-3754 (Salem office and group bookings); 503-854-3314
(information and other reservations)

The Breitenbush Community, a cooperative corporation, heats its buildings by a geothermal system, using deep wells and heat exchangers that the members created themselves. It also generates electricity with an old hydroelectric plant and flume that members rebuilt. Their energy equipment is important to them, because they believe in self-reliance.

Indians held sacred the Breitenbush River Drainage, because of its healing mineral hot springs. In the early twentieth century the area had a hot springs resort. It fell into ruin in the sixties and was purchased in 1977 by a young man, who, with family and friends, restored and reopened it.

The Breitenbush Community now serves as a steward of the land, and is struggling to preserve the old growth forest around it. The community hosts conferences and offers accommodations for personal retreats. A room and organic, vegetarian meals for the latter cost $40-$50 per night.

ENERGY-EFFICIENT PROJECTS

Energy efficiency involves improving the efficiency of lighting and appliances, transportation, and agricultural and industrial production. Here, however, except for an initial example of cogeneration, we are primarily concerned with energy efficient buildings. The last entries comprise a selection of schools and centers that help teach construction of new buildings or the retrofitting of existing buildings to make them conserve energy.

Cogeneration is the combined production of useful heat and electricity. It can be fueled by a wide range of sources, including solar energy; but at present natural gas and coal predominate. In 1988 the United States had approximately 20,000 megawatts of independently owned cogeneration capacity, producing 3.3% of our electricity.

CALIFORNIA INSTITUTE OF TECHNOLOGY
Pasadena, California 91125

The university operates a four-megawatt gas turbine combined cycle cogeneration plant with heat recovery and catalytic reduction. The plant burns natural gas in an electricity-generating turbine. Heat recovered from the turbine exhaust (treated by catalytic reduction to remove nitrogen) is used to make steam that drives another turbine to make more electricity and then goes to the campus for use in preparing food, heating water, heating and cooling space, and for laboratory applications. To visit call George Fielding (818-356-6097).

SOLDIERS GROVE DEVELOPMENT OFFICE
Highway 61, Box 121
Soldiers Grove, Wisconsin 54655
608-624-5209

Soldiers Grove was subject to repeated flooding from the Kickapoo River, until a final devastating flood in 1978. Townspeople then decided to relocate its business district and some residential properties on higher ground and to take advantage of the opportunity to create "America's First Solar Village," where the buildings are designed to obtain at least 50% of their energy from the sun. Here you can see a wide variety of conservation as well as solar measures.

The development office distributes a brochure describing the solar buildings. A guided tour costs $1.

ROCKY MOUNTAIN INSTITUTE (RMI)
1739 Snowmass Creek Road
Snowmass, Colorado 81654
303-927-3851

Energy is one of five areas on which the Rocky Mountain Institute focuses its research and educational activities. (Other major concerns are the related fields of water, economic renewal, agriculture, and security.) Through its Competitek Program it furnishes utilities and large energy users with technical information on advanced methods of saving electricity. Other aspects of its program focus on ideas on how smaller consumers can increase energy efficiency.

Energy-efficient techniques utilized for the building include partially underground construction, door sweeps that eliminate drafts, switches that turn lights on and off as people come and go, a solar clothes dryer, a solar-powered ceiling fan, and insulated cooking vessels. The building includes a semitropical "bioshelter" for growing fish and crops, even bananas.

RMI is open to the public Mon.-Fri. 9:30 A.M.-4:30 P.M., and conducts guided tours Tue. and Fri. at 2:00 P.M. It sells by mail for $5 a Visitors' Guide to its building listing manufacturers of its energy-saving and water-saving equipment. It also publishes a *Resource-Efficient Housing Annotated Bibliography* that lists many additional sources of furnishings ($15).

SOUTHFACE ENERGY INSTITUTE
158 Moreland Avenue SE
Atlanta, Georgia 30307
404-525-7657

Southface houses demonstrations of such energy-saving techniques as radiant heat barriers, moveable window insulation, glazing, solar water heating, and passive solar design. It has an energy library and a building products file, both open to the public; and it runs a homebuilding school, holds seminars and workshops, and publishes a journal and other materials on energy saving design and construction for the Southeast. Its phone number is an Energy Hotline for questions on buildings and energy. The center is open Mon.-Fri. 9:30 A.M.-5:00 P.M. and the last Wed. of every month until 9:00 P.M.

HOUSING RESOURCE CENTER
1820 West 48th Street
Cleveland, Ohio 44102
216-281-4663

This demonstration house, a rehabilitated older building, contains displays on home repair and improvements and energy saving. The staff provides information on home repair and improvement and sponsors weekly workshops on these topics. The house is open to visitors Tues. and Sat. 1:00–5:00 P.M.

URBAN OPTIONS
135 Linden Street
East Lansing, Michigan 48823
612-337-0422

A community service organization centered in a demonstration house, Urban Options was formed in 1978 by people concerned about the energy crisis. They succeeded in gaining the continuing support of the city of East Lansing. Urban Options still works on energy. The house displays methods that people can use to make their homes more energy efficient; funds received for a program to weatherize houses at low cost enables the organization to hire staff. However, Urban Options now also concerns itself with other home-centered questions such as safe disposal of toxics and non-toxic pest control.

Projects of Urban Options include running workshops at the house in the evenings throughout the year, lending tools from a community chest, and operating an environmental library with an information service and its own computerized index of holdings. The house is open to visitors Mon.-Fri. 11:00 A.M.-5:00 P.M.; Sat. 10:00 A.M.-noon.

ENERGY RESOURCE CENTER
427 St. Clair Avenue
St. Paul, Minnesota 55102
612-227-7847

The center gives technical assistance for energy conservation in residential structures and arranges low-interest loans. The staff received national attention for its Shared Savings Rental Energy Conservation Program for large apartment buildings. The staff retrofitted the buildings to save energy, predicted the results, and monitored what actually occurred. The center is glad to talk to people interested in energy conservation and can show a site or two.

ENERGY OUTREACH CENTER
503 West 4th
Olympia, Washington 98507
206-943-4595

A community service agency, the Energy Outreach Center is a walk-in, phone-in information center. It provides objective information about home energy conservation and renewable energy, sponsors workshops that provide hands-on experience in topics like building a solar greenhouse or weatherizing a home, organizes tours of superinsulated homes and homes heated with alternative energy systems, offers consultations for a fee, and operates a library in which the public can browse. The center has a demonstration solar water heater. It is a project of the Olympic Renewable Resources Association and is funded by two cities and one county as well as by fees and donations. Hours are Mon. 9:00 A.M.-4:30 P.M.; Tues.-Fri. 9:00 A.M.-5:30 P.M.

CHAPTER FIVE

"Waste" Management Sites

Recycling was an integral part of the American way of life until the end of World War II. To rural residents composting and re-use were second nature. At least 70% of American cities ran recycling programs before 1920. During the second World War recycling was part of the war effort. Then came the years of abundant material goods, followed inevitably by "the garbage crisis" with which we are now contending.

The Center for the Biology of Natural Systems at Queens College (718-670-4180) estimates that up to 84% of the wastes of a typical suburb can be recycled. Many cities are setting goals of 50%, a rate already reached in Japan; and recycling programs are spreading and becoming increasingly sophisticated. In fact, the market is now glutted with used newsprint. We need to put into operation more factories that recycle paper and need to use more recycled products—or, better still, consume less paper in the first place.

Below are samples of striking efforts to handle "waste" and discarded material. They are listed under the entity that is in charge of the program and are arranged in the following order: drop-off programs, pickup programs, composting, salvage operations, and use of recycled materials. But first, two sites that make the past and present situations vivid:

NORLANDS LIVING HISTORY CENTER
RD 2, Box 3395
Livermore Falls, Maine 04254
207-897-2236 or 207-897-4918

At Norlands visitors learn how Americans used to recycle, as they assume for three days the role of nineteenth-century farm family members. When they harvest crops, prepare meals, and feed livestock, they discover, to quote one participant, that "You never wasted a drop of [nature's] bounty." The center is a year-round working farm on a 445-acre estate. Adult live-ins cost around $200. The farm may be toured in July and August, daily 10:00 A.M.-4:00 P.M. Tours cost $4.50. It is open to groups all year by advance reservation.

HACKENSACK MEADOWLANDS DEVELOPMENT COMMISSION ENVIRONMENT CENTER MUSEUM
2 Dekorte Park Plaza
Lyndhurst, New Jersey 07071
201-460-8300

Interactive exhibits show how and why present-day throw-away lifestyles harm the environment and point toward remedies. Displays include masses of actual trash, "hand-picked" from dumps, and a vertical board game, Composting.

The Meadowlands is an annual migratory stop for thousands of ducks, geese, and shore birds. After examining the trash exhibits, you can study the museum's bird identification panels, the Bird Watcher's Bulletin with information on recent sitings, and a diorama depicting an urban salt marsh and its inhabitants.

The museum is open Mon.-Fri. 9:00 A.M.-5:00 P.M. and Sat. 10:00 A.M.-3:00 P.M. The charge is $1.

DROP-OFF CENTERS

VILLAGE GREEN
West Corner of W. 4th Street and 6th Avenue
New York, New York
212-777-1422

Designed in part as a demonstration project, this voluntary, community-based recycling center is in a park near Greenwich Village. It collects paper, glass, metal, and batteries. Hours are Sat. 10:00 A.M.-3:00 P.M., Mon. 5:00–7:00 P.M., Wed. 11:00 A.M.-2:00 P.M., Fri. 8:00–11:00 A.M. Materials may be left Saturdays at East Side sub stations. Village Green uses "pick-up trikes" to transport materials.

TOWN OF WELLESLEY, PUBLIC WORKS DEPARTMENT
Box 81364, 169 Great Plain Avenue
Wellesley Hills, Massachusetts 02181–0004
617-235-7600

In establishing a state-of-the-art drop-off center, the town of Wellesley took advantage of the fact that residents have never had curbside trash pickup. They must take their refuse to the town's Recycling and Disposal Center (RDF) in order to have the town dispose of it. About 90% of RDF's users put materials into drop boxes marked for a wide range of materials, including mixed paper, tin cans, ferrous metal, batteries, used oil, firewood, and tires. They also use a bottle redemption service, compost area for leaves and grass clippings, corner for reusable items they are willing to give to neighbors, and stations for donating to the Salvation Army and Goodwill Industries, all at the center. The town hauls refuse not destined for recycling, from the RDF to a sanitary landfill.

In a park-like setting, with picnic tables, lawns, trees, and flowers, the center has become a social gathering place. The station was established with the help of local environmentalists in 1971 but is now run entirely by the Department of Public Works. It is located at 169 Great Plain Avenue, on State Highway 135 at the Needham/Wellesley town line.

PICKUP SERVICE

Pickup programs generally recover more waste than drop-in centers, because they require less effort on the part of the public. Pickup at the curb is most common, although special arrangements may be made with large users.

ECOLOGY CENTER OF ANN ARBOR
417 Detroit Street
Ann Arbor, Michigan 48104
313-761-3186

The Ecology Center of Ann Arbor is one of the four independent ecology centers founded on Earth Day 1970 that is still active. Ecology centers grew out of the recycling issue, although they expanded into other areas. The Ann Arbor center works on toxics reduction and alternatives to pesticides. Its recycling program offers free pickups once a month to Ann Arbor residents and operates a drop-off center at 2050 S. Industrial Highway, Wed.-Fri., noon to 7:00 P.M. or dusk, whichever comes first; and Sat. noon-3:00 P.M. The drop-off center houses a display on recycling.

Records of the early activities of the ecology center are housed in the center's public library, also containing books, periodicals, and clippings. The center is open 9:30 A.M.-5 P.M. Mon.- Fri. and 9:30 A.M.-1:00 P.M. Sat. Library hours are Mon.-Fri. 1:00–5:00 P.M. and 9:30 A.M.-1:00 P.M. Sat.

SWIFT COUNTY, MINNESOTA

In Swift County, residents separate waste into three categories: compostable (food, grass clippings, etc.), recyclable, and nonprocessable. Each category is separately picked up at the curbside. The county employs people who for various reasons would otherwise be without jobs to sort the recyclable waste. They pick off a conveyor belt paper, aluminum, glass, plastic, tinfoil, cardboard. Scot Collins, who is in charge of the solid waste program, says that these people, who need help, do "a terrific job." As a result of their work and of the participation of 60%-70% of the county's residents in the recycling program, some 40% of the waste stream is being diverted. The county is experimenting with the compostable material to learn how to make quality compost.

Visitors are welcome at the recyclables sorting center. Call Scot Collins for an appointment (612-843-2356).

SEATTLE, WASHINGTON

After the closing of two landfills operated by the City of Seattle, the city redesigned its solid waste program with the goal of attaining 60% recycling by 1998. Seattle is an environmentally conscious city, and at that time programs operated on a volunteer basis by non-government groups were recycling 24% of the city's wastes. Planners hope that the work of these groups will continue. An additional 8% of waste will be recycled by means of a curbside collection program; 2% through pickup from apartments; and 5% by a program for self-haulers. (The city contracts out garbage collection to private companies.) A three-part composting program will take care of yard waste, which accounts for 10% of the total. Individual households will have the option of paying for curbside pickup of yard waste, of paying to dump it at a transfer station, or of composting it in their back yards. The city has a hazardous waste drop-off point for households, and it operates a special pickup service for appliances and bulky items of furniture ($15 apiece). Many of these items, particularly appliances, are recycled.

Visitors to Seattle see abundant evidence of the pace-setting recycling program along city streets, according to Carl Woestendiek, waste reduction planner for the Seattle Solid Waste Utility. On the north side of town Recycle America provides customers with three stackable bins from which truck crews empty the materials into segmented trucks. On the south side, Recycle Seattle gives customers a single 90-gallon wheeled toter. Materials are sorted at the processing facility. As for regular garbage collection, citizens are charged according to whether they regularly use a minican or one, two or three standard-size cans. For an occasional extra bag, customers must buy a $5 trash tag.

Under contract to the city, Seattle Tilth (described below) educates volunteers who teach householders how to compost, and runs composting demonstration sites, which can be visited.

COMPOSTING

SEATTLE TILTH ASSOCIATION
4649 Sunnyside Avenue N
Seattle, Washington 98103
206-633-0451

An urban chapter of the Western Washington Tilth Association, Seattle Tilth educates the public on organic food production in an urban maritime setting. The chapter offers tours, lectures, and a spring edible landscape sale and fall harvest festival. It has a reference library on alternatives and a garden with raised bed gardening and edible landscaping, espaliered fruit trees, and a solar greenhouse. Visitors are welcome.

Under a grant from the Solid Waste Utility of Seattle, Seattle Tilth is carrying out a compost education program. It has created compost demonstration sites at five locations, including its own garden. The sites show low-cost holding units and worm bins, usually made from recycled materials, and also uses for mulch. Seattle Tilth developed Woodward Park's Zoo Doo program to compost manure, and it has produced a slide show on composting.

The office is open 8:30 A.M.-2:30 P.M. weekdays; the garden is open daily during daylight hours.

CAMPUS CENTER FOR APPROPRIATE TECHNOLOGY
Buck House, # 97, Humboldt State University
Arcata, California 95521
707-826-3551

Campus Center for Appropriate Technology has a diversified program, of which recycling is a strong component. Solar photovoltaic panels and a wind generator supply all the electricity used at Buck House, a demonstration center and home to the directors. With other center members, they tend an organic vegetable garden that they water in part through the use of cisterns. They put fertilizer from a composting toilet around fruit trees; they also run "grey water" (from sinks and showers) through an on-site treatment marsh, where plants absorb nutrients from the water. Periodically they harvest these plants and compost them along with animal manure, other plant waste, and kitchen waste. The resulting fertilizer enriches the vegetable garden.

In the fall of 1987 the center brought quality, inexpensive recycled paper to Arcata—and sold it. The university purchased $40,000 worth of recycled paper for the 1988/89 academic year. The Chamber of Commerce now uses recycled paper for its newsletter, and a print shop offers recycled paper as a printing and copying option. In one year the business grew so large that the Campus Center turned the Paper Project over to a local graphic artist who now runs it.

Buck House is open to the public from 9:00 A.M.-5:00 P.M. weekdays and by appointment. The Paper Project, open weekdays 9:00 A.M.-1:00 P.M., is now at 940 Samoa Boulevard, Suite 204, Arcata, California 95521 (787-822-4338).

Also in Arcata is a firm that accepts, for a fee, organic waste materials from the public and uses them in compost that it sells: Northcoast Quality Compost, South I Street (near Arcata Marsh), Arcata, California 95521 (707-822-4119).

A list of county and community solid waste composting projects is available for $3 from *BioCycle, Journal of Waste Recycling*, Box 351, Emmaus, Pennsylvania 18049 (215-967-4135). A year's subscription to the journal is $55.

USING RECYCLED MATERIALS

EARTH CARE PAPER CO.

P.O. Box 3335
Madison, Wisconsin 53704
608-256-5522

Earth Care sells handsome recycled paper products, ranging from office paper to greeting cards and gift wrap, and also cellulose food storage bags, biodegradable substitutes for plastic. A catalog is free. Earth Care products can be seen at the gift store, Wild Birds Unlimited (Earth Care's first distributor), 6107 Odana Road, Madison, Wisconsin 53719 (608-271-2444). Hours are Mon.-Fri. 9:30 A.M.-5:30 P.M., Sat. 9:00 A.M.-5:00 P.M.

COMPLETE THE CYCLE

3600 East 48th Avenue
Denver, Colorado 80216
303-333-3434

The center exhibits products made from recycled materials and other environmentally friendly merchandise such as compact fluorescent bulbs and low-flush toilets. The multitude of items from used materials includes stained glass and glass containers from recycled glass, and ceiling tiles and stationery from recycled paper. Arnie McKean, the director, plans for the center to become a clearinghouse for information on products and environmentally sound innovations by companies. The center is located in space donated by Tri-R Systems Company, whose business is reprocessing used materials. Visitors to the museum can tour the reprocessing plant. The museum is open Tues.-Sat. 9:00 A.M.-5:00 P.M. and by appointment. There is no charge.

AMERICAN SOIL PRODUCTS, INC.

2222 Third Street
Berkeley, California 94710
415-540-8011

American Soil Products recycles organic wastes into high quality mulches, soil amendments, composts, and topsoils. The wastes come from a variety of local sources: cocoa bean hulls from a chocolate factory, fir bark from saw mills, sand from a local subway construction site, spent compost from mushroom farms, treated sewage sludge (odorless and sterile) from municipal areas.

Visitors to the two-acre site see not only piles of recycled materials but also a greenhouse with drought resistant native grasses. Aquatic Park, where people practice kayaking and canoeing, is next to the site.

SALVAGE/RE-USE

Most communities have ways of circulating usable goods that would otherwise end up in landfills or incinerators: garage sales, rummage sales, flea markets, second-hand clothing stores, collections by churches and charitable associations, trading post programs on radio and tv. . . . Below are a few organizations and businesses that specialize in usable second-hand items, plus two projects that re-use buildings or land.

RESTORE
Route 2
East Montpelier, Vermont 05601
802-229-1930

ReStore sells items rescued from the waste stream for reuse, by teachers and artists in particular. Myriad types of clean, nontoxic industrial scrap and household discards are available for pennies, nickels, and dimes. ReStore is run by Restore Resources, which has offered to schools workshops on using the materials. The store, where you may find wood turnings, pieces of styrofoam, empty thread spools, and lead crystal vases, among other things, is open Wed.-Fri. 1:00–5:00 P.M. and Sat. 9:00 A.M.-2:00 P.M.

RECYCLE, AT THE CHILDRENS' MUSEUM
300 Congress Street
Boston, Massachusetts 02111
617-426-6500

The Childrens' Museum runs a shop similar to ReStore. So appealing are the tubs of computer keyboard keys, sheets of fake fur, and bins of Monopoly hotels, that the store takes in enough money not only to pay its staff but also to help to support the museum as a whole. Hours are Tue.-Thurs. 9:00 A.M.-5:00 P.M., Fri. 9:00 A.M.- 9:00 P.M.

INSTITUTE FOR TRANSPORTATION AND DEVELOPMENT POLICY
P.O. Box 56538 Brightwood Station
Washington, D.C. 20011
301-589-1810

The institute organizes a Bikes Not Bombs Campaign that has sent more than 4,500 used bikes, tools, and spare parts to Nicaragua. It is continuing to ship bicycles and parts to that country and is running Bikes for Africa and Mobility Haiti campaigns. To participate ask the Institute for local contacts. The Boston group, for example, holds a work session every Wed. 7:30–10:00 or 11:00 P.M. at Ferris Wheels, 64 South Street, Jamaica Plain, Massachusetts 02130. Visitors are welcome. It is the best way to find out what the group is doing, according to contact person David Weinstein. Ferris Wheels is the Boston drop-off point for donated bicycles.

The institute works to influence government policy, to obtain assistance from corporations, and to promote bicycle production abroad, as well as to salvage used bicycles for export. A number of the local groups organize special bicycle-centered events for the public to call attention to their work.

YELLOW SPRINGS BIKE CLINIC
Yellow Springs, Ohio
513-767-9393

Run by volunteers, the bike clinic provides free advice and the use of tools to people repairing bikes. It also sells them used parts for a small charge. The money received is used to buy tools and new parts. The clinic accepts donations of used bikes and bike parts that would otherwise be discarded. It is held in the Bryan Community Center. For times and further information call Scott Avnaim at the number above, or 513-767-1339.

APPALACHIAN PEOPLES ACTION COALITION BARGAIN FURNITURE STORE
204 North Plains Road
The Plains, Ohio 45780
614-797-2608; 614-753-1936

To develop jobs and home industries, chronically low-income Appalachian people have organized this furniture store. Here they sell second-hand furniture that they have collected and repaired. At this writing the store is open Fri. noon-7:00 P.M.; Sat. noon-5:00 P.M. Phone to learn of any additional hours.

URBAN ORE
1325 6th Street
Berkeley, California 94710
415-526-7080

A California company with a history of success, Urban Ore accepts or buys from the public building materials, such as doors, windows, and sinks, as well as collectibles, antiques, and scrap metal. It also obtains merchandise through general salvage work and through handling the liquidation of estates. It sells the building materials it collects at its 6th Street store, and other merchandise at the Discard Management Center (1231 2nd Street, Berkeley, California 94710; 415-526-9467). Phone before taking discards to Urban Ore; the staff can tell you whether they want them.

SAVANNAH LANDMARK REHABILITATION PROJECT
c/o Historic Savannah Foundation
212 West Broughton Street
Savannah, Georgia 31402
912-233-7787

A private, nonprofit community development corporation, the Landmark Project was founded in 1974, because "It is far better and cheaper to rehabilitate the sound housing stock that is in the inner cities than to build public housing projects that are antiseptic, impersonal, and give no sense of neighborhood." The most remarkable feature of the project is that it is restoring a neighborhood without displacing the established residents.

Working with the Neighborhood Action Project, a partnership of for-profit groups, Landmark had by 1983 restored or built on vacant lots three hundred housing units in Savannah's Victorian District, a 162-acre neighborhood characterized by dilapidated buildings and absentee landlords. In 1988 it began work on a second two hundred units, of which 60% are restorations. The apartments are rented to low- and middle- income families from the district. Sources of funds for the second stage of work include a Federal Housing Development Grant, and low-interest loans from the National Trust for Historic Preservation, the City of Savannah, and the Ford Foundation.

The Victorian District is located just south of Savannah's National Landmark Historic District. Its boundaries are Gwinnett Street to Anderson Lane and East Broad Street to West Broad Street.

CITY OF BERKELEY
Department of Public Works, Parks/Marina Division
201 University Avenue
Berkeley, California 94710
415-644-6371

Together with a private organization, Design Associates Working with Nature, the City of Berkeley is constructing a California Native Plants Garden on the site of the Berkeley landfill. The garden is designed to replicate coastal plantings of central to northern California and includes some trees and a large variety of shrubs, ground covers, and grasses. They are not labeled. The garden represents a unique attempt to establish a native coastal plant community on a site built of imported soil, in an area with heavy wind and without groundwater; herbicides are not used.

Design Associates Working with Nature operates the California Native Plant Nursery on a site leased from the City of Berkeley in the Berkeley Marina. California native plants are grown for members, contract sales and periodic public sales, and for the city in lieu of rent (1442 A Walnut Street, Box 101, Berkeley, California 94709; 415-644-1315).

CHAPTER SIX

Economic Alternatives

Most environmentalists favor a decentralized economy with small, socially-responsible businesses and self-sustaining communities. Readers wishing to gain a comprehensive picture of alternative economic institutions and organizations, and, in the process, to find a wide variety of types of initiatives to visit should read *Economics as if the Earth Really Mattered: A "Catalyst" Guide to Socially Conscious Investing* by Susan Meeker-Lowry (New Society Publishers, 1988). We refer briefly to benevolent corporations and then turn to a few illustrations of economic alternatives.

Whatever we may think of large corporations in general, not all corporations are equal. *Shopping for a Better World: A Quick and Easy Guide to Socially Responsible Supermarket Shopping* evaluates the social concern of corporations that make consumer products. Attitude to the environment is one area the guide assesses. It is available for $4.95 plus $1.50 postage from the organization that produces it, the Council for Economic Priorities, 30 Irving Place, New York, New York 10003 (800-822-6435). Perhaps the best known example of a socially responsible corporation is:

BEN AND JERRY'S HOMEMADE ICE CREAM
Route 100, P.O. Box 240
Waterbury, Vermont 05676
802-244-5641

Two friends from Long Island founded the firm in an abandoned gas station in Burlington, Vermont in 1978. Now it is a publicly owned corporation selling ice cream to supermarkets throughout the Northeast and through franchise shops as far away as Miami and San Diego. An attitude of social concern has contributed to the popularity of the firm's ice cream.

The ice cream is made of natural ingredients. The firm has established a foundation that receives 7.5% of pre-tax profits, 50% of the proceeds from visitor tours of the factory, and 100% of fees for speaking engagements by members of the firm. The foundation gives grants to organizations furthering social change and community welfare, with an emphasis on Vermont. Furthermore, the firm donates ice cream to non-profit organizations, sponsors community festivities, and earmarks for a community recreation center a portion of its receipts from outlets selling "seconds."

Ben and Jerry's factory is open to visitors 9:00 A.M.-4:00 P.M. Mon.-Sat. A small fee is charged for a thirty-minute tour. One half of the fee goes to the foundation; the other half is applied to a program that encourages the opening of other innovative businesses.

Ben Cohen of Ben and Jerry's Ice Cream has created Community Products, Inc. (RD #2, Box 1950, Montpelier, Vermont 05602; 802-229-1840), which is selling Rainforest Cashew & Brazil Nuts Crunch. The nuts in the crunch are purchased directly, with the aid of Cultural Survival, from forest peoples. The profits are distributed in the following manner: 40% for rainforest preservation and other international environmental projects; 20% to 1% for peace; 10% to employee profit sharing; 30% to reinvestment in the firm.

We can influence corporate behavior by buying from and investing in firms that reflect our social goals and by boycotting those that do not. Even more importantly, we can support initiatives that are moving the nation in the direction of an alternative economy. These initiatives include land trusts, revolving loan funds, sweat equity, cooperative businesses, alternate trading organizations, and community development. A place to do research on such alternatives is the:

ECONOMIC ALTERNATIVES RESOURCE ROOM
P.O. Box 1308
Montpelier, Vermont 05601
802-223-7943

A project of Catalyst, an organization working to increase awareness of the connections between economics, ecology, and human rights, the center houses materials relating to socially responsible investing, the growing "alternative economy," forest destruction, ecophilosophy, and Third World and native peoples issues. It provides information free or at minimal cost and offers workshops, consulting, networking, referrals, and opportunities for small discussion groups. Catalyst is preparing an Impact Corporate America booklet listing fifty of what Catalyst has discovered to be the worst destroyers of Earth, with contact information, company products, and harmful practices. For ordering information contact Catalyst. The center is open Mon.-Fri. 10:00 A.M. -4:00 P.M.

LAND TRUSTS

Land trusts may preserve land for environmental purposes, as described in the chapter on natural areas. They can also be used to provide affordable housing or to both provide housing and conserve land. A private land trust is owned and controlled by the users of the land, while community land trusts have an open membership and an elected board that usually includes people that live on land owned by the trust, other residents of the community, and representatives of the public interest. They are nonprofit corporations that acquire land through donation or purchase with the intention of retaining title in perpetuity, thus removing the land from the speculative real estate market.

A community land trust may lease land on a long-term basis to people who want to build homes or may sell homes already on the land. It will usually impose restrictions on how the owners of buildings on the land can dispose of them. They may have to resell or give first option to the trust and/or may be allowed to obtain only a price that equals their investment (which includes the equity of improvements) plus or minus an allowance for any change in the value of the dollar. This ensures that the homes remain available to low-income people. In order to preserve the environment, the trust may place restrictions also on how the home owners may use the land.

SCHOOL OF LIVING HEADQUARTERS
RD 1, Box 185A
Cochranville, Pennsylvania 19330
215-593-6988

Founded by Ralph Borsodi near Suffern, New York, in 1934, the School of Living has long been an advocate of decentralization, holistic education, and human-scale institutions and activities as solutions to the major problems. One of its specific concerns is community land trusts. The School of Living holds land in trust and welcomes inquiries about putting land into trust. It will conduct workshops and seminars, and meet with people to help them to organize land trusts. It also publishes an explanatory booklet on community land trusts ($2).

A spokesperson for the School of Living describes it as giving "hands-on adult education in organic gardening, global economics, land trusts, and single tax for community use. Individuals visit our communities across the world and discuss the above topics. We can house a few at a time." Visitors who make prior arrangements are welcome at all School of Living centers in the United States: the Heathcote Center, 21300 Heathcote Rd., Freeland, Maryland 21053; Common Ground, Rte. 3, Box 231, Lexington, Virginia 24450; Birthright Leasehold, RD 1, Box 185 A, Cochranville, Pennsylvania 19330.

LIFE CENTER ASSOCIATION LAND TRUST
4722 Baltimore Avenue
Philadelphia, Pennsylvania 19143

The Life Center is an outgrowth of the Movement for a New Society (MNS), a long-time network of social change activists committed to nonviolent direct action, democratic decision-making, liberation from oppression, and production based on human need. Recently MNS disbanded, but the land trust continues with much the same goals as previously. These include providing low-cost housing for social-change activists and others in a neighborhood that is becoming more and more gentrified and taking housing out of the speculation/gentrification process.

The trust owns six properties in West Philadelphia: four communal houses, a hospitality/conference center, and a small office/apartment building. It furnishes housing for social-change activists, and provides space for conferences and low-cost office space for social-change organizations.

The land is owned cooperatively by members of the Life Center Association and managed by the land trust board and the management committee. The by-laws prevent anyone from profiting from the land trust. Individuals do not acquire equity. Rent goes to pay for mortgages, taxes, utilities.

For information, contact Clark Loveridge (215-472-7131).

OZARK REGIONAL LAND TRUST (ORLT)
427 South Main Street
Carthage, Missouri 64836

Ozark Regional Land Trust was founded in 1983 to demonstrate practical means to bring more rural land into community stewardship. There was no suitable model at that time for a regional land trust. In order to integrate environmental and social goals, the organization combined concepts and techniques from conservation land trusts and community land trusts.

The trust has now created five environmental community land trusts on a total of over 800 acres, about 120 of which are reserved exclusively for wildlife. The structure and goals of each vary. Each community land trust, though a title-holding affiliate of ORLT, manages its land according to its own land-use plan.

The largest of the land trusts is the 440-acre Sweetwater Community Land Trust. Here 80 acres are reserved for conservation purposes, including the protection of Sweetwater Spring; 120 acres are set aside for twelve farmsteads with ecological covenants.

Cave Creek Community Land Trust encompasses fifty-five acres of farmland along a tributary of the Buffalo River. Here an educational center in keyline permaculture is being established. (The keyline system involves the construction of thousands of small, gravity-flow, parallel irrigation channels to move water from the center of a valley, the keyline, to the sides.) An agricultural cooperative composed of people living on the land and of area residents will farm the land according to the keyline plan. Five homesteads are sited on forty acres of the trust that are unsuitable for agriculture.

People wishing to tour one or more of ORLT's land trusts should obtain the names and addresses of contacts from the ORLT office.

OREGON WOMEN'S LAND TRUST (OWLT)
P.O. Box 1692
Roseburg, Oregon 97470

The trust was founded in 1975 to acquire land for women and to preserve it in perpetuity. The trust is attempting to provide access to land in all the ways women want, from long-term homesteading and farming to brief periods of recreation and retreat.

In 1976 the trust purchased OWL Farm, 147 acres of woods and pastures with a log home and other structures, garden, spring, and pond. The trust depends on donations, often in the form of monthly pledges, from supporters across the nation for money to meet land payments and property taxes. Members are women who believe in the trust's purpose.

Women and children are welcome to visit the farm, near Days Creek, at any time. Visitors are asked to contribute $3-$5 a night (more if they can, less if they cannot) and to work one hour per day. When asking for information and directions to the farm, please send a self-addressed, stamped envelope.

BENEFICIARIES OF REVOLVING LOAN FUNDS

Revolving loan funds are nonprofit corporations that pool money from lenders and make it available to projects that advance the goals of the fund. ("Revolving" means that the fund continuously receives and disburses money.) The loan funds are often community-based, usually lent at below-market rates to groups that would not otherwise have access to capital, and provide the recipients with technical assistance to help ensure that their projects succeed.

The Institute for Community Economics (ICE), founded in 1967 by Ralph Borsodi and Bob Swann, provides technical and financial assistance to community-based organizations. It manages a revolving loan fund and also works with community land trusts and publishes a *Community Land Trust Handbook*, available for $10 from the institute at 57 School Street, Springfield, Massachusetts 01105 (413-746-8660). The two organizations described below illustrate both of ICE's concerns.

HOME (Home Workers Organized for More Employment)
Box 10
Orland, Maine 04472
207-469-7961

HOME was established in 1970 as a craft cooperative. It still offers craft training, and members still produce a wide variety of crafts, which are sold in a store on Route 1 in Orland, Maine; at a craft and farm fair each August; and by mail. However, with the help of ICE, the cooperative has metamorphized into a multi-faceted organization involved in economic reconstruction and social rehabilitation. Its programs now include day care, a college program (the Rural Education Program), a food cooperative, and a farm cooperative. It also sponsors the Covenant Community Land Trust.

Through the land trust, low-income families can obtain a lease on enough land for a house and for food and fuel production. HOME harvests trees for construction, and processes the wood in its own sawmill and shingle mill. Loans from ICE have financed land acquisition for the trust, construction of homes, and the purchase of the sawmill.

The HOME crafts store is open daily, and offers workshops on crafts Mon.-Fri. Visitors can see pottery, woodworking, and weaving shops, usually with someone at work. The food cooperative, which sells to the public, is open daily. This cooperative houses a greenhouse where plants and, in the spring, seedlings are sold. HOME operates a farmer's market July 15-Oct. 15, Fri. afternoons, where visitors can buy produce from its organic garden.

SOUTH ATLANTA LAND TRUST (SALT)
1523 Jonesboro Road SE
Atlanta, Georgia 30315
404-525-2683

SALT is a community land trust working to revitalize and protect the low income neighborhood of South Atlanta, two miles south of Atlanta's central business district. It purchases properties on the neighborhood's boundaries, rehabilitates or constructs housing on the land, and then sells (or rents) the units to families while retaining land ownership. When a family chooses to sell, it must sell its unit back to the land trust at a price that eliminates speculative increases in value.

The trust receives funds for operating costs, land purchases, and housing development from a variety of sources, including local banks and local and state agencies; but the Institute for Community Economics, which has committed more than $1,000,000 from its revolving loan fund, is its single largest source of funding.

In 1987 it started a program to provide transitional shelter for homeless people. Those selected from shelters are expected to start a savings program for a downpayment on a house, but pay only for utilities for the first three months and pay 25% of their income for the next nine months in a transitional home. If they successfully complete the first year, SALT provides them a house at a heavily subsidized cost.

In addition to providing housing itself, SALT has spawned three other land trusts in Atlanta (Cabbagetown, Chosewood Park, and Pittsburgh neighborhoods).

Visitors are welcome to call at the office on Jonesboro Road, the location of several SALT projects.

PRODUCTS OF SWEAT EQUITY

Sweat equity allows people to pay for their homes totally or in part with labor rather than with cash. It is often a part of a nontraditional financial package that may also involve a land trust, a revolving loan fund, and/or a city's donation of abandoned property.

HABITAT FOR HUMANITY INTERNATIONAL
Habitat and Church Streets
Americus, Georgia 31709
912-924-6935

Habit for Humanity is an ecumenical Christian housing ministry with the objective of eliminating poverty housing from the world and making decent shelter a matter of conscience. By having affluent and poor work together, Habitat hopes to create new understandings.

Habitat builds and renovates houses. Approximately 20% of its projects are renovations, most of which are carried out in big cities. It sells the new or renovated houses at cost with no-interest, no-profit loans, but recipient families are required to put in 500 hours of work on the home they are receiving or on other homes. The remainder of the work is carried out by volunteers.

Because Habitat wants to construct homes that low-income people can afford, the organization is increasingly concerned about building energy-efficient shelter. Construction costs have been cut as much as possible; now the group needs to help buyers save on utility bills, says Patrick Murphy of Habitat's Construction Resources. In Atlanta, Habitat cooperated with Southface Energy Institute in building a passive solar house. Affiliates in Florida, Colorado (Denver), and Kentucky have incorporated into their policies a stipulation that future homes be energy-efficient and have passive solar features. The Kentucky affiliate, Murray-Calloway, states that it is doing so for environmental as well as economic reasons. Affiliates in Yakima, Washington, and Bend, Oregon, are working with efficiency standards set by a utility's Super Good Sense program.

The organization welcomes volunteers both at its Americus headquarters and at its numerous affiliates in this country and abroad. Short-term volunteers at the headquarters receive housing and the use of cooking facilities. Those working there a month or longer are eligible for a food allowance. Volunteers working with affiliates must usually provide their own room and board. For information contact the headquarters.

COOPERATIVES

A cooperative is any business organization that is owned and controlled by its members, who have one vote each in decision-making. There are three basic types of cooperatives. (1) Consumer cooperatives are those whose members have joined together to purchase goods and/or services. They include food cooperatives and housing cooperatives. (2) Marketing cooperatives are those in which businesses or individuals join together to sell their products and services. (3) The members of worker cooperatives join together to produce goods and/or services for sale. Not all businesses described as worker-owned are cooperatives. There are many levels of worker ownership, and the term may be used to indicate businesses in which workers own stock but have no responsibility for making decisions.

Coop America (2100 M St., NW, Suite 403, Washington, D.C. 20063; 202-872-5307), a nationwide network of socially conscious businesses and consumers, publishes an annual directory of its organizational members, which include many cooperatives. It also publishes catalogs ($2) offering for sale selected products of its members, runs an investment service with information on socially responsible opportunities, provides health insurance that covers alternative therapies, and operates a travel service, Travel Links, through which members of the public can buy tickets (800-648-2667).

Below are centers that assist cooperatives, followed by a few cooperatives and other socially conscious small businesses. Additional cooperatives are presented elsewhere in the book.

UNIVERSITY CENTER FOR COOPERATIVES
513 Lowell Hall, 610 Langdon Street
Madison, Wisconsin 53703
608-262-3981

The University Center for Cooperatives is a part of the University of Wisconsin system, which has a special cooperative department or unit with a full-time faculty devoted to education, research, and development of all types of cooperatives. Throughout the year the center holds short courses, workshops, and seminars. It also presents semester-long courses and a correspondence course for university credit. The center's library on cooperatives and cooperation, which is open to the public, includes 7,000 books, 350 periodicals, reference files, and the Rochdale Collection, a collection of rare historical books. The State Historical Society, on the Madison campus, has an archival collection on cooperatives.

THE COOPERATIVE RESOURCES AND SERVICES PROJECT (CRSP)
3551 White House Place
Los Angeles, California 90004
213-738-1254

The Project is a ten-year-old public benefit corporation committed to providing education and training for the development of cooperatives of all kinds and to the expansion of public awareness about cooperatives. The center offers to members and to the general public discussion groups, gatherings, workshops, and technical assistance on a variety of cooperative topics including housing cooperatives, intentional communities, urban communal houses, and worker co-ops, especially with respect to business planning, management, and capitalization strategies. CRSP plans at least two events each week, and announces them in the newsletter that it copublishes, *L.A. Co-ops & Shared Housing Networker.*

The Jerry Voorhis Library at the center, which is open to the public, contains over 2,500 books, other publications, and audio-visual materials on cooperatives of all kinds. Visitors to Los Angeles are welcome to attend CRSP events, and to phone to learn what is going on at a particular time.

Of particular interest, is planning for an Ecological Urban Village (EUV) to be created on an eleven-acre site five miles northeast of downtown Los Angeles. Its purpose will be to demonstrate sustainability, through such features as ecologically integrated systems and social and economic cooperation. Six organizations are acting in an advisory and oversight capacity; CRSP is the lead organization. Interested visitors are invited to attend orientations, meetings, and parties for it.

WORKER OWNED NETWORK
50 South Court Street
Athens, Ohio 45701
614-592-3854

The goal of this association is to connect local people with the resources they need to create worker-owned businesses. The staff of six provides technical assistance and training in business and social process skills. Their major focus is regional, but they also work with groups outside Athens, to whom they provide information, training sessions, and advice by phone. They are creating a cooperative business incubator, and are also trying to start a flexible manufacturing network, a regionally based group of small manufacturers, each of which would make a part of a product. Such a network would benefit from economy of scale, at the same time as it would be able to customize products relatively easily.

The worker-owned businesses in Athens that they have helped start include Crumbs Bakery (219 W Washington), a wholesale natural foods bakery; Shine On Services (50 South Court Street), a cleaning, repair, and maintenance service; Peach Ridge Pedal Power, as its name indicates, a manufacturer of various types of recumbent tandem bicycles (visitors welcome; phone the number above to make arrangements); and Casa Nueva (4 West State Street; 614-592-2016), a restaurant specializing in affordable Mexican food, with a lot of vegetarian dishes and as much locally grown organic produce as possible; breakfast and lunch daily 8:00 or 9:00 A.M.-2:30 P.M., dinner daily 5:00–9:00 or 10:00 P.M., drinks and nachos Wed. and Sat. until midnight.

THE COMMON GROUND
25 Elliot Street
Brattleboro, Vermont 05301
802-257-0855

The Common Ground describes itself as the oldest natural food restaurant in New England. In 1971 more than 200 people donated $50 in money and/or work to begin a restaurant responsive to the needs of the community. During the early years managers appointed by a board of directors ran the restaurant. The staff assumed ownership in 1977, and the restaurant became a collectively run workers cooperative. All business decisions have since been made democratically, and committees carry out management tasks. Seniority is the only basis for differences in pay among workers. Tips are shared.

Since its establishment the restaurant has had the goal of offering wholesome food at a reasonable price in an informal, friendly atmosphere. To vegetarians the menu is extra special—cashew burger, harvest pie, herb and wine roasted potatoes and shallots. . . .

Each Thanksgiving the restaurant sponsors and prepares a community dinner. It continually provides space for music, dances, poetry reading, slide shows, and discussions; and its bulletin board serves as a networking tool. The restaurant is closed Tues. Phone for hours other days.

NESENKEAG COOPERATIVE FARM
650 Boston Post Road
Weston, Massachusetts 02193
617-893-5775; to volunteer 617-648-5117

The farm was established in 1982 as a nonprofit educational partnership for the purpose of providing fresh produce to low-income urban people at a cost below average market prices. Located on the Merrimack River in southern New Hampshire, the farm is run by a farm manager with help from paid farm hands and volunteers. Distribution to low-income people is coordinated by Boston Food Bank. The farm supports itself by selling memberships and by marketing specialty crops to restaurants. All produce is grown by organic methods. To visit, call the manager, Eero Ruuttila (603-886-6587).

DEVA
Box SM88
Burkittsville, Maryland 21718
301-663-4900

A cottage industry that makes and sells cotton clothing, Deva welcomes visitors during the week and most Saturdays. Their headquarters is usually open from 9:00 A.M.-5:00 P.M. Mon.-Sat., but call ahead to be certain. They sell samples, discontinued items, and seconds at reduced prices, and enjoy meeting people. They publish a mail order catalog.

BURLEY DESIGN COOPERATIVE
4080 Stewart Road
Eugene, Oregon 97402
503-687-1644

With approximately fifty worker-owners, Burley designs, manufactures, and markets bicycle trailers, tandem bicycles, and bicyclists' rainwear. In the early eighties the firm passed through a period of not being able to provide workers with a livable income. Now it is growing at a rate of 50% a year and is the nation's largest manufacturer of bike trailers. Workers are represented by an eight-member board of directors of fellow workers. Visitors should call ahead. Tours are not always possible in the busy season, March through August.

GANADOS DEL VALLE
P.O. Box 118
Los Ojos, New Mexico 87551
505-588-7231

Ganados del Valle (Livestock Growers of the Valley) is an agricultural development corporation founded in 1983 by livestock growers and artisans and located in the Rio Chama Valley of northern New Mexico. The organization is demonstrating that a traditional people can draw on cultural and agricultural traditions to revitalize their economy.

One of its projects is a cooperative, self-supporting spinning and weaving enterprise, Tierra Wools. The project is preserving the nearly extinct Rio Grande weaving tradition, while developing clothing and decorator accessories made from local fleece. In an adobe trading post which has been occupied continuously since the 1870s, visitors can see finished products and weavers at work. On certain days they can watch the entire cloth-making process.

Farmers in the valley are working to bring back the Churro sheep, whose wool is especially well suited to weaving. To this end they have bred ewes with Churro characteristics found in local flocks to full-blood Churro-Navajo rams from the Navajo Sheep Project at Utah State University. The farmers operate a cooperative breeding program, a cooperative grazing program, and a revolving loan fund, among other projects.

While some aspects of the Ganados del Valle project are controversial from an ecological standpoint, the Rio Chama Valley of ancient villages, quartzite cliffs, and flower-strewn meadows is itself worth a visit.

ALTERNATIVE TRADING ORGANIZATIONS

Alternative trading organizations market the products of low-income Third World craftspeople and farmers. The organizations pay them a fair price for their work, and educate consumers by providing information on the producers and their situations. Most of these organizations, like the three groups described below, are nonprofit.

JUBILEE CRAFTS
5517 Green Street
Philadelphia, Pennsylvania 19144
215-849-0808

Jubilee sells items from Latin America, Asia, Africa, and North America. To the extent possible it purchases directly from remote groups of craftspeople. It favors groups with local leadership, and crafts that use traditional skills and technologies and have local markets, as it does not want to increase the Third World's dependence on fickle overseas markets. By avoiding middle men, Jubilee is able to pay producers five times what they would earn if their products were sold in retail stores.

Jubilee sells by mail, through a shop at the address above, and through Jubilee Partners across the nation. To become a partner an individual buys a collection of samples. He or she may sell and then replenish these items, or use them only for display and take orders from customers.

TRADE WIND
P.O. Box 380
Summertown, Tennessee 38483
615-964-2334

Created in 1984 as a project of Plenty USA, One World sells products made from fabric handwoven by the Mayas of Gautemala. The items come through Artisanos Mayas, a Guatemalan group that buys the crafts from needy Mayan families, and, when necessary, lends the families money to purchase weaving supplies. The aim of Artisanos Mayas is to help the families provide shelter, education, land, and medicine for themselves. The Mayas are a gentle people who recognize a sacred relationship between themselves and the land and who want to own tillable land to farm in traditional ways.

One World sells through a mail-order catalog and through a small shop at the community, the Farm, where it is located. The shop is open Mon.-Fri., 9:00 A.M.-3:00 P.M.

PUEBLO TO PEOPLE
1616 Montrose Blvd., #4100
Houston, Texas 77006
800-843-5257; in Texas 713-523-1197

Founded in 1979 by two people working in Guatemala for a United Nations affiliated health organization, Pueblo to People purchases products on a regular basis from cooperatives in South and Central America. In 1989 Pueblo to People channeled more than $1 million to poor Latin Americans.

Pueblo to People sells through a mail-order catalog and through a store at 1985 West Gray, Houston, Texas 77019 (713-526-6591).

SELF-SUFFICIENT COMMUNITIES

A sustainable community economy gives security to residents and also assists in environmental preservation. Small businesses sited close to their customers are less likely to degrade the environment than are large, distant corporations. The multitude of places where benign economic development projects can be visited include:

CHARLOTTE, NORTH CAROLINA

The Optimist Park Economic Development Corporation (1320 North Davidson Street, Charlotte, North Carolina 28206–3466) is offering residents of run-down, inner-city sections of Charlotte the opportunity to participate in projects designed to give the area an effective economic base and, in the process, to improve their health and their physical and social environment. A greening project, incorporating the practices of permaculture, is the initial step. Residents are planting fruit and nut trees along roadsides, bikeways, and parks, as well as tending intensive vegetable gardens, engaging in small animal husbandry, and tending fish in ponds filled with water siphoned from the creek that runs through the area. The first year the produce that they raise will go to local markets and the needy. The second year it may be sold through the U.S. Department of Agriculture's Targeted Export Assistance Program.

Entwined with the greening project are programs for giving leadership training and experience to area youth.

For directions to garden spots in the Optimist Park area, phone the corporation president, Angelita Taylor, at 704-332-8732, or Doris Davis at 704-376-2887.

ASHEVILLE, NORTH CAROLINA

In 1984 the Center for Community Self-Help in Durham, North Carolina, founded the Self-Help Credit Union (413 East Chapel Hill Street, P.O. Box 3619, Durham, North Carolina 27702) to lend money to worker-owned and cooperative businesses and to encourage the building of low-income housing. Self-Help is a regulated, federally insured institution with depositors across the country. In 1988 it opened an office in Asheville, North Carolina, to serve the mountain region.

Among the businesses that the western office has helped to finance is the French Broad Food Co-Op (90 Biltmore Avenue, Asheville, North Carolina 28801; 704-255-7650). Organized in 1975, the co-op decided in 1990 to move from cramped quarters in the Old Chesterfield Mill to a larger store, two blocks from downtown. The move required $100,000, $40,000 of which was borrowed from members and $60,000 through the credit union. In the two and a half months after the move, membership increased from 800 to 1,200. The co-op sees itself as educating the public and promoting a sense of community, as well as selling high-quality food. It has a community room and an old-fashioned ceramic water cooler "filled with spring water from up in the mountains." To help people get through the recession it cut its prices for beans and grains to just above cost in January 1991. Hours are Mon.-Fri. 9:00 A.M.-7:00 P.M., Sat. 9:00 A.M.-6 P.M., Sun. noon-6:00 P.M. Non-members can shop.

JAMESPORT, MISSOURI

Local residents of Jamesport, Missouri, have revived their town by attracting visitors who would in the past have driven straight through on their way to see a nearby Amish community. The town has created a series of "Step Back in Time" festivals focusing on the area's heritage and Amish traditions, and has encouraged the opening of stores selling local products. For dates of the festivals or other information, contact the Jamesport Community Association, P.O. Box 215, Jamesport, Missouri 64648 (816-684-6146).

EMBARRASS, MINNESOTA

The town of Embarrass in northern Minnesota's Iron Range has revitalized itself through building on its Finnish heritage to encourage low-impact tourism. Embarrass has the "best quality and quantity of log buildings anywhere" in the United States, a member of the corporation Sisu Heritage told me. The corporation, which now takes in the entire town, offers tours of old Finnish houses and homesteads Mon. and Sat. at 9:00 A.M. and 1:00 P.M. and by appointment (218-984-2672 or 218-984-2601). The cost is $3 per person. A restored Finnish building at the intersection of Route 135N and County Road 21 is the site of an information center, complete with a replica of a sauna (open Memorial Day until snow falls; staffed only on weekends, but brochures are always available).

A craft store, Sisu Tori, sells locally made products, with an emphasis on items in the Finnish tradition, such as hand-loomed rugs and toasters—felted liners for boots or slippers (P.O. Box 111, Highway 21, Embarrass, Minnesota 55732; open at least Fri., Sat., and Sun. 10:00 A.M.-4:00 P.M.).

A Summer Finnish Festival is held the second Sunday in June; a regional fair, which has taken place for over fifty years, attracts visitors towards the end of August; and at Christmas time, in a Finnish ceremony, horsedrawn wagons carry residents to a candlelit cemetery.

The craft store at Embarrass owes something to Voyageur Vision, an organization that residents of Northern Minnesota's Iron Range formed to help educate local craftspeople and assist them in finding markets for their products. The first gift shop in the area was the Tower Voyageur Gift Shop in Tower. It is owned by two Voyageur Vision members and sells the work of 100 to 120 Northern Minnesota craftspeople. Products in the store include jewelry, wild rice, and birch baskets supplied by Native Americans. The Tower shop has helped other craft shops in the area, including Sisu Tori, get started (515 Main Street, Tower, Minnesota 55790; open 9:00 A.M.-5:00 P.M., Mon.-Sat.).

Local Employment Trading Systems (LETS) are a widely used tool for community revival. Members of a LETS group pay each other in "green dollars" for services and purchases. Transactions are reported to a manager who keeps a record, and furnishes members with a monthly statement, similar to a bank statement, showing their balance. The system provides what amounts to a means of barter among more than two people, and also plugs leaks in the local economy, as green dollars can only be spent within the community.

CRSP and Eco-Home in Los Angeles are cosponsors of a LETS project. CRSP has orientation meetings and parties that people interested in LETS can attend, and mails information on LETS in return for a fifty-two-cent self-addressed, stamped envelope.

CHAPTER SEVEN

Intentional Communities

Intentional communities are groups of people who have chosen to live together, usually because they have common views and common purposes. These communities provide members with emotional and intellectual support and enable them to economize and to share responsibilities like parenting. At their best, intentional communities are also kind to the Earth. Members tend to consume fewer resources than normal, as they are likely to share housing, gardens, cars, appliances, and other equipment. Many communities have benign land stewardship as a major goal.

The New Age Community Guidebook: Alternative Choices in Lifestyles (1989) contains descriptions of over 200 communities plus articles and resources. It is available from the publisher, Harbin Springs Publishing, P.O. Box 1132, Middletown, California 95461 (707-987-0477) for $7.95 plus $2 postage. The *Directory of Intentional Communities* (Communities Publications Cooperative and the Fellowship for Intentional Communities, 1990), presents more than three hundred communities; information on visiting, starting, and evaluating communities and resource guides. It can be ordered from Communities Publications Cooperative, 105 Sun Street, Stelle, Illinois 60919 (815-256-2252). Alone it costs $12. For $18 you can receive the directory plus two issues of the periodical, *Communities, Journal of Cooperation.* The journal relays news of intentional communities, discusses their significance, and describes resources.

Experiencing America's Past: A Travel Guide to Museum Villages (Wiley, 1986) by Gerald and Patricia Gutek describes a number of historic intentional communities.

Here I begin with a sampling of intentional communities from America's past. I then describe a resource center and a cross section of contemporary intentional communities. A few communities are described elsewhere—Breitenbush, for example, under hydropower.

The attitudes of contemporary intentional communities to visitors varies. Some are eager to teach the public about their lifestyles; others prefer to host only people who already have a serious interest in intentional communities. Our descriptions note the circumstances under which visitors are welcome.

ZOAR VILLAGE STATE MEMORIAL
P.O. Box 404
Zoar, Ohio 44697
216-874-3011; 216-874-4336

Established by German Separatists in 1817, Zoar was one of the most successful experiments in community living in the United States. The Separatists, on coming to America, bought 5,500 acres in Tuscarawas County, Ohio. As the only means of coping financially during their early years, they formed a corporation to which each member gave all his or her property forever. They prospered because of their industry and their resourcefulness. They paid off their mortgage, for instance, by earning $21,000 shoveling out seven miles of the Ohio Canal. They produced what they needed themselves and were particularly skilled in woodworking and in weaving linen, for which they grew flax. The society went into a gradual decline after the death of their leader Joseph Bimeler, in part, because of an influx of outsiders. It dissolved in 1898.

The Ohio Historical Society now owns and operates the principal buildings. Several buildings have been restored and are open to the public. Visitors can also see the central flower and herb garden, planted in 1828 and embodying religious symbolism.

The Historical Society's buildings are open from early April through late May and from early Sept. through late Oct., Sat. 9:30 A.M.-5:00 P.M. and Sun. noon-5:00 P.M.; from late May to early Sept. Wed.- Sat. 9:30 A.M.-5:00 P.M. and Sun. and holidays noon-5:00·P.M. Admission is $3.

Bimeler Museum is open for information and a walking tour tape Mon.-Fri. 11:00 A.M.-4:00 P.M., when site museums are not open (except for holidays).

SHAKERTOWN AT PLEASANT HILL
3500 Lexington Road
Harrodsburg, Kentucky 40330
606-734-5411

Kentucky's Shakertown is one of a score of Shaker communities that flourished in New England, the Midwest, and the South during the nineteenth century. The Shakers were known for their strict celibacy: men and women occupied different sides of their dwelling. They advocated equality of the sexes and races, pacifism, and simple living. Members of each community held their goods in common.

From 1805 to 1910 Shakers at Pleasant Hill ran their 5,000-acre farm as the nineteenth-century equivalent of an agricultural experiment station. They also sold garden seed and herbs throughout the Midwest and South and, like other Shaker communities, handcrafted furniture.

Pleasant Hill now contains twenty-seven preserved buildings set in peaceful fields on the Kentucky River. By making reservations ahead, visitors can dine and/or stay there overnight ($48-$66). The village is open daily from 9:00 A.M.-5:00 P.M. Admission is $5.50.

Other Shaker communities that can be visited include Hancock Shaker Village, Hancock, Massachusetts (P.O. Box 898, Pittsfield, Massachusetts 01202), which has a Round Stone Barn, as well as other Shaker buildings and a herb garden. Visitors are also welcome at the United Society of Shakers, Sabbathday Lake, Poland Spring, Maine 04274 (207-926-4597), still the home of Shakers. The latter is open Memorial Day through Columbus Day; tours are $3.

A 1973 meeting of Christian retreat center directors and staff at Shakertown led to the drawing up of the Shakertown Pledge, named "in honor of the original gathering place and because the Shaker community had believed wholeheartedly in lives of creative simplicity." The first three of its nine points were "1) I declare myself to be a world citizen. 2) I commit myself to lead an ecologically sound life. 3) I commit myself to lead a life of creative simplicity and to share my personal wealth with the world's poor." The pledge marked a milestone in the movement towards simple living among people of the Christian faith.

FRUITLANDS MUSEUM
102 Prospect Hill Road
Harvard, Massachusetts 01451
508-456-3924

In 1843, at an eighteenth-century farmhouse at Fruitlands, Bronson Alcott, father of Louisa May Alcott (author of *Little Women*), made an abortive attempt to form a Utopian community. He was a despotic overseer. Each morning he gathered members together and assigned tasks. Not liking physical labor himself, he at one point left with Charles Lane, after telling the women and children to harvest the crops. They could not get them all in and went hungry. The community dissolved seven months after it started.

The farmhouse is now a museum of the Transcendental movement, with mementos of Thoreau, Emerson, Alcott, and others. Also on the estate are a Shaker House, an American Indian Museum, and a Picture Gallery, which houses a collection of paintings by members of the Hudson River School, including Thomas Cole, who called attention to the American wilderness through his art. The wooded grounds are lovely for short hikes and picnics.

The Fruitlands Museums are open from mid-May through mid-Oct. Tues. through Sun. and Mon. holidays, from 10:00 A.M.-5:00 P.M. Adult admission is $5.

William G. Scheller's *More Country Walks Near Boston* (Appalachian Mountain Club, 1984) describes a walk to the site of another Transcendental experiment in communal living from the 1840s, Brook Farm in West Roxbury. The meadows and woods at Brook Farm have now been classified as an "urban wild."

SHARED LIVING RESOURCE CENTER
2375 Shattuck Avenue
Berkeley, California 94704
415-548-6608

Directed by Ken Norwood, a former planner/architect for offices in Los Angeles, this nonprofit center provides networking, counseling, and architectural and ecological design and development services to people who wish to form shared-living communities. The staff conducts workshops, consultation sessions, and seminars, and is glad to let visitors consult their library and see designs and slides of cooperative housing projects. The center holds monthly potluck suppers to help form core groups for new housing projects.

SIRIUS COMMUNITY
Baker Road
Shutesbury, Massachusetts 01072
413-259-1251

Sirius is an intentional spiritual community with twenty-two members and thirteen children, located on eighty-six acres of land in Western Massachusetts. Members honor the universal spiritual principles found in the essence of many different teachings and philosophies. Sirius focuses on meditation, educational programs, establishing ecologically sound lifestyles and buildings, ritual celebrations, and ceremonies. Long term work exchange may be arranged for semi-skilled carpenters and organic garden/farm workers.

On the first and third Sunday of the month, there is an open house and potluck lunch (please bring a dish to share), Sunday celebration service from 11:00 A.M.-12:15 P.M., Meditation for Planetary Healing at 12:30 P.M., and a tour of the community at 2:30 P.M. Overnight accommodations, including vegetarian meals, are available weekdays and/or weekends. "For information please call or write" to the Sirius Service Program at the above address.

THE FOUNDATION FOR FEEDBACK LEARNING
135 Corson Avenue
Staten Island, New York 10301
718-720-5378

At this non-religious community, about forty people live together in a cluster of five large, attractive houses that they remodeled. The neighborhood is of lower-middle income and integrated. Although the community is near the Staten Island ferry and a half hour from downtown Manhattan, the community's gardens, fireplaces, porches, and views from the houses give it a rural feel.

Among the community's aims are individual autonomy in cooperative community, better learning skills, and the ability to share thoughts and feelings. Their projects involve innovative use of video and other means of feedback "for learning many things, but mostly for learning how to learn."

Their cooperative businesses market refinished and recycled items as well as new items, many of them purchased at auction. The businesses include Every Thing Goes, a store at 208 Bay Street, in Tompkinsville that sells "new and recycled everything, at as low a cost as possible." Goods are here marketed on consignment for over one hundred people in the neighborhood. The merchandise includes items handmade by area residents. In another building furniture is manufactured or refinished, and sold. An adjacent lot is used as a flea market. The businesses provide one-third of the community's income and are eventually expected to cover all its needs.

A division of the foundation, Community Housing and Other Reclamation Design (CHORD), inaugurated a beautification and neighborhood improvement project on Bay Street in 1984 and has since extended its work to other neighborhoods.

The Foundation for Feedback Learning is glad to receive visitors and needs only a few days' notice. People staying in the community for "anything from a week to a lifetime" can either work with the foundation for room and board or work elsewhere and pay the foundation $400–500 a month for living expenses.

SHANNON FARM COMMUNITY
Route Two, Box 343
Afton, Virginia 22920
804-361-2191 (Wed.-Fri. 9:00 A.M.-9:00 P.M.)

Shannon, a "farm village," is a diverse community with members enjoying personal freedom, yet with the 490 acres and the buildings on them owned in common. Members finance the construction of their own houses and hold them by long-term leases, which they can sell or rent to other members, if they leave. Dues for full members are 7% of after-tax income and one and a half days per month of labor.

Some members participate in two worker-owned businesses, Heartwood Design (cabinetry and lumber sales) and Starburst Computer Group.

Shannon holds open house on Monthly Meeting Days, usually the first Saturday each month. Visitors should plan to be at Shannon at this time. Overnight accommodations are sometimes available. If you want to stay overnight, call ahead. Accommodations are with individual families. The visitor fee is $5 per day per person; $1 for campers.

KOINONIA PARTNERS
Route 2
Americus, Georgia 31709
912-924-0391

Koinonia Partners was founded as Koinonia Farm in rural southwest Georgia in 1942 by Clarence Jordan, author of the Cotton Patch Version of the Bible. Espousing a simple lifestyle and sharing possessions and income, members work with black and white neighbors and with volunteers from around the world.

Providing housing is a major project. Between 1969 and 1990, Koinonia built more than 185 houses and sold them to area families in need. The families purchase them at cost, with no-interest mortgages. Funds from the mortgages help finance the building of additional houses.

The community achieves self-sufficiency by raising fruit and vegetables for its own consumption in a four-acre organic garden and greenhouse; by growing cash crops of peanuts, corn, soybeans, and grapes for sale locally; and by preparing such food products as pecan candy, fruitcake, and granola for mail-order sale. The mail-order business allows Koinonia to provide seasonal employment for sixty people.

Members of Koinonia Partners founded Habitat for Humanity and the community Jubilee Partners.

Visitors may go to Koinonia for a few hours or, with advance arrangements, for a few days. Volunteers work for three or four months in return for a place to live, a food allowance, and a small monthly stipend to cover personal needs.

THE FARM
34, The Farm
Summertown, Tennessee 38483
615-964-3126

The Farm went through a crisis and a profound change before reaching its present sound financial situation. The community was established as a spiritual collective on 1,000 acres in 1971. During its early years it had a traditional communal economy. People joining gave everything that they owned to the common treasury, and anything developed or received by a member belonged to the group. The community grew to 1,400 people on 1,750 acres; but the percentage of members earning money was insufficient. Also the community's businesses experienced reverses. The practice of extreme austerity for several years did not avert a financial crisis. In 1983, to prevent bankruptcy, a new board of directors gave members notice that they must within a few months be responsible for their own family's income and for paying a sum each week towards retiring the common debt and providing community services. The change brought the size of the community by 1986 down to approximately 300, where it remains. The Farm managed to keep not only its land but also its school, clinic, store, bakery, soy dairy, and several other small businesses. Today about a third of the adult residents work in nearby towns and about half make their living on The Farm in community-based businesses and services.

The Farm welcomes tours; and individuals can arrange stays of a week or less, in the fall, spring, or summer. Phone ahead. A small fee is charged for housing, perhaps $15 per person, per night. The Farm store sells food, books published by the community's Book Publishing Company, some of their own vegetarian products, and shirts from their Dye Works. The Farm is a wildlife sanctuary.

EAST WIND COMMUNITY
Box DIC8
Tecumseh, Missouri 65760
417-679-4682

A member of the community writes: "East Wind, est. 1973, is located on 160 acres of Ozark woods and meadows. We want our communal village to serve as a model of a society that is democratic, cooperative and egalitarian.

Income and expenses are communal. The community provides food, clothing, child care, health care, transportation and whatever else the membership deems appropriate. These entitlements are distributed among the members in a fair and equitable manner.

We support ourselves by making hammocks, sandals, and a variety of nut butters. Our sustainable agriculture program is growing. Our ecological awareness is increasing.

We can vary our work by doing different kinds of jobs and are free to make our own work schedules. Gardening, child care, cooking meals and animal husbandry are valued as much as work in industry. We enjoy our natural surroundings, our extensive book and recorded music collections and our many parties. Many of us have an interest in political and environmental activism.

Write to arrange a visit. Potential members visit for three weeks followed by a provisional period of six months."

HIGH WIND FARM
W7136 County Road U
Plymouth, Wisconsin 53073
414-528-7212

Established by High Wind Association, the farm has twenty or so residents living on 128 acres. Since the members feel that people need to live in greater harmony with nature as well as with one another, they have energy efficient buildings including "a bioshelter—a non-consuming micro-farm—one side a passive solar residence, the other side an experimental greenhouse," and practice sustainable agriculture.

People may live at the farm in any of several ways, each with particular responsibilities and benefits. There are householders (residents who build homes); long-term resident volunteers; residents-at-large (people without active responsibilities to the community, usually individuals wanting to pursue private artistic or business initiatives in a sympathetic ambiance); residents in special projects such as sustainable agriculture; and paid staff.

The association offers various educational programs organized around the question of how to transform individuals and society. A particular concern is the creation of an alternative think tank to feed the experience and models of alternative groups to national policy makers to help bring about a shift in values and beliefs. The association has been working on this project with leaders in the United States and abroad since 1986.

To market produce from its farm, High Wind engages in "subscription farming." An outside household can pay a yearly fee and receive an assortment of vegetables, eggs, and honey, at established intervals through the harvesting season.

An overnight stay as a guest at High Wind costs $25 to $30 for room and meals. Open houses, known as Hospitality Days are scheduled on the third Sunday of the month, March through November. A $5 donation is requested from Hospitality Day visitors who are not Associates.

ALPHA FARM
Deadwood, Oregon 97430

Alpha Farm is a "close-knit, extended-family-style community" on 280 acres of land in the Coast Range of Oregon. "Consensus, our decision-making process, is also a metaphor for the ideal world we seek to create here—and so help to create in the larger world. We seek to honor and respect the spirit in all people and in nature; to nurture harmony within ourselves, among people, and with the earth; and to integrate all of life into a balanced whole. We value service, and work as love made visible. Group process is a strong point; we meet regularly for business and sharing."

Founded in 1972, the Farm averages fifteen to twenty adults, plus a few children. New people reside there a year as trial members before they commit themselves to membership. Members and other residents work on the farm, in freelance professional work, and in community-owned businesses: a cafe/bookstore/craft shop, a hardware store, contract mail delivery, and construction. Members hold all income and resources in common. Individuals have private rooms; but other living space is common and evening meals are communal. The community offers workshops on consensus and facilitation several times a year.

The farm is "open to new residents; visitors are welcome for a three-day initial visit. Please call or write well ahead."

ALCYONE LIGHT CENTER
1965 Hilt Road
Hornbrook, California 96044
916-475-3310

Alcyone is a center for living/learning, located on 320 acres amid rolling hills sixty miles north of Mount Shasta, close to opportunities for swimming, rafting, hiking, climbing, and winter sports. A major concern of the community is cooperative living in harmony with the natural world.

Ariesun, the first operational building of the center, is a bioshelter that provides for self reliance in terms of organic food growing, recycling, and renewable energy generation. The 3,300-square-foot structure includes a solar greenhouse and a living compound for up to eighteen people. It features heavy timber roof construction, hand-made tiles, and rammed earth walls.

The center offers workshops in integrated architecture, among other subjects.

Visitors who are environmentally conscious (or who hope to learn how to be) are welcome for stays ranging from a few hours to a week or more. A one-day visit costs $5. A stay of a week in the bioshelter is regularly $200 ($350 for a couple); but guests who stay for at least a week and work twenty hours a week may live at the center for $120 a week and those who participate in an Experience Alcyone program pay $350 a week. Camping costs $15 a day or $90 a week. All these prices include meals.

HARBIN HOT SPRINGS
P.O. Box 82
Middletown, CA 95461
707-987-2477; 800-622-2477 in California only

Harbin Hot Springs is located on 1,160 acres of fields, woods, and streams, two and a half hours north of San Francisco. Once the site of a European-style spa, the land has belonged since 1975 to the Heart Consciousness Church, a non-profit corporation formed by people living in the area at the time. Heart Consciousness serves as an umbrella under which more than a hundred residents of the Springs engage in a variety of activities, including fine woodworking, publishing, and creative arts. The community's major source of income, however, is operating a hot springs resort and hosting conferences and workshop groups.

Harbin Hot Springs has resident and non-resident members. Residents work for the community or pay rent. Many have jobs connected with administering the community and providing for visitors. Decisions affecting the community are made by committees on which residents are encouraged to serve.

Visitors are welcome but should reserve ahead. Fees range from $8 for a daytime visit during the week to $50 for a private room on Friday or Saturday night. Camping facilities and dormitory space are available. Guests have use of hot and warm mineral pools, a spring-fed swimming pool, and a sauna; and are free to explore the land.

Harbin Hot Springs is developing a new community at Sierra Hot Springs in the Sierras, north of Truckee. Here are hot springs in a more natural condition than at Harbin Hot Springs. A three-hour visit costs $5. Camping costs $12-$15 a night. For information contact Sierra Hot Springs, P.O. Box 366, Sierraville, California 96126 (916-994-3773).

CHAPTER EIGHT

Cities

The United Nations predicts that by the year 2000, the world will have sixty cities of over five million, and that 50% of the world's people will inhabit towns and cities. If the planet's ecosystem is to survive, cities will have to be reshaped so that they work *with* rather than *against* the natural world.

The general characteristics of an ecological city are well recognized. To conserve land and energy such a city would have a high population density, and would be three-dimensional rather than flat. It would be self-sufficient in food and energy and would be made up of neighborhoods that mix social classes, if any, and mingle residences, businesses, shops, light manufacturing, and green spaces. Much of the land within the city would be held and used by the people in common. The city would be adapted to and would blend with its environment. Around it, would be a green belt or, preferably, open country.

These characteristics are more readily found in old European cities that evolved gradually over the centuries than in American cities. Many U.S. cities have been constructed in large measure since the development of the automobile, the basic cause of urban sprawl; and in older urban areas the automobile has caused urban boundaries to move ever outwards, while city centers decay.

In his novel *Ecotopia* (Banyon Tree, 1975), Ernest Callenbach describes San Francisco as the capital of an ideal nation, the result of the secession of the northwestern United States. In his San Francisco people travel on bicycles and in battery-driven buses. There are no cars. Creeks that once passed through underground culverts, run above ground along some of the streets. Residents live in the city center in buildings that contain stores, offices, and restaurants, as well as apartments. The central boulevard, Market Street, is a mall with little gardens, fountains, and thousands of trees.

Planet Drum has published *A Green City Program for San Francisco Bay Area Cities and Towns* outlining steps that can be taken to turn San Francisco into an ecological city. The suggestions for action are applicable to other localities (2nd ed., $9 postpaid from Planet Drum Foundation, Box 31251, San Francisco, California 94131).

No U.S. city in its entirety now approaches the ideal ecological city. Nevertheless, we can find glimmerings of the ideal here and there. The following describes two alternative housing developments constructed in different eras, a scattering of other examples of thoughtful planning, and finally three model towns under construction.

RADBURN, New Jersey

The Regional Planning Association of America, to which Lewis Mumford belonged, attempted in the 1920s to create a planned community in New Jersey embodying Ebenezer Howard's conception of a Garden City. It was to be a self-sufficient community of 25,000 people on 1,200 acres, divided into three neighborhoods. Radburn was never completed, in part because of the Depression. Only one neighborhood was built; a planned green belt was not purchased; and businesses and small industries never moved in. Therefore it developed into a bedroom community for white-collar workers.

Certain concerns that would be addressed today in a community seeking self-sufficiency were neglected. Houses were not oriented to the south, and production of food was not integrated into the design. Nevertheless, Radburn was innovative and influential. It had energy-saving curved roads; separated the pedestrian traffic from automobile traffic; and made ample use of commonly-owned green spaces. Houses, attached to one another, were built on cul-de-sacs. Each house had a small back yard, but the rest of the land was given over to paths, lawns, playgrounds, and other recreational facilities for the use of all residents.

Located in Fair Lawn, Radburn today is virtually as it was sixty years ago. For advice on best seeing it contact the Radburn Association, 29–20 Fair Lawn Avenue, P.O. Box 363, Fair Lawn, New Jersey 07410 (201-796-1300).

DAVIS, California

Village Homes in Davis reflects a changed point of view. The designers and developers, Mike and Judy Corbett, were energy conscious. All houses face south, are well insulated, and have large windows on the southern wall. Tile roofs help prevent heat from escaping upwards, north windows allow interior cross-currents in hot weather, and over-hangs admit the sun in the winter but shut it out in summer.

The community has set aside five acres for non-commercial agricul-ture, manages almond and apricot orchards, and has planted fruit trees in green belts. In addition, many residents have vegetable gardens next to their homes. A communal compost pile half a block long symbolizes the dedication to agriculture.

In lay-out the community shares with Radburn curving streets, cul-de-sacs, and common land, though its design is more advanced. Clusters of eight houses share a green space. Bike paths, on which homes front, seem to be everywhere. Roads are narrow to minimize heat absorption and re-radiation during the summer, preventing land from being wasted and discouraging the use of cars. Creeks meandering through the green belts form an above-ground natural drainage system that allows runoff water to be absorbed into the ground instead of car-ried off in pipes. A community building, with a swimming pool, fur-thers socialization among residents.

To find Village Homes, ask anyone in Davis. Visitors can walk through the area.

BOSTON, Massachusetts

Boston's Southwest Corridor Park, inaugurated in 1987, demonstrates, like Davis, how much could be done with the land the United States now devotes to roads. It also shows the usefulness of pedestrian areas that are designed with the help of the people who will use them. It is built on a 4.7-mile strip of land laid waste by an abandoned highway project. In developing the corridor, planners worked with community groups and talked to residents. As a result, the park, which varies in width from sixty feet to a quarter of a mile, contains a variety of spaces – basketball and tennis courts, play areas for toddlers, vegetable gardens, a 3.5-mile bicycle path. Sidewalks, crosswalks, and open spaces connect the park to communities on either side. The park brings these communities together, as people of diverse social classes use it and as residents help to maintain it.

To reach the park, take an orange line rapid transit train to any stop from Back Bay Station to Forest Hills. The orange line runs through the park.

MASHPEE COMMONS, Massachusetts

In Mashpee Commons on Cape Cod a banal, linear shopping center and parking lot have been converted into a pedestrian street, an authentic main street lined with shops, and a plaza. The semicircular plaza and the newly constructed New England-style building behind it are designed to be the town's "heart and gathering place." Landscaped open spaces in the town, which absorb rain, reinforce the region's watershed.

NEW YORK, New York

Pocket-size Paley Park, off East 53rd Street between Fifth Avenue and Madison Avenue illustrates the potential of a single building lot. Honey locust trees and a waterfall make the park a refreshing place to eat lunch or read on a hot summer's day.

SEATTLE, Washington

Seattle is divided by a complex freeway system. To link its two sections symbolically Lawrence Halprin designed a multilevel slab over the freeway. On it stands Freeway Park with greenery, fountains, and a sculptured waterfall, designed by Halprin.

PORTLAND, Oregon

Between 1961 and 1971 Halprin, whose architecture was greatly influenced by land shapes in California's High Sierra, created in Portland a series of open spaces: Lovejoy Plaza and Cascade, Pettigrove Park, and the Auditorium Forecourt Plaza and waterfall. Through erosion forms and falling water, they give people the equivalent of the experience of being in natural areas. Pedestrian malls connect them.

DENVER, Colorado

The South Platte River, which flows through Denver, heavily damaged the city when it flooded in 1965 and in 1973. Instead of engaging in a conventional flood control program, citizens gradually created the

Platte River Greenway. Today extending beyond the city, it includes 450 acres of riverside parks and forty miles of cycling and hiking routes.

SACRAMENTO, California

The Bateson Building and the nearby California Energy Commission Building (1516 Ninth Street) help to make the center of Sacramento livable, while providing a pleasing work environment. Both are built around courtyards where workers and the public socialize. They are also skillfully related to the street. The Bateson Building, named after the anthropologist Gregory Bateson, has two small, sheltered plazas, a small landscaped buffer, and balconies on the street. Both buildings are energy-efficient. The Bateson building, for instance, uses shafts of canvas to move warm and cold air up and down.

A brochure, "A Walking Tour of Energy Efficient State Buildings" in Sacramento is available in return for a business-size, stamped, self-addressed envelope from Public Affairs Office, California Energy Commission, 1516 9th Street, Sacramento, California 95814.

SAN LUIS OBISPO, California

San Luis Obispo constructed Mission Plaza in order to create a focal point for the city, based on its natural asset, San Luis Obispo Creek. California cities usually force the creeks that they have not buried under cement to flow through channels with concrete-lined vertical walls. San Luis Obispo instead widened and recontoured its creek's floodway and built terraced stone walls to protect the banks from high-speed flows. The city landscaped the creek-side plaza with native California plants, and it encouraged shops and restaurants to open second "storefronts" onto the creek walkway.

TUCSON, Arizona

In the center of Tucson is an extensive series of multi-level courtyards linking small stores, a motel, theatres, and an art gallery, and local, state, and federal government office buildings. Pedestrian bridges cross a street that passes through the area. Covered walkways, trees, and pools create a pleasing atmosphere, and tables and benches allow people to sit and work outdoors. The trees should be fruit and nut trees, the city should have planted more of them, and the use of water in a dry climate is a waste; but visitors relaxing away from the sight, noise, and odor of traffic, cannot help but feel that the city is on the right track.

SEASIDE, Florida

Seaside, on the northwest coast of Florida, between Pensacola and Panama City, is a new, small town that looks back to the nineteenth century. A hundred years ago, residents of small U.S. towns could walk to stores, service centers, and schools; and they shared a sense of community. Recapturing these advantages, Seaside, on only eighty acres, is compact. Streets allow cars and parking, but they are designed to make walking more attractive than driving. Residences, stores, and businesses are mingled. The houses, frame structures with tin roofs, revive a northwest Florida tradition of climate-adapted architecture. A beach is shared. The center of the town is still being developed in order for it to provide a maximum of amenities, including a concert hall.

Seaside is expensive. Cottages are available to vacationers, but a one-bedroom cottage rents for from $116 to $242 a day ($446 to $1,042 a week), with a three-day minimum stay from Memorial Day to Labor Day. Furthermore, the Victorian architecture is not everybody's cup of tea. Nevertheless, the town's design set forth a valuable and influential alternative to suburban sprawl.

Visitors can freely walk around the town. For further information contact Seaside, P.O. Box 4730, Seaside, Florida 32459 (904-231-4224). Special Places, Inc., which furnished us with information on Mashpea Commons and Seaside, sells designs for the well-ventilated houses built at Seaside. Its Cottage Catalog costs $5 and comes with a subscription to Special Places' *The Home and Town Gazette* (normally $5 a year) on community-centered urban design.

CERRO GORDO

35587 Row River Rd., Box 569
Cottage Grove, Oregon 97424
503-942-7720

South of Eugene on the north shore of Dorena Lake, an ecological community is being designed and built by the people who will live in it. At present the community is made up of a small number of residents on the 1,158-acre site and a large number of supporters.

The basic design concept of Cerro Gordo is the reintegration of village and natural environment. The houses, community buildings, and businesses will be clustered together to preserve in their natural state 1,000 acres of forest and meadows. Within the overall cluster of buildings will be smaller clusters of residences, each planned by the people who will occupy them. Housing types will vary, from separate, self-sufficient homes to townhouses and boardinghouses.

The underlying philosophy is that of Ian McHarg's *Design with Nature* (Natural History Press, 1969). Using his study and planning method, the community learned the land use limits set by nature. One of their primary goals is to live in a symbiotic relationship with wildlife. They are therefore preserving open spaces; leaving wide, natural corridors along ridges and streams; and landscaping with native species.

Private automobiles will not be allowed in the town. People will walk, cycle, or ride horseback, plus ride a trolley or minibus, and use a delivery service. Residents will recycle wastes, and, to the extent possible, obtain energy from the sun, water, and biofuels.

The community plans to be self-supporting with jobs provided by light production companies, education and publishing, community shops, and intensive agriculture. A forestry cooperative that manages 450 acres earned more than enough money in 1988 to cover the mortgage payment on the land while using a sustainable harvesting system known as Individual Tree Selection Management.

The Cerro Gordo Community Trust has three components: a Cooperative of residents and homeowners, a Community Development Corporation of investors, and a Town Forum of future residents and supporters. Residents own their homes and homesites and together manage common areas, utilities, and facilities.

Visitors are welcome at community gatherings scheduled throughout the year (especially in summer) and at other times by appointment. The community requests that before you go you send for the visitors' guide, and updated Cerro Gordo Community Plan. The Plan is available for $5, or $10 with a year's subscription to the quarterly newsletter.

ARCOSANTI
HC 74, Box 4136
Mayer, Arizona 86333
602-632-7135

In the Arizona desert, Italian-born architect and social philosopher Paolo Soleri is building a prototype for future cities. Called Arcosanti, it is an embodiment of Soleri's concept of arcology (architecture + ecology), according to which architecture and nature can work together as one process.

When completed, Arcosanti will house 5,000 to 6,000 people on only fourteen acres of an 860-acre tract. They will live and work in a series of interconnected structures resembling a single building, in one section twenty-five stories high. The remaining land will be set aside for farming and recreation. The city will have no cars.

Soleri plans for Arcosanti to be in many ways self-sufficient, though maintaining connections to surrounding cities. The city will grow much of its food in greenhouses situated along its lower rim. In the winter, heat from the sun, caught in the greenhouses, will be channeled through the city. All wastes will be recycled.

Approximately 3.5% complete after almost twenty years of work and with only about fifty residents, Arcosanti is still more of a construction site than a community. It may never be finished, but will, nonetheless, serve as an "urban laboratory." Visitors can already see the effectiveness, for instance, of Soleri's quarter-sphere, south-facing structures that in the summer shade and in the winter warm the craftsmen working beneath them.

The center is open to the public seven days a week from 10:00 A.M.-5:00 P.M. It provides tours for a suggested donation of $5 per person. A cafe serving mostly vegetarian food is open daily, 9:00 A.M.-5:00 P.M.

Soleri presents five-week construction workshops during which participants learn about arcology and join in building the city. The cost, including room, board, and seminar fees, is $660. The first week only (seminar week) costs $400. Arcosanti also offers overnight accommodations when guest rooms and apartments are not in use by students. The charge is $15–25 per night, except for a two-bedroom sky suite, which is $60–75 per night.

Soleri raises much of the income for the construction of Arcosanti from the sale of wind-bells, for which he received the American Institute of Architects' Gold Medal of Craftsmanship in 1963. Visitors to Arcosanti can see artisans handcrafting the bells of bronze or ceramics. They can also watch bell making at Cosanti, a complex of half-underground structures that houses Soleri's Cosanti Foundation. Cosanti is open daily, 9:00 A.M.-5:00 P.M. and is located at 6433 Doubletree Ranch Road, Scottsdale, Arizona 85253 (602-948-6145).

Arcosanti can be reached from the Phoenix Sky Harbor Airport by Sedona Transportation Company (602-282-2066; call 24 hours ahead, if possible). Phone Arcosanti also to arrange to be met at the Cordes Junction bus stop two miles from the city.

Unfortunately most American cities and towns have little in common with Village Homes. The following ventures demonstrate that though residents of most present-day cities cannot completely control their use of natural resources, they can contribute to environmental preservation, by living simply themselves and by working to transform their surroundings.

ECO-HOME
4344 Russell Avenue
Los Angeles, California 90027
213-662-5207

In Los Angeles Julia Russell created a demonstration site for ecologically sound living out of an ordinary suburban bungalow. She turned her front yard into a xeriscape: landscaping that requires no artificial watering. She learned how to garden organically; and, although her lot is only 51' x 137', she now obtains about 80% of her food from the garden in the summer and 50% in the winter. She heats her water by solar panels and generates electricity for lights with a photovoltaic system.

The house has become the nucleus of an Eco-Home Network. With the aim of furthering the adoption of appropriate technology and lifestyles, the network publishes a newsletter and other educational materials and offers a consulting service. Membership in the network is open to the public.

Eco-Home gives 1 1/2-hour tours, by reservation only, Sun. and Tues., 10:30 A.M. and 2:00 P.M. (In the summer the second tour may be later in the afternoon.) The cost is $5 per person for up to three people, less per person for groups up to ten people.

ENRIGHT AVENUE
Cincinnati, Ohio

In Cincinnati environmentalists are transforming an ordinary street, Enright Avenue, into a center of sound living. People from the association Imago who live along the street are leading the way, but they are involving their neighbors in their projects to the greatest extent possible. Many families have organic gardens and one owns a solar greenhouse that everyone uses. Others have chickens and bees, and trade their eggs and honey with neighbors. The neighborhood has its own recycling program, and also a buying club for natural food. It holds community dinners monthly and an annual harvest festival.

The street is located on a ridge surrounded by 100 acres of woods, although it is only a few minutes from downtown Cincinnati by bus. The hilliness of the area has prevented development thus far, but condominiums are a threat. The neighborhood is working to preserve the woods, which give the street much of its charm.

Visits can be arranged by contacting Imago (553 Enright Avenue, Cincinnati, Ohio 45205; 513-921-1932).

URBAN ECOLOGY
P.O. Box 10144
Berkeley, California 94709
415-549-1724

Under the leadership of Richard Register, author of *Ecocity Berkeley* (North Atlantic Books, 1987), Urban Ecology is active in such projects to change cities as zoning, creek restoration, tree planting, and city planning. Two of the organization's achievements that can readily be seen by visitors to Berkeley are Milvia Street and Strawberry Creek Park. Using an Urban Ecology design to promote cycling, the city is remaking Milvia into a slow street with new curb lines and new plantings (near Cedar Street and University Avenue). Strawberry Creek Park was once an abandoned patch of land, under which the creek ran through a pipe. Environmentalists brought the water to the surface for a block, and convinced the city to transform the area into a park (one block south of University Avenue and one block west of Sacramento Avenue).

In cooperation with East Bay Citizens for Creek Restoration, Urban Ecology produced stencils, each displaying a "totem" creek animal and the name of the creek associated with it. Over 200 activists spray painted more than 700 of the stencils to mark curbs under which creeks still run. The stencils are still visible.

Readers with a serious interest in city design are invited to visit Urban Ecology itself.

CHAPTER NINE

Peace Sites

Defense policy and international relations concern environmentalists as well as peace activists. Weapons production absorbs money and brainpower that could be better employed in solving environmental crises. Furthermore, conventional warfare and preparations for war as well as nuclear war cause environmental damage.

Below are a few groups protesting the arms race, and then sites representative of three paths toward peace. The chapter closes with examples of visions of peace and of conversion from the military sector of the economy to the civilian.

To find groups working for arms control, disarmament, and world peace in addition to those listed, consult *Peace Resource Book: A Comprehensive Guide to Issues, Groups, and Literature, 1988–1989*, ed. Carl Conetta (Ballinger, 1988) or the *Grassroots Peace Directory*. The *Peace Resource Book* is the work of the Institute for Defense and Disarmament Studies headed by Randall Forsberg, co-founder of the Nuclear Weapons Freeze Campaign. It lists 7,000 national and local groups, with brief descriptions of the national ones. Also included are a descriptive list of peace education programs and a guide to peace-related literature. The *Grassroots Peace Directory* describes more than 7,700 grassroots religious and secular groups. It is published as a group of regional directories. For ordering instructions write to *Grassroots Peace Directory*, c/o ACCESS, 1730 M St. NW, Suite 605, Washington, D.C. 20036 (202-785-6630). It costs between $8.50 and $14 each, depending on region.

When in New York, find out about local disarmament and social justice activities by calling or writing for a copy of the monthly *New York Peace Network Calendar*, New York Peace Network Coalition, 339 Lafayette Street, Room 202, New York, New York 10012 (212-477-5122).

Wilmington College in Ohio is the home of a Peace Resource Center and the Hiroshima/Nagasaki Memorial Collection. The latter is a unique collection of information about the atomic bombings, which displays materials donated to the college in 1975 by Barbara Reynolds, Quaker peace activist and long-time resident of Hiroshima. Research materials include a library in both English and Japanese, documentary film footage, and information on radiation victims in Japan and the United States. The Peace Resource Center contains a wide variety of peace education audiovisual and printed materials, available for rental and for purchase. The college welcomes visitors who wish to use the collections. People at a distance can keep up with the center's acquisitions through a newsletter, free of charge in this country. Contact the center at Wilmington College, Pyle Center Box 1183, 51 College Street, Wilmington, Ohio 45177 (513-382-5338).

PROTEST SITES

In 1989, 5,010 people in the United States were arrested for protesting against civilian and military nuclear programs. As a result of these arrests more than ninety people are serving or have served two weeks to seventeen years in prison, according to the Nuclear Resister (P.O. Box 43383, Tucson, Arizona 85733; 602-323-8697; $18 per year).

KENT STATE UNIVERSITY
Kent, Ohio

On May 4, 1990 Kent State University in Kent, Ohio, dedicated a memorial to the memory of four students killed by members of the Ohio National Guard during a demonstration against the Vietnam War twenty years earlier. At that time antiwar demonstrations were taking place on college and university campuses across the country. The deaths at Kent State increased opposition to the war.

The memorial, which is next to Taylor Hall, is four slabs of pink granite on a hilltop overlooking the Commons, where the shooting occurred. For the dedication ceremony 58,175 daffodils, the number of Americans killed in Vietnam, adorned the hill.

NEVADA TEST SITE
Southern Nevada, northwest of Las Vegas

Activities at the Nevada Test Site epitomize the destructiveness of the current United States defense system and the determination of advocates of other paths.

The Test Site is a part of the Upper Mojave Desert, which is approximately the size of Rhode Island. In 1936 Bob Marshall called the 4.5 million-acre roadless area that now contains the center the finest desert wilderness in the United States and proposed that it be made a preserve. Since 1951 more than seven hundred nuclear tests, above- and belowground, have taken place there. Now it is reminiscent of the "dreary fields of Gorgoroth" in Mordor, the realm of evil depicted by J. R. R. Tolkien in *The Return of the King* (1955). Radioactivity leaks from the bomb tests into the air and into the ground water.

On several occasions small teams of activists, organized by Greenpeace and the American Peace Test have traveled deep into the test site to call attention to the testing and to stop the tests by their presence. They have succeeded in causing postponements. Year after year demonstrations have taken place at the Test Site's boundaries.

The actions at the site are usually coordinated by the American Peace Test (APT), P.O. Box 26725, Las Vegas, Nevada 89126; 702-386-9834. The Nevada Desert Experience, a faith-based nonviolent direct action group, has organized Lenten and Hiroshima/Nagasaki vigils and civil disobedience at the test site for ten years (P.O. Box 4487, Las Vegas, Nevada 89127; 702-646-4814).

MINUTEMAN MISSILE SILO 6 IN FLIGHT L
North of Sturgis, South Dakota

A field of 150 Minuteman missiles abuts the Black Hills, sacred to the Indians of the area. Among the missiles, is L6, named by peace activists the Minds Being Wasted missile. Its silo is at the foot of Bear Butte, a mountain sacred to the Sioux nation.

On Easter Sunday, 2 April 1988, Kathy Jennings and Ladon Sheets, supported by a small group of Sioux and non-Indian Christians from the Rosebud Reservation, climbed over the fence and placed a lily on the lid of the silo. The protesters were convicted of trespassing and sentenced to fifteen days in jail.

The protest is cited in *Nuclear Heartland: A Guide to the 1,000 Missile Silos of the United States* (Nukewatch: The Progressive Foundation,

315 West Gorham Street, Madison, Wisconsin 53703, 1988, $12.50), which gives the precise location of each of the Minuteman silos. To find L6 "From Vale, go west 1 mile, then left 7.4 miles on State Highway 79. Missile is on the right."

VANDENBURG AIR FORCE BASE
West of Lompoc, southern California

Vandenburg occupies 98,400 acres, including 35 miles of Pacific coastline. Among the facilities on the base are the Western Space and Missile Center, which manages the Western Test Range; an Air Force Satellite Control Facility; and the First Strategic Air Division. From the base, missiles are test fired over the Pacific to Kwajalein Atoll and the ocean area north and east of Midway Island. As far as is known, the base stores no nuclear warheads.

In order to protest against nuclear missiles, twenty-eight-year-old Katya Komisaruk walked alone the night of June 2, 1987, through an unguarded gate at the base. There she damaged a computer linked to a missile guidance system. She left cookies and flowers for the guards and spray painted the words "Nuremberg" and "International Law." She hitchhiked to San Francisco, called a press conference, and explained her actions.

The FBI arrested her. In court all references to the fact that Katya acted to help prevent nuclear war were excluded. The judge sentenced her to spend five years in a federal prison and to pay restitution of $500,000. She is now out of prison and attending law school. Attorneys for the Plowshares Defense Fund (36 East 12th Street, New York, New York 10003; 212-475-3232) defended Katya Komisaruk in court, and they help other protesters in difficulty.

SITES COMMEMORATING
NON-VIOLENCE

Martin Luther King, Jr. wrote in his "Letter from Birmingham Jail," "An individual who breaks the law that conscience tells him is unjust and who willingly accepts the penalty of imprisonment in order to arouse the conscience of the community over its injustice is in reality expressing the highest respect for the law." King, who visited India in 1957, was inspired, in part, by the teachings of Mahatma Gandhi. Today members of the peace movement worldwide look to Gandhi and to the United States civil rights movement for examples of how to achieve social goals nonviolently and for suggestions on how citizens can defend a nation without the use of weapons of mass destruction. Environmentalists engaged in nonviolent direct action have also been influenced by the civil rights movement.

Among the memorials in this country to Gandhi is a statue of him in New York City, on the southwest corner of Union Square, across from the Amalgamated Bank. Other memorial sites pay tribute to the heroes of the civil rights struggle.

SOUTHERN POVERTY LAW CENTER

400 Washington Avenue
Montgomery, Alabama 36104
205-264-0286

A sculpture on the grounds of the Southern Poverty Law Center honors the memory of forty black and white people who were killed during the struggle for civil rights. The names of the dead are cut into a circular table in front of a curving wall, down which water cascades. The Southern Poverty Law Center offers legal services, educates, and monitors organizations like the Ku Klux Klan. The designer of the sculpture, Maya Lin, also designed the Vietnam War Memorial near the Lincoln Monument in Washington, D.C.

MARTIN LUTHER KING, JR. NATIONAL HISTORIC SITE AND PRESERVATION DISTRICT

522 Auburn Avenue NE (office of the superintendent)
Atlanta, Georgia 30312

The Preservation District centers on Auburn Avenue, a black business and residential area. Most of the historic buildings are occupied and are thus closed to the public. The house in which King was born in 1929 is open, as is Ebenezer Baptist Church, where King was co-pastor with his father from 1960 to 1968. It was in 1957 at Ebenezer Baptist Church that the organizational meeting for the Southern Christian Leadership Conference was held. King was president of the Conference, a civil rights organization committed to non-violence. King expressed his opposition to the Vietnam War in 1967 (a war that damaged forests and agricultural land, possibly irreparably). His funeral in 1968 took place at the church.

PEACE-ORIENTED COMMUNITIES

Many intentional communities consciously strive to work out ways in which individuals can resolve differences of opinion with a minimum of conflict. They believe that what they are doing is applicable to the larger world. Here we give two examples of communities in which the members live "non-violently" together and act on a concern for global issues of war and peace. Others are described in chapter 7, Intentional Communities.

WOMEN'S ENCAMPMENT FOR A FUTURE OF PEACE AND JUSTICE
5440 Route 96, Romulus
Seneca, New York 14541
607-869-5825

In continuous existence since 1983, the Women's Peace camp is a symbolic protest against nuclear weapons. Adjacent to the camp is the Seneca Army Depot, which has a stockpile of some 1300 nuclear warheads. The camp is also a reflection of Seneca Falls' historic connection with feminism – the city is known as the birthplace of the U.S. women's rights movement.

A member of the camp describes it as "basically an ever-changing group of women striving to live as a feminist, non-hierarchical, non-violent community as an example of what the world could be." Women engage in civil disobedience and direct action, if they want to; and sometimes they are arrested. The camp offers non-violence training, and members work on nonviolent conflict resolution and consensus. There is no formal organization. The camp is located on a 51 acre farm. "All women who want to contribute to the perpetuation of the camp and its ideals are welcome" to stay at the camp, but they are asked to be as self-sufficient as possible and to contribute to the camp by working, participating in activities, or donating money. Men cannot stay on the land.

In the winter all camp members live in two dormitories in an old farmhouse without indoor plumbing. In the summer many stay in tents in the fields. Each year those present plant a garden, and in 1985 they planted an orchard. In the summer there are five to ten women at the camp during the week, many more on weekends. Numbers are lower during the winter.

Also in Seneca Falls are the National Women's Hall of Fame (76 Fall Street; 315-568-8060) and the Women's Rights National Historic Park, which includes a visitor center chronicling the development of the women's rights movement and the restored home of Elizabeth Cady Stanton, organizer of the first Women's Rights Convention (116 Fall Street, 315-568-2991). The Hall of Fame is open all year Mon.-Sat. 10:00 A.M.-4:00 P.M., and, in the summer, also on Sun. noon-4:00 P.M. Donations are appreciated. In the Historic Park the Stanton home is open daily May-Sep. 9:00 A.M.-5:00 P.M.; Oct.-April noon-4:00 P.M. The visitor center is open all year Mon.- Fri. 9:00 A.M.-5:00 P.M. Admission is free.

JUBILEE PARTNERS
P.O. Box 68
Comer, Georgia 30629
404-783-5131

Jubilee Partners is an intentional Christian community that tries to set an example of compassion in a world of conflict. Founded in 1979 on 258 acres in northeast Georgia, the community has as its central mission work with refugees. Jubilee Partners has served also as the coordinating center for the effort in the eastern United States to track the "nuclear train" that carries hydrogen bombs from the assembly plant in Texas to military sites. They consider this weapons work to be both a protest and a means of public education. Members of the community live modestly in order to conserve resources. They hold their overall cost of living to well below $5.00 a day per person by building their own homes, heating with wood and solar power, raising much of their own food, and sharing cars and appliances among themselves. Visitors are welcome, but should get in touch before they go.

INTERNATIONAL CROSSROADS

DUMBARTON OAKS
1703 32nd Street NW
Washington, D.C. 20007
202-342-3234

The Dumbarton Oaks Conferences, two international meetings held in 1944, established the principles later incorporated in the United Nations charter. The meetings were held in the Music Room of the nineteenth-century Dumbarton Oaks mansion, which, along with 16 acres of land, was conveyed to Harvard University by Mr. and Mrs. Robert Woods Bliss.

Beatrix Ferrand in cooperation with the Blisses landscaped 10 acres of formal gardens attached to the mansion. Bright with flowers from early spring through October, they afford a refreshing change from the streets of Washington, D.C.

The public can visit the Music Room from 2:00–5:00 P.M. daily except Mondays. The gardens are open to the public from 2:00–6:00 P.M., April-Oct. and 2:00–5:00 P.M., Nov.-March, except in inclement weather. Admission to the gardens is $2 except in the winter.

UNITED NATIONS HEADQUARTERS
Between First Avenue and the East River, from 42nd to 48th Street
New York, New York 10017
212-963-7713

A limited number of free tickets for meetings of the General Assembly and Councils, when in session, are available on a first-come, first-served basis, shortly before meeting times, 10:30 A.M. and 3:30 P.M. Guided tours of United Nations Headquarters, costing $5.50, are given weekdays and some weekends between 9:15 A.M. and 4:45 P.M. Visitors enter at First Avenue and 46th Street.

VISIONS OF PEACE MADE VIVID

GANONDAGAN STATE HISTORIC SITE
1488 Victor-Holcomb Road
Victor, New York 14564
716-924-5848

The community of Ganondagan was known by the Seneca as the Village of Peace. The site is still important to the Iroquois, who asked that it be preserved and who prepared its interpretive plan which includes three trails: a historical trail, an ethnobotanical trail identifying plants and explaining how the Seneca used them, and an ethnological trail interpreting the cultural history of the Seneca.

According to Seneca oral tradition, during a period of social unrest a Huron man, now referred to as the Peacemaker, traveled among the Iroquois-speaking nations known as the Mohawk, Oneida, Onondaga, Cayuga, and Seneca. Jikohnsaseh, who lived near Ganondagan, was instrumental in assisting him in uniting the five nations in a Confederacy, and it is from her that Ganondagan received its appellation.

The Peacemaker established the Great Law of Peace as the Constitution of the Confederacy. At the heart of the law was a belief that thinking and negotiations can replace violence and warfare as a means of settling conflicts. The Peacemaker, who strongly influenced the thinking of the Seneca, described a world of peace in the fashion of a longhouse, with the earth as its floor and the sky as its roof, in which all nations lived under the Great Law.

Ganondagan included a hundred longhouses (bark lodges that housed members of large, extended families) and a fortified granary. It was burned during a raid by the French in 1687.

According to Iroquois legend, when the Peacemaker formed the confederacy, he uprooted an Eastern White pine, put all the weapons of war into a cave underneath, and replanted the tree, which became a symbol of peace. Jake Swamp, Mohawk Nation Council member, is planting trees of peace around the United States. He can be contacted at Cook Road, Akwesasne Mohawk Reservation, Akwesasne, New York 13655.

PEACE WALL
Martin Luther King, Jr. Park
Martin Luther King, Jr. Way between Addison and Allston
Berkeley, California

Two thousand tiles, each representing one person's vision of peace, are set in cement to form a wall. The project was sponsored by Women for Peace. The creator Carolyn Marks took blank tiles into the local community and asked people to paint them. She also sent tiles to prominent people such as Congressman Ron Dellums and Jesse Jackson. The tiles are arranged in "quilts" according to theme. One quilt depicts the relation of peace to the natural world.

PEACE MUSEUM
430 West Erie Street
Chicago, Illinois 60610
312-440-1860

Among the treasures at the Peace Museum are more than five hundred segments of an 18-mile long peace ribbon created on the theme "what I cannot bear to think of as lost forever in a nuclear war." The Ribbon

Project, in which thousands of people participated, began in 1982 and culminated in 1985 with the symbolic tying of the ribbon around the Pentagon on the fortieth anniversary of the bombing of Hiroshima.

The Peace Museum itself is a non-profit organization providing peace education through the arts and humanities. It presents exhibitions and programs on issues related to war and peace. Every year it mounts four major temporary exhibits.

Hours are daily noon-5:00 P.M., except Thu. noon-8:00 P.M. Admission is $3.50. Phone before going, as the situation may change.

The museum rents exhibitions to organizations and institutions in other parts of the country.

BOISE PEACE QUILT PROJECT
P.O. Box 6469
Boise, Idaho 83707
208-378-0293; 345-2030

The Boise Peace Quilt Project presently involves sixty or so residents of Boise who find quilting a means of reaching out "in friendship, to those with whom we must make peace and in admiration for those who are leading the way." Each year they design and make about three quilts, with thirty people working on each project.

They completed their first quilt, a Soviet friendship quilt, in 1982. The Soviets displayed the quilt in Moscow and then sent it as requested to a smaller city, Alitus in Lithuania. The project has since made a quilt with Soviet quiltmakers. In addition to friendship quilts, members design quilts as awards for specific peacemakers, who are invited to come to Boise to receive their gifts and to talk about their work. Quilt recipients have included Dr. Helen Caldicott, Senator Frank Church, Norman Cousins, Pete Seeger, and Archbishop Raymond Hunthausen. In 1988 John Jeavons of Ecology Action in Willits, California, received the nineteenth quilt for his work in intensive gardening that helps people feed themselves, and one of the 1989 quilts went to Cesar Chavez and the United Farm Workers.

The project sells handsome cards depicting its completed quilts and welcomes nominations for recipients of future awards. Members are always glad to meet with travelers.

CONVERTED MILITARY INSTALLATIONS

Experience in the United States proves that closing military facilities need not, as is commonly thought, cause economic disaster for the areas where they are located. According to the President's Economic Adjustment Committee in the Pentagon, one hundred defense bases were retired to civilian use between 1961 and 1986. New jobs (138,138) more than offset the loss of former Department of Defense civilian jobs (93,424) at these bases. On the former bases twelve four-year colleges and thirty-three post-secondary vocational technical schools have been opened. Industrial and office parks are now located at seventy-five of the bases, and municipal or general aviation airports at forty-two.

Two documents produced by the President's Economic Adjustment Committee cite many specific examples of past conversion: "25 Years of Civilian Reuse, 1961–1986: Summary of Completed Military Base Economic Adjustment Projects" (April-May 1986) and "Communities in Transition: Community Response to Reduced Defense Activity" (1977). They are available from OASD-PA-DDI, Office of the Secretary of Defense, Washington, D.C. 20301.

CROWDER COLLEGE
Neosho, Missouri 64850
417-451-3223

Crowder College was established at Camp Crowder, an army base on the edge of the Ozarks, deactivated after World War II. Along with conventional courses, the college offers an alternate energy program. A cross-continental solar car is one of the program's projects.

DAUPHIN ISLAND SEA LAB
P.O. Box 369–370
Dauphin Island, Alabama 36528
205-861-2141

Dauphin Island Sea Lab is located on 36 acres of a former U.S. Air Force radar base. At the eastern end of Dauphin Island, which can be reached by automobile, the Lab is operated by the Marine Environmental Sciences Consortium, a cooperative project of nineteen Alabama universities and colleges. The Lab conducts marine research and offers students undergraduate and advanced graduate courses. The summer sessions provide five-week college-level courses. Discovery Hall presents a variety of opportunities to high-school students and the lay public, including seminars and field trips. Tours of Dauphin Lab may be arranged by contacting the Lab.

PACIFIC ENERGY AND RESOURCES CENTER (PERC)
Golden Gate National Recreation Area
Fort Cronkhite, Building 1055
Sausalito, California 94965
415-332-8200

PERC is a policy research, public education and conference center committed to conserving energy and promoting sound resource stewardship. Its facilities illustrate its mission.

The center is located in twelve barracks that belonged to Fort Cronkhite, a 400-acre site that includes "fortifications and military installations ranging from World War II sixteen-inch gun emplacements to a deactivated NIKE missile base." The barracks, as constructed on a south-facing slope, exhibited passive solar features. When they were renovated, they were heavily insulated, weatherstripped, and caulked; and buildings in the middle of the group received solar panels and skylights. Pacific Gas and Electric provided an energy-efficient lighting system.

To educate the public the center sponsors briefings, seminars, and conferences, and operates exhibit halls and an environmental education program. Two public exhibit halls, which include changing displays on global environmental issues, wildlife, energy conservation and alternate energy, are open Mon.-Fri. 9:00 A.M.-5:00 P.M. An Education Resource Lab, offering programs on such topics as tropical deforestation and the greenhouse effect is open by appointment.

CHAPTER TEN

Contemporary Arts and Crafts

In coverage of specific sites, no section of this book represents more than the tip of an iceberg. This is particularly true of the following pages. I give only a few examples of some aspects of contemporary arts and crafts. Music and literature are not treated, although some writers and musicians are referred to in other sections of the guide.

"Art is a critical complement to activism, lending soul to a function which is often brain heavy and spirit thin." This perceptive statement is in the handsome catalog of the Syracuse Cultural Workers (SCW). SCW has published works by more than 100 artists and distributed posters for ninety publishers in the United States and abroad. It also creates its own designs celebrating the ideals of justice, peace, and human liberation. For the free catalog picturing the Peace Calendar, posters, prints, and cards, write or call SCW, Box 6367, Syracuse, New York 13217 (315-474-1132).

EARTHWORKS/ENVIRONMENTAL ART

The use of the natural environment as a medium for artistic expression can be traced back to prehistory. Today constructions such as Native American effigy mounds evoke a sense of wonder through their antiquity and suggestions of long-forgotten rituals. Contemporary earthworks, often inspired by ancient examples, reflect a belief that the natural world ultimately remains sacred.

Unfortunately some earthworks obviously harm the land. Environmentalists have recognized this fact and, as a result, may spurn all environmental art. However, earthworks can serve as a means of salvaging already damaged sites. At their best, earthworks draw attention to qualities of the natural world. Furthermore, urban areas benefit from art that reestablishes connections with nature.

For additional examples of earthworks, consult John Beardsley's *Earthworks and Beyond: Contemporary Art in the Landscape*, rev. ed. (Abbeville Press, 1989). Beardsley gives the locations of a selection of the works he describes.

SERPENT MOUND
Locust Grove, Ohio

An early example of earthworks is Ohio's Serpent Mound, an embankment of earth nearly a quarter of a mile long, thought to have been built by the Adena people between 800 B.C. and 1 A.D. The mound represents a gigantic snake uncoiling in seven deep curves. An oval shape at the serpent's head has been interpreted as an egg that is being swallowed or as the open mouth of the snake as it strikes. The mound is on State Route 73 near the village of Locust Grove. For more information contact the Ohio Historical Society, 1985 Velma Avenue, Columbus, Ohio 43211 (614-297-2300).

Effigy Mounds National Monument includes twenty-nine bird and bear likenesses built by the Effigy Mounds People prior to 1300 or 1400 A.D. A visitor center with explanatory material is open 8:00 A.M.-5:00 or 7:00 P.M. daily. Admission is $1. For information contact the monument, RR 1, Box 25A, Harpers Ferry, Iowa 52146.

SUNKEN GARDEN [CHASE MANHATTAN BANK PLAZA], Isamu Noguchi
New York, New York

Noguchi believed that "it is the earth and [the artist's] contact to it which will free him of the artificiality of the present and his dependence on industrial products." Noguchi's sunken garden in New York City's Chase Manhattan Bank Plaza (1961–1964) is reminiscent of a "dry stone" garden in Kyoto, Japan. Black, eroded boulders are scattered on concentric circles of granite paving stone crossed by curved lines suggestive of waves.

GRAND RAPIDS PROJECT, Robert Morris
Grand Rapids, Michigan

Morris's *Grand Rapids Project* (1973–1974) has had a major impact on funding for large-scale environmental art, as it was the first such project in the United States paid for in part with public money. In Belknap Park on Coldbrook Road in Grand Rapids, Morris recontoured an eroded hillside and crossed it with two intersecting paths in the shape of an "x," reaching from top to bottom.

Also paid for with public funds was Morris's early reclamation project for a 3.7-acre gravel pit in southern King County, 10 miles south of Seattle (1979). Morris constructed an amphitheater of concentric terraces and slopes in the middle of the site. Scattered tree stumps at the top of a slope beyond the amphitheater recall the exploitation of natural resources. The site is at the intersection of 40th Place South and South 216th Street, half a mile east of Interstate 5. (For information on the project, contact the King County Arts Commission, 1115 Smith Tower, 506 Second Avenue, Seattle, Washington 98104; 206-296-7580.)

ROCK RINGS, Nancy Holt
Bellingham, Washington

Rock Rings (1979), on the wooded edge of the campus of Western Washington University in Bellingham, consists of two concentric circles of schist quarried in nearby British Columbia. Broken by arched entrances and round windows, the circles both create a cloistered space and place observers in the environment.

BAYER'S MILL CREEK CANYON EARTHWORKS, Herbert Bayer
Kent, Washington

In Kent, Washington, Herbert Bayer created an earthwork to control the flow of water in an eroded canyon after storms (1982). He built a berm to stop the water; upstream, mounds are covered with water during floods and, at other times, form a 2.5-acre park. *Bayer's Mill Creek Canyon Earthworks*, which are dams with "a natural appearance conforming to the landscape," are part of a larger 100-acre park known as Mill Creek Canyon Park, off Kent-Kangley Road on the south slope of East Hill.

PRATT FARM, James Pierce
Clinton, Maine

Employing materials native to the Maine countryside—boulders, sand, clay, and driftwood from the Kennebec River, James Pierce in 1970 began to construct a series of earthworks in which historical references serve as points of departure for his own vision. One work, *Suntreeman*, "was intended, in part, as an ecological symbol," Pierce says. His art derives from such varied sources as a Paleolithic fertility image, seventeenth-century topiary mazes, and Native American kivas and burial mounds. The earthworks occupy a 40-acre park at Pratt Farm in Clinton, Maine, 1 mile south of the Hinckley Bridge on the river road. The park is always open to visitors.

BODARK ARC, Martin Puryear
University Park, Illinois

In *Bodark Arc* (1982) Puryear calls attention to a series of tiny ecosystems at the Nathan Manilow Sculpture Park, Governors State University, University Park, Illinois. The park is on an old farm. Puryear marked a curved path from a hedge of osage orange, across a field to a small pond, and back. Over the pond, the trail becomes a planked walkway. A wooden arch across the path is related to a second path, which is the bow in a bow and arrow pattern that includes the wooden walkway.

The Sculpture Park is on the university campus. It is open daily without charge; but for a map or other information, call 708-534-5368.

VIETNAM VETERANS MEMORIAL, Maya Lin
Washington, D.C.

Maya Lin's *Vietnam Veterans Memorial* (1982) is formed by two 250-foot-long black granite walls that come together in a wide "V." The walls are set into the earth and backed by earth; within the "V" a lawn slopes gently upward. The angle of the ground makes the walls seem to be disappearing into or rising from the earth. On the walls are carved the names of the military personnel killed or missing in action in Vietnam. The memorial is in Constitution Gardens, at the corner of Constitution Avenue and 21st Street NW, in Washington, D.C.

PRIMIST ART

Lee Nading has created across the United States a "Trail of Rising and Falling Birds," a series of highway paintings and totemic sculptures, most of them at sites reflecting the conflict between nature and technology. Rising birds pay homage to nature or to human sanity; falling birds place a jinx on human technology. Nading, a graduate of the Art Institute of Chicago, chose birds as his main image because they are "symbolic of the human spirit and our bond with nature." Birds painted on the road are rising if they are moving away from a car driven in their lane; falling if they are moving towards the car. Nading started painting his trail in 1983. In 1987 he created *The Great Mystery*, a half-mile long strip of symbolic images, as the final work in the series. The painting gave rise to local controversy and "was painted out in black, so I am regarding the half-mile stripe as the finished painting—which 'celebrates the spiritualization of the ecology movement.' " The site is 3 miles east of the Cochiti exit (264) from Interstate 25, south of Santa Fe, New Mexico.

Among Nading's more than two hundred smaller messages are:

Jinx on Agent Orange Producers (on Marshall Road, .2 miles south of Vertac Chem. entrance, Jacksonville, Arkansas)

Jinx on Glen Canyon Damn (on old steel sign at Overlook, Page, Arizona)

Homage to the God of California Gray Whales (US-101, ocean vista 8 miles north of Klamath, California)

Homage to the God of Appropriate Creative Imagination (in front of Frank Lloyd Wright's home Taliesin, Spring Green, Wisconsin)

Homage to the Good God of the Badlands (south rest area on Interstate 90, 3 miles east of Wall, South Dakota).

Nading asks that people who live near his images keep them painted.

In 1989 Nading began work on a *Trail of Sacred Sites*, for which he buries high-fired stoneware tablets bearing pictographic bird images, at cultural, natural, and historic sites. He turned to the tablets to use a more permanent medium than road painting. His precept for his new project is that "there is only one saga common to all people, so all historic sites should be sacred to all people."

COMMUNITY ART

New York, New York

In New York City, Artists in the Gardens brings together city artists and community gardeners in GreenThumb gardens. Eight gardens are chosen annually. Their sponsors (block associations, churches, schools, and other organizations) select the artists they want to work with and are active partners in the design and execution of the projects. Completed art works include Kristi Pfister's mural *Diggers*, which celebrates gardeners at work. In the mural, at Coney Island's La Placita Garden, all of the figures are based on neighborhood people, one of them the late Carole Johnson who organized fifteen gardens on Coney Island. For addresses of the works and the names of contacts, write or call Gina Townsend, Stuart Lowrie or Jane Weissman at Operation Green-Thumb, 49 Chambers Street, Room 1020, New York, New York 10007 (212-233-2926).

Cityarts Workshop in New York is dedicated to the creation of high quality and community-responsive works of art in the five boroughs. Ethnic themes appear frequently in the more than one hundred works that it has sponsored; the natural world is occasionally a subject. One of Cityarts' best known works is the mural, *Louis Armstrong: The Prevalence of Love, Devotion, and Jazz*, designed by Juan Sanchez, located at 107–10 Northern Boulevard, Corona, between 107th and 108th streets. Pedro Silva's mosaic *Sunrise/Sol Naciente* is in Roberto Clemente Park, Bronx, and faces the East River. Cityarts distributes flyers giving the locations of its most frequently visited mosaics, murals, and sculptures. To receive copies send a stamped envelope to the organization at 625 Broadway, New York, New York 10012 (212-673-8670).

Atlanta, Georgia

Atlanta has a mural depicting the sponsors' concerns with the nonviolent struggle for peace and justice. Memorializing past and present leaders of nonviolent action, the *Freedom Quilt Mural* was painted in July 1988 as a joint effort of the American Friends Service Committee, Performing Artists for Nuclear Disarmament, and Arts Pluribus Unum, an organization that brought together visual and performing artists to stage artistic events during the Democratic National Convention in Atlanta. The artist, David Fichter, was assisted by volunteers, including onlookers and neighbors.

Portraits, symbols, and replicas of the fabrics of many continents develop the mural's theme. The focal point is a portrait of a smiling Mahatma Gandhi. Among other leaders depicted are Dr. Martin Luther King, Jr., peace activist Daniel Berrigan, Lucretia Mott (a Quaker who led early abolition and suffragette movements), and Leonard Peltier (an Ogalala Sioux and an organizer for the American Indian Movement, who is on Amnesty International's list of prisoners of conscience). Pictures of hands stitching together the various sections recall Mississippi's freedom quilters, groups of black women organized prior to the civil rights movement.

The mural is on the west wall of the American Friends Service Committee building at the corner of Houston Street and Piedmont Avenue in downtown Atlanta (92 Piedmont Avenue NE, Atlanta, Georgia 30303; 404-586-0460). Atlanta hosts two other Fichter murals: the *Seminole Peace Mural* in Little Five Points and *Sanctuary: the Spirit of Harriet Tubman* at the Arts Exchange.

San Francisco, California

In San Francisco, the old Mission District is the place to go to see murals. Along 24th Street east of Mission Street, you can tour the locally-famous neighborhood murals, featuring some of the best ethnic street art in the nation. A little alley called Balmy Street is completely lined with murals depicting life in San Francisco and Central America.

Los Angeles, California

The longest mural in the world is *The Great Wall of Los Angeles*, which stretches half a mile along the flood control channel for the Los Angeles River in the city of that name. It depicts the history of California from neolithic times through (so far) the 1950s from the point of view of California's ethnic populations. Judith F. Baca, one of the founders of the Social and Public Arts Resource Center (SPARC) in Venice, California, conceived the project and is its artistic director. More than two hundred youths of varied backgrounds have assisted in the planning and have carried out much of the actual painting. The mural is at the intersection of Coldwater Canyon Avenue with Oxnard Street and Burbank Boulevard.

In addition to administering the Great Wall Project, SPARC administers a program for the city of Los Angeles, Neighborhood Pride: Great Walls Unlimited. Under this program twenty-four murals have already been painted by professional artists, assisted by neighborhood youth referred to the program by schools and social service agencies. They include Emily Winters' *Endangered Species* at 801 Ocean Front Walk, Venice. SPARC will furnish a list of the murals, with locations, in return for an SASE.

SPARC is located in a two-story, reinforced concrete Art Deco building that once housed the Venice Division of the Los Angeles Police Department (685 Venice Boulevard, Venice, California 90291; 213-822-9560). It now includes the SPARC Gallery, which exhibits the work of multi-cultural and other traditionally under-represented artists, and a Mural Resource Center with an archive of more than 16,000 slides of public art from around the world. The gallery is open to the public after August 1991, Mon.-Fri., 9:30 A.M.-5:00 P.M. The Mural Resource Center is open to the public by appointment.

CRAFTS

The catalog of Berea College's Student Crafts Program states that the program "maintains the heritage of working with the hands, of respect for natural materials and functional, beautiful products." These phrases sum up values inherent in fine craftwork in general. In *Turtle Island* Gary Snyder demonstrated through the poem "The Jemez Pueblo Ring" that crafts can symbolize the culture that created them.

Areas frequented by tourists contain a plethora of purportedly handmade objects. One way to find items worth treasuring and perhaps also to see craftspeople at work is to visit schools that teach crafts or craft centers run by organizations that require producers to meet fixed standards. They include:

HAYSTACK MOUNTAIN SCHOOL OF CRAFTS
Deer Isle, Maine 04627–0087
207-348-2306

Tours of the studios are conducted Mon.-Fri. at 1:00 P.M. The school runs a gallery where faculty and student work are shown. Shows change every two weeks. Work can be purchased during auctions held several times a year. Areas in which students work include clay, wood, enamels, fibers, glassblowing, and blacksmithing.

VERMONT STATE CRAFT CENTER, FROG HOLLOW
Middlebury, Vermont 05753

Located in a restored mill overlooking Otter Creek Falls, the center's craft gallery features contemporary and traditional work from over 200 Vermont artisans. Classes, workshops, demonstrations, and special exhibitions of the work of artists from other states are offered year round. A pottery studio is open to the public. The gallery is open Mon.-Sat. 9:30 A.M.-5:00 P.M. and, spring through fall, Sun. evenings.

PENLAND SCHOOL
Penland, North Carolina 28765
704-765-2359

Penland operates a Visitors Center which is generally open Tues.-Sun., 9:00 A.M.-Noon and 1:00–4:00 P.M. It also gives tours Tues. at 10:30 and Thurs. at 1:30. Visitors should not enter studios when classes are in session, but Penland can supply a list of studios in the county that receive visitors by appointment. Penland offers advanced courses in clay, glass, graphics, metal, wood, surface design and fiber, drawing and design, and movement.

A grant from the North Carolina Solar Energy and Energy Conservation Program supported the installation of a new solar heating system for the Pines, containing the dining hall and student housing.

BEREA COLLEGE
CPO 2347
Berea, Kentucky 40404
606-986-9341, ext. 5220

Over 150 Berea students work in woodcraft, weaving and needlecraft, broomcraft, ceramics, and wrought iron. Workshops on the campus are open to visitors weekdays. The program sells through a mail order catalog ($2), through the Log House Sales Room and Boone Tavern Gift Shop in Berea, and through Berea College Heritage Crafts in Louisville's Galt House (40 North 4th Street) and in Lexington's Civic Center Shops (410 West Vine).

Berea College serves talented young people of limited financial means, 80% of them from the Appalachian counties of nine states. All students work ten to twenty hours per week instead of paying tuition.

OREGON SCHOOL OF ARTS AND CRAFTS
8245 SW Barnes Road
Portland, Oregon 97225
503-297-5544

Founded in 1906, the Oregon School of Crafts provides full-time, post-secondary studio instruction year round in book arts, ceramics, drawing, fibers, metal, wood, and photography. The campus, which was built in 1979, integrates functional crafts into architecture, through the furniture, handcarved railings and doors, ceramic wash basins and counters, and a fireplace, among other features.

The Exhibition Gallery in Hoffman Gallery mounts a new exhibition of contemporary arts and crafts from local, regional, or national artists approximately every six weeks. On the first Thursday after an opening the public is invited to a reception (5:30–8:30 P.M.). Generally a gallery talk is held on the following Sunday morning. Hoffman Gallery also contains a Sales Gallery that presents juried work. Hours of Hoffman Gallery are Mon.-Sat. 10:00 A.M.-5:00 P.M.; Sun. 9:30 A.M.-4:00 P.M.

Members of the public with a serious interest in crafts can contact the Admissions Office to arrange a campus tour.

ANDERSON RANCH ARTS CENTER
P.O. Box 5598, 5263 Owl Creek Road
Snowmass Village, Colorado 81615
303-923-3181

From May to September this education foundation offers one to three week workshops in ceramics, photography, woodworking, furniture design, and several other fields, including eco-activist art, which combines art, ecology, and community. The gallery in Dows Barn exhibits work by regional, national, and internationally known artists throughout the year and, in the spring, the work of resident artists. The gallery is open 9:00 A.M.-5:00 P.M. weekdays year round. The center presents evening programs in which the public is invited to participate. A brochure is available on request.

BISHOP MUSEUM
P.O. Box 19000-A, 1525 Bernice Street
Honolulu, Hawaii 96817
808-847-3511

At Bishop Museum visitors to Hawaii can learn about the islands' natural history and about their crafts. Hand-crafted articles such as feather caps, barkcloth, and wooden bowls are exhibited; and craftspeople put on demonstrations daily 9:00 A.M.-2:30 or 3:00 P.M.: Mon. and Fri., quilting; Tues. and Thurs., feather *lei* making; Wed., *Lau hala* weaving; Sat., flower *lei* making. The gift shop sells hand-crafted products, among other items. The museum is open daily 9:00 A.M.-5:00 P.M. Admission is $5.95.

Fairs and festivals are an opportunity to meet craftspeople, but if they are not organized by an association that imposes standards, let the inexperienced shopper be wary. The University of Massachusetts' Division of Continuing Education publishes annual directories on the eastern half of the country for people interested in crafts: *Fairs and Festivals in the Northeast* and *Fairs and Festivals in the Southeast.* Order for $7.50 each or $13 for the pair, plus postage ($5 for the pair) from Fairs and Festivals, Arts Extension Service, Division of Continuing Education, University of Massachusetts, Amherst, Massachusetts 01003 (413-545-2360). Suzanne Carmichael's *The Traveler's Guide to American Crafts: East of the Mississippi* and its companion *West of the Mississippi* (E. P. Dutton, 1990) describe museums, studios, galleries, and shows where travelers can view, and often buy, high-quality crafts.

Another approach is to visit craft cooperatives or businesses run by non-profit associations, and/or to buy where you can watch the craftspeople at work. We list a few examples of such outlets here and under Economic Alternatives. (Some of the intentional communities described earlier also make handcrafted products.) In closing the subsection, we present two examples of craftsmen/artists who are creating contemporary products carrying an explicit environmental message.

To find further sources of Indian crafts see the Bureau of the Interior's periodically updated *Source Directory: Indian, Eskimo, Aleut Owned and Operated Arts and Crafts Businesses.* Single copies can be obtained free of charge from the Indian Arts and Crafts Board, Room 4004, U.S. Department of the Interior, Washington, D.C. 20240 (202-208-3773). Most of the businesses listed in the directory operate retail stores. Therefore, the booklet can serve as a travel guide in addition to a source for mail-order catalogs.

QUALLA ARTS AND CRAFTS MUTUAL
P.O. Box 310, Drama Road
Cherokee, North Carolina 28719
704-497-3103

An Indian owned and operated arts and crafts cooperative organized in 1946, Qualla has kept alive the cultural heritage in arts and crafts of the Eastern band of Cherokee. Each of its high-quality products, ranging from fingerwoven scarves and belts to animals carved in walnut, is tagged with a description of the object, the materials used, and the name of the creator. The cooperative sells by mail as well as through its store on the Cherokee Indian Reservation. Store hours are mid-June-mid Aug. 8:00 A.M.-8:00 P.M., Sun. 8:00 A.M.-5:00 P.M.; mid-Aug.-Oct. Mon.-Sat. 8:00 A.M.-6:00 P.M., Sun. 8:00 A.M.-5:00 P.M.; Nov.-May Mon.-Sat. 8:00 A.M.-4:30 P.M., Sun. 9:00 A.M.-5:00 P.M.

When shopping at Qualla Arts and Crafts between mid-May and late October, you may want to stop by the Cherokee Botanical Garden and Nature Trail and Oconaluftee Indian village, where you can see craftspeople at work. There is no charge for the garden and half-mile trail; admission to the village is $7.

DAVID APPALACHIAN CRAFTS
David, Kentucky 41616
606-886-2377

Over one hundred people work in their homes for David Crafts. Traditional mountain products are on display at the shop Mon.-Fri. 10:00 A.M.-4:00 P.M. Visitors on Tuesdays can see women engaged in crafts.

THE HUMMERS
Box 122, Reagan Wells Canyon
Uvalde, Texas 78801
512-232-6167

A family of homesteaders owns this small business in an area of the Texas hill country known as "the country of eleven hundred springs." The Hummers create office and home accessories, hiking staffs, and decorative work out of native deadwood; and they produce green cedar needle items from prunings of juniper trees, and essential oils from deadwood and/or plants by steaming. They also run a printing press.

A shop at the Hummertage, which sells their own products and the work of friends who operate other home-based businesses or small production facilities, is open daily 9:00 A.M.-5:00 P.M. From Memorial Day weekend through Labor Day, the Hummers present woodworking shows free of charge, at 10:00 A.M. and 2:00 P.M. daily. The morning shows emphasize woodturning; and the afternoon, hand-fashioned and band-sawn items. The shows include a tour of the Hummers' woodlot, with trees ranging from walnut and cherry to Pinon Pine and Texas Mahogany. If you are unable to visit, you can order from the store by mail.

OOMINGMAK MUSK OX PRODUCERS' CO-OP
604 H Street
Anchorage, Alaska 99501
907-272-9225

The 200 to 250 Eskimo knitters who are members of this co-op transform *qiviut*, the soft underwool of the Arctic musk ox (*oomingmaka*), into headwear, scarves, and tunics. Most work at home in scattered cottages, but sometimes knitters can be seen at work at the store. It is open 10:00 A.M.-7:00 P.M. in summer; 10:00 A.M.-6:00 P.M. in winter.

The co-op operates a farm with a hundred musk oxen in Palmer (Musk Ox Farm, 50.1 Mile, Glenn Highway, Palmer, Alaska 99645; 907-745-2353, 907-745-4151). Visitors are welcome at the farm and tours are offered, even in winter.

RAMAH NAVAJO WEAVERS
P.O. Box 153
Pine Hill, New Mexico 87321
505-775-3253

The weavings of Ramah Navajo Weavers are sold by appointment in Pine Hill, as well as at the Santa Fe Indian Market, and in retail outlets and museum shops. The association will demonstrate carding, spinning, and weaving by appointment.

ZUNI CRAFTSMEN COOPERATIVE ASSOCIATION
P.O. Box 426
Zuni, New Mexico 87327
505-782-4425

The Zuni are celebrated for inlay jewelry of silver, shell, jet, coral, and turquoise. Their craftspeople established a cooperative in 1967 so that they could control the distribution of their work. It has three main components: a retail showroom on the main street of Zuni, a raw material department from which jewelers can purchase their supplies, and a mail-order catalog business. The cooperative guarantees that each item it sells has been individually handcrafted. Families make the jewelry in their homes.

The Zuni pueblo welcomes visitors during daylight hours. It is made up of one-story adobe dwellings. The oldest part of the pueblo dates back four hundred years.

BOB WALDMIRE
Cardinal Hill Candles and Crafts
RR 2, Box 110
Rochester, Illinois 62563
217-498-9375

Bob Waldmire serves Earth by creating with pen and ink, notecards, leaflets, and posters, picturing and giving facts about plants and animals. His most ambitious undertakings are fantastically detailed poster maps of Arizona, California, Illinois, and New Mexico, crammed with information about the states' natural and human history; and bird's-eye views of the world's tropical rain forests and deserts. He is now beginning to work on bioregional maps.

To observe the subjects for his drawings, Waldmire has spent twenty years on the road in his VW camper-van, concentrating on the desert Southwest. Homebase, where his vintage '66 Chevy schoolbus "house-truck" is parked, is his folks' Cardinal Hill Candle Shop, a family-run business next to a self-designed solar home. He is glad to meet travelers and give a tour, bus and all, if you can catch him in Rochester. If not, you can still visit the shop or order by mail.

JIM MORRIS
Environmental T-Shirts
5660 Valmont
Boulder, Colorado 80301
303-444-6430

If you order a shirt from Jim Morris, you are likely to receive with it information on how to become involved in protecting the environment. The T-shirts are, moreover, messages in themselves. They may display not only graphic illustrations of wildlife but also quotations from nature writers and instructions on lobbying Congress. The designs, often in a rainbow of color, are silkscreened on the shirts. Jim Morris will create shirts to individual specification, if desired.

In the workshop of Environmental T-Shirts is a retail store, where shirts, including seconds, and environmental books are sold. Visitors can watch shirts being printed. If you can't stop by, send for the handsome mail-order catalog (P.O. Box 831, Boulder, Colorado 80306).

PERFORMING ARTS

BREAD AND PUPPET MUSEUM
RD #2 (off route 122, south of Glover)
Glover, Vermont 05839

The Bread and Puppet Museum is a giant collection of puppets, masks, paintings, and graphics used by the Bread and Puppet Theatre, founded by German-born sculptor Peter Schumann in New York City in 1963. In its early years the theater's life-size puppets and masked performers participated in peace rallies and protest marches against social injustice and the Vietnam War. The company now tours extensively in the United States and abroad, and social commentary is an important aspect of its performances.

The museum is housed in a 125-year-old barn, part of a former dairy farm which became the theater's home in 1974. In the barn, puppets recreate dramatic scenes from earlier shows or form compositions with banners, paper-mache reliefs, or old farm equipment. The museum sells a large assortment of printed matter, and at times offers fresh sourdough rye bread from three outdoor Quebec-style clay ovens on the farm.

Admission to the museum is free, but donations are appreciated. It is open daily from mid-May–mid-Oct, 10:00 A.M.–5:00 P.M. For visits in other months, write for appointments and information.

LIVING THEATRE
272 East 3rd Street
New York, New York
212-979-0601

In New York City the Living Theatre stages plays that carry a social message, sometimes on an environmental theme. For the summer of 1991, for example, the theater created street theater on the topic of waste; and in 1988 it produced a play supporting community gardens in some of the gardens themselves. The Living Theatre was founded in 1947 and was among the prime originators of the Off-Broadway movement. The Lincoln Center Branch of the New York Public Library has a collection of materials relating to the Theatre's history.

In addition to repertory and street theater, activities today include workshops on performance techniques, and poetry readings (Tues. eve.), and readings of new and experimental plays (Mon. eve.).

To receive a list of upcoming productions, send a postcard to the office (Box 20180, Tompkins Sq. Station, New York, New York 10009–8959. Office hours are Mon.-Fri. 1:00–5:00 P.M.). Repertory performances begin at 8:00 P.M. Wed. through Sun. Tickets are $10 Fri.-Sun. and pay-what-you-can Wed. and Thurs.

Tribal Warning Theatre, founded by artists who worked with the Living Theatre, presents social theater in San Francisco, as do the San Francisco Mime Troop, Teatro Campesino, and other groups. Watch for announcements of productions in newspapers and on posters.

APPALSHOP
306 Madison Street
Whitesburg, Kentucky 41858
606-633-0108

In eastern Kentucky you can visit the home of a highly successful art organization that began in 1969 as a training program for poor and minority youth in Appalachia. Today Appalshop operates a variety of media programs: Appalshop Films has made over forty-three documentary films relating to rural life; Headwaters Television produces documentaries broadcast in the Central Appalachian region; June Appal Recordings makes and distributes recordings affirming the regional culture; Roadside Theater sends a traveling ensemble across the nation to perform original plays; and WMMT-FM is the only non-commercial community radio station in eastern Kentucky and southwest Virginia. The programs, plus a gallery and a theater, are housed in the Appalshop Center.

Visitors must phone ahead. Appalshop will plan a tour and, if you wish, a showing of films or videos to match your interests. You can view the current display in the art gallery, and, if you time your visit right, attend a program in the theater.

NEW COMMUNITY CINEMA
423 Park Avenue
Huntington, New York 11743
516-423-7653; 800-287-8726

At New Community Cinema on Long Island, first-class films become an integral part of efforts to create a more just and sustainable society.

The cinema hosts benefits for non-profit organizations like Amnesty International, and from time to time combines film showings with discussions and meals. Many of the films it runs cannot be seen elsewhere in the New York suburban area. In 1991 it began offering film-making workshops.

PART III

Natural Areas and Their Wildlife

This section describes a selection of natural sites that are worth visiting and that are or should be protected. I group all except wilderness areas under the entities that control them currently, and I discuss the manner in which these agencies and organizations carry out their roles. A site can be appreciated without knowing whether it is a National Park or a National Monument, but understanding the land-control system helps in preservation efforts. The sites I describe are only a tiny fraction of those worth including. They were chosen for their historical significance to the environmental movement, their importance as habitat for plants and animals, their recreational value, and/or the fact that they represent a particular geographic area.

FEDERAL LANDS

Except for chapter 16, State Parks and Private Preserves, and chapter 17, UNESCO Sites in the U.S., the lands discussed in this section are known as federal lands. These lands date back to the years immediately following the Revolutionary War. Several states claimed large tracts of western land. Maryland refused to sign the Articles of Confederation unless the states donated their claims to the new central government. The Continental Congress supported Maryland's position, and by 1802, 233 million acres were in the public domain.

Through much of the nineteenth century, wars, negotiations, and purchases increased the size of the federal holdings. The public domain at its greatest extent totalled 1.8 billion acres; but it has been subject to subtractions as well as to additions. Individual settlers, railroad and canal companies, states and colleges acquired parts of what were federal lands through purchase, donation, and sometimes theft. Indian reservations also absorbed acreage.

After the federal government has completed a program to turn land over to Native Alaskans, the United States will hold 611 million acres of land—27% of the total of 2.3 billion acres in the fifty states. Of the 611 million public acres, 230 million, more than a third, are in Alaska.

The Department of the Treasury initially administered the lands in the public domain. In 1812 Congress established a General Land Office within this department to handle all aspects of the sale of land. The Office became a part of the Department of Interior, when that department was created in 1849. The Land Office was unable to stay on top of the myriad transactions it was expected to oversee, and it was incapable of preventing ranchers, logging and mining interests, and others from abusing the public domain. Gradually Congress and various presidents transferred to other agencies the administration of lands that they perceived to be of value. In 1946, with the territory that it oversaw reduced, the Land Office was combined with the Grazing Service to become the Bureau of Land Management (BLM).

Regulations governing the use of public land vary with the administering department and agency. The Department of Defense administers more than 25 million acres, most of which are closed to the public for reasons of military security. The bulk of the public domain is administered by the Department of Agriculture and the Department of the Interior. Recreation and preservation are ostensibly among the purposes for which the agencies in these departments administer the lands.

National Marine Sanctuaries and Estuarine Research Reserves are the province of the Department of Commerce. Overseas trade is the origin of the link between this department and the oceans. The department's largest agency is the National Oceanic and Atmospheric Administration (NOAA), which has a variety of environmental responsibilities, including managing the sanctuaries and reserves.

CHAPTER ELEVEN

National Forests

The country's 156 National Forests are administered by the Department of Agriculture through its agency, the U.S. Forest Service (FS). The FS also oversees 19 National Grasslands and 17 land utilization projects; in total, it controls 191 million acres in 44 states, the Virgin Islands, and Puerto Rico. The Department of Agriculture controls the forests, because, at the turn of the century, Gifford Pinchot, a man with an intense desire to manage and utilize the forests, was a close friend of President Theodore Roosevelt.

In the late nineteenth century, timber interests were laying waste to the forests in the public domain. To stem the destruction, Interior Secretary John W. Noble in 1891 persuaded a Congressional conference committee to attach a rider to a general land bill. Unnoticed by most of the members of Congress who voted for it, the rider authorized the president to create "Forest Reserves" on government-owned land. During the next six years Presidents Benjamin Harrison and Grover Cleveland put 39 million acres into reserves. At first the Reserves were administered by the General Land Office in the Department of Interior, but Pinchot, who had managed to become head of a small Division of Forestry in the Department of Agriculture, succeeded in having the Reserves transferred in 1905 to the Department of Agriculture. Shortly thereafter they were renamed National Forests, and the Department of Agriculture's Division of Forestry became the Forest Service.

The federal government did not establish National Grasslands until the early 1930s. At the time of the Depression and the Dust Bowl, farmers in droves were leaving their farms. Congress, seeing an opportunity for the federal government to invest in repairing and restoring the land, passed the Bankhead Jones Farm Tenant Act and related legislation. The Grasslands now total approximately 4 million acres, most of them in the Great Plains.

From the earliest days of the Forest Service (FS), "multiple use" has been its goal. Codifying this approach, the National Forest Management Act of 1976 listed five uses alphabetically: outdoor recreation, range, timber, watershed, and wildlife and fish habitat. However, timber production is, in fact, dominant. "Sustained-yield" is another principle, and, though it does not, in theory, permit harvesting more trees than the Forest Service can replace, it does permit clear-cutting—felling at one time all trees in a given area regardless of age.

In large measure because of the efforts of first Aldo Leopold and later Bob Marshall, both members of the Forest Service, the agency in 1940 adopted regulations establishing three categories of wilderness on roadless sections of its lands. The regulations stated that these areas were, to varying degrees, to be left in their natural condition; but the Forest Service violated its own strictures.

In 1964 Congress came to the rescue by passing the Wilderness Act, designating as "wilderness" nearly 9 million acres classified by the Forest Service previously as "wild" or "canoe" and requiring a study of 5.4 million acres classed as "primitive." Subsequently Congress added to the Wilderness System almost all these "primitive" areas.

Under pressure from environmentalists the Forest Service has since made two reviews of its roadless areas not covered in the 1964 act: Roadless Area Review and Evaluation (RARE) I completed in 1973 and RARE II completed in 1979. In these reviews the Forest Service decided what lands were suitable for addition to the Wilderness Preservation System. Environmentalists do not regard either review as satisfactory,and a U.S. Court of Appeals ruled that RARE II violated the National Environmental Policy Act (NEPA). Congress has nevertheless used RARE II as a starting point for making Wilderness designations on a state by state basis. The National Forests now contain 33.1 million acres of Wilderness.

The 1976 National Forest Management Act required the Forest Service to complete management plans for each National Forest by the end of 1985. The plans govern management of the Forests for fifty years, but are to be revised every ten years. They are subject to public review. Almost all have been appealed by environmentalists.

Under the Forest Service's multiple-use policy, National Forests, National Grasslands, and the National Recreation Areas it administers are open not only to logging, but to livestock grazing, mining and the production of energy, off-road vehicle use, fuel-wood collecting, and hunting. Because the price of a grazing permit for public land is a small fraction of that for private land, cattle and sheep belonging to private ranchers are overgrazing the high meadows and the grasslands under Forest Service control. Mineral extraction is also damaging Forest Service land, as are military facilities. Southeast of Great Falls, Montana, in the Lewis and Clark National Forest are two Minuteman missiles; and the eastern section of the Pawnee National Grasslands in Colorado is the site of more than twenty Minutemen.

Nevertheless, the biggest problems in the National Forests are road building and timber cutting, essentially one problem since roads are built to make harvesting possible. The National Forests are crossed by more than 350,000 miles of logging roads.

The Wilderness Society's *New Directions for the Forest Service* makes recommendations for change. It is available from the society at 900 17th Street NW, Washington, D.C. 20006–2596 ($5).

Robert H. Mohlenbrock's *The Field Guide to U.S. National Forests* (Congdon and Weed, 1984) describes major natural features of each of the National Forests and tells how to reach and to obtain information about the forests.

As a general rule, camping is permitted anywhere in a National Forest. It is free of charge except in established campgrounds, where the Forest Service charges fees of approximately $5-$20 per night, depending on facilities.

The Forest Service's Public Affairs Office responds to questions (P.O. Box 96090, Washington, D.C. 20090–6090; 202-447-3760).

MOUNT WASHINGTON
Northern New Hampshire, east of Bretton Woods

The focal point of the White Mountain National Forest's Presidential Range is Mount Washington, elevation 6,288 feet, the highest mountain in the Northeast. On the occasional clear day, five states, the Atlantic Ocean, and Canada can be seen from the summit. The mountain has the most severe combination of wind, cold, and icing of any inhabited place on Earth. The highest wind recorded anywhere in the world occurred on the summit – 231 mph.

Even in summer the weather can be hazardous. A good starting point for hikes is Pinkham Notch where the Appalachian Mountain Club offers information on weather and trail conditions.

On the way up Mount Washington hikers may want to stop to see the collection of arctic flowers at the Alpine Garden. The Lake of the Woods, the highest alpine lake east of the Rockies is on the Crawford Path, south and west of the summit. Unfortunately visitors who arrive at the peak on foot will meet people who have driven up or arrived by cog railway.

Tuckerman Ravine, two-and-a-half miles from Pinkham Notch, is an amphitheater carved by glaciers. The view from the ravine has changed little since Thoreau camped there July 9–10, 1858.

Concord Trailways carries passengers from Logan Airport to Pinkham Notch via Boston's Park Street bus station. The Appalachian Mountain Club runs a shuttle bus during the summer and winter seasons between Pinkham Notch and several other points in the White Mountains.

For information contact the Appalachian Mountain Club, 5 Joy Street, Boston, Massachusetts 02108 (617-523-0636).

GEORGE WASHINGTON NATIONAL FOREST
[1 million acres]
Northwest Virginia and neighboring West Virginia

The George Washington National Forest is only 3% wilderness, whereas the average for the National Forests as a whole is 17%. Virginia environmentalists are proposing Wilderness status for Laurel Fork Special Management Area and for a 65,000-acre area astride the Shenandoah Mountains. The Shenandoah proposal comprises the already designated Ramsey's Draft Wilderness, the Little River RARE II area, and, to connect them, the upper valley of the North River.

Ramsey's Draft Wilderness is celebrated for the flowers and ferns in the valley of Ramsey's Draft itself and for virgin forests of pine, hemlock, and hardwoods. In the Little River RARE II area, numerous small trout streams flow through a wild forest already administered by the Forest Service essentially as a wilderness because of its unstable soils. The North River, in what would be the connecting area, is a clear trout stream flowing rapidly beneath large hemlock, White pine, and cove hardwoods. On either side of the valley are sandstone cliffs and steep slopes covered with picturesque stunted oaks and Yellow pines.

The remote cliffs and trees would provide breeding habitat for raptors such as the endangered Peregrine falcon and the Golden eagle. After the minor Forest Service roads have been closed, the area would also be appropriate for the reintroduction (or augmentation) of the River otter and the Eastern cougar. Indeed, the cougar may be present, as it has been sighted just to the northeast; and as the proposed wilderness has never been adequately explored for rare animals. The endangered Indiana bat may also survive here.

The proposed wilderness offers fine opportunities for hiking. For information contact R. E. Mueller, Virginians for Wilderness, Rte. 1, Box 250, Staunton, Virginia 24401 (703-885-6983) and the supervisor of the George Washington Forest, P.O. Box 233, Harrisonburg, Virginia 22801 (703-433-2491).

RED RIVER GORGE GEOLOGICAL AREA [26,000 acres]
East central Kentucky, a few miles east of Stanton

The Red River area in Daniel Boone National Forest contains eighty natural arches, the second largest group of arches in the nation. The arches and rock shelters under the cliffs occur where sandstone has resisted the erosion that has caused weaker, lower layers of rock to disappear. The terrain is a mixture of low creek bottoms and high, dry ridges covered with pines and hardwoods. Rock outcrops afford spectacular views. Wendell Berry, poet, essayist, farmer, and Kentucky native, devoted a book, *The Unforeseen Wilderness* (Univ. of Kentucky Press, 1971), to the gorge, "a country of overtowering edges." Canoeing, which Berry describes, is one of the recreational opportunities offered by the area. Another is rock climbing.

The plant population is complex and rich, with 555 species in 100 families. Protected microenvironments in the narrow valleys have allowed the establishment and protection of some southern species. The successive advances and retreats of glaciers caused northern species to migrate to the area. The rare White-Haired goldenrod is endemic, as is the Canadian yew, which is outside its normal range.

In 1985 13,300 acres in the east of the geological area were designated as the Clifty Wilderness Area.

For information contact the supervisor of Daniel Boone National Forest, 100 Vaught Road, Winchester, Kentucky 40391 (606-745-3100).

OZARK NATIONAL FOREST [1,088,000 acres, in five units]
Northwestern Arkansas, north of Clarksville

A land of hardwood forests, deep rivers, and striking limestone bluffs, the Ozark National Forest contains five small Wilderness Areas, one in the Boston Mountains at the head of the Buffalo National River (11,094 acres). The river travels the rest of its journey outside the Forest, but the Forest contains a multitude of springs, mountain creeks, and waterfalls. A hike along Falling Water Creek is a way of seeing the waterfalls at their best.

Among the Forest's spectacular rock formations are two natural bridges. The less accessible, Hurricane Creek Natural Bridge in Hurricane Creek Wilderness Area (15,177 acres) is surrounded by virgin hardwoods. Richland Creek, the longest tributary of Buffalo National River and for which the Richland Creek Wilderness (11,822 acres) was named, flows for 3.2 miles through one of the remotest areas in the Ozarks. A quarter mile above Richland Creek's confluence with Devils Fork are spectacular twin waterfalls, 16–18 feet high, where Big Devils Fork and Long Devils Fork meet. The falls can be reached by a rugged two-mile hike. Hurricane Creek Wilderness is 40 miles north of Russellville, Arkansas. (Richland Creek Wilderness is 36 miles northeast of Russellville.)

The most popular spot in the Forest is Blanchard Springs Caverns, which is located at a recreation area only too thoroughly developed by the Forest Service. Here are six miles of underground corridors and rooms decked with stalactites and stalagmites.

Pressure from environmentalists forced the Pentagon in 1988 to drop plans to use the Ozark and Ouachita National Forests for military training.

For information contact the forest supervisor at P.O. Box 1008, Russellville, Arkansas 72801 (501-968-2354).

HOOSIER NATIONAL FOREST [187,812 acres]
South central Indiana

The Hoosier National Forest has been subject to heavy clearcutting and shows abundant examples of mismanagement. However, it still has attractions, including Hemlock Cliffs and the Pioneer Mothers Memorial Forest.

Hemlock Cliffs, which can be reached by following signs from Grantsburg, Ohio, is a region of bluffs, overhangs, and caves. The hemlocks, beneath which grow mountain laurel, are found along the edge of a sandstone gorge. Adjacent to the National Forest in this area is Arrowhead Arch, where Indiana University excavated an important archeological site. The large sandstone arch is a privately owned, state nature preserve. Those interested in visiting it should contact the state Department of Natural Resources in Indianapolis for information (317-232-4052). Permission from the landowner is required.

The Memorial Forest contains approximately 80 acres of virgin woods: beech, White oak, White ash, Black walnut, and Tulip poplar. The Forest Service says the best specimens may be the walnut trees in a small cove called Walnut Cathedral. The land on which the forest stands was patented by Joseph Cox in 1818 and protected by his family for over a century. In 1940 the land was sold to a lumber company to settle an estate. At the initiative of and with financial help from the Indiana Pioneer Mothers Association and other groups, the Forest Service bought it from the lumber company. A roadside park has been developed on Highway 37 at a corner of the tract.

For information contact the forest supervisor at 3527 10th Street, Bedford, Indiana 47421 (812-275-5987).

BLACK HILLS NATIONAL FOREST [1,233,000 acres]
Southwestern South Dakota and Wyoming, west of Rapid City

The Forest occupies most of the Black Hills, majestic pine-covered mountains that stand out like a cooling oasis in the plains of South Dakota. Here rugged rock formations, canyons and gulches are mingled with lakes and open grassland parks. The most striking of the rock formations, the Needles, comprise a celebrated rock climbing area. Mountain lions, Mountain goats, and Bighorn sheep inhabit the Forest.

Within the Forest are the Black Elk Wilderness (10,700 acres) and the Norbeck Wildlife Preserve (17,066 acres). The Wilderness was named after a holy man of the Ogalala Sioux, because of the vision he held of all peoples, all animals, and plants united as one holy power. The focal point of the Wilderness is Harney Peak, where Black Elk in his old age prayed to the Great Spirit to assist his people. It can be reached by trails from several directions and, at 7,242 feet, is the highest point in the United States east of the Rockies.

For information about Black Hills National Forest contact the supervisor at RR 2, Box 200, Custer, South Dakota 57730.

KALMIOPSIS ROADLESS AREA [408,000 acres]

Southwestern Oregon and northwestern California, west of Grants
  Pass and north of Crescent City

Siskiyou National Forest's Kalmiopsis roadless area and Kalmiopsis
Wilderness (part of the roadless area), take their name from a rare, pink-
flowered heath, *Kalmiopsis leachiana.* The rugged mountains and deep
valleys shelter a wide diversity of flora. More than ninety plant communities are found in the Kalmiopsis. Over a hundred rare and sensitive
plants grow here, as do twenty-eight species of conifers, the most varied
conifer forest in the world. In the Wilderness the ground is red with
peridotite volcanic rock; and the trees, mostly junipers, are dwarfed. In
contrast, the land north of Bald Mountain, north of the Wilderness,
contains the most extensive virgin forest on the coast. The rare Brewer,
or Weeping, spruce and Port Orford cedar are common here. Black
bear, Mountain lions, cougar, and the Northern Spotted owl, among
other species, inhabit the area.

The Forest Service plans to clearcut and road the northern portion
of the Kalmiopsis. In 1983 Earth First! delayed the destruction with
a lawsuit and a blockade, resulting in forty-four arrests. Earth First!ers
and other environmentalists have since renewed the battle.

The Siskiyou National Forest headquarters, at 200 NE Greenfield
Road, P.O. Box 440, Grants Pass, Oregon 97526 (503-479-5301) sells
a topographic map of the Kalmiopsis Wilderness and a map of the
Siskiyou National Forest.

CORONADO NATIONAL FOREST [1,790,000 acres, in several areas]

Southeastern Arizona

The forest is prime territory for studying wildlife, particularly birds.
The Chiricahua National Monument, Mount Graham, and Sycamore
Canyon are outstanding in this and other respects.

The Chiricahua Mountains, site of the Monument and Mount Graham, are two examples of "sky islands" that rise abruptly from flat, dry
desert. Cool and moist and isolated by large expanses of Sonoran Desert, each "island" has a distinctive flora and fauna.

The Chiricahuas, though fifty miles north of Mexico, show strongly
the influence of the southern country. Here such Mexican species as
the Apache Fox squirrel, Mexican chickadee, Sulphur-Bellied
flycatcher and Apache pine intermingle with plants and animals

characteristic of the American Southwest. The wildlife is not the only attraction, moreover. The Monument is the site of stunning rock formations: massive stone columns, rock spires, and huge rocks balancing on tiny pedestals. The rock is rhyolite, for which a popular Monument trail is named.

On 10,700 foot high Mount Graham in the Pinalenos Mountains are found ten endemic species or subspecies of insects, eight of plants, two of snails, the Mount Graham Red squirrel (a subspecies on the federal endangered species list), and an unusually dense population of Black bears. The Pinalenos, which preserve remnants of the Ice Age, exhibit five life zones. The Hudsonian life zone at the top of the range, with its mixture of spruce and fir and delicate wet meadows needs and merits Wilderness protection. Nevertheless, the University of Arizona, the Vatican, and several other institutions are trying to place telescopes on top of Mount Graham, a plan being fiercely contested by local environmentalists.

Sycamore Canyon on Forest Road 39 (not to be confused with the Sycamore Canyon of Sycamore Canyon Wilderness farther north in Arizona) once hosted a flourishing colony of Tarahumara frogs. In April 1973 the Canyon had five hundred to one thousand of the frogs; by April 1975 they had disappeared. None have been seen in Arizona since 1982. Dependent on standing water and having a long reproductive cycle, the frog is thought to have become extinct in the United States because of acid rain. Still to be found in the Canyon are the Goodding Ash tree, Golden-Chested Beehive cactus, Jaguarundi (a native of the cat family), Elegant trogon, and approximately fifteen species of hummingbirds.

The headquarters of the forest is at 301 West Congress, Tucson, Arizona 85701. For information on Chiricahua contact the Monument at Dos Cabezas Route, Box 6500, Willcox, Arizona 85643. On Mount Graham write to the Maricopa Audubon Society (4619 East Arcadia Lane, Phoenix, Arizona 85018) or call the Mount Graham Hotline (602-629-9200).

CHAPTER TWELVE

National Parks, Monuments, and Preserves

In 1849, when Congress created the Department of the Interior, it gave the department varied responsibilities. According to the *United States Government Manual*, Interior was at first a "general housekeeper for the Federal Government." As Congress added and subtracted functions, however, the department's role became that of "custodian of the nation's resources." Today it administers over 500 million acres through its agencies, the National Park Service, the Bureau of Land Management, the U.S. Fish and Wildlife Service, and, to a lesser extent, the Bureau of Reclamation.

NATIONAL PARK SERVICE LANDS

The National Park System had its origin in Congress' designation in 1872 of Yellowstone National Park, the first National Park in the world. Congress did not create the National Park Service, however, until 1916. By that time the United States had seventeen National Parks, twenty-two National Monuments, and military battlefields and cemeteries, each under the agency that controlled the land when the land was set aside.

Today the system consists of 357 areas covering more than 76 million acres, including 47.1 million in Alaska. These areas were designated because of their natural or historic features and are all under the control of the National Park Service; but they bear a bewildering variety of titles, including National Monument, National Military Park, National Battlefield Park, and National Lakeshore. They can be roughly grouped according to method of acquisition and extent of protection.

National Parks in the strict meaning of the term can be established only by act of Congress. Most of the other components of the system are also created by Congress, but there are exceptions. National Monuments are established by presidential proclamation on lands already owned by the federal government. The legal basis for this presidential authority is the Antiquities Act of 1906, passed as a reaction to vandalism among ancient Indian cliff dwellings in the Southwest. Historic Sites can be designated by the Secretary of the Interior. If the property is not in the public domain the secretary can seek authorization from Congress to buy it or can enter into an arrangement with the owner to use it. The earliest National Recreation Areas resulted from agreements between the National Park Service and agencies such as the Bureau of Reclamation. The other agency retained overall jurisdiction but the National Park Service manages the land.

Each area established by Congress or by the President is managed according to the provisions of the specific law or proclamation establishing it. The National Parks and the National Monuments designated because of natural features are, with occasional exceptions, protected from mining and mineral leasing, new mining claims, grazing, farming, commercial cutting of timber, use of off-road recreational vehicles, and hunting. Dams can be erected by the National Park Service to support the purpose for which the given park or monument was created. The main difference between the Seashores and Lakeshores and the Parks is that there is heavier emphasis on recreation in the management of the Seashores and Lakeshores. This may include hunting and fishing. Preserves are a relatively new category that came into being in 1974 with the creation of the Big Thicket and Big Cypress Preserves. They are established primarily to protect specific resources; activities deemed compatible with those resources, including hunting and mining are permitted. Unfortunately use of off-road vehicles is also permitted in Florida's Big Cypress National Preserve, where they are tearing up the land.

In Historic Areas and Parkways, grazing, timber cutting, and farming are permitted if judged appropriate to the unit's historical character. National Recreation Areas are managed primarily for recreation and generally allow timber cutting, mining, grazing, and hunting.

Congress has designated some areas in the National Park System as parts of the National Wilderness Preservation System. They remain in the Park System but enjoy extra protection.

The National Trails System and the Wild and Scenic Rivers System are closely related to the National Park Service, although not all Trails or Rivers are part of the National Park System. The National Park Service administers the river units that belong to the National Park System and the entire Trails System. ("Unit" is used in reference to waterways to indicate a river or a segment of a river.)

The law creating the National Park Service in 1916 required it "to conserve the scenery and the natural and historic objects and the wildlife therein and to provide for the enjoyment of the same in such manner and by such means as will leave them unimpaired for the enjoyment of future generations." There is a conflict inherent in this charge, obvious today. Preservation and use, even for recreational purposes, are not always compatible. Road building in the parks is anathema to many environmentalists, and the greatest current threat to the system may be the crowds of visitors using the roads in the better known parks.

Land acquisitions have not kept pace with public interest in outdoor recreation. Additional Parks and enlargement of existing Parks are urgently needed. Over half of the areas already in the system have privately-owned land (inholdings) within their boundaries. The possibility of development on these lands is always a threat.

Congress set up a Land and Water Conservation Fund for land acquisition in 1965. As the result of subsequent Congressional amendments, the fund now receives $900 million per year, 90% from revenues produced by oil and gas leases on the Outer Continental Shelf. It currently totals more than $7.8 billion – on paper. This money can be and is used for non-conservation purposes. The fund actually has two components: a receipt fund (the $7.8 billion) and an appropriations fund into which Congress annually transfers money from the receipt fund. States, localities, and federal agencies can spend only the appropriations fund. To ensure a stable, consistent source of funding for land purchases, environmentalists contend that Congress should transform the Land and Water Conservation Fund into a dedicated Treasury account or into a true trust.

The biggest enlargement of the public lands system took place under President Carter, and did not involve purchase. In 1978, acting under the 1906 Antiquities Act, Carter designated eleven new monuments and enlarged two existing monuments in Alaska. The Alaska National Interest Lands Conservation Act of 1980 altered boundaries of the units and redesignated most of them as National Parks and National Preserves. The addition of the Alaskan lands more than doubled the acreage of the Park System.

The National Parks and Conservation Association, a private organization devoted to protecting, promoting, and improving the national parks, has published a detailed study of the National Park System with recommendations for improvements, *Investing in Park Futures: A Blueprint for Tomorrow*. Some environmentalists do not believe that the recommendations are sufficiently far-reaching, but the document is a step in the right direction and useful for its analysis of the present situation. It can be ordered from the association at 1015 Thirty-First Street NW, Washington, D.C. 20007 (202-944-8530). The executive summary is $9.95 plus postage.

The Department of the Interior's annual *National Parks: Index*, available from the Government Printing Office that publishes it (Washington, D.C. 20402–9373; 202-783-3238), lists, briefly describes, and gives the addresses of all units in the National Park System. The National Park Service's Public Inquiry Service is P.O. Box 37127, Washington, D.C. 20013–7127 (202-208-4747).

Michael Frome's *National Park Guide*, published annually by Rand McNally, provides a good introduction, with maps, to each National Park. It also contains brief descriptions of other units in the National Park System.

The National Parks and Conservation Association distributes a free catalog of publications describing units of the National Park System. All items can be ordered from the NPCA.

Northern Cartographic in Burlington, Vermont, published in 1988 a large-print book, *Access America: An Atlas and Guide to the National Parks for Visitors with Disabilities*.

Many units of the National Park System and some National Wildlife Refuges have entrance fees. People under sixty-two who frequently visit these lands can save money by buying an annual Golden Eagle Passport for $25. It will admit a carload of people and is available by mail from the Service and at units charging fees. Older people can obtain a free Golden Age Passport. Golden Age Passports must be requested in person and are available at Parks and Wildlife Refuges charging fees, plus the offices of public land agencies. Proof of age must be shown.

Many units of the National Park System operate campgrounds. Some allow primitive camping in their backcountry. Regulations vary from unit to unit. Write or phone ahead for information. A permit for backcountry use may be required.

The units described here are grouped by type.

GREAT SMOKY MOUNTAINS NATIONAL PARK
[520,000 acres]
Western North Carolina and eastern Tennessee

During the Ice Age the Smokies, untouched by glaciers, were a refuge for hundreds of plant and animal species. Today the park contains 1,500 species of vascular plants. The fauna include twenty-three species of salamanders. Three wildlife species are found only in the park: the Red-Cheeked salamander, Cain's Reed-Bent grass, and Rugel's Indian plantain. There they are common. More than a thousand Red-Cheeked salamanders have been seen crossing a road at one time, and the Reed-Bent grass thrives on acidic rock on the top of Mount LeConte (6,593 feet).

In the 1920s when residents of North Carolina and Tennessee became interested in establishing a National Park, the land was in more than 6,000 tracts in private hands and its temperate deciduous forest was being heavily logged. An initial fund-raising campaign netted $500,000, $1,391.72 of which was donated by the children of eastern Tennessee. In 1926 Congress authorized the park without appropriating purchase money. The state legislatures of Tennessee and North Carolina appropriated $2 million each; John D. Rockefeller, Jr. added another $5 million in matching grants. The purchases were made in time to spare the trees in the higher, less accessible locations. Today approximately 20% of the park is virgin forest.

The park contains a variety of restored log structures, reminiscent of the fact that paradoxically many families were forced from their homes when the park was created.

The word "Smoky" refers to a blue-gray haze that used to envelope the mountains as the result of the dense vegetation and high humidity. Visitors today see haze, but it is usually grayish white – the result of air pollution from sulfate compounds. Visibility in the park has decreased 30% since the early 1950s.

In making an itinerary keep in mind that the Appalachian Trail through the park is overused. For information contact the park office in Gatlinburg, Tennessee 37738 (615-436-1200). The phone number for reservations for "rationed" backcountry sites is 615-436-1231, 8:00 A.M.-6:00 P.M., Mon.-Fri.

EVERGLADES NATIONAL PARK [1,506,538 acres]
Southern Florida, south and west of Miami

The subtropical Everglades, a unique ecosystem, is essentially a great curving river up to 60 miles wide, fed by Lake Okeechobee and flowing south to the tip of Florida. In *The Everglades: River of Grass* (Rinehart, 1947) environmental crusader Marjory Stoneman Douglas describes in fascinating detail the "green and brown expanse of saw grass and of water, shining and slow-moving."

The National Park includes land and water adjacent to the "river of grass" and only the lower one-fourth of the river itself. Diversions of water outside the park are threatening the existence of the glades. The Kissimmee River, north of the Everglades is, however, one of the few places in the nation where the Army Corps of Engineers is undertaking a restoration project. The Corps has been asked by Congress to put the river that the Corps previously remade into a straight ditch, back into its original meandering course.

A 38-mile road traverses the park from northeast to southwest. Foot trails leading off it provide an opportunity to see wildlife. The Anhinga Trail, though only half a mile in length, is particularly well located for this purpose. Canoeing is the easiest way to get into the backcountry. The 99-mile Wilderness Waterway from Everglades City to Flamingo makes an excellent trip, normally seven days in length. The Turner River, where West Indies manatees can occasionally be spotted, is a good shorter venture. Many of the hammocks, little humps with unique vegetation, are especially worth seeing. Most of the shallow island-dotted Florida Bay is open to canoeists and other boaters, although, to protect nesting birds, landing on the islands is forbidden. The bay and its islands occupy approximately one-third of the park.

Visit between mid-December and mid-April to avoid the torrential rains of summer and the worst of the mosquitoes and sandflies. The park has two developed campgrounds. Most camping sites in the back-country are chickees, raised wooden platforms, accessible only by boat.

For information, contact the park at P.O. Box 279, Homestead, Florida 33030.

DENALI NATIONAL PARK AND PRESERVE
[6,028,091 acres]
Southcentral Alaska

Congress established the 1.9 million-acre Mount McKinley National Park in 1917, largely to protect the Dall sheep. It was enlarged and received its present name in 1980. The area that formerly constituted the entire park has become the Denali Wilderness Area and is the most heavily used portion of the park.

Since the earliest days of the park, tour buses belonging to concessionaires have provided transportation into the interior. In the 1970s the National Park Service instituted free bus service, and it later stopped almost all use of cars in the park. The buses make round trips from the Riley Creek Information Center to Eielson Visitor Center and Wonder Lake. From Eielson Center, one can see the spectacular 20,320-foot-high Mount McKinley. The scenery on the continuation of the trip to Wonder Lake is worth the extra hours in the bus, if the weather is clear enough for Mount McKinley to be visible. During trips drivers stop to let passengers view wildlife from the buses. They drop people off and pick people up, as requested, at any point along the road.

The park has no trails west of Riley Creek Center. In the backcountry hikers usually follow river bars or ridge systems or walk across tundra. The center provides permits for backcountry camping. The park has seven designated campgrounds.

At Denali visitors can watch moose, caribou, Dall sheep, Grizzly bears, and wolves, in a natural setting. The wolf population, which inhabits the two-thirds of the park not occupied by glaciers and mountains, numbers about 110 animals. As part of a five-year study, rangers fitted twenty-four of them with radio collars. All the wolf packs roam outside the wilderness onto land where they can be hunted legally.

Adjacent to Denali National Park on the southeast is the 324,240-acre Denali State Park. The state park is accessible only by car; but fewer people visit it. Hiking trails cross varied terrain and afford splendid views, and Mount McKinley can be seen from all points.

Unfortunately both the state park and the southern border of the National Park are threatened by the actual and proposed construction of new tourist facilities. Despite the development going on, almost no low- or moderately-priced indoor accommodations are available near the park.

For information on Denali write to the park at P.O. Box 9, Denali Park, Alaska 99755.

OLYMPIC NATIONAL PARK AND NATIONAL FOREST
[914,818 acres of park and 649,979 acres of forest]
On the Olympic Peninsula in northwest Washington

Olympic National Forest and the main body of Olympic National Park, around which the forest forms a semicircle, occupy the center of the Olympic Peninsula. The park also contains a 57-mile strip along the coast. The outstanding feature of the park and the forest are three temperate rainforests in the valleys of the Quinault, Queets, and Hoh Rivers. They result from 145 inches of rain a year, moderate temperatures, and summer fog. Here are old-growth Sitka spruce, Western hemlock, Western Red cedar, and Douglas fir, some of the trees reaching almost 300 feet in height. The Hoh Valley in the national park is a particularly fine area for hiking.

The park was created in part to protect the Roosevelt elk, a northwestern subspecies named after Theodore Roosevelt. Now a herd of 1,400 lives in the park. The Northern Spotted owl, a subspecies that environmentalists say should be listed as endangered, also lives here.

On the peninsula the difference between typical Forest Service management and typical National Park Service management is obvious. Trees in the park are intact, but roaded areas in the Forest have been heavily logged. Roadless areas that do not belong to the Forest's five small Wilderness areas are scheduled for clearcutting.

Port Angeles, where one of the park's visitor centers is located, can be reached by bus and plane. The postal address of the park is 600 East Park Avenue, Port Angeles, Washington 98632. For information on the forest contact the supervisor at P.O. Box 2288, Olympia, Washington 98507.

YELLOWSTONE NATIONAL PARK [2,219,785 acres]
Northwest Wyoming and adjacent Montana and Idaho

Yellowstone National Park is the easiest place in the United States to see large mammals in relatively natural conditions. The animals plus the world's largest thermal basins and the splendidly colored Grand Canyon of the Yellowstone, draw throngs of people to the park each summer.

It is nevertheless possible to enjoy the park's spectacular scenery and wildlife in peace. Yellowstone is essentially a volcanic plateau or caldera between 7,000 and 8,500 feet above sea level, surrounded on the south, north, northwest, and east by mountain ranges rising between 2,000 and 4,000 feet above the plateau. Scattered throughout are lakes and ponds surrounded by dense forests and rivers flowing through broad meadows. More than 90% of this natural wealth is rarely visited. One thousand miles of backcountry trails lead to such choice areas as the upper Firehold River above the Kepler Cascades in the west, the southern arms of Yellowstone Lake in the southeast, and the Mirror Plateau and Lamar River wildlands in the east.

When Congress established the park in 1872, it did not appropriate money for its protection. Vandalism and poaching became so rampant that the Secretary of the Interior asked the Secretary of War to send soldiers to keep order. Cavalry entered Yellowstone in 1886 and remained for thirty-two years, until after the establishment of the Park Service. Troops also went to Yosemite, Sequoia, and General Grant National Parks. They appear to have done an excellent job.

Captain Frazier Augustus Boutelle, acting superintendent of Yellowstone from 1889–1891, was the first black to oversee a National Park. His tenure would have been longer had he been less of a conservationist and more of a politician. Apparently he angered the Interior Secretary by refusing to consent to the installation of an elevator in a conspicuous position in the Grand Canyon of the Yellowstone River and by taking steps to stop a poaching operation connected with preparations for installing steamboat service on Yellowstone Lake.

In 1894 Congress passed the Yellowstone Protection Act, the first federal law protecting wildlife. The act made it a crime to kill or remove wildlife from the park, and forbade other human activities that would disturb wildlife.

A major preservation problem today is protection of the Grizzly bear. No more, and possibly far fewer than 1,000 Grizzlies remain in the lower forty-eight states. The Greater Yellowstone Ecosystem is one of six locations in which they survive. The population in Yellowstone is in decline, most experts agree, as in many recent years deaths have exceeded births. Management of the bears is now a major cause of death, as bears who approach or bother humans are relocated or killed. Bear/human contacts are unnecessarily numerous, because the National Park Service allows major tourist facilities, in particular, Fishing Bridge and Grant Village, to operate in prime Grizzly habitat.

For information on the park contact the superintendent at P.O. Box

168, Yellowstone National Park, Wyoming 82190. For information on Grizzlies, contact the Earth First! Grizzly Bear Task Force, P.O. Box 6151, Bozeman, Montana 59715.

GRAND TETON NATIONAL PARK [310,521 acres]
Northwestern Wyoming, north of Jackson

The Teton Range is a celebrated mountain climbing area, and more than half of the range's roadless area lies within the park. Leigh Ortenburger in the *Climber's Guide to the Teton Range* (Sierra Club Books, 1956) summarized: "These peaks rise steadily at a high angle, bristle with spires and pinnacles, and are topped by sharp summits. . . . There is perhaps no climbing area in the country that can match the Tetons for general mountaineering of an Alpine nature with excellent rock and moderate snow." The mountains also provide spectacular scenery and fine habitat. Climbers pass from sagebrush flats, though coniferous forests dominated by Lodgepole pine, to glaciers and subalpine meadows. Grand Teton Peak is 13,770 feet high.

The nation owes the park to John D. Rockefeller, Jr., whose gift was the subject of fierce controversy. He bought land for the park in the late 1920s and early 1930s secretly under the name of the Snake River Land Company. When Congress tried to combine his purchases with the Teton National Forest and other public lands to create the park, the Forest Service and local ranchers protested so vigorously and successfully that not until 1949 did Rockefeller succeed in presenting his land to the government. Since then, the road between West Thumb in Yellowstone National Park and the South Entrance of Grand Teton has been declared the John D. Rockefeller, Jr. Memorial Parkway.

In *Wapiti Wilderness* (Knopf, 1966) environmentalists Margaret and Olaus Murie describe their experiences in and near the park from 1927 to 1945. The book takes its name from the Wapiti or Elk, which Olaus studied for the U.S. Biological Survey. Olaus is the author of *A Field Guide to Animal Tracks* (Houghton Mifflin, 1974) among other books and was director and then president of the Wilderness Society. Margaret, or Mardie, wrote *Two in the Far North* (Knopf, 1962). She has carried on with environmental work since her husband's death in 1963.

For information write to the park at P.O. Drawer 170, Moose, Wyoming 83012.

REDWOOD NATIONAL PARK [110,178 acres]

Northern California coastline

In 1918 Save the Redwoods League was created to rescue examples of primeval redwood forests and to cooperate with state and national officials in creating redwood parks. One of its first actions was to recommend to Congress the establishment of a Redwood National Park. The park was not created until 1968. Meanwhile the League was purchasing land with old growth redwoods for state parks. It has to date donated over $55 million to protect some 260,000 acres of redwood land, of which 422 acres are now in the National Park.

As created in 1968, the National Park covered only 30,000 acres of federal land. It included the world's tallest tree, a 367.8-foot redwood beside Redwood Creek, and it took in three state parks: Jedediah Smith, Del Norte Coast, and Prairie Creek. However, it did not contain enough land to protect the Redwood Creek and Mill Creek Watersheds. In 1978, Congress passed the National Parks Expansion Act, adding 48,000 acres, including lands essential to the Redwood Creek watershed. The legislation was ground breaking in that it allotted $33 millon for restoration as well as funds for purchase.

Because of heavy logging around the outside of the original park, landslides and erosion were taking place in the Redwood Creek watershed. Of the 48,000 new acres, only 9,000 were old-growth redwood. Prairies and oak woodlands occupied about 2,500 acres. The rest had been recently logged and scarred with logging roads and tractor trails. The Park Service began the process of stabilization and reforestation as soon as the park was expanded.

In addition to redwoods, the park provides opportunities to view uncommon animals. Along the 50-mile shoreline, visitors can watch endangered Gray whales in migration, plus other whales, seals, sea lions, and porpoises. Roosevelt elk and Mountain lions live inland. Since the park is on the Pacific Flyway, it hosts about 300 species of birds, including the Aleutian Canada goose, an endangered subspecies.

The park can be reached by Greyhound bus or by air to Del Norte airport. Along the Coastal Trail that runs the length of the park are three walk-in, primitive campgrounds. Hiker-biker campsites, which need no reservation, are available year round at Prairie Creek and Jedediah Smith state parks. For information on the park, contact the superintendent at 1111 Second Street, Crescent City, California 95531.

The address of Save the Redwoods League is 114 Sansome Street, San Francisco, California 94104.

GREAT BASIN NATIONAL PARK [76,800 acres]
East central Nevada, near the Utah border

The park was created in 1986 to preserve a portion of the Great Basin – a vast area comprising most of Nevada, plus parts of Oregon, Idaho, Utah, and California. Water flowing off the Basin's more than two hundred mountain ranges drains inland rather than to the sea, but as it quickly evaporates or soaks into the ground, the valleys are for the most part dry and barren. Actually the name of the park is rather ironic, as the small protected area comprises mountain peaks but not valleys with their low-elevation flora and fauna.

The South Snake Range, where the park is located, contains a number of unique features. Wheeler Peak, at 13,063 feet the highest mountain entirely within Nevada, hosts one of the park's three groves of Bristlecone pines, and the only glacier in the Great Basin. Several streams coming off the western slope of the range harbor an endangered native subspecies of Cutthroat trout. At the base of the range lies Lehman Caves, one of the largest limestone solution caverns in the western United States.

The range long boasted what was believed to be the oldest tree in the world, a Bristlecone pine, judged to be more than 4,900 years old. On 10 August 1964 the Forest Service cut down the tree to section it and study the growth rings. An approximately 4,300-year-old Bristlecone pine in the White Mountains of California is now thought to be the oldest living tree.

"King Clone," a 70-foot by 25-foot creosote bush in Lucerne Valley, California, is believed to be the oldest living thing. According to carbon dating and other techniques, it has been growing for 11,700 years.

For information on the park contact the office in Baker, Nevada 89311.

ARCHES NATIONAL PARK [73,378 acres]
Southeastern Utah, five miles northwest of Moab

The park (a monument until 1971) takes its name from its more than 200 sandstone arches, the largest group of natural arches anywhere in the world; but the fantastic rocks are only one aspect of the park, as Edward Abbey makes clear in his collection of essays *Desert Solitaire*

(McGraw Hill, 1968). Writing of spring, for instance, he notes the "cliffrose" with its "dense clusters of flowers creamy white or pale yellow, like wild roses, each with its five perfect petals and a golden center" and, in the sand, "tracks of tiger lizards, birds, kangaroo rats, beetles. Circles and semicircles on the red dune where the wind whips the compliant stems of the wild ricegrass." In October he sees "the dead or dying pinyon pines . . . the black-rooted silver-blue sage."

Unfortunately visitors to Arches today have to put up with what Abbey does not like about national parks – development and, in particular, roads. But there are still trails worth taking, and, for Abbey aficionados, yes, Abbey's lost arch does exist.

For information contact the park at P.O. Box 907, Moab, Utah 84532. The park contains a tent and trailer campground.

HALEAKALA NATIONAL PARK [28,655 acres]
Southeastern part of the island of Maui

Created in 1960 to protect the Haleakala Crater, the park was later enlarged to include the Kipahulu Valley, the 'Ohe'o Gulch, and a few miles of coast. Unlike the crater, the added area is green and lush, with abundant water. In 1976, the area of the crater was designated as a 19,270-acre Wilderness.

The half-mile Hosmer Grove Nature Trail in the northwest corner of the park illustrates the park's natural history. The trail begins in Hosmer Grove, trees imported from abroad by Hawaii's first territorial forester, Mark Hosmer. Hosmer created four such forests in Haleakala with the idea of starting timber harvesting. Fortunately the experiment did not work. Beyond the forest is shrubland of native species.

Because of the island's isolation, the native plants – those that colonized the islands before humans arrived – have evolved into forms not found elsewhere. More than 90% of Hawaii's native plant and animal species are endemic. Exotic species, in particular wild pigs and goats, are a major threat to the continued existence of the natives, many of which are endangered.

Among the native birds at Haleakala is the Nene or Hawaiian goose. The feet of this goose have a reduced amount of webbing, an adaptation to walking on lava. The birds apparently once existed on all the main islands, but they were almost completely wiped out, in part by mongoose and other exotic species. As the result of a captive breeding and release program, an estimated 500 Nene now exist in the wild.

The National Park has 36 miles of hiking trails, and there are primitive campgrounds and cabins in the crater. For information and reservations contact the park headquarters, P.O. Box 369, Makawao, Maui, Hawaii 96768.

LAVA BEDS NATIONAL MONUMENT [46,600 acres]
Northern California, 30 miles south of Tulelake

As the name indicates, the land in Lava Beds is volcanic in origin; and, though the most recent lava tubes were formed 30,000 years ago, vegetation is still slight. Grasses cover the north and only gradually give way to junipers and finally to pines in the extreme south. The grasslands provide refuge and food for small animals. These animals and the cliffs on the northern edge of the monument attract raptors. Bald eagles winter here in greater numbers than in any other area in the lower forty-eight states.

The lava tubes themselves may be the monument's most striking feature. As lava flowed from craters, the outside of each flow cooled, slowed, and hardened. When the flow ceased, this shell remained. Later some portions of these surfaces collapsed, creating entrances into caves of lava. The monument contains at least 200 of these caves, some developed to assist exploration, but more than one hundred in their natural state. Among the latter are caves requiring advanced rock climbing skills.

Modoc Indians lived in the area for centuries. The Modocs were driven out by the U.S. Army in 1873, after repeated confrontations with white settlers and after negotiations, which were disastrous for the Modocs. During the Modoc War, fifty-two Modoc warriors held off troops eventually twenty times their number for almost five months.

For information contact the monument at P.O. Box 867, Tulelake, California 96134.

DINOSAUR NATIONAL MONUMENT [211,142 acres]
Northeastern Utah and northwestern Colorado

In 1909 Earl Douglass of the Carnegie Museum discovered in the top of a ledge in the Uinta Mountains "eight of the tail bones of a Brontosaurus in exact position." He and his workers later dug from the site thousands more bones, including nearly complete skeletons. In 1915 the quarry became a National Monument. Today the remainder of the bone-bearing layer forms one wall of the Dinosaur Quarry building at the monument. Visitors can watch paleontologists exposing bones in the wall.

The monument is more than dinosaur remains, however. In 1938 the park was enlarged to include the wild limestone and shale canyons of the Yampa and Green Rivers. The green of cottonwoods and box-elders lining the rivers and their canyons contrasts vividly with the aridness of the surrounding desert. After floating through the monument, David Brower declared, "I have seen a lot of outstanding scenery in the last thirty-five years. I have never had a scenic experience to equal that one."

He was speaking in the context of a battle to save a portion of the monument from flooding. In the late 1940s the Interior Department's Bureau of Reclamation drew up a plan for a billion dollar Colorado River storage project that included construction of a dam at Echo Park within the monument. Before work could start, Congress had to give approval. The conservation movement united against the project, and, galvanized by the energy of Brower, was successful in having the project modified to omit the park.

The battle was a turning point. The various environmental organizations had found that they could work together, and they had found what they needed to do: make our wild places safe from the whims of bureaucrats. The Echo Dam victory prepared the way for the 1964 Wilderness Act.

For information on the monument write to the office at P.O. Box 210, Dinosaur, Colorado 81610. Running the rivers is one of the best ways to see the monument. It contains only a few hiking trails.

COLORADO NATIONAL MONUMENT [20,453 acres]
West central Colorado, near Grand Junction

This monument is less well known than Arches National Park, but contains equally spectacular sandstone rock formations, in the shape of colorful cliffs and spires. It also offers a variety of recreational opportunities. Hikers can readily descend into most of the canyons by means of maintained trails and old deer tracks, yet climbers can find challenges. In the winter Liberty Cap Trail, which crosses the middle of the park, is used by cross-country skiers. Wildlife enthusiasts may see Mountain lions, Mule deer, elk, and bison, especially at twilight. The campgrounds are pleasant. In addition, the monument is near public transportation: the buses and airplanes of Grand Junction.

For information contact the monument at Fruita, Colorado 81521 (303-858-3617).

JOSHUA TREE NATIONAL MONUMENT [558,000 acres]
Southern California, 140 miles east of Los Angeles

At Joshua Tree Monument the Colorado and the Mojave deserts meet. The Colorado, in the eastern half of the monument, below 3,000 feet, is a dry land dominated by the Creosote bush and dotted with cacti. The Mojave, to the west, is higher, slightly cooler, and wetter. Here are found stands of Joshua trees, tall yuccas with erratic branches. The monument includes five fan-palm oases. The 4-mile trail to the largest, Lost Palms Oasis, allows hikers to view a variety of desert scenery in a couple of hours.

Unfortunately a 4-mile-wide Military Training Route passes over the heart of the park. Low-flying jets from Naval Air Station Lemoore near Fresno follow this route. In justifying the flights, Commander General John P. Schoeppner of Edwards Air Force Base noted that there are no restrictions on low-level civilian or military flights over "national parks, monuments, forests, or wilderness areas," except for portions of the Grand Canyon.

Contact the monument at 74485 National Monument Drive, Twenty-nine Palms, California 92277 (619-367-7511).

JAMAICA BAY WILDLIFE REFUGE [9,155 acres]
Within New York City's Gateway National Recreation Area

The ideal wildlife refuge is a completely natural area, but in some parts of the country it is too late to achieve the ideal. Brooklyn is the site of a refuge that though artificial, succeeds in providing needed habitat for plants and animals and refreshment for humans.

The Jamaica Bay Refuge is the work of the New York City Parks Department. In 1951 Parks Commissioner Robert Moses, in consultation with the U.S. Fish and Wildlife Service, ordered the creation of two large fresh water ponds. Later, trees, shrubs, and grass were planted. In 1972, when the Gateway National Recreation Area was established, the refuge became one of its units. Since then, the refuge has been under the supervision of the National Park Service.

From the 1950s the refuge has been managed with the aim of providing diverse habitats. The area now encompasses fresh and brackish ponds, salt marsh, upland fields and woods, islands, and even a portion of Jamaica Bay itself.

During the past twenty-five years more than 325 species of birds have been seen at the refuge. It is at the junction of the Atlantic Coast and Hudson River flyways, and in the spring and autumn thousands of ducks and geese make it one of their stops.

Refuge trails are open daily from sunrise to sunset. Permits are necessary but can be obtained free of charge at the visitor center. A bus stop and a subway station are half a mile from the refuge.

For information contact the Chief Ranger, Jamaica Bay Wildlife Refuge, Gateway National Recreation Area, Floyd Bennett Field, Brooklyn, New York 11234 (718-474-0613).

SANTA MONICA MOUNTAINS NATIONAL RECREATION AREA [150,000 acres]
Forty-six miles along the coast adjacent to Los Angeles

Surrounded by plains, ocean, and population centers, the Santa Monicas are virtually an island. The entire range, one of the few east-west trending ranges in North America, is included in the recreation area. It encloses a Mediterranean ecosystem, of which only five exist in the world, all western coastland.

The mountains are covered with chaparral and sage. Between the mountains are grasslands and woodlands. Steep, rocky canyons shelter waterfalls and streamside groves of sycamore and Valley oak, here at its southernmost extreme. Along the shore are salt and fresh water marshes and sandy beaches of different energy types and exposures interspersed with rocky beaches. Near shore are rock reefs and kelp beds.

The coastal drainages afford spawning runs for Steelhead Rainbow trout; Malibu and Mugu Lagoons shelter birds traveling the Pacific flyway; the mountains provide habitat for the nesting of raptors and for the survival of the Mountain lion in southwestern California.

The Recreation Area, established by Congress in 1978, is still in the course of development. The National Park Service, in charge of planning for the park, owns only 12,000 acres. The remainder includes public parklands, towns, and private camps and estates. The diversity of ownership is illustrated by the fact that the Nature Conservancy owns Cold Creek Canyon Preserve, while the U.S. Navy manages, as part of its Pacific Missile Test Center, Mugu Lagoon, the largest coastal wetland in California outside the San Francisco Bay area. The canyon is open for hiking by prior arrangement only; the missile test center is closed to the public.

Recreational opportunities in the Area include bicycling, swimming, climbing, surfing, and camping. For information on the area contact the headquarters of the National Park Service at 22900 Ventura Boulevard, Woodland Hills, California 91364 (818-888-3770).

SLEEPING BEAR DUNES NATIONAL LAKESHORE [71,132 acres]

Northwest coast of Michigan's Lower Peninsula, west of Traverse
    City

The National Lakeshore protects mainland shoreline and two nearby islands in Lake Michigan, South and North Manitou. The landscape is varied, as massive sand dunes are backed on the mainland by forests and inland lakes and streams. Recreational opportunities vary from dune climbing through canoeing to snowshoeing and cross-country skiing. Visitors in search of seclusion should arrange to visit one of the islands. The northern island has one camping spot with designated sites near the village and docks; the remainder of the island is available for undesignated primitive camping. On the southern island there are three designated camping areas. This island is the site of abandoned farms and the Valley of the Giants, a grove of virgin White Cedar.

The second North American Bioregional Congress took place at Camp Innisfree in the midst of the lakeshore in August 1986.

For information contact Sleeping Bear Dunes National Lakeshore, P.O. Box 277, 9922 Front Street, Empire, Michigan 49630 (616-326-5134).

BIG THICKET NATIONAL PRESERVE [85,773 acres]

Eastern Texas, north of Beaumont

Consisting of eight patches of land and four corridors, this preserve represents a last ditch effort to save an incredibly diverse ecosystem. In eastern Texas elements from eastern forests, the Appalachians, southeastern swamps, central plains, and southwestern deserts meet. The preserve is home to more than 60 shrubs, 85 species of trees, nearly 1,000 other flowering plants, and diverse animal species including coyote, nutria, mink, and beaver. There are huge tupelo and cypress trees, but where rain percolates through sandy soil, desert vegetation grows.

Under pressure from area residents Congress authorized the preserve in 1974. The general area has been subject to exploitation ever since the 1850s, when lumbering began. At one point timber interests even poisoned the land and replanted it with quick growing pine. Rice farmers flooded some forests. Today oil drilling is going on in the preserve. A bill that would add 14,000 acres to the preserve was introduced in the U.S. House of Representatives in 1989.

For information, contact the preserve at 3785 Milam, Beaumont, Texas 77701.

CHAPTER THIRTEEN

National Resource Lands and Wildlife Refuges

The Bureau of Land Management (BLM) in the Department of Interior has exclusive jurisdiction over more than 270 million acres of public land, of which 90 million acres are in Alaska. This is national land that has not been sold; not been withdrawn to form a park, forest, refuge, reservoir, or defense installation; not been granted to a state, railroad, or other entity; or not been made part of the Indian reservation system. These areas are sometimes known as "the leftover lands"; officially they are called the National Resource Lands.

Although the Bureau was formed in 1946 (its predecessor, the General Land Office, dates back to 1812), it did not receive a basic mission statement and policy guideline until 1976, with the passage of the Federal Land Policy and Management Act (FLMPA). This act, which repealed a hodgepodge of earlier statutes, directed the Bureau to follow multiple-use, sustained-yield goals. The agency was to designate "areas of critical environmental concern" (ACECs) and to study its lands for fifteen years to determine which should belong to the National Wilderness Preservation System. As of late 1989, it had designated 429 ACECs containing a total of 6,623,313 acres, for which site-specific management practices and, in some cases, mitigation measures and use limitations had been put into effect. By early 1990 Congress had extended Wilderness protection to 470,000 acres of Bureau land in twenty-six areas.

In addition to exercising exclusive jurisdiction over a large portion of federally owned land, the BLM controls the leasing program and the administration of claims for energy and mineral resources on all federal lands. Despite its enormous responsibilities the BLM is underfunded, understaffed, and, partly as a result of these conditions, unduly subject to the influence of Western miners, developers, politicians, and especially stockmen who graze their animals on public lands.

Much of the limited power of the agency resides in its field offices. To find out exactly what lands the Bureau administers, inquirers must contact these offices. The Department of the Interior annually publishes statistics on the holdings of the BLM and what it is doing with them in *Public Land Statistics,* available from the Government Printing Office.

Under the multiple-use principle, the Bureau permits much the same mixture of land uses as the Forest Service, but it supervises activities on its land even less closely. Except for the agency's Alaskan holdings, most of its lands are in the arid West and are grazed by livestock.

Bureau rules for recreational land use are similar to Forest Service rules. Camping is generally permitted anywhere on BLM land free of charge, except for a few established campgrounds for which a fee is charged. The BLM Public Affairs Office distributes a free map of BLM lands, Recreation Guide to BLM Public Lands, with the addresses of state and district offices. The Public Affairs Office, which also responds to questions, is in Room 5600, 18 and C Streets, Washington, D.C. 20240 (202-208-5717).

BIG SHEEP CREEK SPECIAL RECREATION MANAGEMENT AREA [12,000-plus acres]
Southwestern Montana, south of Dell

Big Sheep Creek, a narrow canyon in mountainous territory, rates an entry in Defenders of Wildlife's *Montana Wildlife Viewing Guide.* Bighorn sheep can often be seen from Big Sheep Creek Road that runs through the canyon. Elk, Mule deer, pronghorn, and Pygmy and Mountain Cottontail rabbits can be found in the vicinity, as can Golden eagles and Sage grouse. The grouse have a strutting ground near Alakali Creek. Hidden Pasture Trail, off Big Sheep Creek Road, affords a hike southwards through open country with fine views.

To the southeast of Big Sheep Creek, on the Montana-Idaho border, lie the magnificent Centennial Mountains. The BLM controls nearly 43,000 acres of this east-west range, almost all of Montana's portion. The mountains, which include 9,000-foot peaks, are thickly forested with Douglas fir, Sub-alpine fir, Lodgepole pine, Rocky Mountain maple, Bigtooth maple, and aspen. Interspersed among the forests are alpine meadows, bright with flowers in the early summer. Animals here include Mule deer, Black bear, elk, moose, Golden Mantled Ground squirrels, and Golden eagles.

For additional information on Big Sheep Creek, contact BLM's Dillon Resource Area Office, 1005 Selway Drive, Dillon, Montana 59725 (406-683-2337).

OWYHEE COUNTRY [3,434,000 acres]
Southeast Oregon, southwest Idaho, and north central Nevada, north of Tusarora, Nevada, and south of Rome, Oregon

These BLM lands, the watershed of the Owyhee River, constitute one of the most remote areas in the United States, despite dirt roads used by ranchers. Rolling grasslands predominate; hikers can gaze for leagues and leagues seeing not a sign of humans. They carry away memories of vastness, spectacular sunsets, coyote howls. . . . It is also a region of deep canyons cut by the Owyhee and its tributaries. Owyhee offers challenging white-water boating during high water seasons.

The area is threatened by overgrazing, which has nearly wiped out the native grasses, allowed cheatgrass to invade, and almost eliminated stream-side cottonwood and willows, shelter for birds and a check on erosion. It is also threatened by the U.S. Air Force, which wants to expand the Saylor Creek Bombing Range across the eastern quarter of the Owyhee. Environmentalists have proposed that the entire Owyhee be made a wilderness national park.

For information contact the Committee for Idaho's High Desert, P.O. Box 732, Mountain Home, Idaho 83647.

BURRO CREEK SPECIAL RECREATION MANAGEMENT AREA [27,588 acres]
Northwest of Phoenix, Arizona, off U.S. 93

The BLM controls vast areas of the Sonoran Desert of southern Arizona, as well as of the Mojave, Chihuahuan, and Great Basin Deserts. Each desert has its own distinctive wildlife. The characteristic feature of the Sonoran Desert is the cacti, more varied than anywhere else on the continent. The most conspicuous are the towering Saguaro. The areas of the Sonoran Desert with the most abundant life, however, are not the dry land where the cacti grow but the riparian zones along creeks.

Burro Creek Canyon is a fine example of the 10% of the surviving creekside areas that are still in an essentially natural state. On the creek banks grow Goodding willow, Fremont cottonwood, and mesquite. Phainopeplas, Yellow and Lucy warblers, and Common blackhawks are among the many birds that shelter and feed there. Blackhawks are candidates for state listing as a threatened species. In the creek itself flourish Round-Tail chub, a native species of fish already listed as threatened in Arizona.

Near the Burro Creek riparian area are dry, sandy washes; hillsides strewn with boulders, amid which agaves and palo verdes grow; and, in the upper watershed, a semi-desert grassland, inhabited by the Black Grama grass, Pronghorn antelope, and Prairie falcon. The desert is far from being the uniform, barren land that BLM is commonly thought to supervise.

For further information contact the BLM, 2475 Beverly Avenue, Kingman, Arizona 86401 (602-757-3161).

NATIONAL WILDLIFE REFUGES

The U.S. Fish and Wildlife Service, was created within the Department of the Interior in 1956. (In 1940 the Biological Survey from the Department of Agriculture had merged with the Bureau of Fisheries from the Department of Commerce to form the Fish and Wildlife Service.) According to the United States Government Manual, the "mission" of the U.S. Fish and Wildlife Service is "to conserve, protect, and enhance fish and wildlife and their habitats for the continuing benefit of the American people." Two of its many responsibilities are thus "identifying, protecting, and restoring" species of plants and animals that are in danger of extinction (Endangered) or in severe decline (Threatened) and managing the National Wildlife Refuge System. I discuss the refuges here.

The National Wildlife Refuge System Administration Act of 1966 was based on the Endangered Species Preservation Act of the same year. The Refuge System was created "for the purpose of consolidating . . . areas . . . administered by the Secretary of the Interior for the conservation of fish and wildlife, including species that are threatened with extinction . . . ."

Theodore Roosevelt had set aside the first refuge, Pelican Island off the coast of Florida, at the request of ornithologists in 1903. Some five thousand brown pelicans, herons, and egrets – which at that time were hunted for their plumes – nested on its 3.5 acres. The island was federal property; Roosevelt used its mangrove thickets as an excuse to invoke the 1891 Forest Reserve Act. Before leaving office in 1909, he had created fifty more refuges by this and other means.

The Fish and Wildlife Service (FWS) administers 466 National Wildlife Refuges comprising a total of 88,273,112 acres. The Fish and Wildlife Service also manages some 2 million acres for other purposes such as fish hatcheries, wildlife research centers, and "waterfowl production areas."

Some of the Refuges have been established to protect a specific endangered species. Roosevelt set aside the Wichita National Forest Reserve in Oklahoma in 1905 as a breeding place for the American buffalo (*Bison bison*), at that time represented in the wild by only twenty-three individuals. A few other refuges were established to permit the reintroduction of a species. Three-fourths, however, have been created and are maintained to benefit waterfowl and other migratory birds.

The main reason for the FWS's focus on birds is that waterfowl hunters have played an active role in the preservation of wildlife and backed up their demands with money at both the federal and state levels. A major source of income for the purchase of National Wildlife Refuges, for instance, has been federal Duck Stamps. Since 1935, waterfowl hunters over sixteen years of age have been required by federal law to purchase a stamp each year; the money from the stamps must go to purchase and lease waterfowl sanctuaries.

Forty states require state Duck Stamps, and sixteen million hunters of all types purchase state hunting licenses annually. The projects and salaries of state wildlife managers depend on the receipts from licenses and stamps, and state managers may put pressure on the national FWS to facilitate hunting.

Hunting is permitted on more than half the refuges; and those refuges are, as a general rule, managed in such a way as to maximize the number of prey. The average National Wildlife Refuge is not a truly natural area. Managers sow crops that attract birds, let water in and out of impoundments, cut trees, and set and control fires.

Production of waterfowl is a benevolent goal, however, compared with some of the activities carried on at refuges. According to the Sierra Club, oil drilling takes place on more than fifty refuges, livestock graze on over one hundred, and the military conducts war games on others. The National Wildlife Refuge System Administration Act of 1966 gave the Secretary of the Interior power to permit any use "compatible" with the system's primary purpose, and Interior secretaries have interpreted "compatible" broadly.

Unfortunately the 1966 act failed to provide for a coherent refuge management system. The National Wildlife Refuge Service lacks a "single overall guiding body of law." At present the only hope for permanently protecting a given refuge is to make it part of the National Wilderness Preservation System. A few refuges and parts of refuges have been declared wilderness areas.

A brochure showing the general location of all national refuges with visitor facilities and indicating the addresses, facilities, recreational uses, and best times to visit can be obtained free of charge from the Office of Public Affairs, United States Fish and Wildlife Service, Department of the Interior, Washington, D.C. 20240 (202-208-5634). This office also answers questions of a general nature.

Each Wildlife Refuge has its own regulations. Many offer splendid hiking, although camping may be prohibited. Some are closed all or part of the year to protect wildlife. Pelican Island in Florida can only be viewed from a distance, for instance. The brochure on the system published by the U.S. Fish and Wildlife Service's Office of Public Affairs indicates what activities are allowed; but contacting the headquarters of the individual refuge for details before going is advisable. Each publishes descriptive information. Refuge addresses can be obtained from the brochure or by calling the refuge office, 703-358-1744.

OKEFENOKEE SWAMP [438,000 acres]
Southeastern Georgia and northeastern Florida

The Okefenokee Swamp is basically a vast peat bog, once part of the ocean floor, though now 103 to 128 feet above sea level. Nine-tenths of the swamp has been made a National Wildlife Refuge, within which is a designated wilderness of 353,981 acres. From the Okefenokee, the Suwanee River flows to the Gulf of Mexico; the St. Mary's to the Atlantic.

The swamp contains only a few short hiking trails. Canoeing is the way to see most of the swamp, and the Fish and Wildlife Service maintains several canoe trails. Designated trips take two to five days, and canoeists spend nights on wooden platforms. Each trail is limited to one party a day. Paddlers pass islands and lakes, but most of the area is "prairie," where vegetation grows through water. Cypress trees draped with Spanish moss dominate the swamp, and at some points canoes must travel through tunnels cleared through vegetation.

American alligators are common. During the winter, when they become relatively inactive, River otters swim carefree in the lakes and boat trails. The endangered Red-Cockaded woodpecker, and the Florida Sandhill crane, osprey, Round-Tailed Water rat, and anhinga are all swamp residents (as is Walt Kelly's Pogo, in his wisdom the first to declare, "We have met the enemy, and it is us").

The swamp has three entrances; one is privately administered and another administered by the state of Georgia. Canoeists should enter through the third, the east entrance managed by the U.S. Fish and Wildlife Service. Reservations for canoe trips can be made by phone as early as two months in advance. Call 912-496-3331. For information contact the refuge at Route 2, Box 338, Folkston, Georgia 31537.

ST. MARKS NATIONAL WILDLIFE REFUGE [97,000 acres]
Northwestern Florida, twenty miles south of Tallahassee

St. Marks, created in 1931, encompasses 65,000 acres of salt marsh, hardwood swamp, fresh water pools, and upland pine, plus 32,000 acres of Apalachee Bay. In 1975, 18,000 acres were designated a Wilderness Area. The refuge provides wintering habitat for waterfowl. Because of the varied habitat, over 300 species of birds, 34 species of snakes, 19 each of turtles and salamanders, 12 of lizards, and 21 of toads and frogs find refuge there, as well as such mammals as the bobcat, mink, and various bats. In addition to wildlife, visitors can see Indian mounds, salt vats from the Civil War, and a lighthouse constructed in 1831 and still operating. The Florida Trail runs through the sanctuary. An entrance fee is charged to visitors on the County Road 59 entrance. For information contact the refuge manager, St. Marks National Wildlife Refuge, P.O. Box 68, St. Marks, Florida 32355 (904-925-6121).

MARK TWAIN NATIONAL WILDLIFE REFUGE
[25,300 acres in nine units]
Along 250 miles of the Mississippi River between Muscatine, Iowa, and Alton, Illinois

In *Life on the Mississippi* Mark Twain shows an impressive knowledge of the geology of the lands along the river. Therefore, it is appropriate that a refuge on the Mississippi flyway is named after him, appropriate except that the land was acquired through a project that changed the river. Most of the land in the refuge was purchased to allow the U.S. Army Corps of Engineers, starting in the 1930s, to construct locks and dams to create a navigation channel for barges. This land was eventually turned over to the U.S. Fish and Wildlife Service, and in 1964 two additional areas were purchased with money from Duck Stamps.

Thousands of migrating birds pass through the refuge, among them the Blue-Winged teal, American Black duck, gadwall, canvasback, redhead, Canada goose, and Snow goose. Wood ducks are one of the few ducks that nest in the refuge; but Bald eagles winter in or near the refuge, five hundred or more in a season; and Great Blue herons, Green herons, and Great egrets are summer residents.

Regulations vary from unit to unit. Many units are closed to the public during migration, and some of the area is permanently off limits; but most provide opportunities to watch birds and other animals and allow hiking and fishing at least part of the year.

The headquarters, Mark Twain National Wildlife Refuge, 311 North Fifth Street, Suite 100, Quincy, Illinois 62301 (217-224-8580), can supply basic information, including the addresses for individual refuges.

AGASSIZ NATIONAL WILDLIFE REFUGE [61,449 acres]
Northwest corner of Minnesota, east of Holt

The bed of glacial Lake Agassiz is the site of the refuge. The largest single public drainage project in the U.S. took place on this land in the early twentieth century. The project, an attempt to turn marshes into farmland, was a failure at a cost of some 1 million dollars. To save Marshall County, its home, from bankruptcy, the state authorized purchase of the land for the development of Mud Lake Migratory Waterfowl Refuge. The refuge was established in 1937 and later renamed to honor Louis Agassiz (1807–73), the Swiss-American zoologist and geologist, whose theory of glaciation strongly influenced John Muir.

The federal government bought the refuge, on the Mississippi flyway, for the purpose of providing habitat for migratory waterfowl. The management therefore embarked on a major program to restore the open water and marsh, now a total of approximately 40,000 acres.

Although the Refuge is still managed "to provide optimum habitat conditions for duck production," to quote a refuge pamphlet, it may be best known for its mammals. The wetland has made it home to a herd of some 250 moose; and it has the only resident pack of Gray wolves in any refuge in the contiguous forty-eight states.

About 4,000 acres of conifers, mainly Black spruce and tamarack in the north central portion of the refuge, belong to the National Wilderness Preservation System.

The refuge welcomes visitors. For information contact the office, Middle River, Minnesota 56737 (218-449-4115).

SANTA ANA AND RIO GRANDE VALLEY NATIONAL WILDLIFE REFUGES [2,000 acres in Santa Ana, plus some 44,000 acres in 75 fragments]
Southeastern Texas

Both the Santa Ana and Rio Grande Valley Refuges are in the Lower Rio Grande Valley, formerly a subtropical paradise for wildlife. Here are still found ten different plant communities and four of the five wildcat species left in the United States: bobcat, jaguarundi, ocelot, and Mountain lion. Nevertheless, 95% of the valley has been cleared, and another wildcat, the jaguar, has disappeared from this country. Environmentalists are trying to save the remaining habitat by urging Congress to appropriate money to complete the purchase of land for the Rio Grande Refuge, planned to cover a total of 107,500 acres, the barest minimum needed. This refuge has been the largest land acquisition program of the Fish and Wildlife Service since the early 1980s. Each year Congress appropriates enough money to add only 5,000 to 10,000 acres. Meanwhile, the desired land is being developed by its private owners. The refuge is closed to the public. Bearing the full burden of visitors, the Santa Ana Refuge, established in 1943, serves as a window to the habitat type being saved.

Santa Ana Refuge is a small island of thorn forest, inhabited by 385 species of birds including the Red-crowned parrot, Elf owl, and Blue bunting; and two endangered wildcats, the ocelot and jaguarundi. It is open to hikers seven days a week from sunrise to sunset, although private cars are forbidden within the refuge at certain times. During these periods tram rides are available. For information contact the Santa Ana/Rio Grande Valley National Wildlife Refuges, Rte. 2, Box 202A, Alamo, Texas 78516 (512-787-3079; 787-7861).

NISQUALLY NATIONAL WILDLIFE REFUGE
A few miles northeast of Olympia, Washington

Nisqually Refuge is "a mosaic of habitats" on the delta where the Nisqually River flows into Puget Sound. The 5.5-mile Brown Farm Dike Trail, along which visitors can walk, separates saltwater and freshwater habitats. Outside the dike are saltmarshes and mudflats where shorebirds, gulls, ducks, and herons feed. Inside the dike are freshwater marshes and open grasslands. Also along the Dike Trail are riparian woodland and brush habitat.

Up to 20,000 ducks and 300 geese visit the refuge during the spring and fall migrations, and many winter there. Goldfinches, warblers, and swallows arrive in the spring and spend the summer. Great Blue herons and Red-tailed hawks are among the year-round residents. The refuge is open to the public daily for walking and bird watching. An observation deck and three photo blinds are available.

The staff of Nisqually also supervises Dungeness Refuge and refuges that consist almost entirely of islands: Protection Island Refuge, Washington Islands, and San Juan Islands Refuge. Like Nisqually, Dungeness is open to the public. It centers in Dungeness Spit, which stretches for 5.5 miles along the Strait of Juan de Fuca, sheltering a bay, sand and gravel beaches, and tideflats, and thus providing protection to a variety of wildlife. The island refuges, which are sanctuaries for seabirds, eagles, and marine mammals, are closed to the public except for Turn Island and five acres on Matia Island (two of the eighty-four islands in the San Juan archipelago that comprise the San Juan Refuge). The public is asked to stay at least 200 yards from these refuges in order not to disturb wildlife.

In 1988 Congress increased the responsibilities of the staff of Nisqually Refuge by providing funding to start acquisition of land for Grays Harbor National Wildlife Refuge, which will be supervised from Nisqually. The Refuge will consist of 1,800 acres of mudflats and saltmarsh, the staging and feeding area for the spring migration of millions of shorebirds. It is located at the mouth of the Chehalis River on the outer coast of Washington about half way between Williams Bay and the Olympic National Park Wilderness Coast strip. In addition to shorebirds, the complex estuary of rivers and streams features colonies of marine mammals, islands of nesting terns, and rainforest.

For information contact the Nisqually Refuge at 100 Brown Farm Road, Olympia, Washington 98506 (206-753-9467).

CABEZA PRIETA NATIONAL WILDLIFE REFUGE
[860,000 acres]
Southwestern Arizona, a few miles west of Ajo

A land of low but rugged mountains and wide valleys containing several lava flows and sand dunes, Cabeza Prieta Refuge was created in 1939 to protect the Desert Bighorn sheep. The endangered Sonoran pronghorn also finds refuge in its arid terrain.

Crossing the southern portion of the Refuge is El Camino del Diablo, the Devil's Highway, which linked the northern frontier of Mexico and the Spanish settlements of California. Indians, Spanish clergy and soldiers, and then miners followed the route, along which many died of thirst.

Today the most obvious hazard is the military. To quote from the brochure supplied by the staff, "No one may enter the refuge without obtaining a valid Refuge Entry Permit and signing a Military Hold Harmless Agreement. Permits are available at the refuge office. . . . Numerous low-flying aircraft cross the refuge on their way to air-to-air bombing and gunnery ranges located north of the refuge. The air-to-air range airspace above the refuge is used to practice aerial gunnery on towed targets. When the air-to-air range . . . is active, all public entry to the refuge under the air-to-air range is prohibited." Ironically, however, the military use of the refuge has kept out off-road vehicle drivers and other land abusers, leaving this part of the Sonoran Desert surprisingly pristine. The Arizona Desert Wilderness Act of 1990 appropriately gave the refuge Wilderness Status.

For information, contact the Refuge at 1611 North Second Avenue, Ajo, Arizona 85321 (602-387-6483).

CHAPTER FOURTEEN

Wilderness Areas

The National Wilderness Preservation System, established by the 1964 Wilderness Act and enlarged by subsequent legislation pertaining to individual states, encompassed 9.1 million acres in 1964 and 94.2 million acres (in 561 different areas) in January 1991. Alaska contains 56.5 million of the current acres. The designated Wilderness Areas are administered by the agency that controlled the land before it was given Wilderness status. Thus there are Wilderness Areas in the hands of the four public land agencies: the Forest Service, National Park Service, Bureau of Land Management, and Fish and Wildlife Service.

The 1964 act states that Wilderness Areas " . . . shall be administered for the use and enjoyment of the American people in such a manner as will leave them unimpaired for future use and enjoyment as wilderness." In Wilderness Areas, logging, off-road vehicle use, and such permanent developments as buildings, roads, and dams are forbidden. Hunting and livestock grazing are usually permitted, as is mining on claims filed before 1984. Many recreational activities are also allowed.

Criteria for Wilderness include pristine character, opportunities for solitude, and sufficient size to allow management as Wilderness. The 1964 act suggests a minimum of 5,000 contiguous roadless acres. The designation process generally begins with an agency studying its holdings and recommending areas for designation.

The language of the Wilderness bills that have been passed for specific states permits areas not designated as Wilderness in the bills to be considered again later for Wilderness status. (Bills that include this stipulation have what is called "soft release" language.)

Most states with significant roadless acreage have passed Wilderness bills. The notable exceptions are Idaho and Montana, where environmentalists are fighting timber companies, miners, and other developers to try to save the remaining roadless lands. Most state Wilderness bills have released more roadless acreage than they have protected, and unless conservationists win unprecedented victories this will be the outcome in these two states.

An open-ended conception of the national wilderness system is a necessity, for the system is still greatly in need of enlargement. No agency has ever looked at all the land in the United States to determine what should be included in the system. Many ecosystems are not represented and most of those included are protected only in fragments, not large enough to sustain all their native inhabitants.

Dave Foreman and Howie Wolke in *The Big Outside* (Tucson, Arizona: Ned Ludd Books, 1989) point out areas that offer splendid opportunities for enlargement of the National Wilderness Preservation System. Their book is the first inventory of U.S. roadless areas since Bob Marshall published an inventory in 1936 in the magazine of the Wilderness Society. The Wilderness Society presents an agenda for the future of the system in its *Wilderness America* (1989, $12.95).

For an overview of the system at present, obtain the U.S. Geological Survey's maps of Wilderness Areas and public lands, which, through color coding, show which agencies of the federal government own what land. They are listed in Appendix I on page 395.

In Wilderness Areas such non-motorized recreational activities as hiking, camping, rafting, fishing, and horseback riding are permitted. Overnight visitors may be required to carry a permit that can be obtained from the regional office of the appropriate management agency.

SIPSEY WILDERNESS [25,906 acres]
Northwestern Alabama, north of Rabbittown

Enlarged by 13,260 acres in 1988, this Wilderness in the Bankhead National Forest encompasses rolling hills cut by steep and narrow canyons that shelter the Sipsey River, a favorite of canoeists. On Bee Branch, which flows into the Sipsey and which can be followed on Forest Route 208, is a one-hundred foot deep, rock-rimmed box canyon with an abundance of waterfalls. Parts of the canyon have never been logged; in it grow Eastern hemlocks, Tulip trees, and beeches. Other tributaries of the Sipsey that can be followed on trails also flow through scenic gorges, with lush vegetation bordering them. Because of the coolness and moistness, trees live in the Sipsey south of their normal range.

For information, contact the supervisor of the National Forests in Alabama, 1765 Highland Avenue, Montgomery, Alabama 36107 or the district ranger for Bankhead National Forest, P.O. Box 278, Double Springs, Alabama 35553.

BOUNDARY WATERS CANOE AREA WILDERNESS (BWCAW) [1,000,000 acres]
Northeastern Minnesota, surrounding Ely and stretching almost 150 miles along the Canadian border

The wilderness, which occupies one-third of Superior National Forest, is understandably but regrettably the most heavily used designated wilderness in the nation. Understandably, because it is prime canoeing country with more than 1,200 miles of canoe routes, including the International Boundary Route, requiring 235 miles of paddling and 9 miles of portaging. Regrettably, because the vast region of lakes and spruce and pine has a mysterious beauty that crowds greatly detract from.

If you go to the Boundary Waters to canoe, avoid the most popular entry points and visit at times other than late May and mid-July through August. To stay overnight you must obtain a permit from an office of the Superior National Forest or a cooperating business. Permits are limited in number and may be requested up to forty-eight hours ahead. If seeing the terrain rather than canoeing is your main goal, consider cross-country skiing in winter, although, be advised, snowmobiles are permitted on 200 miles of trails.

The BWCAW was first set aside as a roadless area in 1926 by the Secretary of Agriculture, after the public protested the Forest Service's goal of building a road to every lake. Sigurd Olson was instrumental in obtaining for it the status of Congressionally designated wilderness in 1978. Olson, an environmental leader, woodsman, and author, lived in Ely.

Recently the Friends of the Boundary Waters Wilderness helped to secure for Minnesota tough anti-acid rain regulations. They are now working to end the flights of military jets in the Snoopy Military Operations Area over much of the National Forest and BWCAW.

For information contact the Friends of the Boundary Waters Wilderness, 1313 Fifth Street S.E., Suite 327, Minneapolis, Minnesota 55414 (612-379-3835) and the supervisor of Superior National Forest, P.O. Box 338, Duluth, Minnesota 55801 (218-720-5440).

SCAPEGOAT WILDERNESS [239,936 acres]

West central Montana, 75 miles northeast of Missoula and 10 miles north of Lincoln

Abutting the better known and more heavily used Bob Marshall Wilderness to the northwest, Scapegoat straddles the Continental Divide and includes portions of the Helena, Lewis and Clark, and Lolo National Forests. Massive limestone cliffs on Scapegoat Mountain are a continuation of the less accessible Chinese Wall in the Bob Marshall, formed when ancient rocks rode up and over more recent deposits. The surrounding areas are less spectacular but still beautiful because of the coloration of soil and rock. Alpine meadows contrast with rugged slopes. Trails follow creeks through dense forest growth. A hike to and from the Indian Meadows Forest Service Station to Heart Lake makes a good day trip.

Grizzly bears, Black bears, Mountain goats, Canada lynx, wolverines, and Mule deer are among the wilderness's residents. In the summer of 1988, the area underwent a major fire known as the Canyon Creek Fire, the aftermath of which will likely benefit some of these large mammals.

For information, contact the forest supervisors in Helena National Forest, Federal Office Building, Drawer 10014, Helena, Montana 59626 (406-449-5201); Lewis and Clark National Forest, P.O. Box 871, Great Falls, Montana 59403 (406-791-7700); or Lolo National Forest, Building 24, Fort Missoula, Missoula, Montana 59801 (406-329-3557). The Lewis and Clark office sells a colored map of the wilderness for $2.00.

SOUTH WARNER WILDERNESS [70,385 acres]

Northeastern California, east of Likely

This designated wilderness in Modoc National Forest encompasses the southern Warner Mountains, including Eagle Peak (9,906 feet) and Warren Peak (8,875 feet). It offers magnificent mountain scenery: lush meadows, clear streams, lakes, canyons, views of Mount Shasta and Lassen Peak. Summit Trail, 27 miles along the crest, is rugged. Yet hikers can find gentler trails leading into the interior that make the scenery accessible without the strenuous climbing necessary in many western wilderness areas.

For information, write to the forest supervisor in Modoc National Forest, 441 North Main Street, Alturas, California 96101 (916-233-5811).

GILA WILDERNESS [557,873 acres]

Southwestern New Mexico, north of Silver City

One of three Wilderness Areas in the Gila National Forest, the Gila was the first designated wilderness in the world. At the suggestion of Aldo Leopold, then a forest ranger in New Mexico, the Forest Service set aside more than 6,000 contiguous acres as a primitive area in 1924. Within a few years, the service had split the tract by constructing the North Star Road through it for management purposes. Nevertheless, the Gila, which is to the west of the road, like the Aldo Leopold Wilderness to the east, is one of the wilder tracts in the Southwest.

The first public action of Earth First! took place in April 1980 in the ghost town of Cooney, near Mogollon in the Gila National Forest, just northwest of the Gila Wilderness. A small group of people set up a plaque commemorating the hundredth anniversary of Apache chief Victorio's raid on the Cooney mining camp. The plaque spoke of "Victorio, Outstanding Preservationist and Great American" who "strove to protect these mountains from mining and other destructive activities of the white race. The present Gila Wilderness is partly a fruit of his efforts."

The Gila Wilderness is dominated by the Mogollon Mountains and cut by the deep, winding gorges of the Gila River. Mimbres Canyon is particularly spectacular. The area contains the nation's largest stand of virgin Ponderosa pine. Wildlife includes the Mountain lion, Black bear, pronghorn, javelina, and Gila trout.

The Gila trout, once common in the area, inhabited only 10 miles of stream when, in 1966, it was listed as endangered. The introduction of Rainbow and Brown trout and degradation of the Gila's habitat were killing it. Thanks to a program managed jointly by the U.S. Forest Service, the U.S. Fish and Wildlife Service, New Mexico State University, and the New Mexico Department of Fish and Game, the endangered trout is now recovering. The program involves erecting barriers in streams, killing Brown and Rainbow trout, and restocking with Gila.

The wilderness contains an extensive network of trails, also archeological sites including cliff dwellings. It is adjacent to the Gila Cliff Dwellings National Monument (533 acres), which preserves cliff dwellings inhabited from about 1280 to the early 1300s. The third wilderness in the forest is the Blue Range Wilderness to the west.

For information contact the Gila National Forest, 2610 North Silver Street, Silver City, New Mexico 88061 (505-388-8201).

CHAPTER FIFTEEN

Wild and Scenic Rivers, Sanctuaries, and Reserves

In 1968 Congress passed two laws regarding inland passageways: the National Trails System Act and the Wild and Scenic Rivers Act. The National Trails, which will be discussed in a later chapter, are primarily recreational in character, though their establishment may entail land preservation. The rivers, on the other hand, are a key element in the national effort to preserve the environment.

The Wild and Scenic Rivers Act designated for protection 8 rivers or river segments totaling 789 miles and called for study of 27 others. As of January 1991, the system had 123 rivers or river segments totaling over 9,318 miles. Of this total, 26 units representing 3,200 miles were in Alaska.

The act set up three categories of protected waterways: wild, scenic, and recreational. A wild river must be free of impoundments; accessible only by foot, on horseback, or by boat; and largely undeveloped along its banks. A scenic river has no impoundments and little development on its shoreline, but may be accessible in places by roads. A recreational river may be dammed, have limited development along its banks, and be fully accessible by roads. Any single river may have segments that belong to each of the categories.

Designated rivers are managed by the entity that is responsible for the land through which they flow. This may be a federal, state, or local agency. The rivers must, however, be managed to preserve or enhance the values that qualified them for protection. Thus there can be no dredging or construction of canals or dams. If land bordering a designated river is privately owned, federal agencies may acquire a corridor that extends, on average, a quarter of a mile on either side of the river.

Despite the existence of the Wild and Scenic Rivers Act, 600,000 miles or 15% of America's free flowing rivers have already been buried behind huge dams. There are 108 dams on "protected" National Park Service land, 172 dams in National Wildlife Refuges, 1,760 dams on property of the Bureau of Land Management, and scores of dam applications pending for the National Forests, according to the public-interest organization American Rivers.

A major reason for the slow pace at which the Wild and Scenic Rivers System is growing is the complexity of the designation process. After a citizen group proposes a river for study, a congressperson must draft a bill calling for the study and Congress must pass it. If it does so, the appropriate agency carries out the study, complete with public hearings and environmental impact statements. The agency then sends a recommendation to the President, who may send it to Congress for a second vote or simply sit on it.

The Wild and Scenic Rivers Act provides an alternative pathway, but it is little known. A governor may ask the Secretary of Interior to add a river without presidential or congressional action, provided the river is already in a state river-protection system. Governor Jerry Brown of California added five rivers totaling 1,235 miles to the system in this way, and his action was upheld by the courts.

Occasionally a river may receive federal protection without being in the Wild and Scenic Rivers System. National Scenic Area status and hydropower bans, which last for varying periods of time, are two means of achieving this end; but the former normally protects only the land along the river and the latter only the water itself.

The National Park Service's *The National Parks: Index* lists the rivers in the Wild and Scenic Rivers System, with a brief description and the address to which to write for information on each. The Sierra Club's booklet "National Wild and Scenic Rivers System," gives the mileage and the management agency for each river and locates the rivers on regional maps. It is available for $2 from the Club's Public Affairs Office at the national headquarters.

A list of the components of the National Wild and Scenic River System with their administering agencies and mileage plus a report on the status of the system is available free of charge from American Rivers, 801 Pennsylvania Avenue SE, Suite 400, Washington, D.C. 20003 (202-547-6900).

Tim Palmer in *Endangered Rivers and the Conservation Movement* (Univ. of California, 1985) makes perceptive proposals on ways of improving management of rivers. Palmer's book also contains a wealth of data on rivers. *These American Lands: Parks, Wilderness, and the Public*

Lands by Dyan Zaslowsky and The Wilderness Society (New York: Henry Holt, 1986) surveys the history of federal lands of all types and makes thoughtful proposals for improving federal land management systems and practices.

ALLAGASH WILDERNESS WATERWAY [95 miles long]
Northern Maine

Winding through forests owned by lumber companies, the waterway was the first state-administered component of the national Wild and Scenic Rivers System. The Maine legislature established it in 1966, and Congress classified it as Wild in 1970. The state of Maine owns an inner zone along each shore, extending back 500 feet from the high-water mark. Here camping, construction, and commercial logging are prohibited. In an outer zone, extending from the 500-foot line to a mile from the high-water mark, timber harvesting according to state-approved management plans is allowed.

The river flows north to meet the St. John River a few miles north of the town of Allagash. Canoeists traveling the full length start at Telos Lake and end at West Twin Brook. Primitive campsites line the waterway. The most challenging stretch is Chase Rapids, 9 miles of fast water. A worthwhile side trip is up the Allagash Stream (3 miles west of Lock Dam) to Allagash Lake, open only to canoes. Generally conditions are suitable for canoeing from around May 20 through October. Henry David Thoreau visited the headwaters in the summer of 1857.

Access to the waterway is by private roads or through Baxter State Park. In either case visitors should learn the regulations ahead of time. The owners of the private roads belong to the organization North Maine Woods, P.O. Box 382, Ashland, Maine 04732 (207-435-6213). For information on the waterway itself, contact the Bureau of Parks and Recreation, Maine Department of Conservation, State House Station 22, Augusta, Maine 04333 (207-289-3821).

HORSEPASTURE RIVER [10 miles]
From Big Sheep Cliffs in southwestern North Carolina to "Lake" Jocassee in South Carolina

Descending 1,500 feet in a space of 3 miles, the Horsepasture plunges down a series of waterfalls, among them the 150-foot-tall Rainbow Falls, where the sun at times paints a rainbow on mist sprayed against rocks. The gorge of the Horsepasture is as much as 2 miles wide and

800 feet deep. Rare ferns and mosses find shelter there, as does *Shortia glacifolia,* a flowering plant endemic to· six counties in the immediate area. French botanist Andre Michaux discovered the plant when he was seeking specimens for the Royal Botanical Garden in France in the late eighteenth century.

The Horsepasture is one of four rivers that drop from the Blue Ridge Escarpment into "Lake" Jocassee, an artificial lake formed in 1970 as a pumped storage project of Duke Power. Others are the Whitewater, the Thompson, and the Toxaway. No trails follow the Thompson and the Toxaway, wild rivers though without the official designation. The Horsepasture is a recreational river. Swimmers and fishers frequent the pools below the waterfalls, and hikers walk a 2.8 mile trail along the bank.

In the early 1980s the firm Carrasan planned to dam the Horsepasture above the gorge and to divert the water to a hydro station, which was to generate electricity for sale to Duke Power. Led by Bill Thomas, Friends of the Horsepasture publicized the threat and generated sufficient public pressure to win state and federal protection in 1986. With the Trust for Public Land in the role of intermediary, the U.S. Forest Service purchased the land on which the dam was to have been built.

The Forest Service now owns approximately 2 miles along the river and is trying to buy additional land from Duke Power. Above the federally protected segment, the river passes along a highway and through developments. Water quality is nominally protected by a state Class B status (maintenance at a level satisfactory for swimming), but enforcement is questionable.

Most of the land through which the Whitewater, Thompson, and Toxaway pass is owned by Duke Power. The Jocassee Watershed Coalition (P.O. Box 272, Cedar Mountain, North Carolina 28718) helped to defeat a second pumped storage project for the area, and hopes to gain protection for all three rivers eventually.

The Foothills Trail, 80 rugged miles from Table Rock State Park to Oconee, South Carolina, crosses the four rivers. Visitors who are not adventurous can drive to the Horsepasture on Route 281.

SNAKE RIVER [1,038 miles long]
Between Idaho and Oregon

Eighteen dams constructed for hydropower and irrigation impede the flow of the Snake. Three of the dams block upper Hells Canyon. Congress created Hells Canyon National Recreation Area and added a portion of the Snake to the Wild and Scenic River System in 1975 to preserve "natural beauty, [and] historical and archaeological values" in the Lower Canyon. A Supreme Court decision years before had cleared the way for the major environmental campaign that culminated in this legislation.

In 1964 the Federal Power Commission had licensed a dam at the High Mountain Sheep site. Three years later the U.S. Supreme Court was asked to rule as to whether this or another dam should be built. Justice William O. Douglas, who wrote the decision, stated that the commission must study not only which site to choose but also whether a dam should be built at all. In doing so, the commission must consider the interest of the public in wildlife and wild rivers as well as the need for power. The landmark decision was the first time that the commission was forced to take into account something other than energy, and it recognized the values of wild rivers.

Hells Canyon was worth the efforts of environmentalists. Averaging 5,500 feet from rim to river, it is North America's deepest or second deepest canyon (King's Canyon is deepest if one counts from the top of the bordering mountains). On the east, tower Idaho's Seven Devils Mountains. The drop from He Devil Peak to the canyon floor is between 7,000 and 8,000 feet. To the west are Oregon's grassy benches and forested ridges. Cacti grow in the hot, dry canyon—within 6 miles of alpine lakes.

Route 86 from Oxbow Crossing to Hells Canyon Dam runs along the Snake River, just before the Wild and Scenic segment; but most of the National Recreation Area is rugged country with few roads. Hat Point Lookout, 7,000 feet above the river on the Oregon side, affords a spectacular view of the river. The Lookout can be reached by a narrow, winding road from Imnaha or by trails up from the river.

Unfortunately dams above the Wild and Scenic River mean that the protected segment is far from pristine. The volume of water in the canyon fluctuates with activities at the dams as well as with the season. A flyer from the U.S. Forest Service, which manages the Wild and Scenic segment, states that "soft white sand bars have given way to black rock rubble. Flood waters no longer replace the beaches every year. . . . The high water mark along lofty ledges has given way to the white-rock line of the daily water fluctuations. Once mighty runs of salmon and steelhead are feeble remnants of better days."

Nevertheless, Hells Canyon still affords splendid whitewater boating, with the degree of difficulty in normal summer flows varying from Class II to Class IV on the international scale. Because of the Snake's popularity, reservations and a trip permit are required from the Friday before Memorial Day through September 15. The five launches permitted daily from the Hells Canyon Creek Recreation Site are allocated by lottery from applications filed between December 1 and January 31. Riverside campsites, most of which are on grassy benches, are limited in number and are available on a first-come, first-served basis.

For further information contact Hells Canyon National Recreation Area, 3620-B Snake River Ave., Lewiston, Idaho 83501 (208-743-3648 for general information; 208-743-2297 for river information and permits).

DEPARTMENT OF COMMERCE SANCTUARIES AND RESERVES

An agency in the Department of Commerce manages National Marine Sanctuaries and National Estuarine Research Reserves. The connection between the department and the ocean arises from the fact that the nation in its early years depended on overseas trade. The first scientific agency in the United States and that of greatest importance up to the Civil War was the Coast Survey founded by Thomas Jefferson, which engaged in research and development for the commercial shipping industry. Renamed the Coast and Geodetic Survey, it was absorbed by the Department of Commerce and Labor, when the department was created in 1903.

National Oceanic and Atmospheric Administration (NOAA):
Office of Ocean and Coastal Resource Management

NOAA was formed in the Department of Commerce by Congress in 1970. The National Ocean Survey, a further renaming of the Coast Survey, became a part of this agency. Also in the agency are the National Marine Fisheries Service, which oversees marine species listed under the Endangered Species Act, and the Office of Ocean and Coastal

Resource Management. According to the *United States Government Manual*, NOAA's mission is "to explore, map, and chart the global ocean and its living resources and to manage, use, and conserve these resources."

The Marine Protection, Research and Sanctuaries Act of 1972 gave NOAA authority to designate and manage National Marine Sanctuaries. Site selection criteria have since been gradually shaped. Sites are to exhibit "values" that give them "national significance." These values may be cultural rather than biological, although all but one of the present sanctuaries center on natural resources. Teams of scientists propose sites for a Site Evaluation List from which NOAA selects active candidates and finally designates sanctuaries, through the Marine and Estuarine Management Division of its Office of Ocean and Coastal Resource Management. The program tries to strike a balance between sites representative of U.S. marine waters and unusual or unique sites.

The United States has seven National Marine Sanctuaries: Key Largo (100 square nautical miles off the Florida Keys, encompassing a portion of the largest coral reef system off North America), Looe Key (a 5.3-square-nautical-mile reef area off the lower Florida Keys), Gray's Reef (17 square nautical miles protecting a limestone outcrop and its wildlife, 17.5 miles off Georgia in a transition zone between the Gulf Stream and more temperate coastal waters), Channel Islands (1,252 square nautical miles off the southern California coast, described below), Point Reyes-Farallon Islands (948 square nautical miles northwest of San Francisco), the *Monitor* (1 square nautical mile surrounding the wreck of the Civil War ironclad ship), and Fagatele Bay (163 acres off American Samoa). Additional areas have been designated as sanctuaries, but the designations are still in the process of being implemented.

On-site management programs normally involve research, educational activities to increase the public's appreciation of the sites and enlist their help in preserving them, and protective programs including surveillance by boat patrols and promulgation and enforcement of regulations. Under a mixed-use approach, recreational activities that are not considered harmful to the sites are permitted.

Under the Coastal Zone Management Act of 1972, NOAA also designates, helps fund, and, in cooperation with the states, manages National Estuarine Research Reserves (NERRs), of which there are eighteen including Great Bay NERR in New Hampshire, Chesapeake Bay NERR in Maryland, Old Woman Creek NERR in Ohio, Apalachicola NERR in Florida, South Slough NERR in Oregon, and Waimanu

Valley NERR in Hawaii. Selection procedures and on-site management programs are similar to those for Marine Sanctuaries.

For addresses and other information about the Marine Sanctuaries and NERRs contact the Marine and Estuarine Management Division, Universal Building, Room 714, 1825 Connecticut Avenue NW, Washington, D.C. 20235 (202-673-5122). For regulations at particular sanctuaries, contact the sanctuaries themselves.

WELLS NATIONAL ESTUARINE RESEARCH RESERVE [1,600 acres]
Along 4 miles of Wells Bay in southern Maine

The Wells Reserve is not typical of National Estuarine Research Reserves in that the land is owned and managed at the federal, state, and local levels. It has three functional components: a portion of the Rachel Carson National Wildlife Refuge, Laudholm State Park, and Laudholm Farm, which are owned by Laudholm Trust in Wells. The trust was set up and funded by local people in 1982 to save from development a nineteenth-century saltwater farm. The U.S. Fish and Wildlife Service, the Maine Bureau of Parks and Recreation, and the town of Wells manage the land in accordance with the guidelines of the National Estuarine Research Reserve program. The trust is restoring the farm, including the farmhouse, an example of Greek Revival architecture. Visitors can tour the restored first floor of the farmhouse and see a slide show.

The Reserve protects and makes accessible to the public one of the last undeveloped stretches of coastal land in southern Maine. It includes the estuaries of the Webhannet and Little Rivers, salt marshes, a sandy beach, fields, and forests. Among the wildlife are Harbor seals, River otters, the endangered Least tern, and the threatened Piping plover.

For information on the reserve, including details about visiting the farmhouse, contact the reserve at RR 2, Box 80, Wells, Maine 04090 (207-646-1555).

CHANNEL ISLANDS NATIONAL MARINE SANCTUARY
Waters extending 6 nautical miles around each of the islands San Miguel, Santa Rosa, Santa Cruz, Anacapa, and Santa Barbara northwest of Los Angeles

The Channel Islands Sanctuary is extraordinarily rich in wildlife because it is in the transition zone between cold water from the arctic and warm water from the tropics. Five species of seals and sea lions (pinnipeds) inhabit the area; twenty-seven species of whales, porpoises, and dolphins (cetaceans) appear at one time of the year or another; and more than twenty-five species of sharks are permanent or occasional residents.

Intertidal zones, tidepools, reefs, and kelp forests teem with life. Each of the five sanctuary islands is surrounded by a bed of Giant kelp (*Macrocystis pyrifera*), a brown alga that can grow two feet a day and reach a length of 200 feet. Among the kelp live 1,000 plant and animal species ranging in size from tiny bryozoans (moss-like animals), which grow on the kelp blades, to Gray whales, which rest among the kelp during migration. More than sixty species of seabirds feed in the Sanctuary during part or all of the year, and eleven species breed there.

In cooperation with the Santa Barbara Museum of Natural History, the sanctuary runs an educational program that does justice to its wildlife. In a Floating Classroom program, Island Packers, the transportation concessionaire, annually takes thousands of students from local schools to the sanctuary for a day. Los Marineros, a multi-disciplinary marine education program, teaches fifth and sixth graders to treasure and care for the ocean environment. Varied trips and workshops for adults are also offered. Since 1988 the sanctuary has held an annual photography contest.

A Sea Center on Stearns Wharf in Santa Barbara introduces visitors to the sanctuary through such exhibits as lifesize models of a Gray whale and a Bottlenose dolphin, aquarium displays, Chumash Indian artifacts, and the remains of ships found in the sanctuary. The center is open in summer, daily 11:00 A.M.-7:00 P.M.; in winter, Mon.-Fri. noon-5:00 P.M. and Sat. and Sun. 11:00 A.M.-6:00 P.M. Admission is $1.50 (211 Stearns Wharf, Santa Barbara, California 93101; 805-963-1067).

Four of the islands that are surrounded by the sanctuary comprise Channel Islands National Park. The fifth, Santa Cruz, is privately owned (90% by The Nature Conservancy). The National Park Service operates its own educational program that includes a live video program, during which visitors can follow a diver 40 feet below them. They see what the diver sees and talk to the diver. The programs, each of which is built around a theme, are held throughout the summer, Tues. and Thurs. at 2:00 P.M. at the Anacapa Island Landing Cove. They are free of charge.

The sanctuary and park (the two share supervision of the nautical mile closest to each island) offer spectacular sites for exploration by snorklers and scuba divers. Boaters can take their crafts to the islands, but first need to find out about restricting regulations.

To reach the sanctuary and national park by commercial boat, contact Island Packers, 1867 Spinnaker Drive, Ventura, California (805-642-1393). For other information get in touch with Channel Islands National Marine Sanctuary, 735 State Street, Santa Barabara, California 93101 (805-966-7107) or Channel Islands National Park, 1901 Spinnaker Drive, Ventura, California 93001 (805-644-8157).

CHAPTER SIXTEEN

State Parks and Recreation Areas, and Private Preserves

State governments own parks and refuges, as do many cities. The states of New York, California, and Michigan even have their own wilderness systems within their state parks. As of 1986, 13,726,000 acres were in state parks and recreation areas nationwide. In addition, several Indian reservations have tribally-designated wildernesses.

Each state regulates its parks as it sees fit. Contact the relevant state agency for information (most distribute free brochures). Addresses of state agencies can be obtained from *The National Directory of State Agencies* (Cambridge Information Group), which is available in libraries.

A quick way of finding out the location of national and state parks and refuges is the American Automobile Association's annual *Road Atlas* on sale in bookstores. It outlines most of these units clearly in color.

The National Parks and Conservation Association publishes regional *Guide[s] to National and State Parks*, listing facilities and sources of information. Order for $2.95 each plus postage from the association.

ADIRONDACK [STATE] PARK [5,693,000 acres]
Upper New York State, north of Gloversville

Adirondack Park is a mixture of private and state-owned land. Forty percent or 2.5 million acres are part of a forest preserve, created by the state legislature in 1885 and since enlarged. An 1894 amendment to the state constitution requires this preserve to "be forever kept as wild forest lands." The remaining 60% is in private hands and includes towns and villages. (Forest preserve lands are also located in Catskill Park.)

An Adirondack Park Agency was created in 1971 and charged with developing a master plan for the care of the state lands and a use and development plan for the private lands. Under the latter plan all private lands are classified according to a six-level system, and guidelines for the development intensity of each level are specified. The Agency, with a governing board made up of landowners residing within the park, non-resident landowners, and state members ex officio, works closely with local governments in implementing the plan. Special regulations protect 1,200 miles of river corridors, designated as part of the State Wild, Scenic and Recreational Rivers System.

The forest preserve was created because New Yorkers feared for their water supply. The Hudson River has its origin at Lake Tear in the Clouds in the northeastern Adirondacks. The headwaters of most or part of four other major basins are also in the region. Nevertheless, during the nineteenth century the Adirondacks were heavily logged; forest fires broke out, because of human carelessness; and erosion silted up streams.

Logging in the Adirondacks caused the loss of wildlife and threatened water supplies. In part because of the destruction of spruce forests, lynx disappeared from the region in the 1880s. Researchers are now trying to reestablish the lynx and have released lynx from the Yukon in the Mount Marcy area.

Mount Marcy, elevation 5,344 feet, is in the northeast portion of the park, where there are forty-two peaks over 4,000 feet in elevation. The western and southern Adirondacks are gentle lands of lakes, ponds, streams, and hills.

The first people to climb all forty-two peaks were young Bob Marshall, his brother, and their guide. Bob Marshall became a cofounder of the Wilderness Society and a Forest Service administrator, and it was he who devised Forest Service regulations designed to prevent the construction of roads in pristine areas (the U Regulations), which anticipated the Wilderness Act. His love of the wilderness went back to his boyhood summers in the Saranac Lake region of the Adirondacks.

The superb recreational opportunities in the park include camping, downhill and cross-country skiing, swimming and scuba diving, horseback riding, and boating. A canoe route almost 140 miles long links Old Forge in the southwest to Tupper Lake and the Saranac Lakes in the north central region; and a 146-mile north-south hiking trail runs between Lake Placid and Northville. The Adirondacks have a total of 2,000 miles of trails.

For information about recreation in the Adirondacks, contact the

New York State Department of Environmental Conservation, 50 Wolf Rd., Albany, New York 12233, the department's regional office in Ray Brook, New York 12977 or the Adirondack Mountain Club, 172 Ridge Street, Glen Falls, New York 12801 (518-523-3441).

Interpretive centers at Paul Smiths and at Newcomb on Rich Lake offer a wealth of educational programs. For information about activities at both centers, contact the Adirondack Park Visitors Information Center, P.O. Box 3000, Paul Smiths, New York 12970 (518-327-3000).

BAXTER STATE PARK [201,018 acres]
North central Maine, northeast of Millinocket

Baxter State Park reflects the vision of one man, Maine's former governor Percival Baxter. In 1920 a few months before he became governor, he climbed to the summit of Mount Katahdin. Looking out over a wilderness scarred by the lumber companies that owned it, he vowed that the land would belong to Maine. At the time, Maine residents ignored or ridiculed the idea of a park. Working alone, Percival bought his first piece in 1930 from Great Northern Paper Company, 5,960 acres, including Mount Katahdin. After making a total of thirty separate purchases, he gave the last section of what is now the park to the people of Maine in 1962 when he was 86. With each gift was a deed of trust saying that the park must remain "forever wild . . . as it was when only the Indians and the animals roamed . . ." Nevertheless, he also wanted the park "used to the fullest extent."

The park is an expanse of evergreen-covered mountains, dense forests, lakes, and alpine bogs. Eighteen peaks exceed 3,000 feet. The northern terminus of the Appalachian Trail, Mount Katahdin has an elevation of 5,267 feet and is a perfect example of a monadnock, a remnant of a former highland that rises above a plain. Thoreau described the view from the top, "the surrounding world looked as if a mirror had been shattered, and glittering bits thrown on the grass." Frederick E. Church of the Hudson River School of artists painted it as presence looming behind a lakeside farm. (The painting is at the Yale University Art Gallery.)

The park is crossed by approximately 150 miles of trails. Rules are quite strict. No all-terrain vehicles or motorcycles are allowed; snowmobiles are restricted to certain areas; and mountain hiking in winter requires advance permission. Camping is limited to authorized camp grounds and sites. Reservations are accepted beginning 1 January of the given year. Would-be visitors are advised to make them months in advance.

For reservations and information contact the park headquarters at 64 Balsam Drive, Millinocket, Maine 04462 (207-723-5140).

STORM KING MOUNTAIN
The west bank of the Hudson River a few miles north of West
    Point, New York

From the brow of Storm King Mountain, 1,335 feet in elevation, hikers have magnificent views of the Hudson River Valley. They can enjoy the mountain today, because for over a decade environmentalists waged a campaign that became a major milestone for the environmental movement.

In 1963 Con Edison announced its intention to build a pumped storage facility at the base of the mountain, connected with the utility's grid by transmission lines mounted on ten-story towers. Environmentalists charged that the project would harm fish—and be an eyesore as well. In 1965 the Sierra Club joined a suit against the utility. The court recognized the club's non-economic interest in the case, a precedent-setting decision that paved the way for suits on other environmental issues. Con Edison agreed to drop its project in 1980 as part of a negotiated settlement.

Storm King Mountain is owned by the Palisades Interstate Park Commission. Stillman Trail, running from Route 32 in Mountainville to Mountain Road in Cornwall-on-Hudson, provides access to the summit. The 10.5-mile trail passes through Black Rock Forest, owned by Harvard University and the site of the highest mountains of the Precambrian Highlands to the west of the Hudson. The forest has been harvested at least twice. Nevertheless it contains a wide variety of species; and hemlocks, spared by loggers, around Mineral Spring Falls are two to three centuries old. The forest's more exposed summits and Storm King Mountain itself provide splendid vantage points for watching the autumnal migration of hawks.

Buses run from the Port of New York Authority Terminal to Mountainville and Cornwall-on-Hudson.

THE NEW JERSEY PINE BARRENS
[Approximately 1.65 million acres]
Southern New Jersey

The New Jersey Pine Barrens are the largest and best known of the world's pine barrens. About twenty examples of this type of ecosystem exist, most of them in the northeastern United States. Within the New Jersey Barrens are Double Trouble State Park, several state forests, natural areas, wildlife management areas, and wild rivers. In 1978 to slow encroaching development the federal government established the Pinelands National Reserve. New Jersey subsequently passed a Pinelands Protection Act dividing the barrens into nine management areas, each with its own type of land use. In the preservation area, which comprises 370,000 contiguous acres centering in Wharton State Forest, the land is to be maintained in its natural state. In the 565,000-acre protection area to the south and east, only development compatible with the essential character of the barrens is to be allowed.

The barrens are level, with white, sandy, acidic soil. Pitch pine, interspersed with Shortleaf pine, dominates the forests that cover most of the area. The vegetation consists for the most part of plants that have inhabited the region since prehistoric days, some of them rare species. Stands of Atlantic White Cedar can be seen at Double Trouble and in the Batsto River drainage of Wharton State Forest among other places. Underlying the barrens are vast aquifers, containing an estimated seventeen trillion gallons of water.

In its underground water supply, the New Jersey Pine Barrens resembles pine barrens on Long Island. The two regions also have in common with each other and with a pine barren in New York's Shawangunk Mountains, dwarf pine plains, where the soil is so inhospitable that trees average only four feet in height.

The New Jersey Barrens are crisscrossed by old sand roads, and traversed by the 40-mile Batona Trail, from Evans Bridge on Route 563 through Wharton and Lebanon State Forests to Ongs Hat on Route 72. Hikers design their own loop walks by starting, for example, at the Batsto Visitors Center on Route 542 or at the headquarters of Lebanon State Forest on Route 72, and following sand roads and portions of the Batona Trail. Canoeists paddle over routes of 1 to 12 miles on the Batsto, Wading, Mullica, and Oswego Rivers. Campgrounds are available along the trail and rivers.

For further information about recreation in the New Jersey and New

York pine barrens contact the New York-New Jersey Trail Conference, 232 Madison Avenue, Room 908, New York, New York 10016 (212-685-9699). The conference publishes the *New York Walk Book* (which includes New Jersey) and Lawrence G. Paul's *The Pine Barrens of Ronkonkoma: A Guide for the Hiker to the Long Island Pine Barrens.*

A Pinelands Preservation Alliance has been formed to protect the New Jersey Pine Barrens. Among its projects are setting up the "Pinelands Watch," a citizens' group in each municipality to monitor enforcement of the Comprehensive Management Plan, and establishing a network to police roads to prevent illegal dumping. The office of the alliance distributes a calendar of programs in the Pinelands (120–34B Whitesbog Road, Browns Mills, New Jersey 08015; 609-893-4747).

John McPhee gives a wealth of cultural and environmental information about the Pine Barrens in *The Pine Barrens*. At Ongs Hat a charming log building houses the historic Ongs Hat restaurant/produce stand. Chatsworth on the edge of the preservation area has an old general store, Buzbys. Albert Hall in Waretown hosts Pinelands musicians. The office of the Pinelands Preservation Alliance is in Historic Whitesbog Village, a turn-of-the-century, agricultural company town in Lebanon State Forest.

CHEYENNE BOTTOMS WILDLIFE AREA [19,857 acres]
Central Kansas, 6 miles northeast of Great Bend

A state-owned and managed area, this wetland is the southeastern portion of a 41,000-acre natural depression just north of the Arkansas River. It "was and probably still is the most important waterbird area in the Central Flyway," according to Marvin Schwilling of Kansas Fish and Game.

An estimated 45% of the North American northward migrating shorebird population stops at the Bottoms; and more than 90% of five species of shorebirds pass through it. Twelve species of ducks nest in the Bottoms, and 600,000 ducks and 40,000 geese have been observed there at one time. The Bottoms provides Critical Habitat for the endangered Whooping crane. It also shelters the endangered Least tern and Peregrine falcon, and has the largest nesting colony of Cattle egrets in Kansas.

Yet all is not well at the wildlife area. Originally it depended on rainfall and runoff for water. In some years it was flooded; in some it remained almost dry. When the state acquired the land, it diverted water from the Arkansas River and built five large ponds. Now, the Arkansas River no longer flows between Garden City and Dodge City and is dying from Dodge City to Great Bend, due to the impoundment of water in reservoirs in Colorado and to increased irrigation and rainwater-retaining land-treatment practices along the river. New, reliable sources of water for the Bottoms must be found, and better ways of storing and handling the water at the Bottoms need to be constructed. Under pressure from environmentalists, the state is conducting a study of means to increase the water supply.

Management encourages bird watchers as well as hunters to visit. For information contact Cheyenne Bottoms, Route 3, Box 301, Great Bend, Kansas 67530 (316-793-7730).

PLATTE RIVER
South central Nebraska, especially the 60 miles between Grand
    Island and Lexington

Each spring from early March through mid-April 500,000 Sandhill cranes, 80% of the continental population, gather on the Platte River to feed and rest from their journey to their breeding grounds in Canada, Alaska, and the Soviet Union. During the day they loaf and forage in the wet meadows along the river, and at night they sleep on sandbars that lie under shallow water.

The entire population of Whooping cranes, an endangered species, visit the Platte in the spring and fall (peak migration occurs 1–20 April and 10 Oct.–1 Nov.). From 150 to 250 endangered Bald eagles winter near ice-free pockets in the river, and the endangered Least tern and the threatened Piping plover occasionally spend the summer there. Five to nine million geese and ducks and thousands of other migrating birds also use the Platte.

Piping plovers and Least terns were once common on the Platte during the summer. They are being driven away, and the Sandhill and Whooping cranes are imperiled by diversions of water that have reduced the river's annual flow by 70%. The birds need an expanse of water and bare sandbars (submerged or above water depending on the species). The diversions, which supply water to Colorado, Wyoming, and western Nebraska, have narrowed the river's channel, allowed vegetation to cover banks, islands, and sandbars; and, by lowering the water table, are drying up formerly wet meadows.

A brochure on watching the Sandhill cranes is distributed by the

Buffalo County Convention and Visitors Bureau, P.O. Box 607, 2001 Avenue "A", Kearney, Nebraska 68848; 308-237-3101. By advance appointment the birds can be seen from the 1,900-acre Mormon Island Crane Meadows sanctuary owned by the Platte River Whooping Crane Habitat Maintenance Trust (2550 North Diers Avenue, Suite H, Grand Island, Nebraska 68803; 308-384-4633) and from the National Audubon Society's Rowe Sanctuary (Route 2, Gibbon, Nebraska 68840). They can also be viewed from roads near the river and from Fort Kearney Hike-Bike Trail and State Historical Park.

The 4,200-square-mile Rainwater Basin area in south central Nebraska near the Platte River also has water problems that endanger migrating birds. When Nebraska was settled, the Basin contained almost 4,000 marshes totaling some 94,000 acres. All but 10% have been drained or filled. In years when the weather causes ducks and geese to crowd into the Basin, severe cholera outbreaks occur. An estimated 72,000 to 80,000 birds died of cholera there in 1980.

For observing birds there is a good basin 2.5 miles south and 2 miles east of the Interstate-80 Aurora interchange. The best times are the first three weeks in March for waterfowl, or the first two weeks in August for shorebirds.

BIG BASIN REDWOODS STATE PARK [16,000-plus acres]
California coast, 20 miles north of Santa Cruz

California has two native species of redwoods: the Coast redwood (*Sequoia sempervirens*) and the Giant sequoia (*Sequoia-dendron giganteum*). Although the trees are closely related, the Coast redwoods are younger—up to 2,200 years old, in contrast to the Giant Sequoias which reach 3,600 years; the Coast redwoods are taller and thinner than the Giant sequoias; and the species grow in different habitats. Needing foggy summers and rainy winters, the Coast redwoods grow only along approximately 450 miles of northern California coast; the Giant sequoias grow in the colder Sierra Nevada.

Congress protected groves of Giant sequoia in 1890 by establishing Sequoia and General Grant National Parks (General Grant later became part of Kings Canyon). Protection for Coast redwoods, more desirable as lumber than the sequoias, was much slower in coming and is still far from complete.

Logging of redwoods began in the 1820s. At first only crude methods were used, but equipment of greater and greater efficiency was introduced, and from 1947 to 1958 a peak of over a billion board feet per year was cut. By 1964 only 300,000 acres of an original 2,000,000 acres of old-growth Coast redwood remained.

Big Basin Park was established in 1902, at the initiative of local citizens and the newly formed Sempervirens Club, to protect a portion of the Coast redwoods. Named at the time California Redwood Park, it was the first state park in California. Where previously logged, it has been reforested by Sempervirens, the Sierra Club, and the Save the Redwoods League.

In the park are stands of virgin redwoods intermixed with Douglas fir, Tan oak, California laurel, and Wax myrtle trees. Beside the redwood communities, Big Basin has chaparral communities on dry, rocky ridges above the cloud layer; mixed evergreen communities between the redwoods and the chaparral; streamside vegetation; and a freshwater marsh, one of the few relatively undisturbed bodies of fresh water on the coast. Hikers pass from one community to another on the 37-mile Skyline to the Sea Trail that runs from Castle Rock State Park in Saratoga, through Big Basin (close to park headquarters), down to the ocean at the mouth of Waddell Creek.

Hikers may catch a bus from Santa Cruz to park headquarters, hike through the park, and catch another bus back to Santa Cruz at Waddell Creek. The park has six trail camps for hikers. Reservations are required and may be made by contacting park headquarters.

The California state parks do not mail brochures free of charge. A price list of material on the parks is available from the Publications Section, Department of Parks and Recreation, State of California, P.O. Box 2390, Sacramento, California 95811. The Santa Cruz Mountains Natural History Association, 101 North Big Trees Park Road, Felton, California 95018, will mail a map and description of Big Basin in return for a stamped envelope and 75 cents.

OVERTON PARK [175 acres]
Memphis, Tennessee

Within the city of Memphis in Overton Park is a virgin forest, a remnant of the primeval hardwood forests that once surrounded the city. At the center of the forest is a mature climax oak-hickory-Tulip poplar stand with trees approximately 200 years old. Around the core, are trees perhaps 50 years younger, which are at or close to reaching the final succession stage. As they age, these are becoming part of the core. Thus the park gives an unusual opportunity to observe mature forest transition.

In its 175 acres the forest contains 50 tree species. The large variety is partly a result of having moist as well as relatively dry habitat and a 30-foot variation in elevation. It hosts scarce birds, including the endangered Mississippi kite, rare Fish crow, and Swainson's and Parula warblers; and such scarce plants as the goldenseal.

For information contact Pepper Marcus, editor of *West Tennessee Forestry and Wildlife News*, P.O. Box 659, Memphis, Tennessee 38101.

PRESERVES OF NON-PROFIT ORGANIZATIONS

Many private non-profit organizations own land for the purpose of protecting it. The Nature Conservancy, with more than 1,200 preserves, has the largest privately-owned nature preserve system in the world. The National Audubon Society also has a system of preserves. There are more than 800 local, state, and regional land trusts of various types. The 549 of these that answered a questionnaire own more than 300,000 acres of land. These land trusts work for the direct protection of specific lands because of their agricultural, historical, natural, recreational, or scenic importance.

Land trusts and national organizations concerned with direct preservation use a wide range of tools in addition to actual purchases. Conservation easements are a major method. Under this approach, the land remains in private hands and can be freely bought and sold. However, an organization receives the right to enforce in perpetuity conservation restrictions on the future use and development of the property. The easement is legally attached to the property's deed. The 549 local, state, and regional land trusts protect more than 290,000 acres by holding easements to them.

As the price of land rises, making it increasingly difficult for land trusts to own land outright, they also employ as tools for preservation, negotiations, land exchanges, and limited development agreements. The latter means that a land owner develops in as appropriate a way as possible a portion of his or her property and arranges for the preservation of the remainder.

The land trusts and national organizations do not retain all the land that they buy or receive as donations. Instead, they may sell or give land to a public body or to another private organization that will conserve it. In certain cases, in fact, they purchase land under an arrangement to turn it over to a public agency that cannot act quickly enough itself to head off development. The number of acres that a trust or national organization saves is likely to be far greater therefore than the number of acres it owns or on which it holds easements. Land trusts at the local, state, and regional levels have protected by one means or another a total of over 2,000,000 acres. The Nature Conservancy has protected 5.5 million acres in 50 states and Canada, in addition to assisting like-minded organizations to preserve land in Latin America and the Caribbean.

Two other national organizations that concentrate on direct protection of land are the American Farmland Trust and the Trust for Public Land. The Farmland Trust protects farmland or potential farmland; the Trust for Public Land preserves urban and rural land for environmental or public-use reasons. These two organizations normally use methods other than holding and managing land themselves. To preserve specific areas, associations concerned with direct protection of land may work with each other and with other types of environmental organizations.

The Nature Conservancy, through its many chapters and field offices, and the American Farmland Trust and the Trust for Public Land, through their regional offices, all work with individuals, groups, and government agencies at the state and local level. To contact them write or call: the Nature Conservancy at 1815 North Lynn Street, Arlington, Virginia 22209 (703-841-5300); the American Farmland Trust at 1920 North Street NW, Suite 400, Washington, D.C. 20036 (202-659-5170); and the Trust for Public Land at 116 New Montgomery St., 4th Floor, San Francisco, California 94105 (415-495-4014). The Land Trust Alliance, a national network of local, state, and regional land trusts, publishes a biannual directory. The 1991–92 *National Directory of Conservation Land Trusts* may be purchased ($15.95 plus $3 postage) from the association at 900 17th St. NW, Suite 410, Washington D.C. 20006 (202-785-1410).

Associations that own land for the purpose of preserving it determine its use; and regulations vary from site to site. The National Audubon Society, for instance, allows full or limited access to some of its preserves, but keeps others completely closed to protect wildlife.

GREAT WASS ISLAND PRESERVE [1,540 acres]
Great Wass Island off the northern Maine coast in Beals

Although only acquired by the Nature Conservancy in 1978, this preserve shows few signs of human activity. Its coastal raised bogs originated when sphagnum moss began collecting in basins left by withdrawing glaciers. These bogs represent a type of peatland peculiar to extreme maritime sites in New Brunswick, Nova Scotia, and eastern Maine. On the south shore of the island, exposed granite bedrock drops steeply into the sea, a sign of the "Fundian Fault," which extends from the Bay of Fundy in southeastern Canada to New Hampshire.

Wildlife is abundant. Here osprey nest and Bald eagles feed and roost. The bogs and spruce forests provide habitat for Palm warblers, Lincoln sparrows, Spruce grouse, and Boreal chickadees. On or near the ocean, Harbor seals, Common eiders, and Great Blue herons can be seen.

In the bogs are unusual carnivorous plants and stunted shrubs. On drier but thin soil is one of Maine's largest stands of Jack pine, at its southern limit in Maine. Several plants rare to Maine including Beach-Head iris, Marsh felwort, and blinks (*Montia fontana*) grow on the exposed headlands.

The island can be reached by a bridge. Day visitors are welcome but must keep to the 3.5 miles of trail and to the rocks around the edge of the island.

For information contact the Maine Chapter of the Nature Conservancy, Box 338, 122 Main Street, Topsham, Maine 04086.

EDGE OF APPALACHIA PRESERVE SYSTEM [5,000 acres]
Southeastern Ohio, 14 miles east of West Union

As its name suggests, the system is a chain of eight preserves straddling the transition zone between the steep unglaciated hills and valleys of the Appalachian Plateau to the east and the rolling, fertile limestone lands of the Interior Low Plain to the west. Included in this geographically and botanically diverse terrain are natural prairies supporting such plants as the bluestem, Little bluestem, and Indian grass characteristic of the Western tallgrass prairies. Lynx Prairie, acquired in 1959 by the Nature Conservancy, is the best known of these plots. Where the soil in the preserve is deep, there are rich mesophytic forests inhabited by abundant bird populations including Pileated woodpeckers, Broad-Winged hawks, and Red-Eyed virios.

Pioneer ecologist E. Lucy Braun, author of the reference work, *The Deciduous Forests of Eastern North America* (1950) and founder and editor of the periodical *Wildflower*, studied the Ohio prairies and assisted the Ohio Chapter of the Nature Conservancy in the development of the Edge Preserve.

Ecologist Reed F. Noss has proposed the establishment of a deciduous forest ecosystem reserve on the wildest land in southern Ohio and northeastern Kentucky. The Edge of Appalachia Preserve would be a key portion of the larger preserve, which would also include Ohio's 70,000-acre Shawnee State Forest and surrounding lands (the "Little Smokies of Ohio"), and Kentucky's Carter Caves State Park.

The Edge of Appalachia Preserve has a network of trails open to the public. For information contact the Cincinnati Museum of Natural History, to which the Nature Conservancy has deeded the land, at 1720 Gilbert Ave., Cincinnati, Ohio 45202 (513-621-3889).

CORKSCREW SWAMP SANCTUARY [11,000 acres]
Southwestern Florida, southwest of Immokalee and off Route 846

A National Audubon Society refuge, Corkscrew Swamp contains the country's largest virgin stand of Bald cypress, the oldest tree in eastern North America. Up to 130 feet in height and 25 feet in girth, many of the cypresses are over 700 years old. They shelter a lush growth of vines, shrubs, aquatic plants, and air plants (*epiphytes*), including orchids.

Visitors walk through the swamp, among the cypress, on a 1.75-mile boardwalk that encompasses 80 acres of the sanctuary. A tour booklet describes the flora and fauna that may be seen along the way. The swamp is the site of the largest rookery of Wood storks in the nation. They nest sometime between November and March, depending on the level of the water. If the water level is such that they cannot obtain an abundant fish supply, the nesting season is a failure. The Wood stork is endangered, yet the South Florida Water Management District, with the approval of the governor of Florida, authorized a television station to build a tower just outside the northwest corner of the sanctuary between the birds' nesting ground and their preferred feeding area. In bad weather when the birds fly low, they will have to find their way around the television tower, a radio tower already in the area, and their guy wires.

For information contact the sanctuary, Route 6, Box 1875A, Sanctuary Road, Naples, Florida 33964 (813-657-3771). It is open 9:00 A.M.-5:00 P.M. daily. Admission is $4.

BLUESTEM PRAIRIE [2,458 acres]
West central Minnesota, 13 miles east of Moorhead

Approximately 80% of this prairie has never been cultivated and is good quality wet and mesic (balanced moisture) tallgrass prairie. Located along the ancient beachline of Glacial Lake Agassiz at the eastern edge of the shortgrass prairie, it contains at least 307 native plant species, including 54 prairie grasses, and is within the range of the Greater Prairie Chicken. (Prairie grass grows taller as one moves from west to east across the country.) The preserve, which belongs to the Minnesota Chapter of the Nature Conservancy, is open to visitors. For information contact the conservancy at RR 2, Box 109, Glyndon, Minnesota 56547 (218-498-2679).

COACHELLA VALLEY PRESERVE [13,000 acres]
South central California, 10 miles east of Palm Springs

An example of cooperation between public and private entities, Coachella is jointly owned and managed by the Bureau of Land Management, U.S. Fish and Wildlife Service, California Department of Fish and Game, and the Nature Conservancy.

The preserve, which straddles the Indio Hills and the San Andreas fault, merits this concentration of effort, as it contains two rare types of habitat: palm oasis woodland and blow-sand fields. The oases are sustained for the most part by water flowing underground from a higher elevation. Fractures and faults in the rock allow the underground streams at certain points to rise to the surface. The blow-sand fields result from torrential rains washing sand and gravel down the mountains and spreading the granite particles in broad alluvial fans. Strong winds blow across the valley and sweep the sand into everchanging dunes.

The preserve was originally established to protect the threatened Coachella Valley Fringe-Toed lizard, which inhabits the dunes; but it also shelters the rare Giant Palm-Boring beetle, Coachella Round-Tailed Ground squirrel, Giant Red Velvet mite, and Coachella Valley Milk vetches.

The preserve has hiking and horseback riding trails of varying lengths and levels of difficulty.

For information contact the preserve at P.O. Box 188, Thousand Palms, California 92276 (619-343-1234).

PRIVATE OWNERS

As a reminder that countless areas that merit protection belong neither to government agencies nor to non-profit organizations, we conclude with an example of land in a multitude of private hands.

NORTHEAST KINGDOM OF VERMONT

Northeastern Vermont, inside Route 2, Route 114, the Connecticut River, and the Canadian border

The northeastern corner of Vermont where the roads end reportedly received the name "Northeast Kingdom" in 1949 from U.S. Senator Aiken of Vermont who was speaking of the area's beauty. In 1988 environmentalists George Wuerthner and Jamie Sayen proposed that it be made a National Park or Wilderness preserve. The terrain is reminiscent of Canada's boreal forest, with bogs, lakes, and spruce and birch-covered hills. The White and Black spruce, rare in Vermont, though common in the sub-arctic, grow here. The region has Vermont's coldest weather and largest moose population. The caribou, cougar, Gray wolf, and lynx once lived in the Kingdom and would be reintroduced, under Sayen's proposal.

Few humans have found the region hospitable, not even the Indians. With soil too thin for profitable farming, the area has always been sparsely settled. Most of the land is now owned by lumber companies, reportedly ready to sell here, as elsewhere in northern New England. The time is ripe for government purchases. Meanwhile, the outdoor enthusiast seeking isolation or the opportunity to study entire ecosystems would do well here.

CHAPTER SEVENTEEN

UNESCO Sites in the U.S.

WORLD HERITAGE SITES

The World Heritage Convention, adopted by the UNESCO (United Nations Educational, Scientific, and Cultural Organization) General Conference in 1972, is a mechanism for safeguarding "outstanding examples of the world's natural and cultural heritage." In signing the convention a nation promises to preserve "the sites and monuments within its borders that are recognized to be of exceptional universal value."

States that have signed the convention are invited to submit nominations for World Heritage Sites to the UNESCO Secretariat. Nominations for natural sites are reviewed by the International Union for the Conservation of Nature and Natural Resources, which reports to the UNESCO Bureau. The Bureau makes recommendations to the World Heritage Committee, which names the World Heritage Sites, and also allocates funds in a World Heritage Fund to countries that have requested assistance. The committee is made up of twenty-one specialists elected by the states that have signed the convention.

A natural heritage property is considered to have universal value if it represents major stages of the Earth's development or processes of biological evolution, displays superlative natural phenomena or scenery, or is the most important habitat of threatened species. It should be large enough to be self-perpetuating.

For further information contact the National Park Service's Office of International Affairs, Room 2137, 1100 L Street NW, Washington, D.C. 20013 (202-343-7063).

The following are the World Heritage Sites in the United States:

Cahokia Mounds State Historic Site (Collinsville, Illinois)
Chaco Culture National Historical Park (Bloomfield, New Mexico)

Everglades National Park
La Fortaleza and San Juan Historic Site in Puerto Rico
Grand Canyon National Park
Great Smoky Mountains National Park
Hawaii Volcanoes National Park (Hawaii National Park, Hawaii)
Independence Hall (Philadelphia, Pennsylvania)
Mammouth Cave National Park (Mammouth Cave, Kentucky)
Mesa Verde
Monticello and the University of Virginia at Charlottesville
Olympic National Park
Redwood National Park
Statue of Liberty
Wrangell–Saint Elias (Alaska)
Yellowstone National Park
Yosemite National Park

BIOSPHERE RESERVES

Launched in 1971 as a program of UNESCO, the Man and the Biosphere (MAB) Program encourages research as a means of solving problems related to resource conservation and use. It also trains specialists and promotes environmental education. Field research takes place in biosphere reserves.

According to MAB criteria, each reserve normally consists of a strictly protected core area, a buffer zone in which uses and activities are managed to help protect the core, and a transition area where conservation knowledge and management skills are applied. The core usually represents a biogeographic unit and is large enough to sustain viable species populations at all levels of the ecosystem. Cluster reserves contain a number of non-contiguous areas and may include laboratories or education centers. The overall spatial arrangement of a cluster reserve is similar to that of a one-unit reserve; the various components are usually administered by different entities linked by coordinating mechanisms.

National MAB committees prepare biosphere reserve nominations. An independent Scientific Advisory Panel for Biosphere Reserves evaluates proposals and makes recommendations to the Bureau (executive committee) of MAB's International Coordinating Council. The Bureau makes the final decision.

For further information on the international program contact the

MAB Secretariat, Division of Ecological Sciences, UNESCO, 7, Place de Fontenoy, 75700 Paris, France (1-45-68-40-68). For information on the program in the United States, including a list of reserves, contact the Secretary of the U.S MAB Project Directorate on Biosphere Reserves, National Park Service, P.O. Box 37127, Washington, D.C. 20013-7127 (202-343-8127).

Examples of the many U.S. biosphere reserves follow. (If the reserve has only one component and the name of the reserve is almost identical to that of this component, only the name of the reserve is stated.)

BIG BEND NATIONAL PARK BIOSPHERE RESERVE

Big Bend National Park, Texas 79843

CAROLINIAN-SOUTH ATLANTIC BIOSPHERE RESERVE

Big Rock Area and Ten Fathom Ledge
Blackbeard and Wolf Island National Wildlife Refuges
Georgia Coast Complex, U.S. Fish and Wildlife Service
P.O. Box 8487, Savannah, Georgia 31412
Cape Lookout National Seashore
P.O. Box 690, Beaufort, North Carolina 28516
Cape Romain National Wildlife Refuge
390 Bull's Island Road, Awendaw, South Carolina 29429
Capers Island Marine Sanctuary, South Carolina Marine Center
P.O. Box 12559, Charleston, South Carolina 29412
Cumberland Island National Seashore
P.O. Box 806, St. Marys, Georgia 31558
Gray's Reef National Marine Sanctuary
Marine and Estuarine Management Division
NOAA, Office of Ocean and Coastal Resource Management
1825 Connecticut Avenue NW, Washington, D.C. 20235
Hobcaw Barony
Belle W. Baruch Institute for Marine Biology and Coastal Research
University of South Carolina
Columbia, South Carolina 29208
Little Saint Simons Island, P&M Cedar Products, Inc.
P.O. Box 7349, Stockton, California 95207336
Santee Coastal Reserve
Box 37, McClellanville, South Carolina 29458

Washo Reserve, South Carolina Nature Conservancy
P.O. Box 5475, Columbia, South Carolina 29250

Yawkey Wildlife Center
Route 2, Box 181, Georgetown, South Carolina 29440

GLACIER NATIONAL PARK BIOSPHERE RESERVE
West Glacier, Montana 59936

HUBBARD BROOK EXPERIMENTAL FOREST BIOSPHERE
RESERVE
Northeastern Forest Experiment Station
P.O. Box 640, Durham, New Hampshire 03824

ISLE ROYALE NATIONAL PARK BIOSPHERE RESERVE
87 North Ripley Street, Houghton, Michigan 49931

JORNADA EXPERIMENTAL RANGE BIOSPHERE RESERVE
P.O. Box 30003, New Mexico State University
Las Cruces, New Mexico 88003-0003

KONZA PRAIRIE RESEARCH NATURAL AREA BIOSPHERE
RESERVE
Division of Biology, Kansas State University
Manhattan, Kansas 66506

LUQUILLO EXPERIMENTAL FOREST BIOSPHERE
RESERVE
Institute of Tropical Forestry, USDA Forest Service
RWU 1152, Call Box 25000
Rio Piedras, Puerto Rico 00928-2500

SAN JOAQUIN EXPERIMENTAL RANGE BIOSPHERE
RESERVE
24075 Highway 41, Coarsegold, California 93614

THREE SISTERS WILDERNESS BIOSPHERE RESERVE
Willamette National Forest
P.O. Box 10607, Eugene, Oregon 97440

VIRGINIA COAST RESERVE BIOSPHERE RESERVE
The Nature Conservancy
Brownsville, Nassawadox, Virginia 23413

YELLOWSTONE NATIONAL PARK BIOSPHERE RESERVE
P.O. Box 168, Yellowstone National Park, Wyoming 82190

PART IV

Environmental Study and Preservation/Restoration Sites

In the battle to preserve the ecosystem, nobody need stand on the sidelines. Not only can we can take steps to conserve resources by simplifying our lifestyles, but we can also have the satisfaction of participating in activities that contribute directly to the welfare of natural areas and wildlife. Numerous organizations and companies are engaged in preservation and restoration projects. Many of them need volunteers. Furthermore, there are countless opportunities for us to enlarge our knowledge of the natural world through taking part in environmental camps and trips, and in programs sponsored by nature centers and other institutions. Such study may point the way to action.

CHAPTER EIGHTEEN

Nature Study Camps and Trips

The following is a sample of organizations and institutions providing trips or camps for adults that emphasize study of the natural world. Sources of information on additional opportunities are becoming numerous. Gerson G. Eisenberg compiles *Learning Vacations* (Peterson's Guides); an April issue of *High Country News* contains a directory to "Outdoor Education in the West" each year; the Jan./Feb. 1991 issue of *Buzzworm* included a "first annual directory" to environmental education programs; and the summer 1990 issue of *Wilderness* lists schools on public lands.

Travelers who would appreciate guidance on locations new to them but who do not want to participate in organized outings would do well to purchase *Nature Guide* by Ilene Marcks. She lists, along with other useful tips, contacts throughout the United States and abroad who have agreed to assist visitors with information about local opportunities in their fields of specialization, from bird watching to geology. The ninth edition of the guide is $8, plus $2 postage, from *Nature Guide*, P.O. Box 1015, Tacoma, Washington 98401–1015 (206-952-4640).

EARTHWATCH
Box 403, 680 Mount Auburn Street
Watertown, Massachusetts 02272
617-926-8200

Since 1971 Earthwatch members have funded scientific research expeditions by becoming members of research teams sponsored by Earthwatch Worldwide and by sharing in both the labor and cost of field research. Individuals can join teams in the arts and humanities, life sciences, marine studies, physical sciences, or social sciences. An individual's share of costs ranges from $800 to $2,000.

ELDERHOSTEL
75 Federal Street
Boston, Massachusetts 02110
617-426-7788

An educational program in the liberal arts and sciences, Elderhostel is open to anyone sixty years of age or older regardless of nationality. Courses normally last a week and take place at educational institutions. Students live in dormitories but classes may involve numerous field trips. The cost of tuition and room and board for a week is approximately $240. Elderhostel places catalogs in public libraries and sends them free of charge to individuals who request them.

MAINE AUDUBON SOCIETY
Gilsland Farm, 118 U.S. Rt. 1
Falmouth, Maine 04105
207-781-2330

The Maine Audubon Society is an example of the various independent Audubon organizations linked only in name to the National Audubon Society. It offers from April to November a full schedule of outings. Non-members may participate but pay at a higher rate. The trips are listed in the April issue of the society's magazine *Habitat*. They fill up early, so, if interested, register well ahead of time.

NATIONAL AUDUBON SOCIETY
National Environmental Education Center
613 Riversville Road
Greenwich, Connecticut 06831
203-869-2017

The National Audubon Society is a leader in environmental education. It offers a wide variety of programs, several of them innovative, for young people and adults. Nature study trips organized by the national office and by local chapters are among the activities. More unusual are the camps that offer one- to two-week sessions in field ecology.

Among them are camps in Todd Wildlife Sanctuary on Hog Island, Maine; lush meadows and woods in Greenwich, Connecticut; and the Wind River Mountains in Wyoming. Special camp programs include field ornithology workshops and a youth ecology camp in Maine; an introduction to field ecology for educators in Connecticut; and nature photography in Wyoming. A week-long ecology camp costs $495-$595. College credit is available.

NATIONAL AUDUBON SOCIETY EXPEDITION INSTITUTE
P.O. Box 67
Mount Vernon, Maine 04352
207-685-3111

In a class by itself, Audubon Expedition Institute operates as a small, investigative camping community with the global environment as classroom and teacher. Groups of students travel from natural area to natural area across the country by bus. As they interact with the environment, with each other, and with people they meet, they learn the academics of the natural and social sciences, education, and traditional music and art, and gain practical competence in such areas as survival, ecology, conservation, values clarification, and critical thinking. They may fulfill a substantial part of the requirements for a B.S. or M.S. degree from Lesley College.

NATURE CONSERVANCY
1815 North Lynn Street
Arlington, Virginia 22209
703-841-5300

The various chapters and field offices of the Nature Conservancy offer trips to allow people to learn about the natural history of lands that the Conservancy is preserving, or, in some cases, simply to enjoy the outdoors while donating to the organization. Programs of special interest are described in the society's bimonthly *Nature Conservancy Magazine.* Others may only be listed in local publications. Examples are five days of cross-country skiing in Yellowstone Park ($1,500) and a week of bird watching in Oregon ($785).

NORTH CASCADES INSTITUTE
2105 Highway 20
Sedro Woolley, Washington 98284
206-856-5700

The institute seeks to increase understanding and appreciation of the rich natural, historical, and cultural legacy of the Northern Cascades. It offers some eighty field seminars, each lasting from two days to two weeks. Topics vary from Wildflowers of Yellow Island by Kayak (tuition $150), through Ethnobotany Field Techniques ($75), to Lost River Sojourns: Nature Writing Workshop ($135). A field camp for grades 5–8 is among the institute's many other programs.

OMEGA INSTITUTE FOR HOLISTIC STUDIES
Lake Drive, RD 2, Box 377
Rhinebeck, New York 12572
914-266-4301 (20 May-20 Sept.); 914-338-6030 (21 Sep.-17 May)

The institute is an educational/retreat center offering weekend and week-long workshops on innovative themes in the arts, health, business, psychology, personal growth, and spirituality. It also offers innovative trips. Programs of particular interest to ecologists include Doug Elliott's Hiking In: Herbs, Woodslore and Foraging; Catskills Wilderness Encounter; and John Seed's Council of All Beings. The cost of a typical five-day course is approximately $240, plus room and board if living at the institute.

SACRED PASSAGE
Drawer CZ
Bisbee, Arizona 85603
602-432-7353

Sacred Passage is a guided wilderness solo experience. Participants, prior to their time alone, receive meditation and awareness training as a group. They rejoin the group for assistance in returning to everyday life. John P. Milton, organizer of Sacred Passage, is a long-time practitioner of Zen, Taoist, and Tibetan Buddhist meditation. The quests last ten days and are conducted in the Rocky Mountains of southern Colorado; the Chiricahua Mountains of Arizona; a West Virginia valley; Baja California and Mainland Mexico. Participants are responsible for their own food. A donation of $480 is requested.

SISKIYOU LAMA EXPEDITIONS
P.O. Box 1330
Jacksonville, Oregon 97530
503-899-1696

Owned and operated by environmentalist Chant Thomas, Siskiyou Llama Expeditions leads small groups (usually four to eight people) on trips in the Siskiyou, Kalmiopsis, Marble, and Cascade Mountain

Ranges. Llamas, which do far less damage to trails than horses and mules, carry the baggage. From mid-May through September, trips range in length from one to six days, with the longer trips costing $75 a day. During other months only one- or two-day trips are offered. Gourmet natural meals with much of the food from Chant Thomas's farm are provided.

THE TRACKER
Tom Brown, Tracker, Inc.
P.O. Box 173
Asbury, New Jersey 08802
201-479-4681

Tom Brown bases his courses on his experience of living in the wilderness and being taught by a Native American, Stalking Wolf, for twenty years. In his courses he "cover[s] equally tracking, nature awareness, and the ancient philosophy of the Earth." The Pine Barrens of New Jersey are the setting for field work. The standard course costs approximately $565.

VICTOR EMANUEL NATURE TOURS (VENT)
P.O. Box 33008
Austin, Texas 78764
800-328-VENT

Birding is the main purpose of nearly all Victor Emanuel Nature Tours. Ornithologists lead trips to prime birding spots in North America and throughout the world. Except for a few wilderness trips, accommodations are in the best hotels and motels available, and participants usually travel from one area to another in a van or small bus. VENT operates weekend trips for the American Birding Association and supports financially leading national and local conservation groups.

WAY OF THE MOUNTAIN LEARNING CENTER
Box 542
Silverton, Colorado 81433

Dolores LaChapelle annually leads an Autumn Equinox Taoist Celebration. The participants learn from the inter-relationships of sky/rock/water/trees in the way the ancient Taoist masters learned. As traditional peoples the world over have done, they ritually circle a sacred mountain by hiking to view it from a different angle each day. Tai Chi is included every day. The celebration lasts four days. Visitors are responsible for their own lodging and meals except for lunches and the final ritual dinner. Write for cost and additional information. This program is offered by Earthwalk: a Wilderness Training Deep Ecology Institute, which is described in the chapter on Emerging Movements.

WILDERNESS SOUTHEAST
711 Sandtown Road
Savannah, Georgia 31410
912-897-5108

A non-profit school of the outdoors, Wilderness Southeast's programs "are dedicated to all who find Nature not an adversary to conquer or destroy, but a storehouse of infinite knowledge and experience . . . ." It offers trips to the Everglades and central Florida, the Great Smokies, the Okefenokee Swamp, the Georgia/South Carolina coast, and abroad. During a Sea Turtle Watch, participants assist in research and conservation efforts. The school conducts environmental camps for teens and arranges customized programs for schools and organizations. The cost of a five-day trip in the Okefenokee Swamp is around $350.

WILD HORIZONS EXPEDITIONS
West Fork Road
Darby, Montana 59829
406-821-3747

Specializing in exploring some of the most remote wildlands in North America, Wild Horizons was founded and is still led by Howie Wolke, co-author of *The Big Outside* and author of *Wilderness on the Rocks*. Wolke and other guides lead backpacking trips in the Greater Yellowstone region, the central Idaho-western Montana wilderness complex, the Colorado Plateau, and the far Southwest. Groups are generally limited to eight participants and travel at an average of six to seven miles a day (depending on the rating of the trip) to allow them to fully enjoy their surroundings. Guides are trained naturalists, who emphasize low-impact hiking and camping techniques. A week-long scheduled trip costs approximately $600. Customized expeditions can be arranged.

CHAPTER NINETEEN

Environmental Study Centers

According to the Natural Science for Youth Foundation there are more than one thousand centers in the United States offering environmental education programs for young people. These include natural science centers in the strict sense of the term, museums, and park visitor centers. Here we give a sampling of centers of various types and in various parts of the country. All those described offer programs for adults as well as for children.

Additional educational centers for young people can be found through sources in the previous section and through a directory published periodically by the Natural Science for Youth Foundation. The 1991 edition costs $75 and can be ordered from the foundation at 130 Azalea Drive, Roswell, Georgia 30075 (404-594-9367).

SHELBURNE FARMS
Shelburne, Vermont 05482
802-985-8686

Landscaped by Frederick Law Olmsted, Shelburne Farms was a private nineteenth-century agricultural estate of some 1,000 acres. It is now owned and managed by a non-profit organization that is striving to set an example for land conservation, agricultural production and marketing, and innovative education.

The board has worked with several land conservation organizations to permanently protect portions of the property, and, in order to obtain revenue, it has transformed Shelburne House into a public inn. As a pioneer of the concept of farmers' markets in Vermont, the farms sell cheese from the estate's dairy and lease space to independent producers and small businesses.

Its educational program includes farm tours, workshops for

teachers, a summer day camp, cultural activities, and presentations in local schools. The *Farms' Project Seasons,* a teachers' manual containing activities grouped by season and grade level, has gained national attention.

The visitor center and farm store are open daily 9:00 A.M.-5:00 P.M. Tours are offered daily Memorial Day through October 20. During these months a walking trail and Farm Animal Area are open daily.

COLLEGE OF THE ATLANTIC
Bar Harbor, Maine 04609
Public affairs: 207-288-5015

A four-year college with Environmental Science as one of its three curriculum areas, College of the Atlantic has a natural history museum in which exhibits, prepared by students, focus on predator-prey relationships and on human impact on the environment. The museum offers interpretive programs, and, for children of 5 to 13 years of age, summer field studies. It is open 9:00 A.M.-4:00 P.M. daily from the day after Commencement to Labor Day. At other times contact the director, Craig Kesselheim, at 207-288-5015. Admission is $2.50.

Also at the college is a nature trail, designed by a student as his senior project and leading to informational displays around the 26-acre, ocean-front campus. Displayed next to the arts and sciences building is a 15-foot skull of a 60-foot Finback whale, whose carcass was recovered by a group of faculty and students in 1983. The whale had apparently been struck by a very large ship a couple of weeks before it washed up on shore near Corea, Maine. A student restored the bones and mounted them in a display as an independent study.

DRUMLIN FARM EDUCATION CENTER AND WILDLIFE SANCTUARY
South Great Road
Lincoln, Massachusetts 01773
617-259-9807

The former owners of Drumlin Farm, Mr. and Mrs. Conrad Hatheway, arranged tours of the farm for Boston-area children from 1940 on. When Mrs. Hatheway died in 1955, she left the farm and an endowment for its operation to the Massachusetts Audubon Society. The 180-acre farm now enables children to become acquainted with a variety of wildflowers and domestic and wild animals, including 200 species of birds. Programs for adults include beginning and advanced birding trips and canoe excursions on the Sudbury River.

The farm can be reached by train from Boston's North Station to Lincoln, followed by a walk. Admission for adults is $5. It is open from 9:00 A.M.-5:00 P.M. every day except Mon. in the summer; 9:00 A.M.-4:00 P.M. in the winter.

Across the road from the farm is Hatheway Environmental Resource Library. Visitors who are not members of the Massachusetts Audubon Society can use materials at the library free of charge or pay $5 a year for check-out privileges. The library is open Mon.-Fri. 9:00 A.M.-5:00 P.M. and Sat. 10:00 A.M.-3:00 P.M.

ALLEY POND ENVIRONMENTAL CENTER
228–06 Northern Boulevard
Douglaston, New York 11363
718-229-4000

Although Alley Pond is an urban environmental center, it encompasses 750 acres of gardens, woodlands, ponds, and salt and fresh water marshes. It offers varied activities, including nature walks on the grounds and field trips. The center can be reached by public transportation from Manhattan. Phone for directions. Open daily 9:00 A.M.-4:00 or 5:00 P.M.

WAVE HILL
675 West 252 Street
Bronx, New York 10471
212-549-3200

Wave Hill was once a magnificent Victorian estate and intellectual center visited by Mark Twain, Theodore Roosevelt, and other noted figures. Now the house and 28 acres of land are owned by the city of New York and serve as a public cultural center. Programs at Wave Hill stress the importance of a sense of place on the land, and demonstrate the many ways—through science, craft, and art—that people can come to know a place, to understand its nature and to express its significance. With its greenhouse, landscaped gardens, and natural area, Wave Hill is an oasis of beauty and peace to New Yorkers.

The center is open from 10:00 A.M.-4:30 P.M. daily (longer in summer) and is accessible by Liberty Lines Express Bus, Metro- North

Commuter Railroad, and subway and city bus. Admission is $2; no charge weekdays, except holidays.

INSTITUTE OF ECOSYSTEM STUDIES
THE NEW YORK BOTANICAL GARDEN
Mary Flagler Cary Arboretum
Box AB
Millbrook, New York 12545
914-677-5358

Established in 1983, the institute has as its focus ecological education and research into the disturbance and recovery of northern temperate ecosystems. Institute educators work with students and their teachers to develop curricula for the schools; set up demonstrations of research projects; and offer workshops, ecological excursions, and formal courses on such topics as landscape design and soil science.

The Institute is located at the 1,924-acre Mary Flagler Cary Arboretum, portions of which are open to the public. These public areas include a fern glen and a garden demonstrating the effective use of low-maintenance perennials. As demonstrations of research in progress, visitors can also see an air pollution garden revealing the effect of ozone on native and cultivated plants, acid rain ponds displaying the influence of rock substrates on sensitivity to acidification and the effect of acidification on pond life, and a display contrasting mowing and burning for meadow management.

Before visiting the arboretum visitors must obtain a permit at the Gifford House Visitor and Education Center. Permits are free. The arboretum is open Mon.-Sat. 9:00 A.M.-4:00 P.M.; Sun. 1:00 P.M.-4:00 P.M. From May through Sept. hours are extended to 6:00 P.M. daily.

SMITHSONIAN INSTITUTION'S NATIONAL MUSEUM OF NATURAL HISTORY/NATIONAL MUSEUM OF MAN
Washington, D.C. 20560
202-357-2627

The museums are responsible for the largest natural history research collections in the world. The exhibits reflect what the collections show about the histories of the earth and of life, nature's diversity, and human cultures. Long-term exhibitions include dinosaurs and other fossil animals and plants; sea life, with a living coral reef and a live exhibit of a rocky coast habitat in Maine; Ice Age mammals and the emergence of man; and an Insect Zoo.

The Office of Education provides free programs for a variety of audiences. A free film and lecture series is held Fridays. Educational facilities include a Discovery Room, where people of all ages may touch and examine natural history objects, and a Naturalist Center, a resource and reference center designed to provide a quiet atmosphere for study by amateur naturalists.

A quarterly calendar of events is available by mail and at the information desk.

ELACHEE NATURE SCIENCE CENTER
2125 Elachee Drive
Gainesville, Georgia 30504
404-535-1976

On a 1200-acre nature preserve, Elachee offers hiking trails, interpretive exhibits, a gift shop, and programs for members and the general public. The building is open Mon.-Fri. 9:00 A.M.-5:00 P.M.; trails are open during daylight hours throughout the week.

LOUISIANA NATURE AND SCIENCE CENTER
P.O. Box 870610
New Orleans, Louisiana 70187–0610
504-246-LNSC

The Louisiana Nature and Science Center has been labeled the central environmental science resource for residents of Louisiana, and it lives up to its role.

Located on an 86-acre bottomland hardwood forest in Joe W. Brown Memorial Park in eastern New Orleans, the center includes an exhibit area, classrooms, planetarium, greenhouse, amphitheaters, discovery loft filled with treasures that children can handle, a garden displaying techniques of gardening for wildlife (visible from inside the interpretive center), and a gift shop emphasizing plants, animals, and habitats of southeastern Louisiana.

Activities for schools are at the heart of the center's programs. The center also sponsors lectures, workshops, and field trips. Annual attendance at the center is nearly 100,000. About 30% of the visitors come as school groups. An estimated 100,000 additional people use the center's nature trails.

SUNROCK FARM
103 Gibson Lane
Wilder, Kentucky 41076
606-781-5502

Sunrock is a 63-acre family farm that doubles as an environmental education center. In 1988 the owners, Franklin Traina and Debbie Pendock, had more than 15,000 visitors, mostly school children from the Cincinnati area. Active in the bioregional movement, Traina and Pendock "offer them a direct experience with nature emphasizing their senses and imagination. They milk goats, take hikes, smell herbs, harvest plants, roll on the grass, touch trees . . . . Most also learn a little Native American lore (wisdom), and take a hayride." Weekend workshops are also occasionally offered.

AULLWOOD CENTER AND FARM
1000 Aullwood Road
Dayton, Ohio 45414
513-890-7360

One of six nature centers across the country owned by the National Audubon Society, Aullwood is a 200-acre sanctuary encompassing a farm, an orchard, vegetable and herb gardens, ponds, prairie, and woods including three-hundred-year-old oaks. The center offers guided and self-guided programs to classes and youth groups and courses for adults. Special events include maple syrup production, woodcock watches, a prairie burn, and a honey harvest. Admission for adult non-members is $2.

OGDEN NATURE CENTER
966 W 12th Street
Ogden, Utah 84404
801-621-7595

The Ogden Nature Center is a 127-acre wildlife habitat, which was farmland from the time the valley was settled until it was purchased in 1940 by the U.S. Government as a defense depot. Now a farmhouse includes a natural history museum. Outside it, can be seen non-releasable birds of prey, including an American Kestrel. The Center cares for injured animals. Classes are held for adults and for children; nature walks led by the center's naturalist can be arranged for a nominal fee. Admission is $1.

ROCKY MOUNTAIN BIOLOGICAL LABORATORY

P.O. Box 519
Crested Butte, Colorado 81224
303-349-7231

A private, nonprofit center for research and education, the Biological Laboratory is located in Gothic. Gothic was a mining community and then a ghost town, before a biology professor purchased it in 1928 to begin creating a center for field biologists. Each summer the laboratory offers intensive college level courses in biology, including Restoration Ecology and Introduction to Field Ecology (no prerequisites). For the general public the laboratory gives field tours and nature walks twice a week in the summer. A fee is charged; reservations should be made at least two days in advance. The public is also welcome to attend scientific seminars, held one or two evenings a week in the summer, and to shop at Gothic's general store located in a building which has been restored to its original state during the mining era.

Gothic is adjacent to the Gunnison and White River National Forests, the Elk Mountain and Maroon Bells-Snowmass Wilderness Areas, and the Gothic Research Natural Area.

RANDALL DAVEY AUDUBON CENTER

P.O. Box 9314
Santa Fe, New Mexico 87504
505-983-4609

At the mouth of Santa Fe Canyon, the center is a state office of the National Audubon Society, an environmental education center, and a 135-acre nature sanctuary. On the site and open for tours Sunday afternoons in July and August is the studio and home of the late Santa Fe artist Randall Davey (once a water-powered saw mill). Since the upper half of Santa Fe Canyon has been closed to public use for more than fifty years, wildlife at the sanctuary is abundant. For a small fee, the public may use the sanctuary's trails, open 9:00 A.M.-5:00 P.M. daily. They can also participate in birdwalks and other programs.

COYOTE POINT MUSEUM FOR ENVIRONMENTAL EDUCATION
Coyote Point
San Mateo, California 94401
415-342-7755

Founded in 1954 as a junior museum of natural history, Coyote Point has evolved into a center devoted to teaching children and adults about the environment. The center museum offers temporary exhibits and a permanent exhibit on four descending levels explaining the six major ecosystems found in the Bay Area: redwood forests, broadleaf forests, grasslands, chaparral, baylands, and coast.

The center is in Coyote Point Park, 6 miles south of San Francisco Airport. Admission to the museum is $2. It is open Wed.-Fri. 10:00 A.M.-5:00 P.M.; Sat. and Sun. 1:00–5:00 P.M.

WILLIAM O. DOUGLAS OUTDOOR CLASSROOM (WODOC)
P.O. Box 2488
Beverly Hills, California 90213
213-858-3834; 213-858-3090

An educational organization, WODOC runs 150 programs in Franklin Canyon, an entry point to the Santa Monica Mountains for residents of the Los Angeles area. Each year thousands of school children, 60% of them from disadvantaged areas, attend a presentation. Youngsters three months to three years in age visit the canyon with their parents to take part in Babes in the Woods and Tikes on Hikes programs that allow them to experience the taste, touch, feel, and smell of the outdoors. Children with handicaps and who are blind follow a twenty-station trail at Heavenly Pond, which is adjacent to Upper Franklin Lake. The organization has signed a thirty-year lease with the Los Angeles Department of Water and Power for the use of the lake and has made this former reservoir a preserve and resting place for migratory waterfowl on the Pacific Flyway.

In 1989 WODOC opened a nature center on the edge of the lake. It includes an auditorium and a 3,800-square-foot exhibition center. Among the exhibits are specimens of animals native to the canyon, and a water and energy conservation display. On Earth Day 1990 WODOC planted 1200 trees, shrubs, and plants that are being watered by a demonstration irrigation and sprinkler system from Israel that operates at only 3 pounds of pressure.

CHAPTER TWENTY

Environmental Preservation/Restoration Projects

Organizations that lend a hand to preserve the environment are necessarily legion in the United States. Here I list only a few examples of specific projects concerned directly with protection or restoration of environmental quality. All the projects described can be visited, have produced results that can be seen, and/or need volunteers. The projects are loosely grouped according to whether the major focus is on water, plants, or animals, although preserving one element of an ecosystem normally involves assisting others. Additional accounts of organizations working directly to improve environmental quality are scattered throughout other chapters on protected natural areas and on emerging movements, as well as in the supplemental resources listed at the end of the book.

Rhode Island Sea Grant College Program publishes a *National Directory of Citizen Volunteer Environmental Monitoring Programs*. It is available free of charge from Publications, Rhode Island Sea Grant Office, Graduate School of Oceanography, the University of Rhode Island, Narragansett, Rhode Island 02882–1197 (401-792-6842).

WATER

PEABODY MUSEUM
East India Square
Salem, Massachusetts 01970
508-745-1876

Standing on the museum's grounds is the Summer School of Biology Building, which was built in 1876. It was the first field-oriented school in the nation for local teachers. Students collected specimens on the shore and dredged from a sailboat. The school lasted only six years, but its leaders remained influential. Edward Sylvester Morse, who lectured there, introduced the study of marine biology to Japan and established the Marine Biological Laboratory at Enoshima. (The relationship between Morse and Japan is presented in an exhibit at the museum.) Museum Curator Alpheus Hyatt went on to establish the Marine Biological Laboratory in Woods Hole.

The museum continues to study the local environment by involving members of the surrounding communities. Volunteers measure dissolved oxygen levels around Salem Harbor in order to get baseline data and to monitor the harbor's general health. During the winter months teams of volunteers monitor the wintering populations of waterfowl in the harbor.

The natural history collections of the museum are limited for the most part to Essex County, an ecologically rich area. The museum can be reached by train from Boston's North Station and by bus from Boston's Haymarket. It is open Mon.-Sat. 10:00 A.M.-5:00 P.M., Sun. noon-5:00 P.M. Admission is $5.

OCEAN ARKS INTERNATIONAL
One Locust Street
Falmouth, Massachusetts 02540
508-540-6801

John Todd of Ocean Arks International designed an innovative waste water treatment process using plants. The process can be seen at projects in Providence, Rhode Island, and in Harwich, Massachusetts. To schedule a visit call Kerry Sullivan Hayes at 508-748-3224.

WEST VIRGINIA MOUNTAIN STREAM MONITORS (MSM)
P.O. Box 170
Morgantown, West Virginia 26507

Mountain Stream Monitors supports voluntary stream monitors around West Virginia by a variety of means, including training through workshops in stream quality assessment. One of its recent projects took place in Monongalia County. MSM documented the condition of Aaron Creek above and below a proposed 45-acre surface mine. The creek is still in quite good condition, and every layer of the overburden proposed for mining is acid-bearing. Testimony of MSM at the hearing helped to cause the proposal's withdrawal.

If you would like to learn about MSM's work, call Craig Mains, MSM President, to arrange a meeting (304-292-3463).

NATIONAL WATER CENTER
P.O. Box 264
Eureka Springs, Arkansas 72632
501-253-9755

The center began as a grassroots effort to protect the healing springs of Eureka Springs from the water-borne sewage flowing from the city's broken sewer lines and septic tank/leach fields. Since the activists realized that the misconceptions that had created a problem there were helping to cause a nationwide water crisis, they incorporated as a nonprofit organization in order to share what they were learning.

The center produces and sells educational materials, including the guidebook *We All Live Downstream* ($8.95 postpaid), and a newsletter. In 1980 the center organized its first National Water Week celebration in Eureka Springs. Held at the autumn equinox, the celebration now consists of a weeklong series of swim meets, canoe and pontoon boat floats, workshops, art shows, movies, music, and dance. The center points out that other communities can replicate or adapt the event to publicize the need for protecting their water resources.

WETLANDS RESEARCH INC.
53 West Jackson Blvd.
Chicago, Illinois 60604
312-922-0777

A not-for-profit corporation affiliated with Chicago's Open Lands Project and governed by elected officials and private citizens, Wetlands Research is investigating the ecosystem approach to restoring the integrity of the Des Plaines River in Wadsworth, Lake County, Illinois. It is reconstructing riverine wetlands on a 450-acre site (owned by the Lake County Forest Preserve District) that borders a 2.8-mile stretch of the upper river. Previously the streambed was channelized, the river polluted and subject to flooding, and the wetlands drained, farmed, grazed, and mined for gravel. Wetlands Research is regrading and broadening the river channel and establishing eight experimental wetland basins, revegetating the site with native plants, and reintroducing native fish and other animals. It is monitoring the work and its results closely with the aim of developing design criteria for the restoration of waterways nationwide. Funding includes $2.2 million from the Army Corps of Engineers.

Experimental research in four of the eight wetland basins began in the spring of 1989. Employees on the site are able to discuss the work with visitors interested in wetland restoration. Hiking trails lead to various restoration projects ranging from savanna to wetland habitats.

RIVERWATCH
The Telluride Institute
P.O. Box 1770
Telluride, Colorado 81435
303-728-4402

In the spring of 1989, Telluride developed a RiverWatch program as a project for the Telluride Middle School. Using the local San Miguel River as the classroom, RiverWatch educates students and their teachers on aquatic ecology, water issues in the arid American West, and most importantly, how citizens can responsibly and ethically manage and conserve water. The program is unusual in its emphasis on water conservation ethics.

RiverWatch takes place over a two-week period in the fall or spring. Teachers first introduce students to the water cycle, wetlands, and worldwide water distribution patterns. Students then map the San Miguel River bottom, test its pH and water quality, and identify aquatic life.

The crucial function of RiverWatch is to give young people an appreciation for the scarcity of Western water, with an emphasis on the way in which aridity has shaped water law, water politics, and development in the West. Students learn about the government agencies concerned with water policy, gain an understanding of water management issues, and are made aware of citizen groups that shape water policy, and are told of water-related career possibilities. By working in teams, students find out how to work effectively as a community to protect a resource.

RiverWatch concludes with student participation in a local river/wetlands remediation project. RiverWatch students and faculty work with members of the Telluride Environmental Commission and interested citizens in a hands-on task to put into practice information learned during the course and to contribute to the health of the San Miguel River.

RiverWatch is now spreading to communities across Colorado, including the Denver area. To see a RiverWatch program in action, contact Telluride in the fall or spring.

CITY OF ARCATA
California

Arcata solved a wastewater problem by creating the 65-acre Arcata Marsh and Wildlife Sanctuary. In the late 1970s the state required the city to upgrade its wastewater treatment system, as the existing 55-acre oxidation pond had been found to be inadequate. The city responded by building a pilot project to demonstrate that wetlands could treat wastewater from the pond. The pilot project led to the development of three freshwater marshes and a lake on land that had once been saltwater marshes but that by 1980 contained an abandoned logging dock, a closed landfill, and an old railroad trestle. Now treated effluent passes through the marshes on its way to adjacent Humboldt Bay. Organisms in the mud and on the marsh plants filter the wastewater; and the nutrients add to the richness of the ecological system. The Arcata Marsh and Wildlife Sanctuary is a home or stop for nearly two hundred species of birds, double the number in the area before its creation.

Additional projects followed the sanctuary. Now Arcata has restored a total of 94 acres of saltwater and freshwater marshes, and uses wastewater to help feed young salmon as well as Steelhead and Cutthroat trout at the local hatching ponds.

The sanctuary, complete with trails and bird blinds, is located at the foot of Arcata's I Street. The Redwood Region Audubon Society sponsors a guided nature walk through the refuge each Saturday at 8:30 A.M.

For information on the restoration contact the city manager at 336 F Street, Arcata, California 95521 (707-822-5953), or the Chamber of Commerce, 1062 G Street (822-3619).

THE MONO LAKE COMMITTEE
P.O. Box 29
Lee Vining, California 93541
818-972-2025

Mono Lake is more than a million years old. Its blue saltwater reflecting the Sierra Nevada to the east is broken by fantastic white towers of tufa, a calcareous deposit, and by islands resulting from volcanic activity. Thousands of California Gulls, which thrive on a species of brine shrimp endemic to the lake, breed on the islands. Millions of migratory birds, including one-third of the world's population of Eared grebes, make the lake a stopping point.

Nevertheless, the Los Angeles Department of Water and Power is threatening Mono Lake's ecosystem by increasing the lake's salinity through diversion of its tributary streams in order to supply the city. The water has dropped a total of forty vertical feet and doubled in salinity since diversions began in 1941. Los Angeles could obtain the water it needs by conservation measures, according to the Mono Lake Committee.

The committee is fighting the diversions by every legal means, including lobbying and the courts. Public education is a major part of its work. It operates the Mono Lake Visitor Center in Lee Vining, where the public can see exhibits and a slide show; in the summer it offers free hour-and-a-half natural history field trips along the lake shore, as well as guided canoe tours ($10 per person). It also presents workshops and classes in the lake's wildlife. Their offices are located at 1207 West Magnolia Blvd., Suite D, Burbank, California 91506.

Since 1980 the committee has organized an annual Los Angeles to Mono Lake Bike-a-thon sponsored by Raleigh Cycle Company. Cyclists fill vials with water at the reflecting pools of the Los Angeles Department of Water and Power and carry the water 350 miles to deposit it in its place of origin, Mono Lake.

The Mono Lake Visitor Center on Highway 395 in Lee Vining is open daily. Hours are 9:00 A.M.-5:00 P.M., longer in summer.

Ten miles north of Mono Lake is the ghost town of Bodie, now Bodie State Historic Park. See it while it is still eerily beautiful. The Canadian company Galactic Resources is planning to mine for residual gold on 20,000 acres of Bureau of Land Management and private land around the park. Some scientists fear that leachate ponds at the mines will poison birds traveling the Pacific Flyway and contaminate Mono Lake.

VEGETATION

CHESTNUT RESTORATION PROJECT
Long Branch Environmental Education Center
Big Sandy Mush Creek, Route 2, Box 132
Leicester, North Carolina 28748
704-683-3662

The Long Branch Environmental Center is assisting in efforts to revive the American chestnut, which once accounted for 80% of the upper forest canopy in Appalachia. The trees succumbed in this century to a fungus imported from the Orient, where it is only a minor disease. Today saplings and suckers grow upwards from the surviving roots of trees felled years ago by the fungus, but the new growth dies before it is mature enough to bear fruit.

For Paul Gallimore, director of Long Branch, the attempt to bring back the trees is an outgrowth of his long-standing work to save the Black bear in North Carolina. The chestnut furnished food and shelter for the bear and other wildlife. Red and White oak, which wildlife rely upon today, are only sporadic producers of mast. Furthermore, there is a threat of oak decline.

Under the direction of the American Chestnut Foundation, a far larger project, the Chestnut Restoration Project is working with backcrosses of American and Chinese chestnut varieties. The idea is to produce a tree with the fungus-resistant qualities of the Chinese and the large size and strength of the American. Long Branch has 3 to 5 acres of young chestnuts. Whether they will survive will not be known for ten to fifteen years. People interested in chestnut restoration can see the trees at the center and join the Chestnut Restoration Project, which provides technical information as well as young trees to grow.

The center, which incorporates elements of permaculture design, also has passive solar buildings, organic gardens, fruit trees, berry patches, and a pond in which Rainbow trout are raised. Call before visiting.

The American Chestnut Cooperators' Foundation, which is intercrossing the few American chestnuts that survived the fungus, is working at the Martin American Chestnut Planting on Salt Pond Mountain in Giles County, Virginia, among other places. This planting contains trees ranging in size from seedlings to 20 feet in height. To visit the site, contact Lucille Griffin, American Chestnut Cooperators' Foundation, 2667 Forest Service Road 708, Newport, Virginia 24128 (703-552-5943). The Foundation is planning an American Chestnut Research Center for Beckley, West Virginia.

FERMI NATIONAL ACCELERATOR LABORATORY
Fermilab Prairie Committee
P.O. Box 500
Batavia, Illinois 60510
708-840-3351

What is probably the largest prairie restoration anywhere is taking place at Fermi National Accelerator Laboratory (Fermilab), a 4-mile, circular, high energy particle accelerator for basic research in particle physics.

Since 1974 a tallgrass prairie has been restored in annual increments in the center of the accelerator ring and in other plots on the 6,800-acre Fermilab site. The plantings total more than 275 hectares, and contain about 145 prairie and prairie marsh species. A herd of one hundred bison is maintained at the laboratory, although not yet in the prairie.

Volunteers are establishing the prairie under the supervision of Dr. Robert F. Betz of Northeastern Illinois University. In accordance with his concept of a "prairie matrix," they plow and disc the land and then, with an all-terrain spreader, plant the seeds of aggressive native species that can survive competition with weeds. After two or three years, they sow the less competitive native species. (They gathered the original seeds from remnants of prairie.) Fermilab opened a 24-hectare restored tallgrass prairie tract to the public in the spring of 1989.

Anyone willing to assist in the restoration should contact the Fermilab Prairie Committee.

NORTH BRANCH PRAIRIE PROJECT
506 South Wabash Ave., Suite 525
Chicago, Illinois 60605
312-431-0158; 869-5966

A "Partial List of Prairies" in Cook County's Forest Preserve District names twenty-two sites in varying conditions. Under the leadership of Stephen Packard, Field Representative of the Illinois Nature Conservancy, volunteers are restoring seven sites scattered along sixteen miles of the North Branch of the Chicago River. The northernmost and largest (150 acres) is Somme Woods Prairie in Northbrook, north of Dundee Road and west of Waukegan Road on both sides of the Chicago River.

Lacking funding for heavy equipment, volunteers have cut brush, raked seed into dense sod, and burned the plots. They are finding that in five or six years they have created a more natural prairie than if they had plowed.

Volunteers are needed to lend a hand on weekend workdays and to help out in a variety of other ways. Contact Steve Packard at the above address or at the Nature Conservancy, 79 West Monroe, Suite 708, Chicago, Illinois 60603 (312-346-8166). The North Branch Prairie Project distributes a brochure describing and giving the location of the seven prairies with which it works.

PRAIRIE PLAINS RESOURCE INSTITUTE
1307 L Street
Aurora, Nebraska 68818
402-694-5535

Prairie Plains Resource Institute is a small land trust with the mission of preserving, managing, and restoring prairie in east-central Nebraska. It has three areas that can be visited.

Lincoln Creek Parkway is a prairie restoration project. The land trust plans to make a two-to-three-mile-long greenway from the north edge of Aurora to a reservoir east of the town. It will include restored prairies and wetlands, a community garden and orchard, trails for hiking and cycling, and a nature center. Thus far a 14-acre work site contains the beginnings of woody plantings and some restored tallgrass prairie, with up to one hundred species of plants.

Bader Memorial Park Natural Area is an 80-acre tract within the 200-acre Bader Memorial Park. Including a stretch of the Platte River, riparian woodlands, sand pits, and tallgrass prairie, the natural area is a microcosm of the Platte Valley. Prairie Plains Institute publishes a handsome book, *Microcosm of the Platte: A Guide to Bader Memorial Park Natural Area* ($10 postpaid), explaining the ecology of the area.

The land trust also owns a thirty-acre virgin tallgrass prairie 6.5 miles south of the Hampton interchange of Interstate 80.

Nebraska contains shortgrass prairie, sandhills prairie, and tallgrass prairie. The Nebraska Game and Parks Commission prints a brochure listing eighteen prairies in Nebraska, with their locations and grass types (2200 North 33rd Street, Lincoln, Nebraska 68503; 402-464-0641).

J. STERLING MORTON ORCHARD AND TREE FARM
100 Arbor Avenue
Nebraska City, Nebraska 68410
402-873-9204

The 220-acre Morton Orchard and Tree Farm are at the headquarters of the National Arbor Day Foundation, an educational organization with the goal of increasing tree planting and improving tree care in urban and rural areas.

Arbor Day was celebrated for the first time in 1872 in Nebraska, when J. Sterling Morton, editor of Nebraska's first newspaper, convinced the Board of Agriculture to set aside a day for planting trees. By 1894 every state had an Arbor Day. Today the Arbor Day Foundation sponsors a number of major projects, including an educational program for elementary school children and a Tree City USA project that helps establish urban forestry programs.

At the J. Sterling Morton Center visitors can see a working apple orchard with a wide variety of trees, a nut arboretum, and a cherry orchard. They can watch cider being made by traditional methods in the fall at the Apple House. The orchard is not organic, but the staff reports that applications of herbicides and pesticides are kept to a minimum. The fruit is not treated after picking.

The Orchard and Tree Farm are open 9:00 A.M.–5:00 P.M. daily. For a guided tour make a reservation in advance. No admission is charged.

TREE PEOPLE
12601 Mulholland Drive
Beverly Hills, California 90210
213-273-8733; 818-753-4600

Tree People exercises leadership in mountain and urban reforestation, environmental education, and community service. Twice a year they conduct a training program called Citizen Forester to teach residents how to lead re-greening campaigns in their neighborhoods. (A valuable part of the training is a book called *The Planter's Guide to the Urban Forest*, which outlines all the steps necessary for planting trees in the city; it is available to the public for a $10 donation, plus $2 postage.) They teach 36,000 children a year how to care for their environment through planting and tending trees. Each child receives a seedling. In addition, Tree People obtains surplus fruit and nut tree stock from local nurseries and distributes it to people in need.

The headquarters of the Tree People is Coldwater Canyon Park—a 45-acre wilderness park that the organization maintains for the city of Los Angeles. Here they have their offices, a small retail nursery, an organic garden, hiking trails, chickens, displays and an education center. The office is open from 9:00 A.M.-5:00 P.M. weekdays and the nursery from noon-5:00 P.M. Sat. and Sun. The staff gives a guided tour of the park at 11:00 A.M. Sun. To volunteer to assist Tree People call the office. Members of Tree People receive six seedlings a year and a bimonthly newsletter.

DESERT BOTANICAL GARDEN
1201 North Galvin Parkway
Phoenix, Arizona 85008
602-941-1225

The Desert Botanical Garden is a fifty-year-old education, conservation, and research institution located on 140 acres in Papago Park. Visitors can see plants from deserts around the world, but a 3-acre exhibit on the plants and people of the Sonoran Desert may be of greatest interest to ecologists. Here are replicated a Saguaro forest, a mesquite thicket, a desert stream environment, and an upland chaparral habitat, each complete with historic and prehistoric structures that help visitors understand how desert plants have been used over the centuries.

Dr. Gary Paul Nabhan, author of *Gathering the Desert* (Univ. of Arizona Press, 1985) and *The Desert Smells like Rain: A Naturalist in Papago Indian Country* (North Point Press, 1982) supervises the Gentry Agroecology Project Farm, located on three acres of the Garden. The project promotes forms of desert agriculture that utilize but do not deplete biological diversity and require minimal inputs of water and little or no fertilizer or pesticides. Week-long training workshops and one-day seminars are held at the garden, and internships are offered to college-age Native American and Mexican students.

The garden is open every day of the year, including holidays, from 9:00 A.M. to sunset. Admission is $4. Readers interested in the Gentry Agroecology Project in particular should write to Liz Ecker, c/o GAP Farm at the Garden.

FOREST WATCH

Wilderness Society
234 North Central Avenue, Suite 430
Phoenix, Arizona 85004
602-256-7921

Forest Watch began in the southeastern United States, where the Atlanta office of the Wilderness Society organized monitoring groups. The first systematic state-wide program was created in Arizona, as the Wilderness Society's Phoenix office put together a broad-based coalition of groups concerned about abusive practices in the state's National Forests. Now the Wilderness Society is developing additional programs; and in northern Arizona, Forest Watch is working hand in hand with an Adopt-a-Timber Sale program, set up by Sharon Galbreath of the Sierra Club.

Forest Watch and Adopt-A-Timber Sale give abundant help to Arizonans wanting to join in their effort. They have offered a conference, workshops, and field trips; they also guide individuals and groups in choosing specific sites to defend. Nevertheless, people in other states need not wait for an organized local program to become active.

Most timber sales are arranged by the offices of Ranger Districts. To identify the Ranger District that controls a given area, contact the supervisor of the National Forest in which the area lies. Ask the Ranger District office for all written materials on timber sales in that section: notices of public meetings, scoping documents, environmental impact statements, decision notices. Walk over your chosen area until you are thoroughly familiar with it. Invite a Forest Service employee to accompany you on one of your visits and to point out what has been planned. Then attend meetings and speak up. Usually the only people at meetings on timber sales are representatives of the Forest Service and logging interests. Sometimes Forest Service employees are pleased to hear from conservationists.

John Wright (address above) will send at no charge copies of instructional materials he has on hand, including a list of timber terms, a checklist of issues to raise about timber sales, and how to respond to scoping documents. He is in the process of putting together a Forest Watch handbook that will be made available to the public. The Wilderness Society already publishes *How to Appeal a Forest Service Decision* ($3 from the national office), which tells how to appeal a timber sale that the Forest Service has already authorized.

To obtain directions to forest areas in Arizona that have been or are being protected by Forest Watch and Adopt-A-Timber Sale or to get into touch with their protectors, contact John Wright or Sharon Galbreath, Plateau Group of the Sierra Club, Box 15, Flagstaff, Arizona 86002 (602-774-1571). Near Heber in the Heber Ranger District of Apache Sitgreaves National Forest two people caused the Forest Service to cut back sales from a planned 10 million board feet to 2.8 million board feet. The forests around Flagstaff are being heavily logged, and virtually every timber sale in the area has been adopted. As a result, the Forest Service's timber selling process is strained nearly to the breaking point there.

ANIMALS

FRATERCULA FUND OF THE NATIONAL AUDUBON SOCIETY
Winter: 159 Sapsucker Woods Road
Ithaca, New York 14850
607-257-7308
Summer: Keene Neck Road
Medomak, Maine 04551
207-529-5828

At Eastern Egg Rock Island (Audubon's Allan D. Cruickshank Wildlife Sanctuary) and the Seal Island National Wildlife Refuge the National Audubon Society is pioneering the transplanting of seabirds.

By 1900 hunters had nearly eliminated the Atlantic puffin from islands off the coast of Maine, their southernmost nesting areas. Under the leadership of Dr. Stephen Kress and in cooperation with the Canadian Wildlife Service, Audubon workers transported chicks from Newfoundland to Eastern Egg Rock, where they were hand-fed in artificial burrows and, when fledged, banded and released. After the puffins had spent their normal two to three years at sea, the Audubon workers lured them back to Eastern Egg Rock to nest, with decoys and tape recordings of terns and Storm petrels. As early as 1987 sixteen of eighteen breeding pairs on the island raised a chick each. Kress is now attempting to reestablish the birds at Seal Island. In the summer of 1990 fifty-two pairs of transplanted puffins returned to Seal Island.

Kress is also testing his seabird restoration methods with different species by working to bring back the Arctic and Endangered Roseate terns to Eastern Egg Rock and Seal Island. In 1990 the Egg Rock tern colony numbered 1,200 pairs of Arctic and Common terns, and thirty-eight pairs of Roseate terns. On Seal Island there were 270 pairs of Arctic terns in mid-1990.

The best time to see the Atlantic puffins is mid-June, July, and the first week of August. Only one island with the puffins can be visited, Machias Seal Island, 12 miles off Cutler, and visits there are not always possible because of the number of people and difficult landing conditions.

Birds on Matinicus Rock and Eastern Egg Rock can be seen from tour boats. An Audubon Society naturalist narrates the tours to Eastern Egg Rock.

For information in the summer on transportation to or near the islands contact the Fratercula Fund at the Maine address.

BAT CONSERVATION INTERNATIONAL
P.O. Box 162603
Austin, Texas 78716
512-327-9721

The world's largest bat colonies are formed by Mexican Free-Tail bats, and the largest North American urban colony of these bats lives from spring to fall in the city that is headquarters for Bat Conservation International. The Mexican Free-Tails winter in central Mexico. By mid-summer 700,000 of them congregate beneath the Congress Avenue Bridge in Austin. To see the bats, be near the bridge when they depart for their evening feeding, usually fifteen to thirty minutes after sunset. The bats fly south under the bridge and then stream eastward. In summer and early fall they eat 14,000 pounds of insects each evening.

Bat Conservation International does yeoman's service in campaigning for the preservation of bats, which are misunderstood, unappreciated, and endangered across the world. Of the approximately 4,000 species of mammals, some 950 or almost one-fourth, are bats. They perform invaluable service pollinating plants, spreading seeds, and devouring insects, yet humans kill countless numbers of them. The bat population is in dangerous decline throughout the world. In 1963 a cave in Arizona housed the world's largest known bat colony, some 30 million Mexican Free-tailed Bats that ate an estimated 350,000 pounds of insects nightly. Within six years the colony was down to

30,000, a reduction of 99.9%, in large part because people fired guns at the roosting bats.

A large part of Bat Conservation's efforts are educational. People wishing to spread the word in their local area can obtain materials from the society.

POINT DEFIANCE ZOO AND AQUARIUM
5400 North Pearl Street
Tacoma, Washington 98407
206-591-5337

Breeding wild animals in captivity is a controversial preservation technique, largely because putting animals in zoos to save them may simply be a way of avoiding doing what is necessary to preserve the species: saving its habitat. Nevertheless, some captive breeding programs are producing positive results, among them the Red wolf program. The Point Defiance Zoo manages this effort in cooperation with the U.S. Fish and Wildlife Service.

The original captive breeding stock was fourteen animals certified as pure Red wolves. (Coyotes apparently interbred with some of the last wild Red wolves.) The last Red wolf known to exist in the wild had been captured in 1980. By early 1990, ninety-seven Red wolves were in captivity, and fourteen were in the wild at Alligator Wildlife Refuge in North Carolina and other selected areas. Sixteen zoos were cooperating in the species survival plan, although forty of the wolves were in the Point Defiance center.

The breeding center belonging to Point Defiance Zoo is 30 miles from Tacoma; but a few pairs of the Red wolves at this center are rotated to the zoo where they can be seen.

The zoo's theme is the Pacific Rim, animals from the volcanic countries bordering the Pacific Ocean. Exhibits include Rocky Shores built to replicate an area near Cape Flattery, Washington, with Pacific walrus, White whales, Sea otters, and puffins, among other animals; and the Pacific Rim Aquarium with an extensive collection of marine invertebrates from the Pacific Northwest.

The Zoo and Aquarium are open from 10:00 A.M.-7:00 P.M. daily in summer; 10:00 A.M.-4:00 P.M. in winter. Admission is $5.50.

WOLF HAVEN
3111 Offut Lake Road
Tenino, Washington 98589
206-264-4695

Wolf Haven has given wooded enclosures on a 65-acre sanctuary to more than forty captive wolves desperately in need of homes. The staff uses these wolves to educate people. It gives tours of the sanctuary, provides programs for schools and civic and professional groups, and publishes a newsletter. In addition, the organization encourages and supports scientific research that will further wolf preservation. For example, it has trained field biologists from several states to recognize signs of wolf and coyote, and it has created a volunteer wolf howling brigade that, on summer weekends, carries out howling surveys in the Cascade mountains to provide needed evidence of the presence of wolves.

Wolf Haven holds hourly tours May-Sep. 10:00 A.M.-5:00 P.M. daily (the last tour starts at 4:00 P.M.); Oct.-April, Wed.-Sun. only, 10:00 A.M.-4:00 P.M. The charge is $5. It holds Howl-Ins May-Sep., Fri. and Sat., 7:00–9:30 P.M. They include a tour, musicians, storytelling, a campfire with a marshmallow roast, and howling with the wolves. The charge is $6.

ARIZONA-SONORA DESERT MUSEUM
2021 North Kinney Road
Tucson, Arizona 85743
602-883-1380

The Arizona-Sonora Desert Museum has as its theme caring about and effectively communicating the totality of the Sonoran desert—from its diverse water and sea life to its mountain ranges. One of its activities is therefore trying to save the many desert animals who are vulnerable to extinction. It breeds the endangered Mexican Gray wolf, and is assisting in saving the endangered Desert pupfish, Sonoran chub, and Gila topminnow among other fishes. It is also breeding the endangered Thick-Billed parrot for reintroduction to its home in Arizona's Chiricahua Mountains. (The Thick-Billed parrot survives in diminished numbers in Sonora, Mexico, and was recently reintroduced by the Fish and Wildlife Service to the Chiricahuas.) These species can be seen at the museum.

Here visitors can observe animals and plants alive in their desert setting and can visit a geological interpretive center that tells the story of the Earth's evolution. The museum operates an outstanding educational program with opportunities ranging from a childrens' toadwatch at desert rain pools to a traditional Saguaro harvest.

The museum opened in 1952, the year that Joseph Wood Krutch (1893–1970) moved to Tucson. Krutch had been a drama critic and professor of English literature in the East. After moving to Arizona, he became an ardent conservationist and the author of essays on the desert, which were respected for both their accuracy and literary quality. His books include *The Desert Year* (1952) and *The Voice of the Desert* (1955), both published by William Sloane Associates. He served on the Board of Directors of the museum through which he influenced some of its early decisions.

The museum is open every day of the year from 8:30 A.M.-5:00 P.M., but has expanded hours in the summer (7:30 A.M.-6:00 P.M.). Visitors are advised to come early in the day when the animals are most active and the number of visitors at a minimum. Admission is $6.

XERXES SOCIETY
10 Southwest Ash Street
Portland, Oregon 97204
503-222-2788

The Xerxes Society is an international organization devoted to protecting threatened and endangered invertebrates and their habitat. Monarch butterfly protection is one of its major projects.

Each fall the entire population of Monarchs west of the Rockies migrates to the California coast, to land that is expensive real estate; and to Mexico, to sites imperiled by deforestation, village growth, and tourism. A decrease in the number of milkweed plants in the United States is reducing the number of butterflies, because the Monarch caterpillars feed only on these plants. The society is trying to protect wintering sites and to learn more about migration routes, wintering patterns, and milkweed. Volunteers are needed to participate July 4th in a butterfly count across the nation. No prior experience with butterflies is necessary.

Readers who simply want to see the Monarchs at a migration site can find thousands of the butterflies from about mid-October through February at Natural Bridges State Beach on West Cliff Drive in Santa Cruz (408-423-4609). Take care not to disturb them.

Gardeners who would like to attract and thus to assist butterflies should order from the Xerxes Society the book, *Butterfly Gardening* (for non-members, $18.95 plus $2.50 shipping).

BAY AREA MOUNTAIN WATCH, SAVE SAN BRUNO MOUNTAIN

P.O. Box BJ
Brisbane, California 94005
415-589-3423

San Bruno Mountain, 4 miles long and 1,300 feet high, is probably the largest natural area adjacent to a major U.S. city and certainly the only remnant of a unique life zone that covered the hills of San Francisco and ended at the southern extension of the mountain.

The unique characteristics of the life zone result in large part from a year-long air pattern. Warm air rising from the valley pulls in cold, wet Pacific air. Where the full force of the cold air makes itself felt, there is a treeless landscape in which Ice Age plants have survived and endemic coastal scrub plants have evolved. In sheltered ravines, on the other hand, rain causes exuberant sub-tropical growth.

The mountain hosts nine plants that the California Native Plant Society has listed as rare and endangered. Three federally listed Endangered animal species inhabit the mountain: the Mission Blue butterfly, the San Bruno Elfin butterfly, and the San Francisco Garter snake. Two other butterflies and a moth are candidates for listing as endangered. The mountain also harbors human treasures – village sites of the Ah-wash-tes Indian tribelet.

Bay Area Mountain Watch is pressing to preserve 850 acres of land adjacent to the existing 2,063-acre mountain park. Whatever the outcome, it will be too late to save the mountain in its entirety, as development is already taking place.

San Bruno was the first site for which developers used a Habitat Conservation Plan (HCP) under a 1982 amendment to the Endangered Species Act, to circumvent the act's prohibition against "taking" endangered species. According to the HCP agreed upon by the developers and the U.S. Fish and Wildlife Service, a 2,700 acre public parkland was to be designated, some of it on land donated by the builder. The builder could destroy habitat on 500 other acres in return for paying for habitat improvements within the park.

Bay Area Mountain Watch points out serious flaws with the HCP: 1) the study on which the HCP was based covered only two seasons and involved only the two endangered butterflies, 2) there is no proof that blue lupines upon which the caterpillars of the Mission Blues depend, will long survive on the land on which they are being replanted, and 3) the firm that made the study on which the HCP was based is now being paid to carry out the mitigation measures.

The environmental group's battle to save the mountains includes lobbying, public education, and research. It offers free nature hikes on the mountain (call 415-589-3423). The mountain provides a fine introduction to the San Francisco Bay area from an ecological perspective, as it offers a splendid view of the whole region.

NEW ENGLAND AQUARIUM
Central Wharf
Boston, Massachusetts 02110
617-973-5200

The New England Aquarium is a prime example of an institution involved in saving marine life. The staff's assistance to distressed and injured mammals includes herding shore-bound cetaceans back to sea and collecting and analyzing tissue samples and data. The New England Aquarium along with College of the Atlantic in Maine and Sealand of Cape Cod respond to reports of strandings in Maine, New Hampshire, and Massachusetts. Visitors to the New England Aquarium can see Harbor Seals that came to the facility as orphaned pups from the New England coast frolicking in an outdoor pool. The aquarium building is open Mon.-Wed., Fri. 9:00 A.M.-5:00 P.M., Thur. 9:00 A.M.- 8:00 P.M., Sat., Sun. 9:00 A.M.-6:00 P.M. Admission is $7.50.

If you find a beached animal – seal or Sea lion, dolphin, whale, manatee, or Sea otter – do not touch it or interfere with it. Under the Marine Mammal Protection Act and Endangered Species Act, it is illegal to give aid without the guidance of an experienced and authorized expert. Identify the animal as accurately as possible and look for obvious problems such as wounds or tangled lines. Then phone the proper authority with your observations as well as the specific location and its accessibility by vehicle. The only proper care is, in the case of a cetacean, to keep the animal's skin moist with seawater.

To identify the stranding network in a given area or for further information on strandings contact one of the following services (Northeast and Southeast are divided at the Virginia/North Carolina border; Northwest and Southwest are divided at the northern border of California):

Stranding Coordinator
New England Aquarium
Central Wharf
Boston, Massachusetts 02110
617-973-5247 (24-hour reporting number)

Regional Stranding Coordinator, Dr. Daniel K. Odell
Sea World
7007 Sea World Drive
Orlando, Florida 32821
407-363-2158

Brent Norberg, Stranding Coordinator, NMFS
7600 Sandpoint Way NE, BIN C157600
Seattle, Washington 98115
206-526-6140
    The general public may also call the local office of the Washington State Patrol for Washington beaches, and the Oregon State Police for Oregon beaches. The number of the resource center in Seattle is 206-285-SEAL.

Joe Codaro, Stranding Coordinator, NMFS
300 South Ferry Street
Terminal Island, California 90731
213-514-6665
    Sea Shepherd (P.O. Box 7000S, Redondo Beach, California 90277) has set up a 24-hour hotline (213-543-2888) to receive reports of marine mammals caught in gill nets, as it has boats that enable it to rescue the animals. It will relay information on strandings. Therefore, strandings can be reported through Sea Shepherd when the NMFS office is closed. Southern California is the territory served by the hotline.

CALIFORNIA CENTER FOR WILDLIFE
76 Albert Park Lane
San Rafael, California 94915
415-456-SAVE

The largest native animal rehabilitation clinic in Northern California, the Marin Wildlife Center is dedicated to increasing human under-standing and respect for wildlife as well as to rehabilitating injured animals. Visitors to the ninety-five-year-old church that houses the facility can see non-releasable animals in the courtyard education center, and can watch animals on the way to recovery through one-way windows in outdoor enclosures. There is also an indoor exhibit hall. The staff answers questions on wildlife injuries, species identification, and conservation; they also offer classes and field trips. The center provides emergency and extended care for 4,000 animals a year. All this with one full-time and one part-time wildlife specialist, working with local veterinarians and other experts, and volunteers, who donate a total of 20,000 hours of work a year.

There is apparently no national network to assist wounded birds and land animals. The Wildlife Clinic at the School of Veterinary Medicine of Tufts University treats anything sick or injured that is brought to them; it also serves as a center for treating endangered animals found anywhere in New England (200 Westboro Road, North Grafton, Massachusetts 01536; 508-839-7918).

The best way of finding the nearest rehabilitation center elsewhere is to ask your state fish and game department or a local humane society. Since such an inquiry may not be speedy, people likely to find injured animals should learn where to take them before they have an emergency on their hands.

CHAPTER TWENTY-ONE

Emerging Environmental Movements and Their Projects

Below I describe three contemporary movements of great importance for environmental preservation: the Green movement, bioregionalism, and biocentrism. None at present has huge numbers of adherents, although, as I indicate, many people who do not call themselves bioregionalists share aspects of the bioregional vision, and the same holds true of the Green and biocentric visions. All are growing, and widespread adoption of and action based on the viewpoint of any one of them would go far to ensuring that the planet remains liveable. Their ideals overlap, and some individuals belong to and work for all three movements. The best hope for the future may lie in these and related movements working together. Among the related movements is Social Ecology, which is represented by the Institute for Social Ecology (found in Appendix IV).

THE GREEN MOVEMENT

In the fall 1988 issue of *Greener Times*, Betty Zisk summed up the characteristics of the Greens that set them apart from other movements and attract new members: "the interconnectedness of our views on environmental, economic, peace and social justice, spiritual and other problems," the aspiration to be a "party along with a movement," and "a genuine commitment to participatory democracy."

Various groups in the United States describe themselves as Green, but the largest Green movement consists of the local Green organizations that make up a network called the Committees of Correspondence. The network originated in 1984 at a meeting in St. Paul, Minnesota, where some sixty people came together to discuss unifying, around a new politics, the many Americans working in peace, environmental, and social change movements. The group took the name Committees of Correspondence from the committees set up by town meetings in the eighteenth century to communicate and to coordinate the actions that were to lead to the American Revolution. The fledgling Greens admired the early committees as models of the spirit of freedom, strong local groups, decentralized coordination, and revolutionary spirit.

At the meeting they adopted ten interrelated values to serve as a basis for future discussion. Still central to any consideration of what it means to be Green in the United States, these values are: ecological wisdom, grassroots democracy, personal and social responsibility, nonviolence, decentralization, community-based economics, postpatriarchal values, respect for diversity, global responsibility, and future focus/sustainability.

The Vermont Greens, who belong to the Green Committees of Correspondence, have adopted a twenty-one-point manifesto, which they discuss at length in *Toward a New Politics: A Statement of Principles of the Vermont Greens*. Though the document expresses the views of only one element of the Green Committees of Correspondence, it provides insights into Green values. The booklet is available from the Vermont Greens, P.O. Box 703, White River Junction, Vermont 05001.

The network of Green Committees of Correspondence consists of more than two hundred local groups in more than twenty-five regions. The regional Green Committees each try to send a balanced representation to an Interregional Committee (IC) that meets quarterly at various locations. The IC encourages local and regional organizing, facilitates the exchange of information and the discussion of issues among Greens, and coordinates local and regional activities. To this end it publishes a quarterly newsletter, distributes organizing aids, coordinates a speakers bureau, and plans national Green meetings. The network has established a clearinghouse in Kansas City.

As this guide went to press, the Greens were considering restructuring the movement. A proposal under consideration would bring about major changes including substituting the name, "The Greens (USA)" for "Committees of Correspondence," and creating a Green Council representing regions and Green political parties.

In September 1990, during a Green Gathering in Boulder, Colorado, the Greens ratified a national program that states the movement's positions on specific topics. The program, which advocates, among other things, the complete phaseout of nuclear power, an end to the use of "pesticide poisons," and a 75% decrease in the military budget, was formulated through a lengthy process involving local groups.

In Europe the Greens engage in politics at the national level. They have been able to attain national political power in many countries, in part because of proportional representation: seats in the national parliament are divided among the parties that receive more than a fixed percentage of the vote (as low as 5%), according to the percentage of votes each party receives.

The United States, with its Congressional seats going to the candidates receiving a majority of the votes in their respective districts, and losers losing completely whether they win 1% or 49% of the vote, is not so kind to alternative parties. The Democratic Socialists of America (formed in 1981 through the merger of the Democratic Socialist Organizing Committee [DSOC] and the New American Movement), while not a political party, have members in the House of Representatives: Ron Dellums (D., California) and Major Owens (D., New York); but the Citizens Party (created in 1980) is fading from sight. American Greens want to become a political force, but many see little hope of winning seats in Congress in the near future, let alone the Presidency.

At the state level Greens in several parts of the country are politically active. The Greens in California voted in February 1990 to form a Green party of California, as sixty delegates from around the state reached consensus on working to get ballot status before 1992. Greens in Michigan are also forming a state party, as are Greens in Texas. The first Green party to receive official recognition by the state in which it is located is the Alaska party. It qualified for state recognition by winning more than 3% of the vote in the 1990 Alaska governor's race.

Building "a grassroots democracy from the bottom up," some local Green groups have already run or supported candidates for public office. The Prairie Greens in Kansas ran a candidate for the state legislature in 1988. In Hartford, Connecticut, in 1987 two out of three candidates on the independent slate, People for a Change, supported by the Greens, were elected to the City Council; and in New Haven, Connecticut, Toni Harp, an independent Green/Democrat, is a member of the Board of Aldermen.

Frank K. Koehn of Wisconsin's Lake Superior Greens was elected to the Bayfield County Board of Supervisors in 1986 and reelected in 1988. There he serves as chair of two county committees and as vice chair of another.

The Greens also engage in campaigns to make government more

responsible to the electorate. Vermont Greens in 1988 defeated a proposal to extend the terms of statewide elected officials from two to four years. In San Francisco, Greens have participated in a coalition to restore district, as opposed to city-wide, elections for city supervisors. In Austin, Texas, Greens are working with other progressive groups to change the city charter to establish proportional representation for the City Council.

Other types of projects of local Green groups include recycling (Houston-Galveston Bay, Texas); protesting the use of styrofoam in fast food establishments (Madison, Wisconsin); and securing the cancellation of a proposed development next to a wetland at the mouth of the Winooski River, and pushing to make the whole wetland area a wildlife refuge (Burlington, Vermont).

The American Friends Service Committee office in St. Petersburg has promoted the Green movement in Florida. The staff has a good collection of Green literature and periodicals, which they are glad to share with people who come to the office (130 19th Ave. SE, St. Petersburg, Florida 33705; 813-822-5522). Please call for an appointment.

Nemaste Greens organize living green summer camps (April through November): "natural farming, soil building, tree planting, gardening, naturism, synergies and celebrations." People wishing to participate should contact Nemaste Greens, Route 2, Box 578, Barnstead, New Hampshire 03225 (603-776-7776).

For a balanced, well-written introduction to the Green movement, read Brian Tokar's *The Green Alternative: Creating an Ecological Future* (R. & E. Miles, 1987). To obtain current news of the Greens subscribe to *Green Letter* (available for the cost of a donation to the Tides Foundation/Green Letter, c/o *Green Letter* at P.O. Box 14141, San Francisco, California 94114).

To find the Committee of Correspondence nearest you contact the Green Committees of Correspondence Clearinghouse, P.O. Box 30208, Kansas City, Missouri 64112 (816-931-9366).

BIOREGIONALISM

The Irish poet George Russell (A.E.) wrote during the Irish revolution: "I believe our best wisdom does not come from without, but arises in the soul and is an emanation of the Earth spirit, a voice speaking directly to us as dwellers in this land." Kirkpatrick Sale, author of *Dwellers in the Land: The Bioregional Vision*, quotes this passage and adds "the alternative to the peril the industrio-scientific paradigm has placed us in . . . is simply to become dwellers in the land" (Sierra Club Books, 1985).

Members of the bioregional movement try "to become dwellers in the land," in other words, "to re-inhabit the land" or "live in place," and they would have others do the same. Dwelling in the land means understanding the ecosystem where you live and understanding the place of humans in that ecosystem. Dwellers in the land are familiar with the plants, animals, waters, soils, climate, and other natural elements of their regions and live in harmony with them. They also value human cultures of the area, try to learn about and preserve past traditions, and work to strengthen current practices that link people to each other and to the land.

Bioregionalists believe that the present division of the planet into nations, states, and counties is artificial. They would loosely divide it into bioregions based on characteristics of the land and of human cultures, which, until recent centuries, were in large measure shaped by the land. Bioregions differ greatly in size, with the smaller fitting into the larger. The largest bioregional unit is the ecoregion, the Sonoran Desert, for example. Ecoregions are divided into georegions, each distinguished by a physical feature such as a mountain range or river. Some georegions can be further divided into morphoregions identified by special landforms and by human developments resulting from the land forms. Sale notes that such a system corresponds to American Indian traditions. The tribe corresponds to the ecoregion; the subtribe to the georegion.

The concept of bioregionalism goes back to indigenous gatherer/hunters. They "developed specific ways to be" in the niches they inhabited, as Gary Snyder describes in *The Old Ways*. The twentieth-century form of bioregionalism originated in the seventies with Peter Berg and Raymond Dasmann and their colleagues at Planet Drum. Today more than eighty organizations in the United States and other parts of the world characterize themselves as bioregional. Their members have met in four North American Bioregional Congresses (NABCs), the first of which took place in May 1984, northeast of Kansas City. At NABC IV in Maine in 1990, the Congress changed its name to the Turtle Island Bioregional Congress. The new name reflects Indian tradition.

Many of the organizations that describe themselves as bioregional do not represent clearly defined bioregions. Such organizations may be working toward defining a bioregion or may simply be learning how to re-inhabit their own land. No map dividing into bioregions all of North America has yet been published. Bioregions will be defined when people living in them come to see themselves and their area as a unit, and this will happen only gradually.

Three bioregions that are already quite clearly delimited are the Ish bioregion (northern Washington and southwest British Columbia), which hosted NABC III in August 1988, the Ozarks (southern Missouri, northern Arkansas, and corners of Kansas and Oklahoma), and Katuah (the southern Appalachian mountains).

The quarterly *Katuah Journal* is helping to make the Katuah bioregion aware of its natural and cultural heritage. The boundaries of this area, named "Katuah" by the Cherokees, are "the Roanoke River Valley to the north; the foothills of the Piedmont area to the east; Yona Mountain and the Georgia hills to the south; and the Tennessee River Valley to the west." Readers wanting to understand the concept of a bioregion, whether or not they are from Katuah, could scarcely do better than subscribe to this handsome publication, which frequently includes descriptions of places open to visitors. The journal's goals include being "a support system for those accepting the challenge of sustainability and the creation of harmony and balance in a total sense, here in this place" (Box 638, Leicester, North Carolina 28748; 704-683-1414).

The Ozark Area Community Congress (OACC) organized the first North American Bioregional Congress. Since October 1980 the OACC itself has convened yearly. The Ozark Resource Center in this bioregion serves people across the country, as it provides general information and organizational help, and can refer questioners to sources of more specialized information (Box 3, Brixey, Missouri 65618; 417-679-4773). The Resource Center sponsors the:

OZARK BENEFICIAL PLANT PROJECT

c/o Steven Foster, Project Research Director
P.O. Box 106
Eureka Springs, Arkansas 72632
501-253-7309

The Plant Project includes an Indigenous Plant Development Program to gather and disseminate information on the economic potential of native Ozark herbs and commonly traded medicinal plants, and an Echinacea Program to stimulate commercial cultivation of Purple coneflowers, which are used for medicinal purposes. Readers interested in seeing small organic herb operations may contact Steven Foster. Serious researchers may use an economic botany library that he owns.

The Turtle Island Office acts as a national clearinghouse to connect people and to give basic bioregional information (P.O. Box 140826, Dallas, Texas 75214). Kirkpatrick Sale, a member of the Hudson Bioregional Council, sells for $4 postpaid a bioregional bibliography (Kirkpatrick Sale, 113 West 11th Street, New York, NY 10011).

The Turtle Island Bioregional Congress's Education Committee, coordinated by Frank Traina, is publishing twice a year *Pollen: Journal of Bioregional Education*. For teachers and bioregionalists, its subject is education dealing with the Earth. Two-year subscriptions are $12 from Frank Traina, Sunrock Farm, 103 Gibson Lane, Wilder, Kentucky 41076.

Planet Drum publishes a semi-annual periodical *Raise the Stakes* (available with a $15 membership), which includes essays on bioregionalism and occasionally a directory of organizations in the bioregional network. The directory, published in 1989, costs $6 postpaid. At Planet Drum's office is an archive of journals that relate ecological thinking to society, politics and culture. The archive is open to members or by appointment (Box 31251, San Francisco, California 94131; 415-285-6556).

Organizations that consider themselves bioregional do not always use the term "bioregionalism" when they are working with the general public, because practical guidance may be a more effective incentive than theory. Furthermore, not all the activities that can be characterized as bioregional are carried out by organizations that link themselves to the bioregional movement, as is illustrated by watershed restoration and preservation projects.

MATTOLE RESTORATION COUNCIL
P.O. Box 160
Petrolia, California 95558

The Mattole Restoration Council is engaged in a classic bioregional effort, often cited as a model for other areas of the country.

A community based, non-profit organization, the Council works to retain and restore natural systems within the Mattole Watershed to health and productivity. Its activities mesh with those of the Mattole Watershed Salmon Support Group, another bioregional organization.

By the 1970s the salmon were dying out in the Mattole River, as silt loosed by clearcutting buried their eggs. Activists have since begun to restore the salmon by catching them as they return to the river to spawn, incubating their eggs, and releasing the fry into the river. By using the eggs from Mattole fish, they are preserving the strain of King Salmon adapted to the river. They are working to stop the source of the siltation by planting trees; preserving trees already in place, in particular those that can be characterized as old growth; building small dams in the river; and repairing the banks. They also engage in public education, as a result of which salmon spawning is becoming an increasingly important part of the valley's culture.

An example of the Mattole Restoration Council's work that can be seen with ease is hand-placed riprap along the headwaters of the Mattole River, upstream of Whitethorn, California, on the county road that leads to Sinkyone Wilderness State Park. Usually riprap—rock to keep a bank from tumbling into a stream—is installed with heavy machinery. This riprap was put in place with a backhoe and a lot of handwork by local people. Every rock, in fact, was placed by hand. Thus, the attractive banks are a source of community pride in the region.

The Restoration Council publishes the *Mattole Restoration Newsletter* and *Elements of Recovery: An Inventory of Upslope Sources of Sedimentation in the Mattole River Watershed with Rehabilitation Prescriptions . . . .* The newsletter is sent to Friends of the Mattole and members of the Restoration Council. *Elements of Recovery* is available for $3 plus postage from the Council.

Other types of organizations may also build broad programs around rivers:

NASHUA RIVER WATERSHED ASSOCIATION
348 Lunenburg Street
Fitchburg, Massachusetts 01420
508-342-3506

In the early 1960s the Nashua River was one of the ten most polluted rivers in the United States. Under the leadership of Marion Stoddart, the Nashua River Cleanup Campaign was founded in 1966, as well as the Nashua River Watershed Association, an outgrowth of the campaign, in 1969. Their efforts succeeded. Today the Massachusetts Department of Environmental Management calls the Nashua a "scenic river." Osprey, Bald eagles, Great Blue herons, and mergansers fish in the river for bass, perch, and pickerel. Cyclists, hikers, birders, and cross country skiers frequent what is now the Nashua River Greenway, comprising 6,000 acres of protected land along nearly 70 miles of shoreline.

The work in the watershed nevertheless continues. The Monoosnoc Brook Greenway Coalition is cleaning up the Monoosnoc Brook, a tributary of the Nashua, and trying to establish a greenway and series of walking trails along the banks. To date nearly 1/2 mile of finished trail exists. The association is still enlarging the Nashua River Greenway, and volunteers monitor acid precipitation.

The Watershed Association publishes a canoe guide to the Nashua River and its tributaries ($6 including postage) and a Greenway Guide ($9 including postage). The office is open from 8:30 A.M.-4:30 P.M. Mon.-Fri. People are welcome to visit to discuss environmental issues or to look through the library of technical publications and slides.

HUDSON RIVER SLOOP CLEARWATER
112 Market Street
Poughkeepsie, New York 12601
914-454-7673

Founded in 1966 Clearwater is dedicated to the restoration and protection of the Hudson River and similar waterways. Over 11,000 members own and operate the 106-foot sloop *Clearwater*, a replica of the Dutch sloops that carried cargo on the Hudson in the eighteenth and nineteenth centuries.

The *Clearwater* sails the Hudson River from April to November. She picks up groups of students and of adults for on-board classes and voyages and leads waterfront festivals and on-shore educational events. Meanwhile, the association's on-shore staff works on waterway topics in traditional ways like filing suits; residents brought together by the sloop form sloop clubs to act on local issues.

The Clearwater Great Hudson River Revival is held during the third week in June at Westchester County Community College. Music has always played an important role in Clearwater—folk singer Pete Seeger was one of its founders—and the festival features singers, dancers, and storytellers from many parts of the world.

Clearwater needs a multitude of volunteers. To become involved call the office.

THE RIVER PROJECT
67 Vestry Street
New York, New York 10013
212-431-5787

The River Project was incorporated in 1987 to establish an oceano-graphic monitoring station in the lower Hudson estuary. Work at the station is in full swing, and the Project has undertaken new programs.

The field station, where the Project works with scientists from several institutions, is at Pier 26 North River, just north of Battery Park City. This station is one of two sites where the Project has undertaken wetland plantings. The other is the Socrates Sculpture Garden, Long Island City. The Project plans an Ecological Reserve Park on the Tribeca waterfront. It operates an education program for "at-risk" chil-dren, and produces community boating and fishing events to teach the importance of the aquatic habitat and wildlife. At Pier 26 it has a Downtown Boat Club, which serves as a center for hand-powered boat-ing in the New York/New Jersey Harbor area. "Members with proven abilities" can store and launch hand-powered boats there. Membership is open to the public.

Botanical gardens, museums, and aquariums that concentrate on lo-cal plants and animals reflect the bioregional point of view, whether or not their directors are aware of the bioregional movement. A sampling of these institutions, many of which need volunteers, follows. (People considering visiting aquariums and also zoos should inquire whether the animals were obtained by capturing individuals in the wild.)

GARDEN IN THE WOODS
Hemenway Road
Framingham, Massachusetts 01701
508-877-6574

On this 45-acre rolling terrain surrounded by woods, 1,500 species and varieties of native American plants plus some exotics grow. The em-phasis is on New England native flowers. Two-thirds of the land is a natural area. The remaining third contains a series of special gardens including a lily pond and rock garden. Open 16 April-31 Oct., Tue.-Sun. 9:00 A.M.-4:00 P.M. Admission is $5.

BROOKLYN BOTANIC GARDEN
1000 Washington Avenue
Brooklyn, New York 11225
718-622-4433

Within the Botanic Garden's 50 acres is a Local Flora Section representing eight distinct ecosystems. Open, Tue.- Fri. 8:00 A.M.-4:30 or 6:00 P.M., Sat.-Sun. and holidays 10:00 A.M.-4:30 or 6:00 P.M. Admission is free.

The garden publishes and sells *American Gardens: A Traveler's Guide* listing 250 gardens throughout the United States open to visitors. It costs $5.95 plus $3.25 shipping.

The Garden's former Research Center in Westchester County has become Kitchawan Preserve, thanks to the efforts of local land trusts and the Trust for Public Land.

NATIONAL ARBORETUM
Entrances at 3501 New York Avenue; 24th and R Streets; the end
    of Maryland Avenue
Washington, DC
202-475-4815

In the middle of the 444-acre National Arboretum is a natural valley through which a spring-fed stream flows. Fern Valley, as it is called, is comprised of approximately 4 acres of woodland and 2.5 acres of meadow. Volunteers and staff have planted in the valley thousands of ferns, wildflowers, shrubs, and trees. Most are native to Eastern North America, though unfortunately a few were introduced from other countries and became naturalized. Several distinct habitats have been created, including the Piedmont, the southern highlands, and the southern lowlands.

At the arboretum, which is directed by the U.S. Department of Agriculture and its Agricultural Research Service, 330 acres of climax Eastern deciduous forest comprise the dominant landscape.

The grounds are open weekdays 8:00 A.M.-5:00 P.M., weekends and holidays 10:00 A.M.-5:00 P.M. Admission is free.

BOWMAN'S HILL STATE WILDFLOWER PRESERVE
Washington Crossing Historic Park
P.O. Box 103, Route 32
Washington Crossing, Pennsylvania 18977
215-862-2924

The 100-acre preserve in the northern section of Washington Crossing Park was founded in 1934 to conserve Pennsylvania's native plants. The preserve includes Penn's Woods, Pennsylvania's first reforestation program, which began in 1944 and covers 9 acres. The visitor center with a museum is open Mon.-Sat. 9:00 A.M.-5:00 P.M., and Sun. noon-5:00 P.M. Admission is free, but a small charge is made for a family nature walk at 2:00 P.M. daily. The grounds are open 8:30 A.M.-sunset daily.

NORTH CAROLINA BOTANICAL GARDEN
Box 3375, Totten Center, University of North Carolina
Chapel Hill, North Carolina 27599
919-962-0522

At the visitor area on Laurel Hill Road, southeastern plants are arranged by habitat. Visitors can walk from a Mountain Habitat, through Piedmont Forest to Sandhill Habitats, to a Coastal Plain. The visitor area is open Mon.-Fri. 8:00 A.M.-5:00 P.M. all year except winter holidays, and from mid-March to mid-Nov. Sat. 10:00 A.M.-5:00 P.M. and Sun. 2:00-5:00 P.M. The Garden offers a one-hour introductory tour of the visitor area from mid-March to mid-Nov. Sat. at 10:30 A.M. and Sun. at 3:00 P.M.

An aim of the Botanical Garden, which is administered by the University of North Carolina at Chapel Hill, is the preservation of North Carolina plants. The 352-acre Mason Farm Biological Reserve, open to members of the public only by special permission, contains diverse native plant communities.

FAIRCHILD TROPICAL GARDEN
10901 Old Cutler Road
Miami, Florida 33156
305-667-1651

In this 83-acre garden, plants indigenous to South Florida, the Florida Keys, and the Bahamas grow in areas simulating their native habitats. For example, a Mangrove Preserve contains Red, White, and Black

Mangroves, which were on the lowland before the garden was created. Also of special interest, though not limited to Florida plants, are the Montgomery Palmetum, with five hundred species of palms; the cycads scattered through the upland area of the garden; and a simulated rain forest.

The garden is open daily 9:30 A.M.-4:30 P.M. Admission is $5.

SANTA BARBARA BOTANIC GARDEN
1212 Mission Canyon Road
Santa Barbara, California 93105
805-682-4726

The Garden, which is devoted entirely to the study of California's native flora, covers 65 acres along Mission Creek. The plants grow in ten settings, including an Arroyo Section; a Canyon Section with plants native to the borders of Mission Creek; a Desert Section; a Redwood Section; and an Island Section with plants from the California islands.

The garden is open from 8:00 A.M.-sunset daily. It offers educational activities. The admission charge for nonmembers is $3, except Tues. and Wed. when admission is free.

A Garden Grower's Nursery sells to the public native California plants and drought-resistant plants from other places Tues., Thurs., Fri., Sat. 10:00 A.M.-3:00 P.M., Sun. 11:00 A.M.-3:00 P.M. A Master Gardener Helpline, 805-682-0988, answers questions Mon. 1:00-4:00 P.M., Wed. 9:00 A.M.-1:00 P.M., Fri. 1:00-4:00 P.M., Sat. 10:00 A.M.-3:00 P.M.

MONTEREY BAY AQUARIUM
886 Cannery Row
Monterey, California 93940
408-649-6466

The goal of the aquarium is to increase understanding of the Monterey Bay marine environment. The major exhibits include a forest of giant kelp (*Macrocystis pyrifera*), Sea otters, the Great Tide Pool, and Monterey Bay Habitats: the open sea, the deep reefs, the sandy sea floor, the shale reefs, and the wharf.

It is open 10:00 A.M.-5:30 P.M. daily. Admission is $8.

THE OAKLAND MUSEUM
1000 Oak Street
Oakland, California 94607
415-273-3884

On the first floor is a 38,000-square-foot gallery of California ecology, arranged as a transect walk across eight biotic zones in the central portion of the state. Visitors pass from the Pacific seashore over the Sierra crest to the desert. For each biotic zone a landscape model gives an eagle's eye view of the topography and vegetation of a representative square mile, and a series of five to six "ecoramas" provides a close-up view of the communities. The museum also includes a Natural Science Changing Gallery for temporary displays on environmental and conservation themes, and a Library of Natural Sounds.

The museum is open Wed.-Sat. 10:00 A.M.-5:00 P.M., and Sun. noon-7:00 P.M. The only charge is for special exhibits.

THE WAIKIKI AQUARIUM
2777 Kalakaua Avenue
Honolulu, Hawaii 96815
808-923-9741

The Waikiki Aquarium is a fine place for visitors to Hawaii to acquaint themselves with the islands' flora and fauna. Founded in 1904 it is the third-oldest aquarium in the United States and is affiliated with the University of Hawaii. The exhibits focus on the marine life of the Hawaiian Islands and the South Pacific. Among them is a collection of artifacts, etchings, and scale models illustrating the ocean's role in Hawaii's early culture. The grounds of the aquarium are landscaped in native Hawaiian coastal flora.

Open daily 9:00 A.M.-5:00 P.M. Admission is a $2.50 donation.

Federal law is now compelling state highway departments to use 0.25% of federal highway funds for landscaping with wildflowers. Florida and Illinois are examples of longstanding programs and Louisiana of a new program for promoting native flowers along highways. A National Wildflower Research Center assists highway departments, among others, in their use of native plants.

NATIONAL WILDLFLOWER RESEARCH CENTER
2600 FM 973 North
Austin, Texas 78725
512-929-3600

"Using wildflowers and native plants helps to ensure the continued survival and balance of ecological systems unique to a particular area," this center points out. Established in 1982 with gifts of money and land from Lady Bird Johnson, it is dedicated to the preservation, propagation, and increased use of wildflowers and other native plants for their economic, environmental, and aesthetic benefits. The center conducts research and educates the public, in part through a clearinghouse, which responds to requests for information and distributes fact sheets on each state.

The center allows visitors to take self-guided tours of the landscape plantings, test plots, and a reconstructed prairie with more than 100 species of grasses and wildflowers, Mon.-Fri. 9:00 A.M.-4:00 P.M.; plus, from early April to early May only, Sat. and Sun. 10:00 A.M.-4:00 P.M. To obtain information about membership, wildflowers, and native plants, send a mailing label and $2 for postage and handling to the clearinghouse at the above address.

FLORIDA DEPARTMENT OF TRANSPORTATION
605 Suwannee Street
Tallahassee, Florida 32399
904-488-2911

Displays of wildflowers in bloom along Florida highways include: March to April, Crimson clover on Interstate 10 from Pensacola to Tallahassee (200 miles); April to May, Annual phlox on Interstate 75 from Tampa (Interstate 275) to the Georgia state line (215 miles); June to August, Blanket flower on A1A from St. Augustine to State Road 201 in Flagler Beach (58 miles); August to December, varieties of coreopsis and goldenrod on US 98 from Panama City County Road 22 to US 19 in Perry (144 miles).

Many of the above displays were not planted by the department, but resulted from years of managing the roadsides specifically for the species mentioned. The best periods are March through May and October through December.

ILLINOIS DEPARTMENT OF TRANSPORTATION
2300 South Dirksen Parkway
Springfield, Illinois 62764

For the past ten years the Illinois Department of Transportation has planted prairie grasses and wildflowers during roadway construction on various sections of the state's highways, including Interstate 474 (Peoria Bypass, around the south and west sides of the city); Interstate 94 (Edens Expressway, on the north side of Chicago); Interstate 55 (Bloomington to Lincoln); Interstate 255 (southeast of St. Louis). As of late 1990 approximately 2,500 acres of Illinois roadsides were seeded to prairie grasses and flowers.

LOUISIANA PROJECT WILDFLOWER
637 Girard Park Drive
Lafayette, Louisiana 70503

In 1987 Louisiana residents involved in successful wildflower planting projects across the state incorporated as Louisiana Project Wildflower. The organization has two long-term programs. The Louisiana Project Wildflower Trace entails dividing the state into districts and letting each district stimulate local planting projects based on a district-wide scheme for the use of particular species. A second project involves seeking and preserving natural stands of wildflowers.

With support from the Project, the Louisiana Department of Transportation is revising its maintenance practices to encourage the growth of wildflowers along highways, and communities are yearly increasing their plantings. Three of the many communities with planting programs are Lafayette, Monroe, and Alexandria. Designated wildflower management areas along highways for 1988–89 were State Roads 28 (Alexandria to Leesville), 118 (near Peason), 112 (west of Sugartown), and 167 (north of Turkey Creek), and Interstate 49 (northwest of Alexandria and south of Opelousas). Native stands of verbena, coreopsis, penstemon and other flowers are returning as the Department of Transportation revises its maintenance practices.

BIOCENTRISM

Biocentrism is closely related to bioregionalism, as adherents to the biocentric view, like adherents to the bioregional movement, regard human beings as members of ecosystems. While bioregionalists emphasize relationships to place, however, biocentrists stress the relationships between humans and wildlife—plants and animals. All are part of a complex web of life; no one aspect, including humans, is more important than the others.

The biocentric point of view has been expressed in the lives of indigenous peoples and in the works of numerous writers, including John Muir. In *A Thousand-Mile Walk to the Gulf* (1916), Muir says, "Now, it never seems to occur to these far-seeing [anthropocentric] teachers that Nature's object in making animals and plants might possibly be first of all the happiness of each one of them, not the creation of all for the happiness of one. . . . And what creature of all that the Lord has taken the pains to make is not essential to the completeness of that unit— the cosmos?"

D. H. Lawrence, the celebrated early twentieth-century British novelist, wrote from a biocentric point of view, which he expressed particularly clearly in an essay "Pan in America" written outside a cabin (still standing) near Taos, New Mexico: "What can a man do with his life but live it? And what does life consist in, save a vivid relatedness between the man and the living universe that surrounds him? Yet man insulates himself more and more into mechanism, and repudiates everything but the machine and the contrivance of which he himself is master, god in the machine" (*Phoenix: The Posthumous Papers*, 1936).

Many people who adhere to the biocentric view call themselves deep ecologists, and the main periodical in the United States expressing the biocentric point of view is *Wild Earth* (P.O. Box 7, Canton, New York 13617; 315-379-9940; $20 a year).

Some deep ecologists believe that destruction of machines or other harmful private property (monkey wrenching), is a valuable tool for achieving environmental aims. From their point of view, life, including that of plants and animals, is sacred; private property is not. This outlook is commonly associated with the Earth First! movement but goes far beyond Earth First!. Henry David Thoreau in an 1849 essay "Salmon, Shad, and Alewives" lamented the fact that fish once abundant in the Concord River could no longer reach their old spawning grounds because of a dam at Billerica (still in existence). "I for one am with thee [shad], and who knows what may avail a crowbar against that Billerica dam?" In parts of Europe and the Third World, ecological sabotage is more common than it is in the United States, although its major literary expressions are two American novels, Edward Abbey's *The*

Monkey Wrench Gang (Avon, 1975) and *Hayduke Lives!* (Little, Brown, 1990).

Biocentrism and also bioregionalism are embodied in Ursula K. LeGuin's utopian vision of the future, *Always Coming Home* (Harper and Row, 1985), set in a valley of the northern Pacific coast, possibly near California's Trinity Alps Wilderness. LeGuin writes of the Kesh, a people who travel outside their valley: their "sense of community, of continuity with the dirt, water, air, and living creatures of the Valley determines them to overcome any ordeals to get home to die; the idea of dying and being buried in foreign lands is black despair." Before a Kesh takes any life, even that of a flower or mosquito, he or she briefly addresses the being that is to die. Uttering a brief formula "maintained and contained the idea of need and fulfillment, demand and response, relationship and interdependence."

Biocentrists regard ritual as a key means of linking people to one another and to the natural world. A powerful reflection of this point of view is the contemporary Council of All Beings. The term is used in two ways: for a one-and-a-half to three-hour ritual in which participants represent other species and for a workshop of one or more days that includes the ritual and activities leading up to and flowing from it. In the workshops the participants mourn for the destruction that humans are inflicting on the environment, remember the rootedness of humans in nature, and finally, losing their human identities, speak from the perspective of other life forms. Out of a deepened sense of identification with the Earth, they experience renewed energy to work for its protection.

Thinking like a Mountain: Towards a Council of All Beings (New Society, 1988), a collection of prose, poetry, and drawings, helps readers to work back into a vital relationship with the Earth and enables them to organize and guide a Council. Two of the co-authors, Australian John Seed and American Joanna Macy, author of *Despair and Personal Power in the Nuclear Age* (New Society, 1983), occasionally conduct Councils in this country. For information contact John Seed, Rainforest Information Centre, POB 368, Lismore, New South Wales 2480, Australia (066-21-85-05).

Three organizations/institutes that represent the biocentric point of view and a program that uses the related term "deep ecology" follow:

ALL SPECIES PROJECTS
804 Apodaca Hill
Santa Fe, New Mexico 87501
505-982-2768

"Beyond human-centered behavior to a healthy biosphere" is the motto of All Species Projects. Its most visible manifestation is All Species Day.

The first All Species Day was held in San Francisco in 1978. Now it is celebrated in some thirty locations, including Greenville, North Carolina, and New York City, where in 1988 a parade took place on Broadway. The celebration in Santa Fe, an annual event since 1982, is the largest.

The Santa Fe project takes six months of preparations, including educational workshops for teachers, parents, and community organizations. "The values we commemorate are nurtured in preparation," organizer Chris Wells says. On the day itself there is a great parade including floats propelled by marchers, cyclists, and solar power; and in Fort Marcy Park, an ecological pageant.

In Santa Fe All Species Day takes place in May; other communities choose their own dates, often also in May. Readers able to volunteer in Santa Fe should contact the above address; in Kansas City contact Heartland All Species Project (816-523-2784).

All Species Projects has established an All Species Foundation which is creating model programs that can be replicated and introduced into school systems and communities throughout the country. The Santa Fe team has published a handbook and is distributing it to schools.

THE TRACKING PROJECT
P.O. Box 266
Corrales, New Mexico 87048
505-898-6967

The Tracking Project, like All Species Projects, works on a broad front. Organizer John Stokes reports that its "program involves teaching survival skills and the art of tracking" but that the "emphasis [is] on the 'arts of life,'—music, story, dance." "In addition to training people in how to live with the natural world, we work with native people in this country and many others, we perform benefit performances for endangered species and natural habitats and we try to network around the globe with others . . . interested in so-called 'deep ecology.' "

The Tracking Project offers programs for children in the schools and for adults. In partnership with Jake and Judy Swamp, the Project presents Tracking the Roots of Peace gatherings for natural and cultural awareness in locations from Hawaii to New York state. During these programs Jake Swamp plants a tree of peace. Under the auspices of the Omega Institute, the Project also offers to the general public tracking trips and classes lasting several days each.

For a list of events contact the Project.

GAIA INSTITUTE
Cathedral of St. John the Divine
1047 Amsterdam Avenue at 112th Street
New York, New York 10025
212-295-1930

The Gaia Institute is devoted to the study of the Gaia hypothesis, which states that "conditions on the surface of the earth are maintained within the bounds of the physiological requirements of organisms by feedback relations between ecological communities and regulative concentrations of gases, solutes and salts in the atmosphere and hydrosphere." The Institute is committed to realizing the goal of the human community to restructure itself in Nature.

The institute "aims to participate in the discovery of fundamental connections between the organic realm and the regulation of global conditions." It presents seminars on the Gaia concept's theoretical and practical ramifications. These seminars are open to the public. Contact the institute for a schedule. To cover expenses the organizers request a donation from those who attend and who can afford to contribute.

The Cathedral of St. John the Divine holds services of particular interest to ecologists. These have included a Blessing of the Animals and a Thanksgiving service of spiritual reconciliation with American Indians. The Paul Winter Consort, celebrated for its environmental music, makes the cathedral its New York home.

In early 1990 the institute began publishing a newsletter. Subscriptions, which include institute membership, are $25.

OUTDOOR LEADERSHIP TRAINING SEMINARS
Breaking Through Adventures
P.O. Box 20281
Denver, Colorado 80220
Toll free number: 800-331-7238

A set of special courses, Breaking Through, draws on a variety of skills as participants experience the relationship between wilderness and personal growth. Dolores LaChapelle—author of *Finn Hill Arts' Earth Wisdom* (1978) and *Sacred Land Sacred Sex—Rapture of the Deep* (1988)—and Rick Medrick, Ed.D., are among the leaders.

In "The Original" Breaking Through and Deep Ecology: Outdoor Celebration and Transformation, participants relive the vision of a time when humans lived in harmony with nature and one another. Through camping, climbing, rafting, and wilderness travel—and through the exploration of myth and ritual—they create a tribal community. Southern Colorado's Sangre de Cristo Range and the Arkansas River provide the vehicle for this endeavor. The many other Breaking Through courses include a Women's Canyon Quest.

Each trip lasts approximately a week and costs $550-$825. For Dolores LaChapelle's Autumn Equinox Taoist Celebration see the Nature Study chapter.

PART V

Outdoor Recreation

CHAPTER TWENTY-TWO

Outdoor Clubs and Associations

Participating in planned programs is a good way to get started in outdoor activities. The organizations listed below each lead a variety of outings. Organizations that emphasize one particular type of activity are described later in the discussion of that activity.

SIERRA CLUB
730 Polk Street
San Francisco, California 94109
415-776-2211

The Sierra Club was founded in 1892 to preserve California's Yosemite Valley and environs. After several years of environmental battles, many members began to lose enthusiasm. To revive interest the group in 1901 organized an outing – a month of excursions with John Muir from a base camp in Tuolumne Valley. The innovation was such a success that the club has been sponsoring outings ever since, and now with half a million members, the Sierra Club is known for both its conservation work and its outdoor activities.

Outings are organized on three levels: national, chapter (chapters usually cover a state), and group. Outings within the United States sponsored at the national level are listed each year in the January/February issue of the club's bimonthly magazine, *Sierra*. Backpacking trips in wilderness areas are the heart of the offering, though there are a variety of other opportunities. The cost per week ranges from a few hundred dollars to over one thousand dollars. For those who want to work in the outdoors, the club offers service trips which are subsidized and therefore less expensive than regular trips. Only club members can go on national outings.

Chapters and groups organize their own trips, usually in their geographic area, and varying in length from a few hours up to weeks. They may open their trips to non-members.

New York State's Atlantic Chapter (217 East 85th Street, Suite 200, New York, New York 10028) organizes a wide variety of free outings open to the public. A three-month schedule, which costs non-members $3, lists and rates the difficulty of the various trips. For a recorded announcement, including information on obtaining the schedule, call 212-749-3740. For activities of the New York City group in particular, call 212-473-7986.

APPALACHIAN MOUNTAIN CLUB (AMC)
5 Joy Street
Boston, Massachusetts 02108
617-523-0636

With almost 39,000 members, the Appalachian Mountain Club is the oldest permanent conservation/outdoor organization in the United States. It was founded in 1876 and served as a model for the Sierra Club in the Club's early years. The AMC organizes trips in the Northeast through its headquarters and through its eleven local chapters, which are scattered from Washington, D.C. to Maine. Hiking trips, using as shelter eight huts owned by the club, form the core of its offering at the national level; but the headquarters also organizes workshops in cycling, canoeing, mountain leadership, and nature lore. Like the Sierra Club, the AMC is involved in trail maintenance. In addition, it uses volunteers for search and rescue teams. Non-members may go on outings. For information on trips organized by the main office and the location of local chapters, contact the club's headquarters.

THE MOUNTAINEERS
300 Third Avenue West
Seattle, Washington 98119
206-6284-6310

Founded in 1906, the Mountaineers is now the third largest conservation/outdoor organization in the United States, with more than 11,000 members. Regularly scheduled activities—all conducted by volunteers—include mountain climbing, hiking, cross-country skiing, cycling, canoeing, sailing, and nature study. It teaches courses in mountain climbing and in skiing. Activities center in the northwestern

United States, but the club also leads trips in foreign countries. Trips are open to non-members who have the necessary skills and stamina.

Every spring since the 1920s the Mountaineers have presented a play in an outdoor theatre in the club's 208-acre Rhododendron Preserve, eight miles west of Bremerton, on the Kitsap Peninsula.

The club has branches in Bellingham, Tacoma, Olympia, and Everett, Washington; but the Seattle office handles registration and car pooling for activities.

AMERICAN YOUTH HOSTELS (AYH)
P.O. Box 37613
Washington, DC 20013
202-783-6161

American Youth Hostels sponsors a wide variety of outings, at the national level and through AYH Councils (regional offices), and, in some cases, individual hostels. The headquarters will provide needed addresses. By joining the association through a local office you will pay the regular membership price but receive future publications of that office at no extra cost. The Ozark Area Council of American Youth Hostels, 7187 Manchester Road, St. Louis, Missouri 63143 (314-644-4660) furnishes information on its numerous hiking and biking trips, for example.

Discovery Tours, sponsored by the national AYH office, are bicycle and hiking tours, some with and some without a van. They last from nine to thirty-eight days, are rated for level of skill, and are usually limited to nine participants and a leader. The cost of twenty-three days of cycling along the California coast is $750; twenty-one days of hiking in Alaska, $1300.

WOODSWOMEN
25 W Diamond Lake Rd.
Minneapolis, Minnesota 55419
612-822-3809

Woodswomen organizes biking, canoeing, skiing, climbing, llama packing, trekking, and sun vacations for women. The majority of the trips are in the Midwest and West, but Woodswomen also goes to the East and abroad. Most trips have a natural history component. The association provides an opportunity to join a network of women interested in the outdoors. Members receive a directory of members and a newsletter that includes information on other outdoor programs for women, and for women and men with women leaders. A week's backpacking on Mount Ranier costs $555; a weekend of canoe instruction in northern Wisconsin $145.

AMERICAN VOLKSSPORT ASSOCIATION
1001 Pat Booker Rd., Suite 203
Universal City, Texas 78148
512-659-2112

The American Volkssport Association, a branch of the International Volkssportsverband (People's Sports Association), offers opportunities to join others in day walks, bike rides, swims, and cross-country ski trips. Though the U.S. branch was founded only in 1979, the organization already has chapters throughout the country. The events are free, as is a list of local chapters. The association's bimonthly newsletter, *The American Wanderer* ($8 a year) lists events.

NATIONAL OUTDOOR LEADERSHIP SCHOOL
P.O. Box AA
Lander, Wyoming 82520
307-332-6973

Founded by mountaineer Paul Petzoldt, this school offers courses designed to teach minimum impact camping, travel techniques, safety, environmental awareness and expedition dynamics. Major activities include wilderness backpacking, mountaineering, sea kayaking, skiing, and winter camping. Courses range in length from two weeks to three months. College credit is available on selected courses. Courses take place in the western United States and abroad. Tuition is $1,250 and up; financial aid is available on a merit and need basis.

CHAPTER TWENTY-THREE

Hiking Trails

The American Hiking Society is the place to start for information on trails and the organizations building and maintaining them. People phoning or writing with a question on a trail will receive a brochure and the facts they need or information on where to obtain them. A computerized data base of more than 4,500 trail-using groups, from hikers to horseback riders, enables the society to put people in touch with local outdoor organizations. The society can be contacted at 1015 31st St. NW, Washington, D.C. 20007 (703-385-3252).

NATIONAL TRAILS

The United States has an ambitious but incomplete national system of trails. The 1968 National Trails System Act called for the establishment of three classes of trails: scenic, recreational, and side or connecting. Congress added a fourth class, historic, to the system in 1978.

Today there are more than 750 national recreation trails, totaling over 8,100 miles. These trails, which vary in length, are designated by the Secretary of the Interior or, if within the National Forests, by the Secretary of Agriculture, after they have been certified by the agency or private party that has jurisdiction over the land. They must be ready for use when designated. A computerized inventory is maintained by the Recreation Resources Assistance Division (code 765), National Park Service, P.O. Box 37127, Washington, DC 20013 (202-343-3780), which makes available a printed listing.

National historic trails and national scenic trails, like National Parks, can only be designated by Congress. The National Park Service administers the National Trails System, but another federal agency whose land is crossed by a given trail, may be designated manager of that particular trail. We specify the managing agency, unless it is the National Park Service.

There are eight national historic trails. Much of their mileage is over roads, and planning for several of them is only beginning. The first three of the trails listed below are the historic trails of greatest interest to hikers and paddlers.

The 1968 Trails System Act established two scenic trails, the Appalachian Trail and the Pacific Crest Trail, and it mandated study of fourteen more trails for possible designation as scenic. Congress eventually added four of these trails, plus two additional trails. None of the scenic trails has yet been completed. Congress did not begin appropriating funds to buy or develop land until 1978, and much of the money appropriated has gone to the Appalachian Trail. In designating several of the trails, Congress forbade the purchase of private land. The last seven of the trails below are scenic. The Natchez Trace Scenic Trail is omitted, because it will actually be a parkway rather than a trail.

LEWIS AND CLARK TRAIL

This trail travels 4,500 miles from the Mississippi River to the Pacific Ocean and back by a different route, and includes water routes, marked highways, and planned trails. Information can be obtained from the National Park Service, P.O. Box 5463, Madison, Wisconsin 53705-0463 (608-833-2788) and from the Lewis and Clark Trail Heritage Foundation, P.O. Box 3434, Great Falls, Montana 59403.

NEZ PERCE TRAIL

Almost 1,000 miles long, this trail commemorates the march of Chief Joseph and his people from their reservation in Oregon, through Idaho, Wyoming, and Montana, almost to the Canadian border. Several hundred miles of the historic route in Idaho and western Montana can be walked on pre-existing trails. For information contact the Northern Regional Office of the Forest Service (the managing agency) Federal Building, P.O. Box 7669, Missoula, Montana 59807 (406-329-3582).

IDITAROD TRAIL

The Iditarod commemorates the route from Seward to Nome, Alaska, that prospectors, following ancient hunting paths, used during the Gold Rush. The main route is 900 miles long, but the system contains 2,300 miles of trail, for in most areas the trail is simply a network of paths traversing the wilderness and connecting native villages. The famous dog sled race held on the trail each winter follows frozen rivers and even ocean.

The one area in which the Iditarod is a standard trail is the Seward to Anchorage region. Beginning at the Eagle River Visitor Center outside Anchorage, travelers can take a 25-mile hike southward to Crow Pass. On the way they pass from a white spruce forest, up to alpine vegetation, through tundra, then finally down to a hemlock forest lush with ferns. For information contact the Anchorage District of the Bureau of Land Management, which manages the trail, at 6881 Abbott Lupe Road, Anchorage, Alaska 99507 (907-267-1248).

APPALACHIAN TRAIL

No more than 149 miles of this 2,110-mile trail, from Mount Katahdin in Maine to Spring Mountain in Georgia, is still in need of protection. The rest of the corridor is in the hands of federal and state agencies. Protection is scheduled to be completed in the 1990s.

The AT is the oldest of the scenic trails. Benton MacKaye first proposed the trail in an article in the *Journal of the American Institute of Architects* in 1921. Volunteers began construction in 1922. The trail incorporated sections of preexisting trails, the longest being the lower 95 miles of the Long Trail in Vermont.

In 1925 volunteers working on the trail formed a federation of clubs, called the Appalachian Trail Conference (ATC), with each assigned a section of the trail to develop and maintain. The ATC now consists of 31 clubs plus 22,000 individual members and has become a model for other trail organizations. The conference recruits volunteers to maintain trails in the summer and is usually able to pay their expenses, apart from transportation to and from home. It has organized a land trust, the Trust for Appalachian Trail Lands, to purchase land along unprotected sections of the trail. The clubs operate a system of shelters, one approximately every ten miles, except in the White Mountains where the Appalachian Mountain Club has huts. It also has a major publications program, featuring trail guides and maps. Members receive the general interest periodical, Appalachian Trailway News.

Hiking the complete trail takes four to six months on the average. Many people who go the whole way begin in Georgia in late March or early April and follow spring north.

To relieve congestion on the AT, volunteers, in cooperation with the

National Park Service and Forest Service, are completing a 250-mile Benton MacKaye Trail, which will form a figure "8" with the southern portion of the AT. The new trail starts just north of Springer Mountain, crosses the AT near Shuckstack Mountain in Great Smoky Mountains National Park, and returns to the AT at the park's northern boundary.

The ATC headquarters is located at Washington and Jackson Sts., P.O. Box 807, Harpers Ferry, West Virginia 25425 (304-535-6331).

CONTINENTAL DIVIDE TRAIL

The Continental Divide Trail, which is managed by the U.S. Forest Service, extends almost 3,000 miles along the crest of the Rocky Mountains from the Canadian to the Mexican border. The trail passes through Glacier, Yellowstone, and Rocky Mountain National Parks and through more than twenty established and proposed National Forest Wilderness Areas. It is not for the faint-hearted, since it is remote and often climbs above timberline, but the scenery and the opportunities to see wildlife are outstanding. Much of the trail route is only accessible from late June through September.

The trail is far from complete but hikers can find their way with a series of guidebooks published by the Continental Divide Trail Society. Directed by Jim Wolf, the society also produces a semi-annual newsletter "DIVIDEnds." The address is P.O. Box 30002, Bethesda, Maryland 20824.

FLORIDA TRAIL

Construction of the Florida Trail began over two decades ago, under the leadership of Miami's James A. Kern, a wildlife writer and photographer. Now the Florida Trail Association, which works on the National Scenic Trail and on other routes, has some 5,000 members. When finished, the Florida Trail will extend more than 1,300 miles: from the Gulf Island National Seashore near Pensacola to the Big Cypress National Preserve. It is managed by the U.S. Forest Service.

The longest completed section covers 800 miles, 109 miles of which have been certified by the Forest Service. The segment passes from the Apalachicola River in Apalachicola National Forest, through Osceola and Ocala National Forests, to North Orlando.

Besides building and maintaining the trail, the Florida Trail Association sponsors outings and conferences and distributes to members a guidebook and bimonthly newsletter. Only members can hike on certain sections of the trail that are in private hands. The association can be reached at P.O. Box 13708, Gainesville, Florida 32604 (904-378-8823).

ICE AGE TRAIL

Limited to the state of Wisconsin, the Ice Age Trail "generally follows the end moraines of the most recent glaciation." In other words, it follows what were dumps of debris formed at the edge of a moving ice sheet. It also detours to take in other glacial features.

When finished the trail will meander 1,000 miles, from Green Bay south, then north, and finally west. Langlade County in the north is so full of lakes and bogs formed by the melting glacier that the trail here frequently crosses swamps on beaver dams.

The nine sections of the Ice Age National Scientific Reserve serve as anchors for the trail. The best known of the nine are Devil's Lake, springfed with no visible outlet and surrounded on three sides by quartzite cliffs, popular with climbers; and Horicon Marsh, site of the Horicon Marsh National Wildlife Refuge and the state-run Horicon Marsh Wildlife Area. The marsh, a stop-over for migrating Canada Geese, is a prime bird watching area.

The reserve and the trail are results of a proposal for an Ice Age Glacier National Forest made by the late Ray Zilmer of Milwaukee in the 1950s. The trail still consists only of fragments. About 500 miles of trail are open for use, although the National Park Service has only certified about half of them.

The Ice Age Park and Trail Foundation, 333 West Miflin, Madison, Wisconsin 53703 (608-251-5550) is coordinating efforts to complete the trail. It distributes trail maps and newsletters and sponsors interpretive tours and educational conferences. The superintendent can be reached at the National Park Service, P.O. Box 5463, Madison, Wisconsin 53705-0463 (608-833-2788).

NORTH COUNTRY TRAIL

Running across the grain of the country, the North Country Trail will eventually start at Lake Champlain in New York and end at Lake Sakakawea, North Dakota, where it will join the Lewis and Clark National Historic Trail. Planners hope that one day it will connect with the Appalachian and Long Trails in the East to form one continuous trail from the east to west coasts across the northern tier of states. The trail meanders, as is indicated by the fact that it will cover more than 3,200 miles in only seven states. It features many historic sites and a great diversity of scenery, as it passes from the Adirondack Mountains to the plains of the upper midwest.

The trail runs along several pre-existing trails, including segments of the Finger Lakes Trail in New York and the Buckeye Trail in Ohio, plus the Pictured Rocks Lakeshore Trail in Michigan's Upper Peninsula. More than one third of the trail has been completed.

The North Country Trail Association, P.O. Box 311, White Cloud, Michigan 49349, publishes a quarterly newsletter for its membership, provides an information service, and organizes hikes along various sections of the trail and work parties for trail construction and maintenance. The supervisor can be reached at the National Park Service, P.O. Box 5463, Madison, Wisconsin 53705-0463 (608-833-2788).

Information on the New York and Ohio sections of the trail may be obtained by writing the Finger Lakes Trail Conference, P.O. Box 18048, Rochester, New York 14618, and/or the Buckeye Trail Association, P.O. Box 254, Worthington, Ohio 43085.

PACIFIC CREST TRAIL

The farthest west of the scenic trails, the Pacific Crest Trail traverses 2,627 miles, from the Canadian border to Mexico. Following mountain ranges, it offers the most spectacular scenery of any of the eight trails. Elevations range from 173 feet at the Columbia River Gorge between Washington and Oregon to 13,200 feet at Forester Pass in the High Sierra of California. Some of the most scenic and least used portions are in California, north of Lake Tahoe. Since much of it lies in National Forests, the U.S. Forest Service is the primary managing agency.

The trail takes in three major pre-existing trails: the Cascade Crest Trail in Washington, the Oregon Skyline Trail in Oregon, and the John Muir Trail, which runs from northern Yosemite Park to Mount Whitney, passing on its way through the John Muir Wilderness. Only 25 miles of the trail in Southern California have not yet been constructed. In these stretches, where there are right of way problems, hikers use roads.

A Pacific Trail Conference (PCT) cooperates with the Forest Service in maintaining the trail and offers to members and the public advice on maps and on other matters connected with hiking the trail. The

PCT can be contacted at 365 West 29th Ave., Eugene, Oregon 97405 (503-686-1365). Permits necessary for camping in wilderness areas and for lighting fires can be obtained by writing to the Forest Service or the National Park Service office nearest the point of entry.

POTOMAC HERITAGE TRAIL

Congress intended the Potomac Heritage Trail to stretch across the Potomac Basin from Chesapeake Bay to the tributaries of the Ohio River in western Pennsylvania. Construction will entail linking several established trails: the National Park Service's Mount Vernon Trail, which runs 17 miles from the Abraham Lincoln Memorial near the Capitol to George Washington's home in Virginia; the Northern Virginia Regional Park Authority's Washington & Old Dominion Trail; the Appalachian Trail; the Chesapeake and Ohio Canal Trail; and Pennsylvania's 70-mile long Laurel Highlands Hiking Trail. To complete the eastern end beyond the Mount Vernon Trail, planners may need to use canoe and boat links.

Congress has forbidden the National Park Service to acquire land for this trail, even as a gift. Volunteers and state and local governments must spend the needed money and do all the work. A hiking route westward from Cumberland, Maryland, to connect with the Laurel Highlands Trail is being established by the Potomac Heritage Trail Association. A guide and maps for the 50-mile portion of it from Cumberland to Mount Davis in Pennsylvania is available. For information contact Thurston Griggs, Potomac Heritage Trail Association, 1718 N Street NW, Washington, D.C. 20036, and the National Capital Regional Office of the National Park Service, 1100 Ohio Drive, SW, Washington, D.C. 20242 (202-426-7704).

To learn about the Mount Vernon Trail, popular with Washington area hikers, cyclists, and joggers, contact the Superintendent, George Washington Memorial Parkway, Turkey Run Park, McLean, Virginia 22101.

OTHER TRAILS

The U.S. Forest Service manages 107,000 miles of trail, enough miles to circle the globe four times. Nevertheless, this figure represents a loss. The agency managed 145,000 miles of trails in 1945, when the mileage was at its peak.

Moreover, the Forest Service does not keep its trails in good condition. Forest roads have gained what trails have lost. Between 1974 and 1983 the Forest Service built or reconstructed 89,000 miles of roads as opposed to 9,000 miles of trails. Furthermore, for each of fiscal years 1990 and 1991 the Bush administration requested approximately $390 million for forest road maintenance and construction and less than $40 million for trails.

The recent sums for trails, nevertheless, represent increases that reflect the work of the National Trails Coalition, which includes the American Hiking Society, National Audubon Society, Sierra Club, and Wilderness Society. Under the Reagan administration the Forest Service asked for zero dollars for new trails and little for maintenance.

In addition to the trails managed by federal agencies, the United States has trails that are owned and managed by states, localities, and private parties, such as land trusts.

Iowa is an example of a state with good trails. It has a total of almost 3,000 miles, including more than 650 miles of equestrian trails and 860 miles of trails suitable for cycling. The Iowa Trails Council, which has assumed a leadership role in trail creation, publishes the *RIBBIT* (Ride Intriguingly Beautiful & Bodacious Iowa Trails) guide to 140 miles of trails for cycling and also for hiking. It is available for a $5 donation from the Iowa Trails Council, 1201 Central Avenue, Center Point, Iowa 52213 (319-849-1844).

Hawaii likewise has an impressive trail system, described by Robert Smith in five books on hiking in Hawaii, published by Wilderness Press. *Hawaii's Best Hiking Trails* (2nd ed., 1985) includes the finest trails in the other four. Despite the high population density on Oahu, trails into the Koolau and Wainae mountain ranges provide good hiking. On Kauai, the Waimea Canyon in Kokee State Park and the Kalalau Valley on the Na Pali Coast afford choice trails, the latter a two-day cliff edge trail to what has been called "one of the most beautiful and powerful places on Earth." The Kaupo Gap Trail in Haleakala National Park on Maui descends from approximately 10,000 feet to sea level. A recommended hike on Hawaii is through backcountry along the northern Kohala Peninsula from Waipo Valley to Waimanu Valley, otherworldly in its beauty.

David Stanley's and Deke Castleman's *Alaska-Yukon Handbook Including the Canadian Rockies* guides hikers and environmentalists in Alaska (Moon Publications, 722 Wall Street, Chico, California 95928, 1988). The Chilkoot Trail, though much traveled, is unsurpassed in

Alaska and western Canada for scenery and history. Passing from tidewater at Dyea near Skagway to the headwaters of the Yukon River at Bennett in Canada, it covers 33 miles of an old Indian trail across the Chilkoot Pass.

Some states through their tourist or recreation departments distribute maps giving overviews of trails in the state. The New England Trail Conference, 33 Knollwood Drive, East Longmeadow, Massachusetts 01028, sells for $3, a map showing New England trails and listing the principle maps and guidebooks for these trails.

For hiking possibilities around major northeastern cities, the Appalachian Mountain Club is helpful. It publishes a series of guides for Baltimore, Boston (two books), New York, Philadelphia, and Washington. The books include maps, directions, and comments on natural history and can be ordered from the club's main office. Guides to use around San Francisco include Sierra Club Books' *Adventuring in the San Francisco Bay Area* (1987) and *To Walk with a Quiet Mind* (1975).

The strongest possibility for increasing trail mileage in general in the United States is through the conversion of abandoned railroad tracks to trails. Rail to trail conversions are discussed under cycling in the next section.

CHAPTER TWENTY-FOUR

Cycling Trails

As is discussed in the chapter covering transportation, certain localities have created paths for the exclusive use of cyclists; but most cycling routes consist of roads or trails that cyclists share with motorized vehicles and/or hikers. Many of these routes have been created by the associations Bikecentennial and the Rails-to-Trails Conservancy. Many others have been developed by the agencies that manage state and national parks and forests.

Whether or not trails on public lands should be open to cyclists is controversial. *Mountain Bike* magazine reports that 44% of the national forests, state forests, and state parks that it has surveyed forbid mountain biking. States are passing legislation on the subject. California, Maryland, and Michigan now forbid mountain biking on trails, except where it is explicitly permitted. On the other hand, Washington, Oregon, Colorado, Delaware, and West Virginia permit mountain biking, except where specific circumstances necessitate closure.

Whatever the official position, people who want to preserve natural areas do not cycle on hiking trails, because such cycling can cause severe erosion. Do not cycle at all in designated Wilderness Areas. Where cycling is permitted, use dirt Forest Service roads, which are constructed to withstand use by motor vehicles; they offer splendid opportunities for mountain bikes.

TRANSAMERICA BICYCLE TRAIL

A 4,500-mile trail stretching from Astoria, Oregon to Yorktown, Virginia, the TransAmerica Trail was the first project of Bikecentennial. The association inaugurated it in 1976 to celebrate both the 100th anniversary of the arrival of bicycles in America and the nation's bicentennial. The trail crosses the country by way of Missoula, Montana; West

Yellowstone, Montana; Rawlins, Wyoming; Pueblo, Colorado; Farmington, Missouri; and Berea, Kentucky, among other places.

Since 1976 Bikecentennial has developed a 1,700-mile National Bicycle Route Network. In creating trails Bikecentennial staff plots routes that link together existing backroads. The routes pass through varied terrain and through highly scenic areas rather than go directly from one terminus to another. Bikecentennial sells detailed maps of the routes it creates.

The set of twelve maps for the TransAmerica Trail costs nonmembers $64.95 plus postage. A single map is $6.95 plus postage. The maps can be ordered from Bikecentennial, P.O. Box 8308, Missoula, Montana 59807 (406-721-8719).

MAINE TO VIRGINIA BICYCLE ROUTE

This 1,110-mile Bikecentennial route connects Bar Harbor, Maine, to Richmond, Virginia. It passes through dense hardwood forests and picturesque New England towns and through the cities of Hartford, Philadelphia, Baltimore, and Washington. Spurs take riders into Boston and New York. A set of three maps costs nonmembers $16.95 plus postage.

CALIFORNIA TO FLORIDA BICYCLE ROUTE

The National Bicycle Route Network is still growing. Bikecentennial has plotted only 950 miles of the California to Florida Route: from San Diego, California to El Paso, Texas, by way of Mesa, Arizona. When its staff has completed the research now underway, the route will reach Ormond Beach, Florida. Two maps of the completed section are available, for $6.95 each plus postage.

WASHINGTON AND OLD DOMINION TRAIL

Perhaps the best known and most heavily used example of the conversion of an abandoned railway corridor to recreational use, the 44-mile W&OD Trail runs from the Potomac River in Washington, D.C., to Purcellville, Virginia, in the foothills of the Blue Ridge Mountains. It has over one million users a year. Most of the trail is paved, making it excellent for cycling; from Vienna to Leesburg a separate bridle path runs alongside the main trail. Since the trail is somewhat congested inside Washington, a good starting point is the intersection of Sandburg Street and the W&OD path, near Vienna. A W&OD trail guide can be purchased from the Northern Virginia Regional Park Authority, 5400 Ox Road, Fairfax Station, Virginia 22039 (703-352-5900).

CANNON VALLEY TRAIL

The Cannon Valley Trail follows the route of the abandoned Chicago/ North Western railroad for 19.2 miles between Cannon Falls and Red Wing, Minnesota. Cyclists, hikers, and cross-country skiers travel beneath north-facing bluffs and above the Cannon River, which empties into the Mississippi River near Red Wing. Trail users can continue beyond the trail into Red Wing and picnic beside the Mississippi.

IRON HORSE STATE PARK

A 113-mile corridor along a segment of the old Chicago, Milwaukee, St. Paul and Pacific Railroad in the state of Washington, Iron Horse State Park may eventually become the longest rail to trail conversion in the nation. The state acquired 213 miles of railway line east of Easton, when the railway company went bankrupt in 1977. Under the management of the Washington State Parks and Recreation Commission, the first 25-mile section of Iron Horse Park, a non-motorized trail, was opened to the public in 1984. This section starts in Easton, amid a pine and Douglas fir forest at an elevation of 2,200 feet, and, descending 500 feet, traverses rolling farmlands and canyons along the Upper Yakima River. The park has recently been enlarged by an agreement with AT&T for use of 36 miles of rail corridor to the west of Easton and by the Department of Natural Resources's turning over 46 miles in the east to the Parks and Recreation Commission. The Department of Natural Resources still manages 142 miles of the railroad corridor east of the Columbia River, for the recreational use of which it charges a fee of $10-$100.

Because of weather and maintenance problems, the condition of the 213-mile corridor, even in Iron Horse State Park, varies from month to month. Overnight use is not permitted. Cyclists and hikers wishing to travel any section of the corridor must obtain permits. For information and the addresses of the agencies that grant permits, contact the office of Ange Taylor, Supervisor of Region III, Washington State Parks and Recreation Commission, 2201 North Duncan Drive, Wenatchee, Washington 98801-1007 (509-663-9719).

The Rails-to-Trails Conservancy publishes a *Guide to America's Rail-Trails*, describing the nation's 245 rail to trail conversions. It is available for $6.75 to nonmembers from the Conservancy at 1400 16th Street, NW, Washington, D.C. 20036 (202-797-5400). In part due to the work of the Conservancy, rail to trail conversions now provide 3,245 miles of recreational trails in thirty-five states.

WHITE RIM TRAIL

In Canyonlands National Park, the 110-mile White Rim Trail skirts the escarpments of the giant Island in the Sky mesa. White Rim is a jeep trail. Park officials, conscious of the problem of cycling on trails, allow bicycles on jeep trails but not on other types of trails. For information, contact Canyonlands National Park, 125 West 200 South, Moab, Utah 84532.

ROUTES IN LOLO NATIONAL FOREST

Covering more than two million acres in western Montana, Lolo National Forest is the site of towering mountains, flower-splashed meadows, rushing streams and waterfalls, and wild backcountry. It is also a prime area for viewing wildlife, from Peregrine falcons to the occasional Rocky Mountain wolf. As a pilot project, Bikecentennial has mapped the mountain biking routes in the forest. The product of their research is available to the public for $3.95 from their office.

The *Cyclists' Yellow Pages* published by Bikecentennial and the *Bicycle USA Almanac* published by the League of American Wheelmen (Suite 209, 6707 Whitestone Road, Baltimore, Maryland 21207-4106; 301-944-3399), provide a wealth of information for cyclists. The emphasis in each reflects the fact that while Bikecentennial is an organization for recreational cyclists, the League of American Wheelmen works with both commuters and touring cyclists. The *Yellow Pages* includes such information as personal contacts for up-to-date recreation and cycling information on the fifty states and abroad, opportunities for mountain biking, an overview of interstate bicycle routes, and lists of information sources for recreational cyclists. The *Almanac* publishes for each state the names and addresses of volunteers specializing in various types of assistance, summaries of key bicycle laws, a comprehensive list of published resources, updates on local advocacy efforts, and special events, among other topics. Each annual is free to the members of the association that publishes it.

Both organizations sell to the public guides on operators of bicycle tours: *Bicycle USA Tour Finder* from the League of American Wheelmen, with 150 plus listings ($5 postpaid) and the *Bicycle Vacations Guide* from Bikecentennial with nearly 150 listings ($2 postpaid). Tours exist to fit every taste. For cyclists who want to travel in comfort through picturesque scenery, the offerings of Vermont Bicycle Touring (Box 711, Bristol, Vermont 05443; 802-453-4811) may well appeal. Participants can eat breakfast and dinner and spend the nights at inns to which a van carries their baggage, and they can travel at their own pace during the day. The tours take place not only in Vermont, but also in Maine, Virginia, California, Hawaii, and overseas. Tours last from two to twenty-one days. Five days of cycling in Vermont in midsummer costs approximately $700. Bikecentennial offers a few "light touring" opportunities in the West, but most of its trips are self-contained (cyclists carry the baggage). A ninety-day Bikecentennial tour across the country on the TransAmerica Trail costs $2,000. The phone number for the tours department is 406-721-1776.

The League of American Wheelmen conducts and sanctions rallies. Typically a rally is based at a college or university and lasts three to five days. A variety of day cycling trips, workshops, and purely social events are offered to participants. The League's national office organizes a National Rally and National Congress of Bicyclists in early July and the Great Eastern Rally (GEAR), usually in June. Locations differ from year to year. Local affiliates of the League also offer rallies. For instance, central Kentucky's Bluegrass Wheelmen has held several rallies based at Georgetown College, with rides through the surrounding horse country. The League office can supply information on upcoming rallies.

Long-distance "rides" are organized by a variety of organizations and businesses. The *Des Moines Register* has sponsored a trans-Iowa bicycle event known as RAGBRAI annually since 1973. Cyclists ride 490 miles through fields of corn that were once tall-grass prairie, from the Missouri River to the Mississippi River. The event always takes place during the last week of July, but riders can start when they want to and go at their own pace. For information send a business-size, stamped envelope to RAGBRAI, P.O. Box 622, Des Moines, Iowa 50303 before 1 March. The event has become so popular that the newspaper has had to establish a limit of 7,500 cyclists and chooses them by lottery. To enter the lottery cyclists pay the event's registration fee, which is refunded to unsuccessful applicants. Other annual rides that attract widespread interest include the New York Ride across the State

(NYRATS) from Buffalo to New York City (914-454-5803); Ride around Wyoming (307-672-6323); and Pedal across Lower Michigan (PALM; 313-665-6327).

Cyclists who wish to travel alone or with companions of their choosing can find a wealth of books about cycling routes. Among the top books on regional routes are *Bicycling the Pacific Coast: A Complete Route Guide, Canada to Mexico* by Tom Kirkendall and Vicky Spring, 2nd ed. (Mountaineers Books) and *The Best Bike Rides in New England* by Paul Thomas (Globe Pequot Press). In *Mountain Bike Adventures in the Northern Rockies* and *Mountain Bike Adventures in the Four Corners Region*, Michael McCoy (Mountaineers Books) describes "guilt-free" rides on logging roads, jeep paths, and single-track trails on which off-road vehicles are already allowed.

The League of American Wheelmen sells to members a list of Hospitality Homes, members who volunteer to put up other members ($5).

John Mosley maintains a computerized *Touring Cyclists' Hospitality Directory*, listing cyclists willing to let fellow cyclists have a place to stay and a shower. The service is reciprocal. Only cyclists who send in their names for listing can obtain the directory. There is no fee for listing, but contributions help keep the network going. John Mosley can be reached at 13623 Sylvan Street, Van Nuys, California 91401 (818-781-5865).

In 1990, in cooperation with the Buffalo Ranger District of Wyoming's Bridger-Teton National Forest, Bikecentennial built a campground on the TransAmerica Bicycle Trail, only a few miles from the east entrance to Grand Teton National Park. The campground, Blackrock Creek, is open only to self-propelled travelers.

California and Oregon reserve special sections for hikers and bikers in many of their state campgrounds. These spaces rarely fill up, so late arriving hikers and bikers can stay, even though recreational vehicles are being turned away at the gate. The sites are usually away from the camping loops, and camaraderie often develops among the users. Washington also has "primitive" sites reserved for auto-free travelers, but these often do fill up.

Bikecentennial in cooperation with Wide World of Travel in Missoula, Montana, offers members a travel service that specializes in the needs of cyclists. In addition to selling tickets, the service can give information on such matters as taking a bicycle on a plane or bus and getting from an airport to a trail.

CHAPTER TWENTY-FIVE

Canoeing, Kayaking, and Rafting Opportunities

Paddlers without knowledge of choice places for paddling and rowing can orient themselves by picking a major outfitter and using their facilities and the water near them; or, in reverse, by picking a river or lake and then finding local organizations and firms near that body of water who can give them advice.

A newcomer who takes the latter approach cannot go far wrong by starting with one of the national Wild and Scenic Rivers or by picking one of the national or state recreation water routes. The state of Oregon has established the Willamette River Greenway, extending over 255 miles from Saint Helens to Cottage Grove. A free map is available from the Oregon State Parks and Recreation Division, Department of Transportation, 525 Trade Street SE, Salem, Oregon 97310. Missouri has the 134-mile Ozark National Scenic Riverways—the Current and Jacks Fork Rivers, flowing through the Ozark hills, complete with huge freshwater springs and numerous caves (Ozark National Scenic Riverways, P.O. Box 490, Van Buren, Missouri 63965).

The Upper Mississippi River and several of its tributaries in Minnesota, which have been protected by local ordinances and zoning regulations, offer good boating, as does the 56-mile Edisto Canoe and Kayak Trail on the small blackwater Edisto River in South Carolina—from U.S. Highway 21 to Givhans Ferry State Park. For details of the Edisto contact the South Carolina Department of Parks, Recreation and Tourism, 1205 Pendleton Street, Columbia, South Carolina 29201 (803-734-0166).

Popular places for sea kayaking are the San Juan Islands off the northwest coast of Washington State, Alaska's Glacier Bay, and around the islands of Hawaii. In 1988 Mountaineers Press published a guide to the latter, *Audrey Sutherland's Paddling Hawaii*. The Maine Island

Trail Association (60 Ocean Street, Rockland, Maine 04841) is establishing a 300-mile route along the Maine coast from Portland to Jonesport. Paddlers stop for the night on islands, a few of which already have camping facilities. Membership includes a guidebook.

To locate groups of paddlers in these and other locations, consult one of the following three national paddling associations. All have affiliates.

The American Canoe Association (8580 Cinderbed Road, Suite 1900, P.O. Box 1190, Newington, Virginia 22122; 703-550-7495) is a good place to turn to for answers to questions about water sports. The staff is most familiar with whitewater, and will answer queries asked in person, by mail, and over the phone from members and nonmembers. The association operates a bookstore, for which it will mail a catalog free of charge upon request.

Through its Regional Coordinator Network, American Whitewater Affiliation (AWA; P.O. Box 85, Phoenicia, New York 12464; 914-688-5569) engages in programs of river conservation, access and management, keeps the public abreast of the issues, assists local river activists, and publishes reference tools such as the AWA Nationwide Whitewater Inventory. AWA brings boaters together for fun and competition annually at the Ocoee Whitewater Rodeo in Tennessee (June) and the Gauley River Festival in West Virginia (September). Proceeds from these events further the organization's conservation efforts.

The specialty of the United States Canoe Association (c/o Jim Mack, 606 Ross Street, Middletown, Ohio 45044; 513-422-3739), an all-volunteer organization, is marathon canoe racing. The association organizes National Marathon Canoe and Kayak Championships and National Triathlon Canoe Championships in August each year, among other events. Affiliates help implement the club's "five-star program": "competition-cruising-conservation-camping-camaraderie."

The prime center for whitewater sports in the Southeast and perhaps in the entire country is a worker-owned company:

NANTAHALA OUTDOOR CENTER
41 Highway 19 West
Bryson City, North Carolina 28713
704-488-2175

Founded in 1972, the center offers instruction at all levels of whitewater canoeing and kayaking and offers guided canoe, kayak, and raft trips. Frequently used rivers in the Southeast include the Nantahala, French Broad, Ocoee, Chattooga, and Nolichucky. The center also leads adventure trips in the western United States and abroad. Though Nantahala is known for water sports, it now also offers hiking and cycling trips and beginning and intermediate rock climbing.

At its headquarters in Bryson City, North Carolina, it has a basecamp with cabins, a store, and three bunkhouses that can accommodate a total of fifty people. The lodgings are available to the general public when not occupied by course and trip participants. It also operates there three restaurants: River's End (breakfast, lunch and dinner in summer; shorter hours in winter), Slow Joe's, an outdoor sandwich shop (daily, Memorial Day to Labor Day); Relia's Garden, featuring vegetables from a garden on the slope below the restaurant (breakfast and dinner, Memorial Day through Oct.).

Another major center for instruction and guided trips is Whitewater Specialty, N3984, Hwy. 55, White Lake, Wisconsin 54491 (715-882-5400). The National Outdoor College and the Outdoor Center of New England each specialize in whitewater and flatwater instruction (11383 Pyrites Way, Rancho Cordova, California 95670; 916-638-7900, and 8 Pleasant St., Millers Falls, Massachusetts 01349; 413-659-3926). For other large paddling schools, some offering trips, see the back pages of *Canoe* magazine (Subscriptions: P.O. Box 10748, Des Moines, Iowa 50349), a basic source of information for canoeists and kayakers.

For additional suggestions for guided trips by water, contact:

NEW ROUTES
RFD 5, Box 2030
Brunswick, Maine 04011
207-729-7900

New Routes offers year round outdoor trips for women of all ages and all levels of experience and ability. The trips are of two types. One is the purely recreational trip where relaxation and enjoying the outdoors are the only agenda. The second emphasizes personal and/or professional growth around themes of recovery, empowerment, and spirituality. The company operates an outdoor center at Harwell, where sea kayak and canoe instruction is given. Trips are varied, but canoeing and kayaking in the Northeast predominate for both recreational and growth-oriented trips. A typical week's trip costs about $600.

NORTH WOODS WAYS
Box 286
Dover-Foxcroft, Maine 04426
207-564-3032

North Woods Ways offers canoe trips in the Maine woods, including the St. John and the Chesuncook Rivers, and in Labrador. Conducted in the spirit of classic Maine guiding, the trips leave time for exploration. Canoes are wood and canvas, and paddles are handmade. The cost of a five-day trip in Maine is approximately $550.

In the winter North Woods Ways leads trips by snowshoe and toboggan on frozen rivers.

FIGARO CRUISES
P.O. Box 1336
Camden, Maine 04843
800-473-6169

The *Figaro* is a 51-foot centerboard yawl built in 1965 for ocean racing and rebuilt to accommodate six passengers. It now carries vacationers on three- and six-day cruises. Specialty voyages include yoga, men's, sailing and seamanship, photography, and natural history. Passengers have time ashore each day to walk, stretch, or maybe swim in a fresh water quarry. Cuisine is vegetarian gourmet, with seafood an option for non-vegetarians. Phone or write for prices and other details.

WILDERNESS ALASKA/MEXICO
1231 Sundance Loop
Fairbanks, Alaska 99709
907-479-8203; 907-452-1821

Wilderness Alaska/Mexico offers paddling and backpacking trips in the Brooks Range of Alaska and in Mexico and Belize. Owner/operator Ron Yarnell, who leads many of the trips himself, is keen on birding and plant identification. Among the Alaskan trips is the Hulahula Backpack and Paddle Raft (in the Arctic National Wildlife Refuge)— ten days of backpacking followed by a 100-mile paddle raft trip to the Arctic Ocean ($2,700 including transportation from Fairbanks). Southern trips include a week-long kayak trip on uninhabited Espiritu Santo Island in the Sea of Cortez ($800), and a week of whale watching from kayaks in Magdalena Bay ($700). Ron Yarnell has supported the Northern Alaska Environmental Center by conducting major trips as fund-raisers for the center.

WILLAPA BAY TOURS
P.O. Box 22
Nahcotta, Washington 98637
206-642-4892

Willapa Bay Tours offers guided and non-guided half-day or overnight trips by kayak to Long Island in Willapa Bay, Sand Island in the Columbia River, Island Lake, and Loomis Lake. Long Island, the largest estuarine island on the Pacific Coast, is the site of a 274-acre grove of old growth Red cedars. Individual trees in the grove have come and gone but the grove as a whole has existed as it can be seen now for 4,000 years. In the recent past the grove was threatened by logging. Under heavy pressure from environmentalists, the U.S. Fish and Wildlife Service acquired the grove, part in 1983 in a land-for-timber exchange with Weyerhaeuser and the remainder in 1985/86 by purchase.

ROCKY MOUNTAIN RIVER TOURS
P.O. Box 2552
Boise, Idaho 83701
208-344-6668; 756-4808 (June-Sept.)

Dave and Sheila Mills' Rocky Mountain River Tours takes people on the Middle Fork of the Salmon in oar-powered rafts. The river is the best route through 105 miles of rugged, relatively untouched country in the Frank Church River of No Return Wilderness. Tour guides, all of whom have a science background, practice low-impact camping and teach respect for the land. Time off-river allows for personal outdoor experience. Expert Dutch oven cuisine is a special attraction. A six-day trip costs $1,067.

Sheila Mills has published two books of recipes she has tested on river trips: *Rocky Mountain Kettle Cuisine* and the new *Rocky Mountain Kettle Cuisine 2* ($15.95 plus $2 postage).

FRIENDS OF THE RIVER
Building C, Fort Mason
San Francisco, California 94123
415-771-0400

Working to save western rivers, Friends of the River charters kayaking and rafting trips to raise money for their conservation work.

The National Association of Canoe Liveries and Outfitters, c/o Jim Thaxton, Route 2, Box 249, Butler, Kentucky 41006 (606-472-2205; fax 606-472-2030) publishes a directory of its members, updated yearly ($2 postpaid). Furthermore, Jim Thaxton will refer people to liveries and outfitters in specific areas. The following member livery illustrates canoe/kayak rental services at their best:

MORGAN'S FORT ANCIENT LIVERY
5701 State Route 350, At Fort Ancient State Park
Oregonia, Ohio 45054
513-932-7658; 800-WE-CANOE

Morgan's operates three liveries, each of which has a camp ground and will prepare dinners for groups to eat on the river. The staff keeps up to date on river conditions, and briefs paddlers on river safety. The Fort Ancient Livery is on the Little Miami River. The other two liveries are on the Mad River: Morgan's Mad River Outpost, 5605 Lower Valley Pike, Springfield, Ohio 45502, and the Whitewater River: Morgan's Brookville Canoe Center, 7018 Whitewater River Lane, Brookville, Indiana 47012. Trips for which Morgan's outfits paddlers last from three hours to three days.

If you are interested in building a canoe, contact:

WoodenBoat School
P.O. Box 78, Naskeag Point
Brooklyn, Maine 04616
207-359-4651

People who would like to own a handcrafted canoe, kayak, pram, or sloop can learn how to build their own, while attending a one- or two-week course at the WoodenBoat School. The school, an offshoot of *WoodenBoat Magazine*, also offers courses in sailing and celestial navigation. Cost of building your own DK 14 kayak in six days is $390, plus the cost of materials. Optional room and board at the school are $245 a week. The Rockport Apprenticeship, a nonprofit school of wooden boatbuilding, offers workshops between sessions of its two-year apprentice program (P.O. Box 539, Sea Street, Rockport, Maine 04856 (207-236-6071).

PART VI

Moving Around

CHAPTER TWENTY-SIX

Alternative Forms of Transportation

"When policies encourage their full use, van pools, public cars, buses, and railroads require a quarter as much fuel to move each passenger a kilometer as private cars or airplanes do," according to *State of the World 1988*. Unfortunately, traveling the United States without using either cars or planes is, in many places, impossible unless you can take the time to cycle or walk.

Let's Go: USA, compiled annually by Harvard Student Agencies (St. Martin's Press), is helpful in regard to public transportation in the locations it covers. Here I discuss briefly alternatives to owning or renting a car or flying and, in the process, I point out a few places where travelers can get around quite well on public transportation.

CARS

To travel by car while giving minimal or no encouragement to the automobile industry, take a car that is going to your destination whether or not you are in it.

Auto Driveaway (310 South Michigan Ave., Suite 1401, Chicago, Illinois 60604; 312-341-1900) matches drivers with cars that are to be moved from one location to another. Drivers pay a cash deposit (usually $250), refundable when they reach their destination. They must be twenty-one years of age or older, must fill out an application in advance, and must allow themselves to be fingerprinted. They can take passengers with them. Auto Driveaway, however, carries insurance on the vehicles but not on drivers and passengers. For each trip an itinerary and arrival time are agreed upon by an agent and the driver. The distance covered each day usually averages around 400 miles. For the names and addresses of local branches of this and similar firms, look in the Yellow Pages of the telephone book under Driveaways, Auto Driveaways, or Auto Transporters.

In the winter, southern car rental agencies, particularly those in vacation areas, often find themselves with an excess number of cars that have been dropped off by northerners. To get the cars back up north they may allow drivers wanting to head north, to rent a car for a week at a substantial discount and then give the driver a plane ticket for the return home. Inquire at car rental agencies in the South. Arrangements vary from agency to agency of a company.

Another approach is to look for announcements from people who are seeking riders/drivers for car trips. You can find them on co-op and campus bulletin boards (student centers often have ride boards), and sometimes in the classified advertising sections of newspapers. You can also place an announcement yourself. Of course, exercise judgment in deciding to whose driving to trust your life.

Hitchhiking is decidedly dangerous, and is illegal along interstate highways among other places. If you are doing it in the United States for the first time, read the relevant section of *Let's Go: USA* before you start.

BUSES

Buses are more likely to be going to small towns and to parks than are trains and planes; but the only nationwide bus company, Greyhound, has been eliminating lightly used services and routes. (Greyhound purchased Trailways, another national firm.) Greyhound has been trying to improve transportation to and from rural areas by cooperating with public and private local carriers that are willing to take rural passengers to depots where they can catch cross-country buses. An example of such a service is Jaunt, Inc. (1138 East High, Charlottesville, Virginia 22901; 804-296-6174). A private, nonprofit line, Jaunt uses passenger cars and vans to transport the elderly, retired, and handicapped for the federal government and also to carry members of the general public. When going by Greyhound, double check any information on schedules and routes that you receive. Horror stories abound from people who have been misinformed about buses.

An appealing alternative to Greyhound, where available, is:

GREEN TORTOISE
P.O. Box 24459
San Francisco, California 94124
800-227-4766, outside the San Francisco Bay area; 415-821-0803

Green Tortoise offers community living on wheels. During long trips, passengers sleep on the buses and help prepare two hearty meals a day, usually vegetarian. Planned stops include parks and forests, where passengers have time for walks or swims. Trips are made in standard coaches with the seats and luggage racks removed to make room for seat-high platforms with foam mattresses, facing sofa benches, and bunks. The buses travel up and down the West Coast; and between San Francisco and Boston-New York in the spring, summer, and fall. They also occasionally go to special destinations. The journey between San Francisco and New York or Boston lasts eleven to fourteen days.

The cost for a one-way, cross-country trip is approximately $279. Taking a bike along is $10 or more extra. Passengers contribute approximately $3 a meal toward food purchases. Reservations and deposits on the ticket price are required for long trips, and are advisable for short trips.

U.S. cities with good local bus systems are few and far between, but they do exist. The National Association of Transit Consumer Organizations (NATCO) cites Syracuse, New York; Duluth, Minnesota; Madison, Wisconsin; and Bellingham, Washington, as leaders in buses among medium-sized cities. The California Transit League has given high marks to the bus systems in Los Angeles, San Diego, San Jose, Oakland, Marin County, Santa Barbara, Monterey, and Santa Cruz.

New York City's Mass Transit Authority runs buses that will take you to where you want to go, but that are so slow that you are sorely tempted to splurge on a cab or to brave a subway system so complex that even New York residents sometimes lose their way.

Portland, Oregon, on the other hand, has a system that is rapid and well thought out. It is divided into seven districts, each with its own color-coded symbol. The Tri-County Metropolitan Transportation District of Oregon (Tri-Met; 4012 SE 17th Avenue, Portland, Oregon 97202) publishes an annual *Tri-Met Guide*, in the form of a thick paperback book and folded map. It includes directions to major points from all parts of the city.

The Chicago Transit Authority (CTA) estimates that 90% of Chicago's population lives within a five minute walk of a bus or train stop. A dollar fifty ($1.25 plus a transfer for 25 cents) will get you to almost every part of the city. "Unlike New York's system, the CTA is safe and clean and reasonably efficient," a Chicago resident told me. "We don't have a car and have little problem getting around on the CTA. Now if we could just get half a million people out of their cars and into a bus!"

The Metropolitan Transit Commission (MTC) of Minneapolis, Minnesota, has nearly a thousand buses traveling 114 bus routes over a seven-county area that includes St. Paul and several suburbs. Fares are $1.10 during peak hours on non-express buses, less if tickets are bought ahead. To help the environment, MTC uses biodegradable cleaning chemicals and recycles oil, batteries, tires, and outdated bus bodies. It is researching other means. A particulate trap installed on an older bus successfully reduced the amount of soot emitted from the bus, for instance.

TRAINS

Long-distance intercity trains in the contiguous states belong to the Amtrak System, a quasi-public agency formed by Congress in 1970. Amtrak is growing, despite budget cuts in recent years. In 1990 passenger-miles of travel were up for the eighth consecutive year for a record of 6 billion; ridership was 22.2 million. The reliability index (trains on time) rose from 75.1% in 1989 to 76.1% in 1990 despite a need for funds to spend on operating equipment. As in 1989, Amtrak recouped 72% of its costs with revenues. The most heavily traveled Amtrak route is between Boston and Washington, in particular New York to Washington.

One of the most scenic routes is that taken by the California Zephyr between Chicago and San Francisco. The train crosses the Sierras in California by daylight whether it is traveling east or west, and passengers going west see the full splendor of the Rocky Mountains. Another scenic route is that taken by the Coast Starlight between Seattle and Los Angeles.

Any trip from Chicago to the west coast takes two nights and one to two days. The fastest train is the Southwest Chief, which goes through Kansas City and Flagstaff on the way to Los Angeles. A passenger leaving Chicago Monday would arrive in Los Angeles Wednesday morning.

The Empire Builder from Seattle or Portland to Chicago is a fine way to see Glacier National Park without hiking. Check the timetable, however, to make sure that it passes through the park in daylight during the time of year that you are traveling.

If you want to take a car from Washington, DC, or points south to Florida and to economize on gasoline, ride the auto train, which runs from Lorton, Virginia (near Washington, D.C.) to Sanford, Florida.

Amtrak carries bicycles on trains that handle checked baggage. It charges $5, which covers the use of a bicycle box. Handlebars and pedals must be removed.

For information and reservations call 800-USA-RAIL (872-7245), Amtrak offices in major cities, or a travel agent. To obtain a national timetable, call the 800 (toll-free) number. The All Aboard America coach fare from the East to the West Coast is $259 off season; $309 during the summer.

Lines that are not part of the Amtrak system carry commuters in various parts of the nation, and some non-Amtrak lines travel through areas that appeal to hikers and sightseers. The Empire State Railway Museum publishes an annual Steam Passenger Service Directory that covers tourist railway lines and live steam operations in the U.S. and Canada, with details on routes, fares and schedules. Order from Steam Passenger Service Directory, P.O. Box 95, Richmond, Vermont 05477 ($8.95 plus $1.75 shipping within the U.S.).

DURANGO AND SILVERTON NARROW GAUGE R. R. CO.
479 Main Avenue
Durango, Colorado 81301
303-247-2733

From May through October trains make a 90-mile round trip from Durango to Silverton in approximately 9 hours with a 2 1/4 hour layover in Silverton. They follow the Animas River through the San Juan National Forest. Passengers can get off at the Needleton flag stop, and hike from there into the Weminuche Wilderness. The adult round-trip train fare is $37.15.

ALASKA RAILROAD
P.O. Box 107500
Anchorage, Alaska 99510–7500
800-544-0552 from outside Alaska

Owned by the state, the Alaska Railroad carries passengers between Fairbanks and Anchorage with a stop at Denali National Park and Preserve. It also runs between Portage and Whittier, a route on which it carries automobiles, and between Anchorage and Seward. Anchorage to Fairbanks, a 350-mile route, takes all day, allowing time to admire the scenery. Service is year round, except for the Anchorage-Seward route; but it is reduced from September to May. The one-way fare from Anchorage to Fairbanks with a stop at Denali, for example, is $108.

INTRACITY HEAVY RAIL LINES

Intracity rail lines are of two basic types: heavy rail and light rail (trolleys and streetcars). With both, cars run on pairs of track. Heavy rail systems are usually powered, however, by a third rail that carries electricity; light rail, by overhead catenary wires. Light rail can operate on city streets whereas heavy rail usually runs under the ground or on raised tracks, because it must be separated from pedestrian and auto traffic. The need for keeping heavy rail apart from streets and also a high level of automation makes it more expensive than light rail and means that it is best suited to densely populated areas.

Atlanta, Boston, Chicago, Miami, San Francisco, Philadelphia, Washington, and Baltimore have heavy rail lines.

The BART system (Bay Area Rapid Transit) connects San Francisco with Oakland, Berkeley, Concord, and Fremont. It is clean, modern, and relatively speedy although not inexpensive; and a ride on BART can be an opportunity for sightseeing. From the Concord line riders see Mount Diablo and surroundings; from the Fremont line riders can see grassy hills above which sailplanes, at times, glide.

The 70-mile Washington Metrorail is generally considered the finest system in the nation. The service is frequent, the stations and cars are clean and attractive, riders pay according to distance traveled and time of day, the explanatory maps are relatively easy to understand, and the system is fully accessible to the handicapped. Among the subway's many stops are Washington's National Airport, the Capitol, and

Dupont Circle, near which a variety of environmental offices are located.

A subway line takes people from downtown Chicago into the bowels of O'Hare Airport in less than twenty minutes. Taking a car or taxi to O'Hare, on the other hand, "can be a nightmare during rush hour and cost you a fortune," a Chicago resident reports.

Cities recently constructing light rail lines include Buffalo, Pittsburgh, Sacramento, San Diego, and San Jose. Portland has a light rail line, MAX, connecting with its bus lines at transit centers and at a transit mall.

The San Francisco Municipal Railway (MUNI) runs light rail underneath Market Street, through tunnels, and out to the beach, among other places. MUNI also operates above-ground streetcars, plus celebrated cable cars, and buses. As a result, San Francisco is one of the easiest places in the United States for traveling without a car.

The San Diego Trolley links downtown San Diego and an Amtrak station with the Mexican border at Tijuana. Passengers need only walk a couple of blocks from the terminal to the central district of Tijuana. San Diego plans to have 113 miles of light rail eventually.

FERRIES

One of the greatest bargains in U.S. transportation is the ferry ride from Battery Park at the tip of New York City's Manhattan Island to Staten Island – 50 cents round trip. The Staten Island Ferry, which leaves the park every half hour, is a good way to see the harbor and the Statue of Liberty and takes passengers to an island that, though largely urban, offers a Green Belt with good hiking. Battery Park itself, where you can smell the saltwater and feel the sea breezes, is a refreshing change from mid-Manhattan.

The Alaska Marine Highway System offers an enjoyable and relatively benign way to travel to Alaska. You can catch the Southeast Alaska ferry at Bellingham, Washington; Prince Rupert, British Columbia; or, 15 May-30 Sep., Stewart, British Columbia. It stops at Ketchikan, Wrangell, Petersburg, Sitka, Juneau, Haines, and Skagway. Feeder vessels serve several smaller communities. The Southcentral Alaska ferry, which is not linked to the Southeast route, stops at Kodiak, Port Lions, Homer, Seldovia, Seward, Valdez, Cordova, and Whittier. At Whittier passengers can transfer to and from the Alaska Railroad. In summer, ferries link Kodiak and the Aleutian Islands.

Service on the major routes is year-round, though more expensive in the summer than at other times of the year. The line requires reservations and full payment prior to sailing. The summer one-way fare, excluding meals and berth, from Bellingham to Juneau, is $216; and from Kodiak to Whittier via Valdez, $152. If you cannot afford a stateroom, you can sleep in public lounges or in lawn chairs on deck. The ferries carry cars. For information and reservations, write to Alaska Marine Highway, P.O. Box R, Juneau, Alaska 99811, or phone 907-465-3941; from the United States, 800-642-0066.

HUMAN-POWERED VEHICLES

Bicycles are the most widely-used human-powered vehicles, and in the United States they are becoming increasingly popular. Today, in addition to being a form of recreation, they serve as a means of commuting to work for 3.2 million people, twice the number who commuted to work five years ago. This, despite the fact, that relatively few U.S. cities encourage the pollution-preventing practice. In many, roads are so rough and glass-strewn that a mountain bike, with its heavy, broad tires, is recommended equipment; and cycling lanes, if existent, are so often used by cars, particularly at curves, that riding in them can be more dangerous than riding in standard lanes. Paths devoted entirely to cycling are rare.

More than half of all commuters travel five miles or less to work. If cities would make cycling safer and more pleasant, cycling would increase sharply. Madison, Wisconsin, for instance, increased the share of bicycles in traffic from 4% to 11% between 1974 and 1980 by providing bike lanes.

Government at the national and local level is beginning to take cycling seriously. Congress included in its 1991 transportation appropriations bill $1 million for a study of bicycle use; and in 1987 Seattle, for instance, pioneered the concept of police on bikes. Cycling police can now be seen in some 100 cities, including Boston, Miami Beach, Dallas, and Los Angeles. (In Lexington, Kentucky, police ride horses.)

The cities that are friendly to commuting cyclists tend to be university towns in the Midwest or West. Here are a few places in which cyclists will feel welcome:

GAINESVILLE, FLORIDA

According to the 1980 census, 6.4% of workers commute by bicycle. The city has an ordinance that requires developers to provide bicycle parking.

BOULDER, COLORADO

Boulder has 18 miles of bike paths including 6-mile Boulder Creek through the center of the city. The city is adding six new bike paths totaling 15 miles, several of them feeding into Boulder Creek. An information rack at 2026 11th Street offers maps for cyclists and information on cycling regulations and trails. City employees can check out bicycles.

MISSOULA, MONTANA

The home of Bikecentennial (described in chapter 24, Cycling Trails), Missoula encourages cycling without creating bike paths and lanes. The streets are wide and well maintained; ample parking facilities for bicycles are available downtown. Half of the 60,000 residents own bicycles.

SEATTLE, WASHINGTON

Bicycling Magazine, which named Seattle first in a list of the ten U.S. cities that do the most to promote cycling, reports that Seattle spends $100,000 each year to improve streets for cycling. All new developments must have parking for bicycles, and every new or renovated bridge must be accessible to bicycles. Half the population cycles; and 90% of the riding "is on city streets."

EUGENE, OREGON

Eugene has 18 miles of designated bike routes, 36 miles of bike lanes, and 21 miles of bike paths. The city employs a full-time bicycle coordinator, has had a bicycle advisory committee since 1970, and runs a bike-on-buses program.

DAVIS, CALIFORNIA

Davis prides itself on being the "Bicycle Capitol" of the United States. With more than 40,000 bicycles, it claims to have more per capita than any other U.S. city. The city and university together have approximately 30 miles of paths separated from roads, and special lanes for cycling. They are depicted on a map distributed by the Chamber of Commerce.

PALO ALTO, CALIFORNIA

The city has 65 kilometers of bikeways, and a central 3.2 kilometer boulevard for bicycles only. Since 1980, it has spent some $1 million on lighted paths, bike bridges, and bike lockers and racks. An ordinance forces developers to include bicycle parking space for each new apartment, and to put showers for cyclists and joggers in new office buildings.

The Bicycle Parking Foundation (P.O. Box 7342, Philadelphia, Pennsylvania 19101; 215-222-1253) assists bicycling organizations in making their communities more "bike friendly" by installing attractive new bike racks as a public service. Among other projects, the foundation designs and fabricates racks and makes them available to participants. The more handsome a rack, the more easily it can be installed in a location offering maximum surveillance, the foundation reasons.

The foundation's hitching post rack can be seen in downtown Portland, Palo Alto, and Providence and at the Philadelphia and Baltimore Art Museums, among other places. More than two hundred are in use in Philadelphia at sites ranging from the Liberty Bell Pavilion to the Reading Terminal Market.

Most commuters are accustomed to cycling at a modest speed. Nevertheless, human-powered vehicles have potential as a means of relatively high-speed transportation. The Gold Rush bicycle was clocked at 65.48 mph in 1986. It is recumbent and fully faired (covered to cut wind resistance). A group of engineering students from MIT traveled 72 miles, from Crete to Greece, in a human-powered plane in 1989. Propellers may increase the speed of human-powered boats; already a pedal-powered hydrofoil has traveled for short distances at almost 15 mph.

An association facilitating these feats is the International Human-Powered Vehicle Association (P.O. Box 51255, Indianapolis, Indiana 46251; 317-876-9478). This organization is dedicated to promoting improvement, innovation, and creativity in the design and development of human-powered transportation, as well as encouraging public interest in physical fitness and good health through exercise. In the past, sports vehicles, particularly bicycles and rowing shells, have been restricted in their design to ensure that athletics were primary. Organizers of bike races only allow standard bicycles, for instance. This has inhibited improvements in engineering. IHPVA provides a forum where inventors can test and evaluate new machines in races, symposia, and contests. Anything goes, as long as the vehicle is powered solely by its rider(s).

Each year the IHPVA sponsors, among other things, the International Human-Powered Speed Championships, which are producing technically advanced vehicles and possibly the commuting vehicles of the future. Du Pont has established a prize fund for human-powered watercraft, which the IHPVA administers.

The association publishes an annual *HPV Source Guide* ($6), a newsletter, and the quarterly technical journal *Human Power*. An information package on the organization costs $1.

TRANSIT GUIDES

Car-Free in Boston: The Guide to Public Transit in Greater Boston & New England makes it reasonable to recommend New England, like San Francisco, to visitors wanting to travel without automobiles. Boston and Cambridge are particularly difficult cities in which to find one's way because they are not laid out in rectangular blocks. *Car-Free* tells you how to get where you want to go in these cities and also gives basic information about transportation in New England as a whole (Association for Public Transportation, P.O. Box 192, Cambridge, Massachusetts 02238; $4.95 plus $1.25 postage). Membership in the association, $15 a year, brings with it a free copy of the next guide, a quarterly newsletter *Mass. Transit*, and *Car-Free Updates*. Non-members can obtain a subscription to the updates between successive editions for $1.

For public transit in the area around New York City, purchase *The Carefree Getaway Guide for New Yorkers* (The Harvard Common Press, 535 Albany Street, Boston, Massachusetts 02118; 617-423-5803; $9.95 plus $3 shipping).

The *San Francisco Bay Area Regional Transit Guide* is designed to answer all basic questions about using mass transit in the nine-county area. Compiled by the Metropolitan Transportation Commission (MTC), it lists small private carriers as well as the major public operators. The MTC, which hopes to update it annually, sells it for $5.25 postpaid (MTC, Metrocenter, Technical Services, 101 8th Street, Oakland, California 94607).

The *California Transit Guide*, published by California Transit Publications in cooperation with the California Transit League, contains descriptions of California's local, rural, and intercity transit systems in a regional format. The second edition was published in 1989. California Transit Publications (P.O. Box 11657, San Francisco, California 94101) did not respond to our query as to current availability.

How to Get from the Airport to the City All Around the World, the Airport Transit Guide, 1989–90 edition (M. Evans; $4.95) describes the possibilities for getting into each of 375 U.S. and foreign cities.

Fly/Ride USA and Canada by Ed Perkins and the Editors of Consumer Report Books (Consumers Union of the United States) though published in 1977 contains much still-useful information on getting into and around 40 U.S. and Canadian cities.

CHAPTER TWENTY-SEVEN

Food Markets and Cooperatives

John Robbins, son of the founder of Baskin-Robbins Ice Cream Company, explains that a given acreage can feed twenty times as many people abstaining from animal products as it can Americans eating standard meals (*Diet for a New America*, $16.45 including postage, from EarthSave, Dept. GC, P.O. Box 2030, Cameron Park, California 95682). Consumers can further environmental preservation, moreover, in ways other than through vegetarianism: purchasing in bulk, buying locally, and eating organic produce.

It is difficult to live up to ideals concerning food when you're travelling. But it's not impossible. Across the country there is a growing network of cooperatives, farmers' markets, health food stores, and vegetarian restaurants where you can get good, healthy food at reasonable prices. They're also good places to meet people.

MARKETS

In 1990 Congress passed a bill requiring that federal standards for organic food production be implemented in 1992. The bill gives some guidelines as to what constitutes organic production, although details must be worked out by a National Organic Standards Board.

In the meantime, certification is carried out by states, associations of growers, and even private firms, all with their own definitions of organic. As a general rule, whatever the criteria, certification depends on records provided by farmers and on inspections carried out by an inspector employed by the certifying body. However, some private firms analyze food for pesticide residue.

An international certifying association of farmers, the Organic Crop Improvement Association (OCIA) headquartered in the United States, certifies products on over 100,000 acres in North, South, and Central

America. Its good reputation stems in part from the fact that it has a detailed audit-trailing system that enables it to trace any certified item from the store shelf back to the seed. State and regional growers' associations may join OCIA if they adopt its strict standards (3185 Twp Road 179, Bellefontaine, Ohio 43311; 513-592-4983). An information packet costs $10.

Biodynamic farming has its own certification system. Farms and other organizations producing biodynamic foods are evaluated by experts in biodynamics through the auspices of the Demeter Association, 4214 National Avenue, Burbank, California 91505 (818-843-5521). Evaluators belong to the Demeter Evaluation Circle and are recognized by the Biodynamic Farming and Gardening Association of North America, P.O. Box 550, Kimberton, Pennsylvania 19442 (215-327-2420). The Demeter Association distributes a list of certified biodynamic farmers and their products.

In 1985 various individuals and organizations concerned with the growing, processing, and marketing of organic food founded a trade organization, Organic Foods Production Association of North America (OFPANA), to establish and maintain standards of excellence for organic food businesses. It has published a set of guidelines for certification programs, available for $12.50 plus $2.50 shipping from OFPANA, P.O. Box 1078, Greenfield, Massachusetts 01301 (413-774-7511).

To locate sales outlets for organic food, contact the regional or state certifying association for the area in question. The California Certified Organic Farmers (CCOF), for example, distributes (for an SASE or $1) a list of retailers and wholesalers of its certified foods in California (CCOF, State Office, P.O. Box 8136, Santa Cruz, California 95061–8136; 408-423-2263). ATTRA can supply a list of all certification organizations (call 800-346-9140.)

Foods certified as organic can be purchased by mail. The Center for Science in the Public Interest distributes a list of Organic Food Mail-Order Suppliers (send $1.50 plus a long SASE with 52 cents in stamps); the California Action Network publishes the *Organic Wholesalers Directory and Yearbook* for $25 plus $3 shipping and handling from the association at P.O. Box 464, Davis, California 95617; 916-756-8518. It includes farms selling to individuals and a section on resources.

When advice is lacking, the best bets for ecologically sound food shopping are farms and farmers' markets; locally owned food stores; and cooperatives.

Below are examples of farmers' markets listed by the sponsoring body, which can supply further information.

COUNCIL ON THE ENVIRONMENT OF NEW YORK CITY
51 Chambers St., Room 228
New York, New York 10007
212-566-0990

Since 1976 New York City's Council on the Environment has sponsored farmers' markets called Greenmarkets. A few, including markets at the World Trade Center on Church Street (Thursday) and in front of the Manhattan Municipal Building on Center Street (Friday), are held year around. "The cheeses are wonderful," a Council employee reports. Permanent signs with the market logo and the days for the market have been placed at market sites.

Operation Green Thumb (49 Chambers Street, Room 1020, New York, New York 10007; 212-233-2926) sponsors a City Gardeners Harvest Fair, which includes a farmers' market, each August at Floyd Bennett Field in Brooklyn.

THE HARTFORD FOOD SYSTEM
509 Wethersfield Avenue
Hartford, Connecticut 06114
203-296-9325

A public service organization, the Food System stitches together government and social service agencies, farmers' markets, and retail and wholesale enterprises with the aim of helping people in the city to control their food supply. Its many projects include organizing farmers' markets and urban farmstands (for locations contact the office); establishing a community canning facility in a public housing project; running two small convenient stores at housing for the elderly: Smith Tower Apartments, 80 Charter Oak, and Betty Knox, 141 Woodland Street; and constructing a 13,200-square-foot commercial hydroponic greenhouse (now Hartford Fresh, on Elliott Street), which can be seen by appointment.

MAINE ORGANIC FARMERS AND GARDENERS ASSOCIATION
P.O. Box 2176
Augusta, Maine 04330
207-622-3118

The third weekend after Labor Day, MOFGA calls attention to its programs and to organic agriculture in general with a hugely successful Common Ground Country Fair at the Windsor Fairgrounds in Windsor. A farmers' market is a part of the fair. As at other Maine farmers' markets, approximately half of the growers are organic producers.

SOUTHLAND FARMERS MARKET ASSOCIATION
1010 South Flower, Room 402
Los Angeles, California 90015
213-749-9551

California has approximately 110 farmers' markets certified by county agricultural commissioners. They are open only to farmers who are also certified by the commissioners. Agents of city governments, non-profit organizations, or one or more farmers organize the markets.

In Los Angeles County 15 of 21 markets are organized by Southland Farmers Market Association, a non-profit group funded by farmers. Each farmer at a Southland market pays 1.5% of gross sales to the association, which recruits farmers, trains managers, publicizes the markets, and sees to it that regulations are followed. The largest of the Los Angeles County markets is held at the corner of Arizona and 2nd Street in Santa Monica, Wed. 10:00 A.M.-2:00 P.M. The oldest is the Gardena Market, created in 1980. It is held Sat. 6:30 A.M. to noon, at 1300 Van Ness. A market is held in Venice at the corner of Pacific Ave. and Venice Blvd. 7:00–10:30 A.M. Fri. For a complete list of markets contact the association.

COOPERATIVES

In areas with a population that is conscious of health and environmental issues, private businesses may operate stores selling natural grown produce. Nationwide, however, the top choice for ecologically sound grocery shopping at reasonable prices are food cooperatives. They are of two main types: retail stores (storefronts) and buying clubs (pre-order co-ops that periodically place orders directly with a wholesaler). Increasingly items traditionally stocked by co-ops can be found at supermarkets owned by chains; but in patronizing these stores rather than co-ops customers are losing control of their food supply.

The national directory *Finding Co-ops*, lists food co-ops and co-ops of other types (North America Students of Cooperation, NASCO, P.O. Box 7715, Ann Arbor, Michigan 48107; $9.95 plus 15% shipping). However, the directory was published in 1984 so is going out of date. For every area except southern California, you can identify local co-ops by calling the wholesaler(s) that sell(s) to cooperatives in the region. For southern California contact the Cooperative Resources and Services Project, 3551 White House Place, Los Angeles, California 90004 (213-738-1254). The wholesalers listed below are cooperative businesses:

NORTHEAST COOPERATIVES
P.O. Box 8188, Quinn Road
Brattleboro, Vermont 05304
802-257-5856

New England and eastern New York.

CLEAR EYE
Route 89 South
Savannah, New York 13146
315-365-2816

Chiefly northern and western New York State.

HUDSON VALLEY FEDERATION
P.O. Box 367
Clintondale, New York 12515
914-883-6848

Southeastern New York state and New Jersey.

MOUNTAIN WAREHOUSE
1400 East Geer Street, Warehouse #3
Durham, North Carolina 27704
919-682-9234

North and South Carolina and parts of Georgia, Virginia, West Virginia, and Tennessee.

ORANGE BLOSSOM
P.O. Box 4159
Gainesville, Florida 32613
904-372-7061

Florida, Georgia, and Alabama.

FEDERATION OF OHIO RIVER COOPERATIVES (FORC)
320 Outer Belt Street
Columbus, Ohio 43213
614-861-2446

Indiana, Kentucky, Maryland, Ohio, Pennsylvania, Tennessee, and West Virginia, with a few stores in Washington, D.C.

OZARK COOPERATIVE WAREHOUSE
P.O. Box 1528
Fayetteville, Arkansas 72702
501-521-4920

Alabama, Arkansas, Georgia, Kansas, Louisiana, Mississippi, Missouri, Oklahoma, western Tennessee, and Texas.

BLOOMING PRAIRIE
2340 Heinz Road
Iowa City, Iowa 52240
319-337-6448

Illinois, Indiana, Iowa, Kansas, Michigan, Minnesota, Missouri, Nebraska, South Dakota, Wyoming.

MICHIGAN FEDERATION OF FOOD CO-OPS
727 West Ellsworth, Building 15
Ann Arbor, Michigan 48108
313-761-4642

Michigan (mostly lower Michigan) and some cooperatives (mostly buying clubs) in Indiana and Ohio.

NORTH FARM COOPERATIVES
204 Regas Road
Madison, Wisconsin 53714
608-241-2667

Upper Midwest (mostly Illinois and Wisconsin) and northeast Iowa.

COMMON HEALTH WAREHOUSE COOPERATIVE
1505 North 8th Street
Superior, Wisconsin 54880
715-392-9862

Northern Minnesota, Montana, Upper Peninsula of Michigan, North Dakota, northwest South Dakota, northern Wisconsin, northeast Wyoming.

BLOOMING PRAIRIE NATURAL FOODS
510 Kasota Avenue, SE
Minneapolis, Minnesota 55414
612-378-9774

(A subsidiary of Blooming Prairie in Iowa.) Minnesota and other parts of the Upper Midwest.

NUTRASOURCE
4005 Sixth Avenue South, P.O. Box 81106
Seattle, Washington 98108
206-467-7190

Alaska, Hawaii, Idaho, Montana, Oregon, and Washington.

NORTH COAST FOOD EXPRESS
3134 Jacobs Avenue
Eureka, California 95501
707-445-3185

Oregon and northern California. (Owned by the North Coast Cooperative.)

TUCSON COOPERATIVE WAREHOUSE
350 South Toole Avenue
Tucson, Arizona 85701
602-884-9951

Arizona, a little of California, parts of Colorado, New Mexico, and parts of Texas. (Will refer inquirers about stores outside its area, to the relevant wholesaler.)

The following are examples of retail coops. Unless otherwise indicated, they sell to non-members.

CENTRAL SQUARE MARKET
581 Massachusetts Avenue
Cambridge, Massachusetts 02139
617-661-1580

Formerly called the Cambridge Food Co-op, this co-op now has a deli
with a lot of take-out foods, and a salad bar with many vegetarian
dishes. Hours are Mon.-Sat. 9:00 A.M.-9:00 P.M., Sun. noon-8:00 P.M.

GOOD FOOD COOP
58 East 4th Street
New York, New York 10003
212-260-4045

Good Food is the only storefront co-op in Manhattan. According to the
New York State Department of Agriculture and Markets, New York's
five burroughs had thirty food co-ops in 1982. Today many New Yorkers who might use co-ops, buy instead at the city's numerous small
health-food stores and the farmers' markets. Good Food purchases
some of its produce, most of which is organic, from Amish farmers at
these markets. Good Food owes its survival in part to being located in
a low-rent, city-owned building. Hours are Mon.-Fri. 1:00-9:00 P.M.,
Sat. 10:00 A.M.-8:00 P.M., Sun. 2:00-6:00 P.M.

FLATBUSH FOOD CO-OP
1318 Cortelyou Road
Brooklyn, New York 11226
718-284-9486

At this 500 household co-op, 99% of the produce is organic. The co-op
sponsors social and educational activities, and often takes part in Brooklyn civic events and street fairs. It is near bus and subway stops. Phone
for directions. Hours are Mon.-Fri. 9:30 A.M.-8:00 P.M., Sat. and Sun.
9:30 A.M.-7:00 P.M. Non-members can shop.

PARK SLOPE FOOD CO-OP
782 Union Street
Brooklyn, New York 11215
718-783-8819

Non-members cannot buy at this co-op, New York's largest; but the co-
op holds frequent orientations for potential members and visitors are
welcome at the store. With annual sales of $1.5 million, the co-op is a

sophisticated operation. Each adult member of a co-op household works as part of a squad three hours every four weeks. The co-op owns a two-story building. Open Mon.-Thurs. 5:00 P.M.-9:45 P.M., Sat. 9:00 A.M.-7:30 P.M., Sun. 9:00 A.M.-5:00 P.M.

KNOXVILLE COMMUNITY FOOD CO-OP
937 Broadway
Knoxville, Tennessee 37917
615-525-2069

Open Mon.-Sat. 9:30 A.M.-7:30 P.M., Sun. 1:00–6:00 P.M.

WHEATSVILLE
3101 Guadalupe Street
Austin, Texas 78705
512-478-2667

Wheatsville serves as a gathering point for environmentalists in Austin. Open from 9:00 A.M.-11:00 P.M. daily, it holds an open house the last Saturday of every month, when non-members can shop at member prices. Normally non-members pay a 7% markup.

EAST DAKOTAH FOOD CO-OP
420 South First Avenue
Sioux Falls, South Dakota 57102
605-339-9506

Hours are Mon.-Sat. 9:00 A.M.-7:00 P.M., Sun. 11:00 A.M.-4:00 P.M.

OLYMPIA FOOD CO-OP
921 North Rogers
Olympia, Washington 98502
206-754-7666

The store includes a deli, and is open 9:00 A.M.-8:00 P.M. every day.

ARCATA CO-OP
811 I Street
Arcata, California 95521
707-445-3185 (in the Eureka office)

The Arcata Co-op is the pivot around which Arcata and much of the county move, the premiere meeting place. It stocks virtually all one could need in foodstuffs, including organic produce bought locally.

Prices are competitive. Open 9:00 A.M.-9:00 P.M. daily, except 9:00 A.M.-8:00 P.M. Sunday.

North Coast Cooperative, which owns this co-op, also owns a neighborhood market in Eureka (333 First Street) and a store on Main Street in Fortuna, plus its wholesale operation. North Coast started out as a small Arcata buying club in 1973.

CO-OPPORTUNITY
1530 Broadway Street
Santa Monica, California 90404
213-451-8902

This natural food coop has more than 4,000 members and does more than $4 million in business each year. Open Mon.-Sat. 9:00 A.M.-8:00 P.M.; Sun. 10:00 A.M.-7:00 P.M.

FOOD CONSPIRACY CO-OP
412 North 4th Avenue
Tucson, Arizona 85705
602-624-4821

Hours are Mon.-Sat. 9:00 A.M.-7:30 P.M., Sun. 9:00 A.M.-6:00 P.M.

CHAPTER TWENTY-EIGHT

Vegetarian Restaurants

Vegetarian Times' Guide to Natural Food Restaurants in the U.S. and Canada (The Book Publishing Co., 1989) is the book for locating vegetarian and natural foods restaurants across the United States. I describe a few exemplary restaurants and cafes below. A few others are in the section of the guide on economic alternatives. The restaurants and cafes range from the casual to the formal.

WILLOW ISLAND RESTAURANT
1 West Main Street
Canton, New York 13617
315-386-8822

The cozy interior of this restaurant belies its history – the building is a converted gas station. Willow Island serves a variety of tasty main dishes, soups, salads, deserts, and breads, all made from scratch at the restaurant, with organic produce, almost no salt, and, when a sweetener is desirable, maple syrup. A typical main dish costs $7 or $8. Open Tues.-Sat. 11:00 A.M.-9:00 P.M.

HORN OF THE MOON CAFE
8 Langdon Street
Montpelier, Vermont 05602
802-223-2895

At Horn of the Moon travelers can find progressive periodicals and leaflets and petitions as well as tasty vegetarian meals. The cafe, which inspired *The Horn of the Moon Cookbook*, is open Mon.-Thurs. 7:00 A.M.-4:00 P.M.; Fri.-Sat. 7:00 A.M.-9:00 P.M.; Sun. 10:00 A.M.-2:00 P.M.

CABBAGETOWN CAFE
404 Eddy Street
Ithaca, New York 14850
607-273-2847

In business for more than seventeen years, Cabbagetown serves such vegetarian treats as cashew chili and Vietnamese salads. Ethnic dishes are a specialty. Hours are Mon.-Fri. 11:30 A.M.-8:30 or 9:00 P.M.; Sat. 10:00 A.M.-9:00 P.M.; Sun. 10:30 A.M.-9:00 P.M.

MOOSEWOOD RESTAURANT
214 North Cayuga, Dewitt Mall
Ithaca, New York 14850
607-273-9610

A worker-owned restaurant, Moosewood specializes in international vegetarian cuisine, with fish Friday and Saturday and an ethnic specialty Sunday. It is open for lunch 11:30 A.M.-2:00 P.M. except Sun. and for dinner 5:30-8:30 P.M. weekdays and 6:00-9:00 P.M. weekends.

BLOODROOT
85 Ferris Street
Bridgeport, Connecticut 06605
203-576-9168

At this fourteen-year-old feminist collective, you can shop for feminist books while waiting to eat. On the waterfront, Bloodroot serves a seasonal vegetarian menu. It offers lunch (11:30 A.M.-2:30 P.M.) and dinner (6:00-9:00 or 10:00 P.M.) Tues., Thurs., Fri., Sat.; brunch 11:30 A.M.-2:30 P.M. Sun. For dinner Wed., phone ahead.

ANGELICA KITCHEN
300 East 12th Street
New York, New York 10003
212-228-2909

Typical and delicious fare at this vegan restaurant are millet vegetable salad; a herbal lentil walnut pate served with rice and crackers; a three squash stew; and walnut pear cookies. The restaurant is open 11:30 A.M.-10:30 P.M. every day.

SPRING STREET NATURAL
62 Spring Street
New York, New York 10012
212-966-0290

A favorite for fourteen years, Spring Street Natural prides itself on using organic ingredients to the extent possible. The menu includes vegetarian pasta dishes and a complete line of herbal teas. It opens at noon daily and closes at midnight or 1:00 A.M.

FOOD FOR THOUGHT
1738 Connecticut Avenue NW
Washington, D.C. 20009
202-797-1095

An informal restaurant and favorite of the public-interest community, Food for Thought has a bulletin board with personal notices and information on events. Open from mid-day to midnight daily, except closed at lunch time Sun.

RED SEA
2463 18th Street NW
Washington, D.C. 20009
202-483-5000

This inexpensive Ethiopian restaurant is popular with students. Open from 11:30 A.M. to midnight daily.

STONE SOUP
50 Broadway and 8 Wall Street
Asheville, North Carolina 28801
704-255-7687

Stone Soup is a thirteen-year-old, worker-owned restaurant. It serves breakfast and lunch each weekday and brunch Sunday (9:30 A.M.-1:30 P.M. at the Broadway location). Thurs., Fri., and Sat. 5:00–9:30 P.M. Stone Soup is open as a cafe. Wholesome soups, sandwiches, and deserts are its staples.

ALFALFA
557 South Limestone
Lexington, Kentucky 40508
606-253-0014

If a progressive group in Lexington wants to hold a benefit dinner or a reception, Alfalfa is the place. It serves both vegetarian and meat entrees; and presents entertainment nightly. It is open for lunch Mon.-Fri., dinner, Tue.-Sat. (5:30–9:30 or 10:00 P.M.), and brunch (10:00 A.M.-2:00 P.M.) Sat. and Sun.

EAT YOUR VEGETABLES CAFE
438 Moreland Avenue, NE
Atlanta, Georgia 30307
404-523-2671

The cafe offers such specials as tofu manicotti, vegetable Wellington, and an African platter, including black bean fritters. Macrobiotic dishes are served. Open for lunch and dinner Mon.-Sat.; lunch Sat. 11:30 A.M.-3:00 P.M.; brunch Sun. 11:00 A.M.-3:00 P.M.

HIGH NOON CAFE
4147 Northview Drive
Jackson, Mississippi 39206
601-366-1602

Owned by Rainbow Whole Foods Co-op, the cafe is vegan. Hours are Mon.-Fri. 11:30 A.M.-2:00 P.M. It serves a variety of sandwiches, a different fresh-made soup and a different plate lunch special each day. The adjacent co-op is open Mon.-Sat. 10:00 A.M.-6:00 or 7:00 P.M.

HARVEST CAFE AND BAKERY
1112 1/2 Van Buren
Oxford, Mississippi 38655
601-236-3757

Meals at this vegetarian restaurant range from brown rice with vegetables to upscale gourmet dinners. Lunch is served Mon.-Fri.; dinner Thurs.-Sat. (5:30–10:00 P.M.); brunch Sun. Organic produce is used whenever possible.

BLIND FAITH CAFE

525 Dempster Street
Evanston, Illinois 60201
708-328-6875

A vegetarian restaurant, Blind Faith serves nightly specials, including walnut loaf, chickpea stew, and an Indian dinner. A macrobiotic dish is offered each evening. Open Mon.- Thurs. 10:00 A.M.-9:00 P.M., Fri. 10:00 A.M.-10:00 P.M., Sat. 8:00 A.M.-10:00 P.M., Sun. 8:00 A.M.-9:00 P.M.

COUNTRY LIFE

2465 Perry Street
Madison, Wisconsin 53713
608-257-3286

This top-notch restaurant is one of many Country Life restaurants across the United States and in other nations operated by various Seventh Day Adventist "corporations." All are vegan. The Madison restaurant is closed Fri. and Sat.; phone for hours the remainder of the week. It waits on guests, but many Country Life restaurants are buffets. The addresses of a few other Country Life restaurants are 112 Broad Street, Boston 02110 (617-350-8846); 3748 Ringold Road, Chattanooga, Tennessee 37412 (615-622-2451); and 888 Figueroa, Los Angeles, California 90017 (213-489-4118).

NEW RIVERSIDE CAFE

329 Cedar Avenue
Minneapolis, Minnesota 55454
612-333-4814

A worker-owned restaurant for twenty years, Riverside Cafe justifiably prides itself on its wok dishes, wholesome deserts, ethnic specialties, and whole wheat crepes and omelets. It is vegetarian and serves some foods free of wheat, eggs, and dairy products. Customers can learn ingredients through signs in the cafeteria line where food is served. It is open throughout the day every day, but hours vary somewhat.

SEWARD COMMUNITY CAFE
2129 East Franklin Avenue
Minneapolis, Minnesota 55404
612-332-1011

Founded in 1974 to provide whole foods at a reasonable price to the Seward community, Seward Cafe is owned by the community and managed by a worker collective. It supports the extensive co-op movement in the Twin Cities in such ways as buying from cooperative wholesalers and providing deli items and baked goods to retail cooperatives. Its menu includes vegan dishes. In the summer the cafe has tables outdoors in a secluded area. Hours are 7:00 A.M.-8:00 P.M. weekdays and 8:00 A.M.-8:00 P.M. weekends.

HOT LICKS
3549 College Road
Fairbanks, Alaska 99709
907-479-7813

As the name indicates, Hot Licks specializes in ice cream. It also serves home made bread and soups (one meat and one vegetarian every day). A great place to meet people and find out about activities in Fairbanks, it is open daily from 7:00 A.M.-11:00 or 12:00 P.M. in summer; shorter hours in winter.

SOURDOUGH EXPRESS BAKERY
1316 Ocean Drive
Homer, Alaska 99603
907-235-7571

Sourdough specializes in seafood, although it also offers meatless fare. The baked goods made from grain ground at the bakery, are celebrated. The owner cooperates with the Center for Alaskan Coastal Studies which offers day-long excursions to study the ecology of Kachemak Bay (for information on the trips call China Poot Bay Society 907-235-6667). Hours are 6:00 A.M.-10:00 P.M. Closed 1 Oct.-1 April.

GRAVITY BAR

415 Broadway Avenue East
Seattle, Washington 98102
206-325-7186
and
86 Pine Street, Seattle, Washington 98101
206-443-9694

The Gravity Bars serve vegetarian breakfast, lunch, and dinner, with lots of organic food. Despite the name, they do not serve alcohol; and smoking is not allowed. Wheat grass is grown on their restaurants' own organic farm. In a corner of each restaurant, health and world eco-sensitive products and books are sold. The entrance way to the Broadway store sports a huge bulletin board. Hours are Mon.-Thur. 8:00 A.M.-10:00 P.M., Fri.-Sat. 8:00 A.M.-11:00 P.M.; Sun. 9:00 A.M.-11:00 P.M.

HONEY BEAR BAKERY

2106 North 55th
Seattle, Washington 98103
206-545-7296

A vegan restaurant, Honey Bear serves hot cereal and baked goods for breakfast; two soups, three salads, and a dinner special for lunch or dinner. It is open daily, 6:00 A.M.-10:00 or 11:00 P.M.

THE COTTAGE — A RESTAURANT

2915 Row River Road
Cottage Grove, Oregon 97424
503-942-3091

Owners of the Cottage have received awards for the passive solar design of its building from both the state of Oregon and the U.S. Department of Energy. Vegetarian meals are popular, but meats are also served. Open Mon.-Fri. 11:00 A.M.-8:30 or 9:00 P.M., Sat. 5:00–9:00 P.M.

THE TOFU SHOP DELI AND GROCERY

768 18th Street
Arcata, California 95521
707-822-7409

Fashioned after the neighborhood tofu shops of Japan, this deli/grocery makes tofu daily. It sells light meals including a wide variety of tasty soy products. Hours are Mon.-Sat. 8:00 A.M.-8:00 P.M.; Sun. 11:00 A.M.-6:00 P.M.

GREENS
Fort Mason, Building A
San Francisco, California 97123
415-771-6222

A gourmet vegetarian restaurant, Greens obtains much of its food from Green Gulch Farm. Both restaurant and farm are part of the San Francisco Zen Center. It is open for lunch and dinner Tues.-Sat. and for brunch Sun. 10:00 A.M.-2:00 P.M. Reservations are recommended. Prices are somewhat higher than those of most of the restaurants on this list.

GUARANGA'S VEGETARIAN CUISINE
503 Water Street
Santa Cruz, California 95060
408-427-0294

At Guaranga's it's "all you care to eat," self-served. The restaurant rotates fourteen-day specialties showing a Far Eastern influence. It offers a delicious salad bar with vegan and non-vegan dressings, and is very reasonably priced. Open for lunch Tue.-Sat. 11:30 A.M.-2:30 P.M.; and for dinner Tues.-Sat. 5:00–8:00 or 9:00 P.M.

INDIAN SUMMER DELI & JUICE BAR
2724 Soquel Avenue
Santa Cruz, California 95062
408-476-9840

According to a Santa Fe vegan, food at Indian Summer is "almost exclusively vegan, fairly macrobiotic . . . very delicious and large portions served." Hours are 11:00 A.M.-5:30 P.M. daily.

KEFFI
1245 East Cliff Drive
Santa Cruz, California 95062
408-476-5571

Influenced by the "Living Foods" philosophy, Keffi has a large selection of live gourmet cuisine. As Santa Fe's only full-service vegetarian restaurant, Keffi charges somewhat more than many of the restaurants on our list. Expect to pay $8-$9 for an entree. Open for lunch Tue.-Sat. 11:30 A.M.-2:30 P.M. and for brunch Sun. 10:30 A.M.-2:30 P.M. Dinner is Tues.-Sun. 5:00–8:00 or 9:00 P.M.

Santa Cruz is reputed to have the largest number of vegetarian restaurants per capita of any city in the country. Two other restaurants that visitors may want to sample are Zanzibar (seafood and vegan and vegetarian dishes; 2332 Mission Street; 408-423-9999); and Staff of Life (cafeteria-style natural foods cuisine and a bakery with vegan and non-vegan treats; 1305 Water Street; 408-423-8068).

CLOUD CLIFF BAKERY AND CAFE
1805 Second Street
Santa Fe, New Mexico 87504
505-983-6254

Cloud Cliff is "the main gravitation spot in Santa Fe for artists, activists, and people who are tired of the city's overly chic atmosphere." It serves a full breakfast and sandwiches and pizzas, among other items—vegetarian except for fish and organic chicken. Open daily 7:00 A.M.-2:00 P.M.

NATURAL DELI
2525 South King Street
Honolulu, Hawaii 96826
808-949-8188

A vegan restaurant open 10 A.M.-9:00 P.M. daily, the Natural Deli shares a building with a large health food store, Down to Earth Natural Foods, selling organic and bulk products.

CHAPTER TWENTY-NINE

Lodging

Youth hostels are a bargain. The one drawback is their relative scarcity. The United States has approximately 220. For $5 and up a night, the hostels offer dormitory-style accommodations and kitchen facilities to travelers of all ages. You should be a member of American Youth Hostels (AYH) and carry with you linens or a "sleep sack," a folded and sewn sheet. Advance reservations are advisable, especially in the summer.

Joining the AYH for a year costs people between the ages of eighteen and fifty-four $25; youth $10; and senior citizens $15. Members receive a handbook describing all U.S. hostels and a membership card good for 5,300 hostels worldwide. Visitors to the United States can use AYH membership cards, which can be purchased from International Youth Hostel Federation affiliates. To join the AYH contact the national headquarters at P.O. Box 37613, Washington, D.C. 20013 (202-783-6161). You may join through this office or through any AYH Council.

In cities, two alternatives to hostels are lodging with the Young Men's Christian Association (YMCA) or Young Women's Christian Association (YWCA). Some YMCA's accommodate women and children as well as men; the YWCA's are normally limited to women. The YMCA of Greater New York books reservations at numerous YMCAs throughout North America, and offers package programs including room, some meals, and sightseeing in several major cities. Reserving ahead is advised. Contact The Y's Way, 356 West 34th Street, New York, New York 10001; 212-760-5856. For $3 the YWCA sells a directory of its facilities to women wanting to stay at a YWCA. Call or write to the National Board, Young Women's Christian Association of the USA, 726 Broadway, New York, New York 10003 (212-614-2700).

Accommodations on college and university campuses are an excellent buy. A few campuses offer rooms year round, although most do so only during the summer. The *U.S. and World Wide Travel Accommodations Guide* lists, with prices ($12-$24 per day) and dates, 700 colleges and universities in the United States and abroad that welcome guests; it also describes many YMCA lodging centers open to the general public of all ages and gives tips on economical travel. Order, for $13 (plus $1.50 for first class postage) from Campus Travel Service, P.O. Box 8355, Newport Beach, California 92660 (714-720-3729). For colleges and universities advance reservations are necessary.

Bed and breakfasts (rooms, including breakfast, in private homes) are a great way to meet people around the country, but are not necessarily an economical way to travel. Bed and breakfast rooms may cost only half the price of equivalent accommodations in hotels; but hotel prices can be exorbitant.

Among the many printed guides to bed and breakfasts, Pamela Lanier's *The Complete Guide to Bed and Breakfasts, Inns and Guesthouses* stands out. It lists around 6,000 lodgings, with brief descriptions of the significant features of each, including availability of bicycles and opportunities for outdoor recreation. It includes classified indexes: nature, skiing, farm vacations, vegetarian, among other topics. (Unfortunately few of the bed and breakfasts fall into the vegetarian category.) It also lists by region and by state, bed and breakfast reservation services. Order from the publisher, John Muir, P.O. Box 613, Santa Fe, New Mexico 87504; 505-982-4078.

Bed and Breakfast: The National Network, an association of regional bed and breakfast reservation services, will furnish a list of its members with addresses and phone numbers. Write to the Network at Box 4616, Springfield, Massachusetts 01101. Bed and breakfast reservation services include:

NEW WORLD BED AND BREAKFAST
150 Fifth Avenue, Suite 711
New York, New York 10011
212-675-5600; 800-443-3800 except in New York and Canada

Places travelers in rooms in private homes and in unoccupied, furnished apartments in New York City. A room for one person in a home is $40–70.

URBAN VENTURES
P.O. Box 426
New York, New York 10024
212-594-5650

Specializes in accommodations in New York City. The prices for a single start at $45.

THE BED AND BREAKFAST LEAGUE, LTD./
SWEET DREAMS AND TOAST
P.O. Box 9490
Washington, D.C. 20016

Specializes in Washington and its suburbs. A room for one person with a shared bath costs $35–65. The service charges a $10 booking fee per reservation.

BED AND BREAKFAST HAWAII
P.O. Box 449
Kapaa, Hawaii 96746
808-822-7771; 800-733-1632

Produces and distributes a book describing more than a hundred bed and breakfasts (on all the islands) for which the service makes reservations. The book also suggests restaurants, out-of-the-way places to visit, and opportunities for outdoor recreation.

The Maine Farm Bed and Breakfast Association offers vacations at farms. For information contact Sally Godfrey at her referral service, Bed and Breakfast Down East, Ltd., Box 547, Eastbrook, Maine 04634 (207-565-3517).

The annual directory, *Homecomings,* can help "Unitarians, Quakers, Ethical Culturists, and other religious liberals" to find low-cost accommodations in the homes of like-minded people. The cost of the directory plus a membership ID and postage is $11.95. The directory covers the United States and also lists some homes in Canada. It is available from Homecomings, Box 1545, New Milford, Connecticut 06776.

To promote peace and international understanding, the international organization Servas assists people in staying in homes in countries other than their own. Servas was founded in 1948 as a work/study/travel program by an international group of young peacemakers studying in Denmark. Stays are usually for two nights, and no money is exchanged between host and traveler. Travelers are invited to participate in the life of the home and the community, and to share ideas, questions, interests, and concerns with their hosts.

Both hosts and travelers receive orientation from volunteer interviewers. The fee for travelers is $45 per year, plus a refundable deposit of $15 for host lists. The organization suggests that hosts make a voluntary contribution of $15. Residents of the United States interested in participating, should contact the U.S. Servas Committee, 11 John Street, New York, New York 10038 (212-267-0252). People living abroad should contact the Servas office in their own country; you can obtain the address from the U.S. office. Contact your national office one to four months before starting a trip.

Exchanging housing is a way of cutting the cost of vacations. The International Home Exchange Service/INTERVAC is among the services that help people find others with whom to exchange. For a $35 annual fee, plus postage and handling, it supplies three books of listings, in one or two of which it describes the subscriber's dwelling. Subscribers contact each other directly and make their own arrangements. The address in the U.S. is P.O. Box 190070, San Francisco, California 94119 (415-435-3497).

Camping on public land is discussed in Part III, Natural Areas and Their Wildlife. To locate public and private campgrounds consult *Woodall's Campground Directory* or regional directories from the Woodall Publishing Company (11 North Skokie Highway, Lake Bluff, Illinois 60044). Private campgrounds tend to be more crowded and more expensive than campgrounds in public parks and forests. At Kampgrounds of America (KOA) sites, hot showers and telephones are standard, but the price may be $15 or more for two people for a night.

A sampling of lodgings follows:

APPALACHIAN MOUNTAIN CLUB (AMC)
5 Joy Street
Boston, Massachusetts 02108
617-523-0636

The AMC owns and/or operates a wide variety of camps in Maine, New Hampshire, Massachusetts, and Vermont. They are open to non-members, although at most facilities non-members pay more than members. Some are primitive campgrounds where only tents, or, in some cases, folding tent trailers are permitted. Others have cabins or lodges. Some of the camps are self-service facilities; others provide all meals. Only camps with good skiing and snowshoeing are open year round.

The best known of the AMC facilities may be the eight huts about a day's hike apart, along the Appalachian Trail, and Pinkham Notch Camp. They are among fifteen AMC facilities in New Hampshire. Sleeping over a hundred people, Pinkham Notch serves as a base camp for thousands of hikers, campers, and skiers each year and as an educational facility. The only Vermont camp is Wheeler Pond Camp at Barton, a self-service camp with two cabins. Along the Maine coast are four campgrounds frequented by tidewater canoeists; three are on islands: Beal, Swan, and Fort. The club operates full-service facilities on Mount Desert Island, which is the site of Acadia National Park, and on the top of Mount Greylock in the Berkshires of western Massachusetts, among other places.

For information, contact the club. Reservations for a given year cannot be mailed until 1 April, but the camps fill up quickly after that date. Prices vary from a few dollars a night for the Saco River campgrounds in New Hampshire and Maine, through $10 a night ($15 for nonmembers) for New Hampshire's Crawford Notch Hostel, to more than $35 a night for a single, including meals, at a full-service camp on an island in New Hampshire's Lake Winnipesaukee. Some camps only accept reservations for one or more weeks.

ROWE CAMP AND CONFERENCE CENTER
Kings Highway Road
Rowe, Massachusetts 01367
413-339-4216

The center describes itself as "a warm, non-competitive environment in which people can experience joy, creativity and learning, as well as personal and spiritual growth." Guests participate in summer camp sessions or attend fall, winter, or spring retreat workshops, usually with nationally known leaders. In addition, between September and June on days when no conference is scheduled, they may use the center as a place for retreat, alone or with a group.

The center is surrounded by 1,400 acres of forest and wilderness preserve. Orchard House, where guests often stay, is nestled at the top of an orchard next to pine woods. Rowe is near prime areas for downhill and cross-country skiing. A private room for one person during the week costs $30, on a weekend $40.

TEMENOS
Box 84A, Star Route
Shutesbury, Massachusetts 01072
413-367-9779, Wed. 11:00 A.M.-1:00 P.M., or leave a message

Temenos, southeast of Greenfield, is a retreat center where individuals have personal retreats and groups hold workshops, training sessions. Here one finds silence, a wooded setting, an atmosphere of reverence for all living creatures and all spiritual traditions, and healing energies from the past, through power spots, including mineral springs and a monk's cave.

Temenos rents four cabins with woodstoves for cooking and heating and with access to water and wood. They are available for retreats of up to three months from November to April and for shorter retreats from May to November. The fee is on a sliding scale based on income, $8-$30 for a single night, with lower rates for longer visits. Reserve in advance. You may also stay in your own tent or on the floor of a lodge. The property has no phone or electricity.

ADIRONDACK MOUNTAIN CLUB
Box 867
Lake Placid, New York 12946
518-523-3441

The club operates Adirondak Loj on the edge of the High Peaks wilderness area, eight miles south of Lake Placid, and Johns Brook Lodge in the backcountry of the High Peaks and reachable only by a three and a half mile hike. It also has two cabins accessible by foot trail, deep in the Johns Brook Valley of the High Peaks. The lodges offer leantos as well as more elaborate accommodations. Adirondak Loj, which, unlike Johns Brook Lodge, is open year round, has a campground.

To reach the vicinity of the lodges take an Adirondack Trailways bus to Keene Valley or Lake Placid. The lodges and cabins are open to the public; Adirondack Mountain Club members receive a 10% discount. A bed or private room at Adirondack Lodge costs $20-$48 per person, depending on the season, the accommodations, and the meals requested.

THE CROSSING
906 South 49th Street
Philadelphia, Pennsylvania 19143
215-726-0743

A spinoff of the Movement for a New Society, the Crossing provides peace and social justice workers visiting Philadelphia with dormitory-style accommodations. The cost is $10–16 per night, based on ability to pay. Kitchen facilities are available.

PENDLE HILL
Wallingford, Pennsylvania 19086–6099
215-566-4507

A Quaker center for study and contemplation. Pendle Hill offers a resident study program with three ten-week terms; an extension program of short-term conferences and events; and the opportunity to be a sojourner. Sojourners stay at Pendle Hill for periods of one day to three weeks. They are free to participate in the life of the community, including classes, meetings for worship, and cooperative work in an organic garden, or to remain apart. Libraries and craft facilities are available. The 22- acre campus is in a suburban area, accessible by public transport. Room and board for a sojourner are $45 a day for the first week, $43 a day thereafter.

INDIAN VALLEY RETREAT
Route 2, Box 58
Willis, Virginia 24380
703-789-4295

Indian Valley offers individual or group retreats on 140 acres of rolling meadows, woodlands and mountain streams in the beautiful Blue Ridge Mountains of southwest Virginia, 15 miles north of the Blue Ridge Parkway. For guests the center has two relatively primitive cabins and three rooms in an old farmhouse. The cost of a night and breakfast is only $12.50.

The center presents workshops, including a Women's Wellness Week.

CIRCLE PINES CENTER
8650 Mullen Road
Delton, Michigan 49046
616-623-5555

Situated on 360 acres of rolling meadows and woodland, and fronting on spring-fed Stewart Lake, Circle Pines is a place to relax as well as to gain from the center's mission of teaching cooperation. The center offers weekend programs on such varied topics as maple sugaring and peace education. In the summer, as space is available, people can make individual stays at the center. The cost per night for individual accommodations is $5 for camping privileges, $17.50 for a bed in a hostel-style lodge. For the price of meals contact the center.

NEAHTAWANTA INN
1308 Neahtawanta Road
Traverse City, Michigan 49684
616-223-7315

First opened in 1906, the inn is now a bed and breakfast, which also houses the Neahtawanta Research and Education Center, an organization working on peace, community, sustainable use of resources, and personal growth issues. The inn is on a peninsula in Grand Traverse Bay north of Traverse City. Depending on the season, visitors can rent a boat or sailboard nearby or enjoy cross-country or downhill skiing. A single room with breakfast is $45 or $50 a night, a double $55 or $60. Children are welcome. A family suite is available.

INTERNATIONAL HOUSE
1414 East 59th Street
Chicago, Illinois 60637
312-753-2280

The International House in the heart of the University of Chicago campus is a splendid gothic building that houses both American and international students. Most of the guests are students attending the university, but rooms are available for travelers of all ilks looking for cheap—and nice—lodgings throughout the year. In addition to single rooms for rent, the building has a cafeteria, a reading room, and a large public room, where everything from dance courses to movie nights are held. Rooms rent for $14 a night (which includes towels and linens) for students with Youth Hostel cards, $25 a night for others; discounts are available for stays that last longer than a week. Reservations are encouraged. No advance payment is needed. Transportation to and from O'Hare and Midway airports is available. Contact International House Reservations at the above address.

PINE BUTTE GUEST RANCH
HC58, Box 34C
Choteau, Montana 59422
406-466-2158

Owned by the Nature Conservancy, Pine Butte combines a traditional western guest ranch milieu with a natural history program. During the summer a full-time naturalist conducts daily hikes. The lodge and eight rustic but comfortable cabins are surrounded by land protected for wildlife. The rate for room, board, and the naturalist program in the summer is $775 per person per week. Starting 10 June the minimum stay is one week. The off season rate is lower. Proceeds from the ranch support the work of the Conservancy.

THE MOUNTAINEERS
300 Third Avenue W
Seattle, Washington 98119
206-284-8484

The Mountaineers operate Kitsap Cabin in the Rhododendron Preserve and four lodges primarily for skiing. All are in the state of Washington. The ski lodges are Meany Ski Hut, three miles from Stampede Overpass; Mount Baker Lodge near the Mount Baker ski area east of Bellingham; Snoqualmie Lodge; and Stevens Lodge at Stevens Pass. The lodges are open to non-members, but members pay lower fees. The prices for a weekend for a non-member are $12 at Baker, $13 at Stevens, $20 at Snoqualmie, and $32 at Meany.

SHENOA RETREAT CENTER
P.O. Box 43
Philo, California 95466
707-895-3156

Shenoa is a retreat center operated in accordance with the ideals and principles of the Findhorn Community in northern Scotland. It occupies 160 acres of open meadows interspersed with forests of redwood, fir, laurel, and oak, set amongst gently rolling hills. The staff and invited faculty periodically present events and programs. Individuals, families, and groups are welcome to make use of the facilities for their own retreats and workshops. Vegetarian meals are served. Inquire as to rates which vary with the season. Write or phone before visiting.

WELLSPRING RENEWAL CENTER
Box 332
Philo, California 95466
707-895-3893

An interfaith retreat and conference center, Wellspring is located on 50 acres in the coastal hills of Mendocino County beside a redwood forest. It sponsors events such as canoeing and backpacking trips and a harvest work session and celebration. "Wellspring cabins are available for vacations when not superseded by programs." Camping is also available. Write for dates and fees.

CLAIR TAPPAN LODGE
P.O. Box 36
Norden, California 95724
916-426-3632

For Sierra Club members and their guests, the club operates a rustic mountain lodge at an elevation of 7,000 feet on Donner Summit. Volunteers built the lodge in 1934 and have since expanded and maintained it. In the summer the lodge provides a base for hiking and rock climbing. In the winter it offers skiers the highest average snowfall in the Sierra, instruction, 5–7 kilometers of groomed cross-country ski trails, and equipment rental.

For a reservation form, contact the lodge. The charge for a member, including meals, is $26 midweek and $30 Fri. and Sat.

Across a ravine from Tappan is a smaller lodge for groups. Four huts are located about a day's ski or hike apart, around Tappan. Reserve with Tappan.

THE MILE HI
27 Ramsey Canyon Road, RR 1, Box 84
Hereford, Arizona 85615
602-378-2785

Owned and operated by the Nature Conservancy, the Mile Hi is a choice spot for birding. More species of hummingbirds have been seen here – fourteen – than at any other place in the United States. The Mile Hi includes 20 acres and six modern housekeeping cabins. It is adjacent to the 280-acre Ramsey Canyon Preserve, also Nature Conservancy property. In Ramsey Canyon are five major biotic communities: pine-fir, pine-oak, oak woodland, mesquite grassland, and riparian.

The price per night for a cabin is $60 for one or two people. From April to August advance reservations must be for a minimum of three nights, if space is available.

KALANI HONUA CONFERENCE CENTER AND RETREAT
RR 2, Box 4500
Kalapana, Hawaii 96778
808-965-7828

Kalani Honua is 30 miles southeast of Hilo, on the tropical windward coast of the Big Island of Hawaii. It provides lodging and meals for groups, as well as for individual guests. "This is a very eclectic center. We are off the beaten path and away from the tourist centers, a wonderful base for exploration into the mysteries and beauty of this volcanic island." Phone or write to receive a brochure or to check on available space and upcoming events. A double occupancy room with shared bath is $54 per night May 1-Dec. 14, $58 per night Dec. 15-April 30. Meals cost about $25 per day. Private baths and cottages are also available.

CHAPTER THIRTY

Environmentally-Related Employment: Getting Away to Work

Earning room and board while away from home is a way of making travel affordable. A wide variety of volunteer positions enable travelers to assist in a worthwhile project while seeing a new part of the country or world and meeting people with common interests.

The book *Volunteer!*, published by the Council on International Educational Exchange and the Commission on Voluntary Service and Action (CVSA), describes over two hundred service agencies in the United States and abroad with openings for volunteers for periods ranging from a weekend to three years. Openings covered include activities related to environmental preservation, although social work is predominant. Order, for $6.95 plus $1.35 postage, from *Volunteer!* Distribution, Box 347, Newton, Kansas 67114 (checks payable to CVSA).

The American Hiking Society annually publishes *Helping out in the Outdoors: A Volunteer Directory to American Parks and Forests*. It lists internships and volunteer jobs on all types of land open to the public. Most positions are for campground hosts, trail maintenance and construction crews, and wilderness rangers and backcountry guards; but there are also opportunities for office workers and others. An issue costs $5 mailed to the United States and $8 abroad. Order from the society at 1015 31st Street, NW, Washington, D.C. 20007.

Below is a sampling of programs using volunteers, listed by organization. It closes with an account of the youth conservation corps. Corps members are not strictly volunteers and are more likely to work in their communities than to travel; but the movement is described, because of its growing importance for youth and for the environment.

AMERICAN HIKING SOCIETY – VOLUNTEER VACATIONS

P.O. Box 86

North Scituate, Massachusetts 02060

In addition to publishing a directory, the American Hiking Society runs a volunteer program. Participants in its Volunteer Vacations work in teams for ten days of a two-week vacation, usually in a national park, national forest, or state park. The most common project is trail building or maintenance. Participants provide their own camping equipment and generally pay for their own transportation to the project area, but are normally given their food. Teams work at all seasons of the year, and locations include Alaska and Hawaii. Applicants should be experienced backpackers in good physical condition. Information on the program is free, but $30 must accompany an application.

APPALACHIAN TRAIL CONFERENCE

P.O. Box 807

Harpers Ferry, West Virginia 25425

304-535-6331

Members of Appalachian Trail Volunteer Crews work on trail building and preservation for periods ranging from a week to a whole season. The normal work week is Thursday through Monday, with a Tuesday/Wednesday "weekend." Anyone in good condition and over eighteen may apply. (Contact the technical assistance coordinator.) Once a volunteer reaches a work and training center, most of his/her expenses are met.

Other trail associations welcome volunteers but do not usually have the resources to organize summer-long volunteer programs that pay the on-the-job expenses of participants.

COUNCIL ON INTERNATIONAL EDUCATIONAL EXCHANGE

205 East 42nd Street

New York, New York 10017

212-661-1414

The council sponsors International Workcamps for young people in Europe and North America. Volunteers generally work forty hours a week in exchange for room and board. Work falls into two general categories – manual/physical and social service. U.S. and European volunteers participate in the camps in this country, which run for three weeks each in July and August. Most U.S. camps are conservation oriented. Work in the past has included general park maintenance and tending a native-plant garden. Applications are accepted as early as January for the following summer and must be accompanied by a $125 fee, partially refunded if the applicant is not placed. Placement is on a first-come, first-served basis.

GESUNDHEIT INSTITUTE
2630 Robert Walker Place
Arlington, Virginia 22207
703-525-8169

Led by Dr. Hunter D. (Patch) Adams, a physician who is friends with his patients, the institute is constructing a model health care community in Pocahontas County, West Virginia. Volunteers, skilled or unskilled, who can stay at least a week are needed in West Virginia, but must phone or write to the Arlington address to make arrangements ahead of time. In return for hard work, they receive room and board and the chance to contribute to an exciting project. The community is designed to stimulate patients toward health; and it will include, in addition to a forty-bed hospital, such pleasures as a theater and a 30,000 volume library.

MENNONITE VOLUNTARY SERVICE
General Conference Mennonite Church
722 Main Street, Box 347
Newton, Kansas 67114
316-283-5100

Most of the Mennonite Voluntary Service assignments are for one or two years, but a limited number of openings for shorter-term workers exist. Short-term volunteers receive only room and board; those working for twelve months or more receive additional benefits. The program is open to Christians of all denominations and traditions. Environmental positions include work in weatherization of low-income housing, an office manager position with an environmental association, and a post as environmentalist with a nature-study center.

STUDENT CONSERVATION ASSOCIATION
P.O. Box 550C
Charlestown, New Hampshire 03603
603-826-4301

The association assists college students and other adults in obtaining volunteer seasonal positions as resource assistants with federal land agencies and also with some state agencies and private organizations. Applicants receive a catalog describing open positions. When they return the completed application, they select four jobs for which they want to apply. The association screens the applications; the agency offering a given position makes the final choice. In return for work, successful candidates receive funds to cover travel to and from the work site, free housing, a subsistence allowance to help offset the cost of food, and an allowance for any required uniforms. Positions are diverse and are available for all seasons.

TRAVELER'S EARTH REPAIR NETWORK (TERN)
Friends of the Trees Society
P.O. Box 1064
Tonasket, Washington 98855

Friends of the Trees has established a computerized listing of people and organizations around the world who seek visitors to assist in earth repair work such as reforestation, erosion control, agroforestry, and sustainable agriculture. Many of the hosts can supply housing and food, though not always free of charge.

To participate travelers obtain from TERN an application that asks them to describe their qualifications and needs; and return it with a basic $50 fee. TERN then runs a computer search for the countries or areas requested. (Individual states in the United States and provinces in Canada can be searched.) The traveler receives a printout, annotated by the TERN staff. Potential hosts must fill out an application but hosts do not pay to be listed.

VOLUNTEERS FOR PEACE (VFP)
43 Tiffany Road
Belmont, Vermont 05730
802-259-2759

This association places volunteers in workcamps run by a variety of organizations, primarily in Europe but also in the United States and a few other countries. For a $10 annual membership contribution, applicants receive a directory from which they can select one or more workcamps, each of which lasts two or three weeks. Registration costs $100 per camp. Volunteers pay for and arrange their own travel but usually receive room and board in return for labor. Placement is on a first-come, first-served basis. Anyone can write or call to receive a free newsletter.

VFP organizes its own workcamps in the United States for American and foreign volunteers. Foreign applicants pay no registration fee. Many of the American volunteers for these camps are recruited locally. Projects at the camps have included maintaining a trail, roofing an old farmhouse and reconstructing a yurt, and doing general maintenance at an environmental study center.

NATIONAL ASSOCIATION OF SERVICE AND CONSERVATION CORPS (NASCC)
1001 Connecticut Avenue, NW, Suite 827
Washington, D.C. 20036
202-331-9647

Year-round and summer youth corps, many of them working on conservation projects, exist now in more than twenty states and in many localities. Currently they employ some 60,000 people a year. More than 80% of the participants are disadvantaged; high school dropouts represent more than 40% of the participants in most programs and 80% in others. Usually corps members receive minimum wage for working full-time at least four days a week, and spend part of the fifth day on general education and preparation for obtaining a job when they are ready to leave the corps. Administrative arrangements differ from corps to corps. Funding comes from cities, states, private sources, and federal job training and community development block grants.

The state-funded California Conservation Corps operates a Training Academy and seventeen residential centers with thirty-two satellites. Its Mendocino Center (707-463-2822) provides public conservation work and operates the Napa Native Plant Nursery, which propagates plants for distribution throughout the state. The Placer Energy Center (916-823-4902) in Auburn, overseas an energy program through which corps members monitor energy use, and install energy saving devices in office buildings and low-income homes throughout the state. Del Norte Center (707-482-2941) in Klamath works in fisheries restoration and sends corpsmembers to Yosemite and other wilderness areas to construct trails and reforest meadows.

An example of a smaller program, the Montana Conservation Corps was organized in 1990 as a private, nonprofit corporation to provide employment opportunities for youth as well as to enhance their environmental awareness. Among the corps's projects during its first summer were cleaning up the East Gallatin State Recreation Area and constructing a trail for the handicapped. For further information contact Larry Dominick (406-752-6565).

NASCC is participating with the Student Conservation Association and the National Park Service in a program to repair damage caused by fires and fire-fighting in Yellowstone National Park in 1989. Crews of corpsmembers are serving in the park.

A network of operators and advocates of youth corps, NASCC is a voice for youth corps in Washington, provides for exchange of information among corps, and offers technical assistance to those interested in launching new corps. Its publications include the quarterly newsletter *Youth Can!,* including information on innovative projects and legislative initiatives ($25 yearly); and *Conservation and Service Corps Profiles,* a descriptive listing of existing conservation and service corps programs ($5).

Cultivation on organic farms tends to be labor intensive. Thus organic growers often need assistance. The organizations described below bring together growers and people wanting to work on farms. As a general rule, the workers exchange labor for room, board, and farming experience. Each worker/farmer pair make their own arrangements, which can range from weekend work stays to long-term apprenticeships.

The earlier section of the guide on alternative agriculture includes farms that may be contacted directly in regard to apprenticeships.

MOFGA APPRENTICESHIP PLACEMENT SERVICE
P.O. Box 2176, 283 Water Street
Augusta, Maine 04330
207-622-3118

To participate in this service of the Maine Organic Farmers and Gardeners Association, growers and prospective workers fill out applications. The placement service matches a grower with a worker and sends each a copy of the other's application. If they do not make an agreement, they can receive information on other possibilities. The service costs apprentices $15, and growers $30 ($20 for MOFGA members). Only growers willing to train an apprentice should take part.

NATURAL ORGANIC FARMERS ASSOCIATION (NOFA)—VERMONT
15 Barre Street
Montpelier, Vermont 05602
802-223-7222

NOFA will provide to anyone interested in working, a list of certified growers who hire people and will assist in making the farmer-worker hookup.

NORTH EAST WORKERS ON ORGANIC FARMS (NEWOOF)
c/o New England Small Farm Institute
Box 937
Belchertown, Massachusetts 01007
413-323-4531

Descriptions of each of the growers' farms are printed in a spring newsletter or in updates that are mailed to the workers. The workers are responsible for contacting farms. The focus is on the northeastern United States. Receiving lists costs $5; listing a farm $10.

OHIO ECOLOGICAL FOOD AND FARM ASSOCIATION
65 Plymouth Street
Plymouth, Ohio 44865
419-687-7665

Would-be farm apprentices fill out an application and pay $15. In return they receive a list of possible farm situations. Farmers pay $20 for being listed.

SOUTH ORGANIC APPRENTICESHIP PROGRAM (SOAP)
Utopia Organic Gardens
School Street, P.O. Box 45
Utopia, Texas 78884
512-966-3724

SOAP serves the southern United States. For $10 a year a grower or
worker is entitled to a fifty-word description in the SOAP newsletter
and to the four issues of the newsletter published that year.

Utopia Organic Gardens, which serves as the SOAP office, are
demonstration gardens, open to visitors except Sunday mornings.
Herbs are the specialty, but asparagus, which is harvested in March and
April, is the biggest crop. Other vegetables are also grown.

TILTH PLACEMENT SERVICE
P.O. Box 95261
Seattle, Washington 98145
Attention: Lee LaCroix
206-524-5620

Tilth facilitates work arrangements in Washington, Oregon, Idaho, and
northern California. It publishes a bimonthly newsletter containing
descriptions of growers and potential workers. Either a worker or a
grower can initiate a contact. The annual fee is $8 in the United States
and $12 to a foreign address.

CALIFORNIA CERTIFIED ORGANIC FARMERS (CCOF)
State Office, P.O. Box 8136
Santa Cruz, California 95061
408-423-2263

The CCOF publishes a grower-members list that indicates which
growers want apprentices. The list is for sale to the general public for
$6. A list of apprenticeships only costs $1.

The following periodicals are among the sources of information on
permanent and temporary environmental jobs:

Community Jobs
1601 Connecticut NW, #600
Washington, D.C. 20009
202-667-0661

Published monthly by Community Careers Resource Center, this periodical lists "socially responsible jobs and internships" across the nation. Subscriptions are $20 for 6 months; $25 per year. A single issue is $3.95.

Environmental Job Opportunities
Institute for Environmental Studies, University of Wisconsin-Madison
550 North Park Street, 15 Science Hall
Madison, Wisconsin 53706
608-263-3185

This periodical emphasizes openings for candidates with a strong academic background and/or management experience, but it also lists beginning positions and internships. Subscriptions cost $10 a year (10 issues).

Environmental Opportunities
P.O. Box 4957
Arcata, California 95521
707-839-4640

Sponsored by the Environmental Studies Department of Antioch/New England Graduate School in Keene, New Hampshire, this monthly bulletin presents a wide variety of positions throughout the country. Listings include openings in organizations, outdoor education, research, and seasonal positions and internships. The periodical closes with announcements of upcoming conferences and educational opportunities. Subscriptions are $24 for six months; $44 for a year.

Earth Work
Student Conservation Association
P.O. Box 550
Charlestown, New Hampshire 03603-9985

Published monthly by the Student Conservation Association, *Earth Work* lists professional and entry-level full-time positions and internships and seasonal openings. It also prints articles with information on careers in conservation and environmental work. A one-year subscription is $29.95. A single issue costs $6.

The Job Seeker
Department A, Route 2, Box 16
Warrens, Wisconsin 54666

Two issues each month list environmental and natural resource vacancies nationwide. A three-month trial subscription is $19.50.

CHAPTER THIRTY-ONE

Contacts

The following individuals, organizations, and businesses can orient newcomers to environmental/ecological activities in their respective areas. Many of the associations and firms listed earlier can also fill this role.

Friends of Earth Island Institute has established Earth Island Centers across the country, which carry on ecological projects compatible with the institute's work. The centers want to hear from and meet fellow ecologists. For addresses read *Earth Island Journal* or contact the institute (300 Broadway, Suite 28, San Francisco, California 94133; 415-788-3666).

GULF OF MAINE
61 Main Street
Brunswick, Maine 04011
207-729-5083

Gulf of Maine is an independent alternative bookstore owned by Beth Leonard and Gary Lawless. It serves as the Maine contact for Earth First! and for the bioregional movement. Store hours are Mon.-Sat. 9:30 A.M.-5:30 P.M.

LEARNING ALLIANCE
494 Broadway
New York, New York 10012
212-226-7171

The Learning Alliance receives visitors and links them to activities in the New York area. It can make referrals to a wide variety of organizations, mainstream and avant-garde.

Creating ties among people and among ideas is a central concern of the Learning Alliance. Thus it offers a comprehensive program of workshops, conferences, travel, and action/study groups, through cooperating with over a hundred community organizations.

The workshops bring together people with varying backgrounds. The alliance encourages them to create on-going groups, and it offers these groups support. Those already formed include alternative economics and Green politics study groups and a network of holistic health and community health practitioners.

The alliance publishes a free calendar of its programs. Phone to get on the mailing list. Prices of events in New York range from free to about $45 and vary with ability to pay.

WETLANDS PRESERVE
161 Hudson St. (Corner of Laight)
New York, New York 10013
212-966-4225; for a tape of environmental notices 212-966-5244

Wetlands Preserve opened in early 1989 as an environmental rhythm and blues nightclub. It features the Earth Station, an information center with bulletin boards, brochure holders, a calendar, and a concession stand for eco-material. Each Sunday at 5:00 P.M. it hosts the Eco-Salon, an ecological networking social club to which everyone is invited; and the second Wednesday of every month, 5:00–8:00 P.M., is given to eco-networking. Sundays after 6:00 P.M. speakers, films, and musicians take the stage. Natural, vegetarian snacks are on sale, along with draft beer. The club is open from 5:00 P.M. until the early morning hours daily, except Sat. when it opens at 9:00 P.M.

CENTER FOR GLOBAL SUSTAINABILITY
1817 White Avenue
Knoxville, Tennessee 37916
615-524-4771; 615-573-2322

The center is the focal point for activities of the Foundation for Global Sustainability, with clean water, forest preservation, and peace projects. It also serves as an office for the Shaconage Greens and the Oak Ridge Environmental Peace Alliance, as well as a resource pool for other organizations and individuals concerned with regional ecological issues. Visitors are welcome. Call or write for hours.

THE MISSISSIPPI 2020 NETWORK
P.O. Box 31292
Jackson, Mississippi 39286
601-366-8467; 800-844-8467 in Mississippi

For an orientation to Mississippi, contact the 2020 Network, a statewide community of active visionaries. The Network created and is a member of the state's first environmental coalition, ECO-MS, the Environmental Coalition of Mississippi. It holds a monthly workshop in Jackson on a topic of concern to the public, has established a bookstore and an audiovisual resource center, and is organizing an affordable housing project. In addition, it is assisting groups that are fighting waste incinerators. An emerging project is creating a statewide women's political network that will encourage and train women to seek elective office, with the aim of transforming state politics. Another is an after-school youth environmental studies program.

RENAISSANCE BOOKSTORE
1337 East Montclair
Springfield, Missouri 65804
417-883-5161

An alternative bookstore, Renaissance has a bulletin board and publishes the quarterly *Imagine Magazine* to publicize area activities. Open Mon.-Sat. 10 A.M.-7:00 P.M., Sun. noon-5:00 P.M.

SLAUGHTER ENERGY ENTERPRISES
3517 Virginia
Kansas City, Missouri 64109
816-931-0742

An avid networker with contacts in the North American Bioregional Congress, All Species Project, and other organizations, Stan Slaughter would like to meet eco-wanderers. A major interest at Slaughter Energy Enterprises is insulating and otherwise making old buildings energy efficient. Stan Slaughter also works in eco-theater and collects, learns, and performs topical eco-music. He has produced a cassette and matching song book, "In Tune with All Species" ($10).

HIGH WIND BOOKS AND RECORDS
3041 North Oakland Avenue
Milwaukee, Wisconsin 53211
414-332-8288

Selling alternative literature, with an emphasis on health and new age music, High Wind has become a networking center in Milwaukee for the High Wind Association that owns High Wind Farm and for other alternative groups and individuals. Hours are Mon.-Thurs. 10:00 A.M.-7:00 P.M.; Fri. 10:00 A.M.-9:00 P.M., Sat. 10:00 A.M.-7:00 P.M., Sun. noon-5:00 P.M.

NORTHERN SUN ALLIANCE
1519 East Franklin Avenue
Minneapolis, Minnesota 55404
612-874-1540

A hundred-year-old building at 1519 East Franklin houses the Alliance's Rainbow Rags, Honor the Earth Recycling Center, and *Northern SunNews*, and provides temporary office space for other environmental and alternative organizations. Stop by to learn what is going on in Minneapolis. Rainbow Rags sells used clothing and household items, an excellent supply of second-hand books, and new environmental cards and tee shirts. It is open Mon.-Sat. 11:00 A.M.-5:30 P.M.

At this writing, Northern Sun is raising money to buy the building. If the Alliance cannot do so, it will have to move. Phone before going.

NORTHERN ALASKA ENVIRONMENTAL CENTER
218 Driveway
Fairbanks, Alaska 99701
907-452-5021

Since 1971 the center has been the U.S.'s northernmost environmental group working on the issues facing arctic and interior Alaska. The staff is happy to receive visitors. Call ahead, as office hours vary.

ECOLOGY HOUSE
341 SW Morrison
Portland, Oregon 97204
503-223-4883

Founded in 1983, Ecology House features gifts with environmental themes, including windchimes, educational games, synthetic scrimshaw, and fine art prints. Products and services support a vegetarian-based, cruelty-free lifestyle.

The store does not represent any particular environmental or animal issues organization, but the staff can direct people to organizations that focus on their areas of concern. Also, the store provides free literature on environmental and animal issues.

Ecology House #1 is at 1441 Pearl Street, Boulder, Colorado 80302 (303-444-7023); Ecology House #2 is at 49 Exchange Street, Portland, Maine 04101 (207-775-1281).

NORTHCOAST ENVIRONMENTAL CENTER (NEC)
879 9th Street
Arcata, California 95521
707-822-6918

The center welcomes visitors, including those who want to know about meetings and outings in northern California or whom to contact for help with environmental problems. It has a library of 7,500 volumes and extensive files in which members of the public can do research. Its monthly *Econews* is basic reading for environmentalists throughout California.

Among the many accomplishments of NEC since its founding in 1971 is a state-wide Adopt-a-Beach program, started by NEC to clean local beaches. It played a leading role in the successful campaign to prevent the construction of the G-O (Gasquet-Orleans) Road through the Six Rivers National Forest, a road that would have desecrated an area sacred to Indians. The center is run by a coalition of ten organizations, each of which has a member on the board. The office is open Mon.-Sat. 10 A.M.-5:00 P.M.

ASHKENAZ
1317 San Pablo Avenue
Berkeley, California 94702
415-525-5054

Ashkenaz serves vegetarian lunch Tuesday through Friday. Evenings, except Monday, it offers music, dancing, and vegetarian snack bar food. Half the programs "are folk dances from other cultures; the rest, music from the Third World." Alternative groups occasionally hold benefits there; and they post notices on a bulletin-board wall. Office hours, when the building is always open, are Tue.-Thur. 11:00 A.M.-5:00 P.M.

ECOLOGY CENTER
2530 San Pablo Avenue (just south of Dwight)
Berkeley, California 94702
415-548-2220

The Berkeley Ecology Center handles some four hundred queries a month on environmental matters, and will be glad to answer questions from traveling ecologists. Its monthly newsletter includes current environmental information, directories, and a comprehensive list of upcoming regional environmental events. The center has a large library of books, periodicals, and files of clippings on more than six hundred topics. The public may consult the materials at the center, but only members can borrow books. The center's store stocks books, environmental periodicals and journals, organic gardening supplies and recycled paper.

The center's work in Berkeley includes sponsoring the city's farmers' markets (Derby Street between Milvia and Martin Luther King, Tues. 2:00–7:00 P.M.; Center Street between Milvia and Martin Luther King, Sat. 10:00 A.M.-2:00 P.M.) and operating a curbside recycling program, through which trucks visit each Berkeley neighborhood weekly. The center is open Tue.-Sat. 11:00 A.M.-5:00 P.M.

BACK OF BEYOND BOOKSTORE
P.O. Box 387, 83 North Main Street
Moab, Utah 84532
801-259-5154

The bookstore, which opened in early 1990, is intended to be a tribute to and a legacy of Edward Abbey. Its collection emphasizes the outdoors, natural history, the environment, and the Colorado Plateau. The store serves as a distribution point for information on the West's environment and public lands and offers numerous newsletters from organizations. Open from approximately 10 A.M.-9:00 P.M. daily in summer; 10:00 A.M.-6:30 P.M. in winter.

THE EARTH STORE
2369 Westwood Boulevard
Los Angeles California 90064
213-441-1758

The Earth Store sells a complete array of earth-sensitive products: water saving devices, 100% recycled computer paper, cruelty-free cosmetics, solar batteries, environmental magazines, etc. It has a bulletin board for announcements. Hours are 10:00 A.M.-6:30 P.M. daily.

THE GREEN STORE
2232 Sunset Cliffs Boulevard
Ocean Beach, California 92107
619-225-1083

The Green Store sells and distributes material for organizations and sells Guatemalan clothing, recycled paper items, and other environmentally benign products such as energy-efficient light bulbs. It is open Tues.-Sat. 10:00 A.M.-7:00 P.M.; Sun. noon-7:00 P.M.

PROJECT EARTH RESOURCES CENTER
127 West Drachman
Tucson, Arizona 85705
602-882-5341

Staffed by volunteers, Project Earth Resources Center includes an information center, library with books and videos, viewing room, bookstore, and gift shop. The Center hopes to evolve into an umbrella organization for the local environmental movement. Current programs include recycling, monitoring ozone levels, and organizing field trips and hikes. Hours are 9:00 A.M.-9:00 P.M. daily.

Appendix

APPENDIX I

Sources of Outdoor Equipment, Maps, and Information

If you're looking for equipment one of the first places to consult is Recreational Equipment, Inc. (REI), the nation's largest consumer cooperative with more than 711,000 members. Founded in Seattle in 1938, REI sells outdoor gear and clothing through nineteen stores, most in the West, and a mail-order catalog.

In 1984 REI founded the Wilderness Campaign with a $100,000 grant, and in 1985 provided a grant of $103,000 to establish a National Trails Coalition to lobby Congress on behalf of trails. It continues to support these and related organizations; in 1988, with a $35,000 grant, it established a coalition headed by American Rivers to protect the nation's free-flowing rivers.

A lifetime membership in REI costs $10. Members own the company and elect the governing board. At the end of each year they receive a dividend based on the sum of their purchases. To sign up, contact REI, P.O. Box 88125, Seattle, Washington 98138 (800-426-4840).

Equipment stores are a grand place to meet fellow outdoor enthusiasts and to receive tips on events and sites in the local area as well as advice on purchases, as the better stores employ sales people active in the sports for which they sell equipment. Army and navy surplus stores may yield bargains, although they are not generally the place to go for advice. Some local outdoor stores subsidize with money or goods local conservation activities. Patronizing these stores and letting them know why is a way of voting with your dollars.

A brand of outdoor clothing to choose to support the environment is Patagonia. The company, owned by the climber Yvon Chouinard, is generous with donations to environmental organizations and encourages other firms to give also. For a catalog, write to Patagonia, Mail Order, P.O. Box 8900, Bozeman, MT 59715.

The principal federal mapping agency is the Department of Interior's Geological Survey (USGS), but other federal, state, and local agencies, and private companies also produce maps useful for recreational and environmental purposes. A one-stop source of information on maps and cartographic data is the USGS's National Cartographic Information Center, U.S. Geological Survey, 507 National Center, 12201 Sunrise Valley Drive, Reston, Virginia 22092; 703-860-6045. The NCIC, which compiles information on the work of all government agencies and of private companies, also operates regional offices. The offices accept orders for aerial photographs and satellite imagery and sell custom cartographic products.

U.S. GEOLOGICAL SURVEY

The best known maps of the USGS are its 7.5 minute topographic quadrangles, the "topo maps" commonly used by hikers. The scale of these maps is 1:24,000, like other such expressions of scale, a ratio. For the 7.5 minute map, 1 unit on the map equals 24,000 units on the ground; 1 inch on the map equals 2,000 feet. The area portrayed varies between 49 square miles and 71 square miles, depending on the latitude.

Not all parts of the country have yet been mapped to this scale. Between 1910 and 1950 the standard topographic quadrangles were 15-minute maps with a scale of 1:62,500 (1 inch = approximately 1 mile). Many of the 15-minute maps are still available. Each 15-minute map shows between 197 and 282 square miles. The USGS also issues topographical map series in intermediate scale: 1:100,000 quadrangle and county maps; and in small scale: 1:250,000 and 1:1,000,000 quadrangles.

Other USGS publications include a series of topographical maps showing areas in the National Park System and National Wildlife Refuges; a series of land use maps; various thematic maps, including the National Wilderness Preservation System and Alaska National Interest Lands; and National Atlas Separates. The National Atlas was published in 1970 and is out of print, but separate sheets of selected reference and thematic maps are still available, some of them in updated editions.

An outstanding example of the updated separates is the handsome "Potential Natural Vegetation" by A. W. Kuchler. The map is color keyed to show "the vegetation that would exist [in the United States] today if man were removed from the scene and if the plant succession after his removal were telescoped into a single moment." It thus "reveals the biological potential of all sites." Other National Atlas Separates of interest include Major Forest Types, and Federal Lands.

The USGS offers free indexes and catalogs to the maps of each state and also free indexes to a number of its series, including the *Index to Small-Scale Maps of the United States* and the *Index to Intermediate-Scale Mapping/Index to County Mapping.* Indexes are sheets showing an outline of the state or nation. Marked on them are the areas covered by individual maps, usually with their names and dates.

The indexes, like the maps themselves, can be ordered by mail from Map Sales, U.S. Geological Survey, Box 25286, Federal Center, Denver, Colorado 80225; 303-236-7477. They can also be obtained over the counter from USGS Public Inquiries Offices across the country, which double as sales and information centers. Filling mail orders takes at least three weeks. Therefore, purchasers may prefer to buy from a Public Inquiries Office or commercial distributor.

The best way to gain a grasp of the variety of information offered by the USGS is to obtain their free brochures. Geological Survey Circular 900, "Guide to Obtaining USGS Information," describing the organization of the USGS and its services, is available from the survey's Books and Open File Department, P.O. Box 25425, Federal Center, Denver, Colorado 80225; 303-236-7476. Also available from this office is a booklet explaining "Topographic Maps." The Map Sales office distributes the valuable brochures, "Catalog of Maps," explaining the types of maps sold and where to get them, and "Catalog of Cartographic Data," describing types of information other than maps. Requests for material must be made in writing. For assistance in selecting or ordering maps call 800-USA-MAPS.

The Mid-Continent Mapping Center of the USGS's National Cartographic Information Center gives tours of its facilities during which visitors can see all phases of the mapping process. For a tour, go to the center between 8:00 A.M. and 3:00 P.M., 1400 Independence Road, Rolla, Missouri 65401; 314-341-0851.

NATIONAL PARK SERVICE

The USGS is the main source for maps of the National Park system. However, the National Park Service issues some recreational and historic maps available at the parks themselves or from the service's

Public Information Office, P.O. Box 37127, Washington, D.C. 20013-7127; 202-208-4747.

U.S. FISH AND WILDLIFE SERVICE

In cooperation with the USGS, the Fish and Wildlife Service produced eighty-three Coastal Ecological Inventory Maps at 1:250,000 scale, indicating important species and their habitat. These are sold by the USGS.

U.S. FOREST SERVICE

The Forest Service sells maps of the National Forests, National Forest Wilderness Areas, and other special designated areas, usually at a scale of 1/2 inch or 1 inch = 1 mile, plus visitor maps with points of interest and camping and recreational facilities marked. The maps can be ordered from the appropriate regional office of the Forest Service or from the supervisor of the Forest in question.

BUREAU OF LAND MANAGEMENT (BLM)

The BLM publishes 1:100,000 quadrangle maps of surface management and surface minerals management, distributed by the USGS. BLM state and district offices distribute free recreational maps, usually one for each district, showing land ownership, major roads, campgrounds, and points of interest. BLM also puts out excellent, small-scale, statewide maps for the Western states, indicating Wilderness Areas and Wilderness Study Areas. They can be ordered from BLM's state offices.

DEPARTMENT OF AGRICULTURE

The Aerial Photography Field Office of the Agricultural Stabilization and Conservation Service is the depository and reproduction center for photographic film acquired by this service, the Soil Conservation Service, and the U.S. Forest Service. Their combined aerial photography covers about 95% of the 48 contiguous states. Reproductions are available at scales ranging from 1 inch = 4,833 feet to 1 inch = 200 feet for costs of $3 to $50 each. Obtain ordering information from the Aerial Photography Field Office, P.O. Box 30010, 2222 West 2300 South, Salt Lake City, Utah 84130 (801-524-5856), or from your local Agricultural Stabilization Conservation Service office.

OTHER SOURCES

Each state has a geological survey, which works with the USGS. Much, but not all, state geological mapping is available from the USGS. State agencies involved in environmental protection and in fish and game management may also produce maps, as may state transportation departments.

DeLorme Mapping Company is bringing out an Atlas and Gazetteer Series "mapping America's back roads – one state at a time." Completed volumes contain a wealth of information on recreational possibilities (P.O. Box 298-88, Freeport, Maine 04032; 207-865-4171).

A relatively inexpensive source of satellite photography is the National Oceanic and Atmospheric Administration, Satellite Data Services Division, Room 100, Princeton Executive Center, Washington, D.C. 20233 (301-763-8400), which distributes images taken by U.S. oceanographic and meteorological satellites.

The Department of Commerce's National Oceanic and Atmospheric Administration is the source for information on weather patterns. Available data is described in the 338-page *Selective Guide to Climatic Data Sources*, free of charge from the National Climatic Data Center, Federal Building, Asheville, North Carolina 28801. The customer service staff at this center answers written or phone (704-259-0682) questions in regard to the availability of information. For the cost of reproduction (minimum charge $5), they will furnish available climatic summaries for specific sites.

The agency's series, "Climatological Data," includes monthly bulletins and an annual bulletin for each state. Together these bulletins trace temperature, precipitation, evaporation, soil temperature at a specific depth, and wind movement for well over eight thousand weather stations. Departures from the norm are stated, allowing the norms to be calculated. As a general rule, "Climatological Data" can be found only in large libraries. More accessible, commercially published almanacs, including the World Almanac, contain weather summaries for selected places. The National Atlas includes climatological maps.

Major publishers of books on hiking, paddling, cycling, and other outdoor recreation include the Appalachian Mountain Club (5 Joy Street, Boston, Massachusetts 02108; 603-466-2721), Menasha Ridge Press (P.O. Box 7, Carborro, North Carolina 27510; 919-967-8920); Mountaineers Books (306 Second Avenue W, Seattle, Washington

98119), Sierra Club Books (730 Polk Street, San Francisco, California 94109), and Wilderness Press (2440 Bancroft Way, Berkeley, California 94704; 415-843-8080). They send catalogs on request.

Environmental Magazines and Computer Networks

The following list is intended to guide readers to a few basic written resources and is by no means comprehensive. Prices are given only for items that individuals would be likely to purchase rather than to consult in a library.

MAGAZINES

Many additional periodicals are listed with the associations that publish them. Prices are for a one year subscription to an individual within the United States.

Alternative Energy Sourcebook and Real Goods News
Published by Real Goods Trading Company, 966 Mazzoni Street, Ukiah, California 95482 (707-468-9214). *Real Goods News*, published three times a year, updates the annual *Sourcebook*. The *Sourcebook* costs $10 postpaid; a subscription to Real Goods, which includes the Sourcebook, is $20. These publications are catalogs of a firm selling alternative energy products. They are excellent sources of basic information about alternative energy equipment in general and tell the pros and cons of specific items as experienced during actual use.

The Animals' Agenda
Published by Animal Rights Network, 456 Monroe Turnpike, Monroe, Connecticut 06468 (203-452-0446); subscriptions: P.O. Box 6809, Syracuse, New York 13217. $22. Discusses all types of animal abuse. Gives notes on events and campaigns to stop this abuse.

The Animals' Voice Magazine

Published bimonthly by the Compassion for Animals Foundation, 3960 Landmark Street, Culver City, California 90232. Subscriptions from P.O. Box 16955, North Hollywood, California 91615. $20. *Animals' Voice* speaks out against all forms of cruelty to animals.

Buzzworm: The Environmental Journal

Published bimonthly by Buzzworm, Inc., 2305 Canyon Blvd., Suite 206, Boulder, Colorado 80302. $18. Subscriptions from P.O. Box 6853, Syracuse, New York 13217. Articles in this handsome magazine emphasize enjoying and preserving the great outdoors.

Catalyst

Published quarterly by Catalyst Press, P.O. Box 1308, Montpelier, Vermont 05601. $25. Edited by Susan Meeker-Lowry, this newsletter discusses investing in social change.

Climbing

Published bimonthly. Order from Climbing, P.O. Box 339, Carbondale, Colorado 81623 (303-963-9449). $24. Gives an overview of the U.S. climbing scene. Includes news, equipment surveys, columns on technique and medicine, and reviews of outdoor books.

Continuing the Conversation: A Newsletter on the Ideas of Gregory Bateson

Published quarterly by HortIdeas Publishing, Route 1, Box 302, Gravel Switch, Kentucky 40328. $8. Coverage includes topics in ecology, psychology, and religion and their interrelationships.

Creation

Published six times a year by Friends of Creation Spirituality. The Circulation Office: 160 East Virginia St., Suite 290, San Jose, California 95112–5848. $20. Brings fresh insights into the Western religious tradition through scripture, the creation mystics of the West, the wisdom of earth-centered native spiritualities, dialogue with Eastern religions, and creative contemporary thinkers in such fields as Green politics, the new physics, bioregionalism, and creation spirituality.

E. The Environmental Magazine

Published bimonthly by Earth Action Network, P.O. Box 5098, Westport, Connecticut 06881 (203-854-5559). Subscriptions, P.O. Box 6667, Syracuse, New York 13217. $20. A nonprofit publication, *E* serves as a clearinghouse magazine for the environmental advocacy community, and reports on the spectrum of environmental issues and organizations. It is directed to concerned members of the general public as well as to environmental activists.

Environment

Published ten times a year by Heldref Publications, a division of the Helen Dwight Reid Educational Foundation in cooperation with the Scientists' Institute for Public Information, 4000 Albemarle Street NW, Washington, D.C. 20016. $24. Each issue includes three major articles on national and international topics, news notes, and book reviews.

Environmental Ethics

Published quarterly by Environmental Philosophy, Inc., Chestnut Hall, 1926 Chestnut Street, University of North Texas, Denton, Texas 76203-3496. $18. Articles discuss the philosophical aspects of environmental problems.

Garbage: The Practical Journal for the Environment

Published Bimonthly by Old House Journal Corporation, 435 9th St., Brooklyn, New York 11215 (718-788-1700). $21. Garbage tells consumers how to reduce the negative impact their households make on the environment.

High Country News

Biweekly, Box 1090, Paonia, Colorado 81428 (303-527-4898). $24. High Country News is a highly respected voice on environmental issues in the West.

Home Power

Published bimonthly by *Home Power Magazine* (A Division of Electron Connection, Inc.), P.O. Box 130, Hornbrook, California 96044 (916-

475-3179). $10. Contains practical, hands-on information about using renewable resources in home sized, stand-alone electrical systems.

HortIdeas

Published monthly by HortIdeas Publishing, Route 1, Box 302, Gravel Switch, Kentucky 40328. $15. Emphasizing ecological ideas, this periodical is packed with information for both organic and non-organic gardeners and horticulturists. Summaries of reports of useful recent research are a major element.

Native Nations

Published monthly by the Solidarity Foundation, P.O. Box 1201, Radio City Station, New York, New York 10101 (212-765-9731). Subscriptions from 175 5th Avenue, New York, New York 10010. $20. Presents a full spectrum of news and opinion from Native Americans. Coverage includes environmental issues.

Natural History

Published monthly by the American Museum of Natural History, Central Park West at 79th Street, New York, New York 10024. $22. Conveys the fascination of the natural world through colored photographs and texts written by professional scientists for the educated layperson. Harvard University professor Stephen Jay Gould's monthly column is particularly fine.

New Options

Published monthly; P.O. Box 19324, Washington, D.C. 20036 (202-822-0929). $25, less depending on your financial situation. Discusses post-liberal approaches to politics.

Northern Sun News

Published monthly by Northern Sun Alliance, 1519 East Franklin Ave., Minneapolis, Minnesota 55404 (612-874-1540). Since 1978 *Northern Sun News* has been a voice for the Midwest on alternative energy and alternative politics. Free, but for mailing to an address a $15 donation is requested.

Nuclear Times

Published quarterly by Nuclear Times, Inc., 401 Commonwealth Avenue, Boston, Massachusetts 02215 (617-266-1193). $15. Created in 1982 to serve the peace movement, *Nuclear Times* suspended publication in the spring of 1989. When it recommenced a year later, it had a broadened coverage: peace, justice, and the environment—issues that affect global security.

Organic Gardening Magazine

Published monthly by Rodale Press, Inc., 33 East Minor Street, Emmaus, Pennsylvania 18098 (215-967-5171). $25. Through *Organic Gardening* Rodale Press has been teaching Americans how to garden without using synthetic chemicals since the 1940s.

Soil Remineralization: A Network Newsletter

Published three times a year by Joanna Campe, 152 South Street, Northampton, Massachusetts 01060 (413-586-4429). $12. Provides a means of keeping up with the soil remineralization movement, which contends that human activities and demineralization of our soils over thousands of years are bringing on another Ice Age, through causing a decline in the vegetation biomass and an increase in the level of carbon dioxide in the atmosphere.

Solar Age or Ice Age? Bulletin

Published almost annually by Don Weaver, P.O. Box 1961, Burlingame, California 94010 (415-342-0329). Inquire as to price. The *Bulletin* is a lengthy resource book of the remineralization movement.

Utne Reader

Published bimonthly by LENS Publishing Company, The Fawkes Building, 1624 Harmon Place, Minneapolis, Minnesota 55403 (612-338-5040). Subscriptions from Box 1974, Marion, Ohio 43305. $18. Consists, for the most part, of articles first published in other alternative publications.

Whole Earth Review

Published quarterly by Point, 27 Gate Five Road, Sausalito, California 94965 (415-332-1716). $20. Articles and book reviews cover a wide variety of holistic topics as well as computer technology. Editors J. Baldwin and Stewart Brand published in 1990 the excellent *Whole Earth Ecolog*.

Wild Earth

Published by the Wild Earth Association, P.O. Box 492, Canton, New York 13617 (315-379-9940). $20. Quarterly in 1991; frequency may subsequently increase. Created in 1991, *Wild Earth* takes an uncompromising position on issues relating to wilderness, wildlife, and biodiversity. The perspective is biocentric. Editors are Dave Foreman and John Davis, formerly editors of *Earth First! Journal*.

COMPUTER NETWORKS

The major U.S. computer networks for environmentalists and peace activists are those operated by the Institute for Global Communications (IGN): EcoNet and PeaceNet. A member of one network is able to use the other and to be reached by members of the other. The networks offer several services: *Electronic mail* allows members to send private to one another and to members of many other computer networks around the world. *Conferences* give users access to information on a specific topic posted by conference managers and other users and allow discussion among members on the same general subject. *Databases* allow users to consult compilations of information on specific topics. A *user directory* permits a member to obtain a list of all other members except those requesting anonymity.

The charge for EcoNet or PeaceNet is modest. Econet costs $15 for signing up, a monthly fee of $10 allowing one free off-peak hour of use per month; $10 for every additional hour of peak use and $5 for every additional hour of off-peak use. However, if you do not live in a city with a node of Telenet (the data network that supports EcoNet and PeaceNet) you have to pay a phone company for a call to the nearest node whenever you use EcoNet or PeaceNet.

One of the greatest advantages of PeaceNet and EcoNet for somebody involved in international work is that a hookup with GreenNet, which serves the European environmental and peace movements, allows users to communicate with European activists for the same cost and as easily as with U.S. activists.

PeaceNet and EcoNet have the same address and phone number: 18 De Boom Street, San Francisco, California 94107 (415-923-0900).

Greenpeace invites the public to participate free of charge in its Environet computer bulletin board. For information contact Greenpeace Action, 139 Townsend Street, 4th Floor, San Francisco, California 94107 (415-512-9025).

National and Local Environmental Organizations

The lists of associations below are designed to provide resources in addition to those in the text rather than to serve as a directory of key organizations. With a few exceptions they do not include the associations described in the earlier chapters. The organizations that appear here are not necessarily more important than those described previously. Most of them are in this chapter, instead of earlier, because they do not operate projects that the general public can visit.

I emphasize national organizations here, because the previous chapters were devoted almost exclusively to local and regional entities. Most of the national organizations listed below offer publications, services, or opportunities for involvement (in addition to donating money) to individuals and local groups.

I list first general environmental associations (national and then regional or local), then associations working on the environment among other topics.

NATIONAL ENVIRONMENTAL ORGANIZATIONS

AMERICAN RIVERS CONSERVATION COUNCIL
801 Pennsylvania Avenue SE, Suite 400
Washington, D.C. 20003
202-547-6900

Since 1973, American Rivers, the only national organization devoted to preserving rivers and their landscapes, has helped gain permanent protection under the Federal Wild and Scenic Rivers Act for more than 7,000 miles of water. Among its projects is a Dam Early Warning System to inform local activists of proposed developments.

EARTH FIRST!

P.O. Box 5176
Missoula, Montana 59806-5716
406-728-8114

Earth First! takes a no compromise position on environmental issues. Earth First!ers use confrontation, guerrilla theater, and civil disobedience as well as more conventional tactics. A movement rather than an organization, Earth First! is made up of autonomous but cooperating elements including local Earth First! groups, the Earth First! Foundation, various task forces, and the periodical *Earth First!* ($20/year), one of two successors to the *Earth First! Journal* (1980–1990). The other is *Wild Earth* (see Appendix II). To find the nearest Earth First! group, look at the directory in *Earth First!* or call the above number.

EARTH ISLAND INSTITUTE

300 Broadway, Suite 28
San Francisco, California 94133
415-788-3666

Earth Island focuses on global issues, including the slaughter of dolphin by tuna fishermen and the damage that the military does to the environment. It sponsors a variety of projects, almost all of which welcome the involvement of activists; but each must be contacted separately to learn of opportunities. Obtain a list from the Earth Island office or read *Earth Island Journal*, published quarterly and mailed to members.

THE ECO-JUSTICE PROJECT AND NETWORK

Center for Religion, Ethics and Social Policy (CRESP)
Anabel Taylor Hall, Cornell University
Ithaca, New York 14853
607-255-4225

"Eco-justice" means working simultaneously for the ecology of the planet and the well-being of all its people. Through the project, ministers and social and physical scientists pool their knowledge and skills to serve churches, communities, and colleges. The organization offers a consulting service, presents conferences, and produces programs and program materials. Members receive *The Egg: A Journal of Eco-Justice* quarterly.

EDUCATIONAL COMMUNICATIONS
P.O. Box 35473
Los Angeles, California 90035-0473
213-559-9160

The many projects of the center include "Ecoview" newspaper articles; the bimonthly Compendium Newsletter with international, national, and southern California news ($20); the Directory of Environmental Organizations; and radio and television series produced and hosted by Nancy Pearlman.

"Environmental Directions" is a half-hour public affairs radio series that airs weekly in the United States and Canada. The programs are distributed to National Public Radio, American Public Radio, listener-sponsored, university-sponsored, and Indian stations. A list of the stations carrying "Environmental Directions" is available from the center. Audiocassettes of each program can be purchased ($15).

"Econews" is an innovative news, interview, and documentary television series. It covers all types of environmental issues and is aired weekly on some 65 outlets in 350 cities and hundreds of communities. Videocassettes can be purchased ($32).

ENVIRONMENTAL ACTION (EA) and
ENVIRONMENTAL ACTION FOUNDATION (EAF)
1525 New Hampshire Avenue NW
Washington, D.C. 20036
202-745-4870

Environmental Action engages in lobbying and political campaigning. EAF promotes citizen action through written material, technical assistance, and workshops. Areas of recent concern include the Right to Know Act, drinking water quality, reduction and recycling of solid waste, least-cost energy planning, and utility accountability. Publications include the bimonthly *Environmental Action* sent to members, the bimonthly *Power Line* (energy, $20), and the quarterly *Wasteline* (solid waste, $10).

ENVIRONMENTAL DEFENSE FUND (EDF)
257 Park Avenue South
New York, New York 10010
212-505-2100

EDF influences state and national policy through the work of its lawyers, scientists, and economists. Founded in 1968, it helped ban the use
of DDT in the United States. It still works on toxics issues—it drafted
and is pushing for the enforcement of California's Proposition 65,
which requires public disclosure of significant risks. It is also active on
such varied topics as Antarctica and energy conservation.

FRIENDS OF THE EARTH (FOE)
218 D Street SE
Washington, D.C. 20003
202-544-2600

In 1990 Friends of the Earth merged with the Environmental Policy
Institute and the Oceanic Society to form a new organization named
Friends of the Earth. Founded by David Browder, FOE had 37 international affiliates, which it brought to the new organization. The current
FOE describes itself as "an independent global advocacy organization
that works at local, national, and international levels to: protect the
planet, preserve biological, cultural, and ethnic diversity; and empower
citizens to have a voice in decisions affecting their environment and
lives." Publications include the general newsmagazine *Not Man Apart*
and three newsletters: "Atmosphere," "Community Plume" (on chemical safety), and "Groundwater News."

GREENPEACE USA
1436 U Street NW
Washington, D.C. 20009
202-462-1177

Greenpeace is best known for its non-violent direct actions designed to
call attention to environmental problems; but it also conducts research
and disseminates information on the results. It is the one nongovernmental organization that maintains a base in Antarctica. Nuclear
testing and whaling are major concerns.

NATIONAL AUDUBON SOCIETY
950 Third Avenue
New York, New York 10022
212-832-3200

Despite its name, the National Audubon Society does far more than study birds. Activities include lobbying on a wide range of issues, running a multi-level educational program, and acquiring and maintaining wildlife sanctuaries. Among its projects is an acid rain monitoring network. It has local chapters, not to be confused with independent organizations that also use "Audubon" as part of their names. Members receive *Audubon*, published six times a year. Subscriptions to the *Audubon Activist* ($20), published eleven times a year by the society, are sold to both members and non-members. The society's information service answers questions from the public on environmental topics.

NATIONAL WILDLIFE FEDERATION
1400 Sixteenth Street NW
Washington, D.C. 20036–2266
202-797-6800

The federation was founded in 1936 with the backing of businesses that had a financial interest in hunting. It still tends to represent the point of view of hunters; but, with a membership of some five million, is an influential voice for conservation. Among the society's many programs are Wildlife Camps for children and Teen Adventures. Its publications include the bimonthly *National Wildlife* and *International Wildlife* ($16 each) and, for children, the monthly *Ranger Rick* ($15), and *Big Backyard* ($12).

NATURAL RESOURCES DEFENSE COUNCIL (NRDC)
40 West 20th Street
New York, New York 10011
212-727-2700

The NRDC combines legal action, scientific research, and citizen education. Its many projects have included working with Soviet scientists in a nuclear test ban verification project, demanding environmental impact statements on nuclear reactors used in the production of nuclear weapons, and challenging U.S. Forest Service management plans. Members receive a newsletter and the quarterly *Amicus Journal*.

THE NATURE CONSERVANCY
1815 North Lynn Street
Arlington, Virginia 22209
703-841-5300

The Conservancy has as its "mission to find, protect, and maintain the best examples of communities, ecosystems, and endangered species in the natural world." Under agreements for the protection of land, it turns some of the land it obtains over to other organizations or agencies. It uses volunteers to help manage, monitor, and, if necessary, restore the preserves over which it retains ownership. To volunteer contact your local chapter or field office.

PROJECT LIGHTHAWK
P.O. Box 8163
Santa Fe, New Mexico 87504
505-982-9656

Lighthawk's pilots fly activists, journalists, legislators, and lawyers to and over areas they need to study and to meetings and hearings they would otherwise miss. Its tools include grassroots organizing, aerial photography, aerial surveys, and media coverage. Write or call if you need Lighthawk's help or want to offer support.

RENEW AMERICA
1400 Sixteenth Street, NW, Suite 710
Washington, D.C.
202-232-2252

An outgrowth of the organization Solar Action, Renew America is an education and networking forum for the efficient use of natural resources. Its *State of the States* (SOS) reports detail the performance of individual states on specific environmental issues. Renew America conducted campaigns in 1989 and 1990 to locate and publicize effective environmental projects. *Searching for Success*, the report of the 1990 campaign, costs $10.

STUDENT ENVIRONMENTAL ACTION COALITION (SEAC)
P.O. Box 1168
Chapel Hill, North Carolina 27514-1168
919-967-4600

"SEAC is a grassroots democratic network of students and student groups" on more than 1,000 campuses, "all working together to build a strong student movement to save the planet." It offers to help student activists with information and contacts. The newsletter *Threshold* helps keep members in touch with one another.

SIERRA CLUB
730 Polk Street
San Francisco, California 94109
415-776-2211

In this environmental organization policies on issues are developed by the membership through a procedure involving local groups, state chapters, regional councils, and the board of directors. Members receive *Sierra* every other month. The club's *National News Report*, published 24 times a year, is available by subscription ($18). At the headquarters is a bookstore and a library open to the public by appointment.

SOCIETY FOR CONSERVATION BIOLOGY
Blackwell Scientific Publications
Three Cambridge Center, Suite 208
Cambridge, Massachusetts 02142

Membership in this relatively new interdisciplinary society brings with it a subscription to the quarterly, *Conservation Biology*, worthwhile for all concerned with the preservation of natural systems.

SOCIETY FOR ECOLOGICAL RESTORATION AND MANAGEMENT
University of Wisconsin Arboretum
1207 Seminole Highway
Madison, Wisconsin 53711
608-263-7889

Members receive a monthly newsletter and the semi-annual *Restoration and Management Notes*, a forum for the exchange of news, views, and information. The office responds to questions on restoration, with information or with assistance in finding people who can answer.

WILDERNESS SOCIETY
900 17th Street NW
Washington, D.C. 20006–2596
202-833-2300

The work of the society centers in public lands issues, about which it serves as an information resource. Members receive the quarterly *Wilderness*. The society sells a variety of valuable publications that can help activists to impact the management of specific tracts of public land as well as overall policy.

UNITED NATIONS ENVIRONMENT PROGRAM (UNEP)—NORTH AMERICA OFFICE
Room DC2–0803, United Nations
New York, New York 10017
212-963-8093

UNEP has its headquarters in Kenya and an office in New York. Its mandate is to encourage and coordinate sound environmental practices. Among its projects is an environmental sabbath each June. At this time all faith communities are asked to examine their own traditions to find wisdom and guidance to inspire action. UNEP assists with publicity, materials, and leadership training.

The New York Office of UNEP publishes *UNEP North America News*, distributed free of charge (call or write to be put on the mailing list).

WORLD RESOURCES INSTITUTE
1735 New York Avenue NW, Suite 400
Washington, D.C. 20006
202-638-6300

The institute conducts policy research and analysis addressed to global resource and environmental issues. Every two years it issues a documented report on the status of the planet's resources, *World Resources*. Each report contains basic facts on all areas and more detailed treatment of "focus" areas, which vary with each issue.

WORLDWATCH INSTITUTE
1776 Massachusetts Avenue NW
Washington, D.C. 20036
202-452-1999

The institute researches and informs the public about trends in the global economy and the natural systems on which it depends. It publishes the bimonthly periodical *World Watch* ($15), a series of papers on specific topics, and the annual *State of the World, A Worldwatch Report on Progress toward a Sustainable Society* ($10.95 paperback).

LOCAL AND REGIONAL ENVIRONMENTAL ORGANIZATIONS

The list below is a small sample. For groups described elsewhere in the guide, check the indexes. In some states the most active general-interest environmental organizations are chapters or groups of national organizations/movements. When seeking local groups, do not overlook this possibility. Normally the national offices will give addresses for local groups. Also remember that the American Hiking Society has a database of trail-user groups. For additional leads consult the directories listed in this and earlier chapters, inquire at the local food co-op or other alternative business/association, or ask the state's department of environmental protection.

PRESERVE APPALACHIAN WILDERNESS (PAW)
P.O. Box 52A
Bondville, Vermont 05340
802-297-1022

A network of biocentric wilderness preservation and restoration groups in the eastern United States, PAW works to implement a vision of a vast wilderness corridor stretching from Canada to Florida. SouthPaw in the southeast and Preserve Adirondack Wilderness in New York state are affiliates.

AUDUBON SOCIETY OF RHODE ISLAND
12 Sanderson Road
Smithfield, Rhode Island 02911
401-231-6444

Founded in 1897, the society has a many-faceted environmental program including maintaining sanctuaries and organizing an annual fall birding weekend on Block Island.

CONNECTICUT AUDUBON SOCIETY
2325 Burr Street
Fairfield, Connecticut 06430
203-259-6305

Among its other activities the Connecticut Audubon Society manages fourteen sanctuaries, some of which offer educational programs to the public.

CHESAPEAKE BAY FOUNDATION
162 Prince George Street
Annapolis, Maryland 21401
301-268-8816

With 60,000 members this society works to protect the Chesapeake Bay and its tidal tributaries.

CONSERVATION COUNCIL OF NORTH CAROLINA
P.O. Box 37564
Raleigh, North Carolina 27627
919-851-5870

Over 45 organizations and 500 individuals make up the council, which is active in energy and environmental issues.

TENNESSEE ENVIRONMENTAL COUNCIL
1725 Church Street
Nashville, Tennessee 37203
615-321-5075

With a membership of 49 organizations and over 1,500 individuals, this umbrella association provides information, coordination, and leadership to Tennessee environmentalists.

HEARTWOOD
Route 3, Box 402
Paoli, Indiana 47454
812-723-2430

Formed in 1990 by activists from Kentucky, Illinois, and Indiana, Heartwood has as its mission the broadening of public understanding of the politics and ecology of the midwestern forests. It works for an end to logging of the public forests in the midwest.

NATIVE AMERICANS FOR A CLEAN ENVIRONMENT (NACE)
P.O. Box 1671
Tahlequah, Oklahoma 74465
918-458-4322

Founded in 1985 for the purpose of raising the consciousness of the general public about environmental issues with emphasis on the nuclear industry, this effective organization networks with environmental and Indian groups around the world. Industry projects of major concern include Kerr-McGee's uranium conversion facility. It publishes a monthly newsletter ($5).

CENTER FOR RURAL AFFAIRS
P.O. Box 405
Walthill, Nebraska 68067
402-846-5428

The purpose of the center is to provoke public thought about social, economic, and environmental issues affecting rural America, especially the Midwest and Plains regions. Projects include producing a curriculum in sustainable agriculture for high schools, studying and reporting on the federal Conservation Reserve Program, and conducting seminars, for people engaged in rural policy making.

MONTANA ENVIRONMENTAL INFORMATION CENTER
P.O. Box 1184
Helena, Montana 59624
406-443-2520

In addition to lobbying and monitoring the implementation of environmental laws, the center helps people in Montana communities with information and organizing advice.

GREATER ECOSYSTEM ALLIANCE

P.O. Box 2813
Bellingham, Washington 98227
206-671-9950

The alliance encourages a higher level of ecological understanding of Pacific Northwest issues through combining activism with conservation biology. It works to preserve the North Cascades, Selkirk, Olympic, and Central Cascades ecosystems.

OREGON NATURAL RESOURCES COUNCIL

Yeon Building, Suite 1050, 522 Southwest Fifth Avenue
Portland, Oregon 97204
503-223-9001

The council works in particular on wilderness, wild rivers, oceans, and wildlife issues.

COLORADO ENVIRONMENTAL COALITION

777 Grant Street, Suite 606
Denver, Colorado 80203
303-837-8701

The coalition coordinates work of the Colorado environmental community. It publishes the *Colorado Environmental Directory* (1990 ed. $5) to groups, coalitions, and public agencies.

CITIZEN ALERT

P.O. Box 5391
Reno, Nevada 89513
702-827-4200
or
P.O. Box 1681
Las Vegas, Nevada 89125
702-649-4384

Citizen Alert distributes a quarterly newspaper on environmental, nuclear, and military issues that confront Nevada, plus notices of relevant events. It has successfully countered such varied threats as a plan by Nevada National Guard to build a tank training range in central Nevada and the Thousand Springs coal-fired power plant.

ECOLOGY CENTER OF SOUTHERN CALIFORNIA
P.O. Box 35473
Los Angeles, California 90035
213-559-9160

This regional conservation organization is a project of Educational Communications, founded and overseen by Nancy Pearlman. Members receive *The Compendium Newsletter*.

SOUTHWEST RESEARCH AND INFORMATION CENTER
P.O. Box 4524
Albuquerque, New Mexico 87106
505-262-1862

In New Mexico the center works on such varied issues as forest planning, water quality, and the Waste Isolation Pilot Project (WIPP) for radioactive waste. Through its Washington office (110 Maryland Ave. NE, Box 21, Washington, D.C. 20002; 202-547-7040) it coordinates a national citizens' network of groups working to ensure that high-level radioactive waste is handled and disposed of safely. The offices welcome questions. The center publishes quarterly the *Workbook* ($12), focusing on social change and the environment.

NATIONAL ORGANIZATIONS THAT WORK ON THE ENVIRONMENT, AMONG OTHER ISSUES

CLERGY AND LAITY CONCERNED (CALC)
198 Broadway, Suite 305
New York, New York 10038
212-964-6730

CALC is a nation-wide, multi-racial network for people of faith and conscience from all walks of life. It exists to help build a movement of justice and peace. Among the issues on which it is active are toxics and nuclear weapons. CALC has local chapters in approximately thirty states.

FREEDOM OF INFORMATION CLEARINGHOUSE
P.O. Box 19367
Washington, D.C. 20036
202-833-3000

A project of Ralph Nader's Center for Study of Responsive Law, the clearinghouse provides technical and legal assistance to all who seek access to information held by government agencies. The staff is available for phone or mail consultations. The clearinghouse also litigates to protect the public's right to government information.

GOVERNMENT ACCOUNTABILITY PROJECT (GAP)
25 E Street NW, Suite #700
Washington, D.C. 20001
202-347-0460

GAP works with "whistle blowers," government employees who reveal problems in their agencies. It investigates their charges and, if found valid, publicizes them and, through litigation if necessary, sees to it that they are acted on. GAP is doing valuable work on nuclear reactors, food safety, and other issues.

NATIONAL CENTER FOR POLICY ALTERNATIVES (NCPA)
1875 Connecticut Ave. NW, Suite 710
Washington, D.C. 20009
202-387-6030

NCPA is a public policy center focusing on accomplishing positive changes at the state and local level. One of its main functions is helping legislators to draft legislative initiatives and to build the support necessary for passage. Environmental security is among the areas in which it works. Its State Support Center on Environmental Hazards publishes a newsletter on developments in the states, *Environmental State Report* ($30).

INTERFAITH IMPACT FOR JUSTICE AND PEACE
110 Maryland Avenue NE, Suite 509
Washington, D.C. 20002
202-543-2800

IMPACT is an ecumenical information/action network for influencing legislation and public policy. Its tools are testimony on Capitol Hill, congressional briefings, and letters and calls from members. It works on a cross section of issues of concern to the nation's churches and synagogues. One of its subnetworks is Environmental Stewardship. Members of National IMPACT receive Prepare (periodic background papers on emerging issues), Update (a monthly newsletter on the status of legislation), and Action Alerts for the network to which they belong. State IMPACT affiliates work on state issues.

NATIONAL SPELEOLOGICAL SOCIETY
Cave Avenue
Huntsville, Alabama 35810
205-852-1300

The society has more than 200 local chapters across the country, providing caving trips, training, and information. The national office will put you in touch with the nearest chapter and also offer opportunities to participate in their extensive program for the protection of caves, which are uniquely fragile ecosystems. One of the concepts promoted by the conservation committee is that of caves as underground wilderness.

PUBLIC CITIZEN
2000 P Street NW, Suite 605
Washington, D.C. 20036
202-833-3000

A membership organization, Public Citizen represents consumer interests through lobbying, litigation, research, and publications. It works through five divisions: Congress Watch; the Health Research Group; the Litigation Group; the Critical Mass Energy Project; and Buyers Up, a group-buying organization.

THE UNITED STATES PUBLIC INTEREST RESEARCH GROUP (US PIRG)
215 Pennsylvania Avenue SE
Washington, D.C. 20003
202-546-9707

Working in the fields of the environment/public health, consumer protection, energy policy, and government reform, US PIRG includes campus-based local groups, some of which have off-campus offices, and the national advocacy office at the above address. The campus-based groups control the national office. Call this office to locate the group nearest you. An example of a local campaign is Maryland PIRG's stopping of the construction of a mass-burn incinerator. US PIRG's quarterly report is *Citizen Agenda*.

Organizations Working in Specific Areas Related to Environmental Preservation

AGRICULTURE

AG ACCESS
603 4th Street
Davis, California 95616
916-756-7177

The firm Ag Access sells by mail and in its store "all available agricultural and horticultural books," and offers an out-of-print book service and an agricultural research service.

AMERICAN MINOR BREEDS CONSERVANCY
Box 477
Pittsboro, North Carolina 27312
919-542-5704

The Conservancy seeks to preserve endangered and minor breeds of farm animals through identifying them and making surveys of existing populations; promoting the use of rare breeds in appropriate commercial operations, homesteads, and living history museums and farms; and encouraging the formation of breed registry associations. It publishes a newsletter and annual Breeders Directory.

APPROPRIATE TECHNOLOGY TRANSFER FOR RURAL AREAS (ATTRA)
P.O. Box 3657
Fayetteville, Arkansas 72703
800-346-9140

A project of the U.S. Department of Interior, managed by the National Center for Appropriate Technology (NCAT), ATTRA fields questions on sustainable agricultural practices. It responds by sending information or providing referrals. Call 8:00 A.M.-5:00 P.M. Central Time.

BIO-DYNAMIC FARMING AND GARDENING ASSOCIATION
P.O. Box 550
Kimberton, Pennsylvania 19442
215-935-7797

The association supports training programs and scientific research; publishes and sells books; puts out the quarterly magazine *Bio-Dynamics* (a subscription is equivalent to membership) and a bimonthly newsletter; rents films and videos; sells compost preparations and starter; and operates an advisory service. The service is open to the public without charge, although donations are welcomed. Questions are referred to a network of specialists who answer by phone, letter, or even a farm visit.

INSTITUTE FOR ALTERNATIVE AGRICULTURE
9200 Edmonston Rd., Suite 117
Greenbelt, Maryland 20770
301-441-8777

Financed by nongovernmental sources, the institute serves as a sponsor of research and education outreach programs, a voice for alternative agriculture in Washington, a publisher, and a contact for people seeking information on sustainable farming systems. Its publications include the monthly *Alternative Agriculture News* and the quarterly *American Journal of Alternative Agriculture* ($20 for nonmembers). It responds to inquiries from individuals and groups.

OFFICE OF SMALL SCALE AGRICULTURE
Cooperative State Research Service
U.S. Department of Agriculture
Washington, D.C. 20251
202-447-3640

Opened in 1986, this office is interested in sustainable techniques as a means of helping small farmers. Its ongoing and planned initiatives include a quarterly newsletter; a series of one-page fact sheets, "A Small-Scale Agriculture Alternative"; a directory of small-scale agricultural specialists in research and education; and a video about making money on small-scale agriculture. The newsletter and fact sheets are free; the video can be rented.

SEED SAVERS EXCHANGE
Rural Route 3
Box 239, Decorah, Iowa 52101

Members of the exchange save old-fashioned food crops from extinction by locating gardeners who are keeping seeds that are family heirlooms, traditional American Indian crops, garden varieties of the Amish or Mennonites, varieties dropped from seed catalogs, or outstanding foreign vegetables. The exchange publishes an annual *Winter Yearbook* which contains the names and addresses of members and lists the more than 4,000 varieties that they are helping to maintain. It also publishes *The Garden Seed Inventory* (2nd edition), which lists nonhybrid varieties still commercially available and shows which the commercial sources are most likely to discontinue offering.

ANIMAL PROTECTION AND RIGHTS

FARM ANIMAL REFORM MOVEMENT (FARM)
10101 Ashburton Lane
Bethesda, Maryland 20817
301-530-1737

FARM seeks to reform today's intensive animal agriculture through regulatory legislation and a national boycott of animal products raised in an inhumane or unhealthful manner. Its campaigns include the annual Great American Meatout, 20 March (the first day of spring), when Americans are asked to "kick the meat habit"; World Farm Animals Day when the suffering and slaughter of animals is memorialized, 2 October (Mahatma Gandhi's birthday); a Veal Ban Campaign; and a Public Awareness Campaign using advertising and distributing literature.

ANIMAL LEGAL DEFENSE FUND (ALDF)
1363 Lincoln Avenue
San Rafael, California 94901
415-459-0885

ALDF seeks through litigation to further the interests of and establish rights for animals. An Emergency Response Network, responding to more than fifty calls a week, provides legal expertise on behalf of animals and animal advocates nationwide. Its booklet, "The Animals' Advocate: Investigating Animal Abuse," is available for $2.50 from the office.

DEFENDERS OF WILDLIFE
1244 19th Street NW
Washington, D.C. 20036
202-659-9510

Defenders works to preserve wildlife and wildlife habitat through education, litigation, research, and advocacy. It publishes *Defenders* bimonthly.

PEOPLE FOR THE ETHICAL TREATMENT OF ANIMALS (PETA)
P.O. Box 42516
Washington, D.C. 20015
301-770-7444

An educational and activist group, PETA opposes all forms of animal exploitation. It distributes much information that helps individuals to make a difference where they live, including free fact sheets, videos (rent or buy), a packet for setting up a literature table ($15), an activist manual ($5), a national list of phone tree nodes, and a suggestion-packed brochure "Once a Week, Once a Month, Get Active for Animals." *Peta News* is the organization's bimonthly periodical.

WILDLIFE DAMAGE REVIEW
P.O. Box 2541
Tucson, Arizona 85702-2541
602-882-4218

Wildlife Damage Review was founded in 1991 for the purpose of bringing widespread public scrutiny and critical review to the Animal Damage Control (ADC) Program, under which federal authorities harass and kill predators and other wild animals. The organization serves as a clearinghouse to store and share information about ADC activities and offers coordination and support to a broad range of groups and individuals working on the issue.

APPROPRIATE TECHNOLOGY

TRANSNATIONAL NETWORK FOR APPROPRIATE/ ALTERNATIVE TECHNOLOGIES (TRANET)
Box 567
Rangeley, Maine 04970
207-864-2252

TRANET links autonomous individuals and organizations directly with one another. The Rangeley office acts as a clearinghouse and switchboard to help create the linkages and promote mutual aid among members. Six times a year it publishes TRANET, a newsletter/directory. Each issue contains short news items from around the world on alternative technology and related topics, and also a directory of organizations working on a given topic. The membership fee ($30 for an individual) covers a year's subscription for the subscriber and one for an individual, group, or library in the Third World. TRANET has developed a mini library of 100 do-it-yourself manuals and other resources on self reliance. Donations are placed in a fund for the library. The organization is 100% volunteer.

ECONOMICS

E. F. SCHUMACHER SOCIETY
Box 76, R.D. 3
Great Barrington, Massachusetts 01230
413-528-1737

An educational organization to promote the ideas in E. F. Schumacher's *Small Is Beautiful* (1973), the society sponsors the Annual E. F. Schumacher Lectures, organizes seminars, and sponsors and develops local programs such as the Community Land Trust in the South Berkshires and the Self-Help Association for a Regional Economy (SHARE). SHARE collateralizes loans to small businesses and is issuing a regional currency, Berkshares. The society sells copies of the lectures for $3 each. It is initiating a library devoted to collections of books and papers on decentralism. The public may consult materials in the library by appointment and may call the library at the above number with reference questions.

GOOD MONEY PUBLICATIONS
Box 363
Worcester, Vermont 05682
800-535-3551

This company will furnish information on the social responsibility of corporations. It charges a fee for the service and provides free estimates of the cost of answering specific requests. It publishes the bimonthly *Good Money* and the bimonthly *Netback News* for socially conscious investors ($75 for both). It is also putting out a series of issue papers, *Environmental Issue and Investment Strategies,* with information on publicly traded companies that pollute the environment and corporations that respond best to ecological concerns ($20 each).

THE SEVENTH GENERATION FUND
P.O. Box 10
Forestville, California 95436
707-887-7420

The fund provides financial and technical assistance to rebuild the political, cultural, and economic infrastructure of Native American nations. It publishes *Native Self-Sufficiency* quarterly ($8).

ENERGY

CRITICAL MASS ENERGY PROJECT
215 Pennsylvania Avenue SE
Washington D.C. 20003
202-546-4996

A division of Public Citizen, the Critical Mass Energy Project conducts research and publishes reports on nuclear and alternative energy. Among its reports is an annual assessment of nuclear power plant safety ($7.50 for activists).

CONSERVATION AND RENEWABLE ENERGY INQUIRY AND REFERRAL SERVICE (CAREIRS)
Box 8900
Silver Spring, Maryland 20907
800-523-2929

CAREIRS answers questions and publishes informational brochures on conservation and renewable energy. It refers technical questions to NATAS and other sources.

ENERGY CONSERVATION COALITION
1325 New Hampshire Avenue NW
Washington, D.C. 20036
202-745-4874

An alliance of 20 organizations, this coalition engages in lobbying and public education for energy conservation. Updates on its campaign are included in Environmental Action's *Powerline*. Send an SASE for a list of its publications.

NATIONAL APPROPRIATE TECHNOLOGY ASSISTANCE SERVICE (NATAS)
P.O. Box 2525
Butte, Montana 59702
800-428-2525; in Montana, 800-428-1718

NATAS provides tailored information and technical assistance on energy conservation and energy-related appropriate technologies, including the marketing of energy-related inventions. It can be reached weekdays 8:00 A.M.-5:00 P.M. Mountain Time.

SAFE ENERGY COMMUNICATION COUNCIL
1717 Massachusetts Avenue NW, Suite LL215
Washington, D.C. 20036
202-483-8491

The Council assists public interest organizations in obtaining time to air their views on television and radio and in generally sharpening their approach to the media. It presents workshops on working with the media, for local public-interest organizations, environmental and otherwise. Its publications include occasional Myth-Busters, factual brochures on energy issues.

HEALTH

CALIFORNIA SCHOOL OF HERBAL STUDIES
Box 39
Forestville, California 95436
707-887-7457

Dedicated to the exploration and development of healing with herbs, the school offers a comprehensive range of long-term, week, weekend, and one-day events in San Francisco and in Forestville. Each September it sponsors a herb retreat at Breitenbush in Oregon. The retreat is a celebration of herbalism, with herb walks, workshops, and demonstrations.

HUMAN ECOLOGY ACTION LEAGUE (HEAL)
P.O. Box 49126
Atlanta, Georgia 30359
312-665-6575

HEAL concerns itself with an illness known as chemical hypersensitivity or environmental or ecological illness. Victims of chemical hypersensitivity become ill when in contact with small amounts of widely used "safe" chemicals. HEAL promotes research, publicizes chemical sensitivity, works to curb the use of pesticides and other toxic or sensitizing chemicals, and establishes local chapters that provide emotional support for members and educate their communities. It publishes a quarterly, the *Human Ecologist*, and operates an information service that answers questions. A safe lodging directory for people with chemical sensitivity is available for $3.50.

THE NATIONAL FOUNDATION FOR THE CHEMICALLY HYPERSENSITIVE
P.O. Box 9
Wrightsville Beach, North Carolina 28480

With chapters in 40 states, the Foundation helps people who know or fear that they may have become ill from 302 chemicals, to locate a physician and puts them in contact with others who can give them support. In order to publicize chemical hypersensitivity, it compiles information on people with the illness and conducts research on pollution and its effects Memberships and newsletter subscriptions are available.

INTERNATIONAL OUTREACH

CONSERVATION INTERNATIONAL
1015 18th Street NW, Suite 1000
Washington, D.C. 20036
202-429-5660

Conservation International acts as a catalyst for conservation action by bolstering local and national organizations in tropical nations. It was the first nonprofit conservation organization to transact a debt-for-nature swap. It used a foundation donation to purchase Bolivian debt, which was then converted into local currency to support a large conservation project in Bolivia. It has since formed a Conservation Financing Program to transact additional debt conversions and to explore other opportunities for tapping new or little used sources of local currency. Members receive the quarterly report *Tropicus* and other special publications.

FOOD FIRST
Institute for Food and Development Policy
145 Ninth Street
San Francisco, California 94103
415-864-8555

A research and education center, Food First is dedicated to finding and revealing the causes of hunger and to ending the problem. In the past it has chiefly worked abroad, but it is now also working within the United States. The newsletter, "Food First News," is sent to members. The association encourages activists to develop local Food First Associates groups.

RAINFOREST ACTION NETWORK (RAN)
301 Broadway, Suite #A
San Francisco, California 94133
415-398-4404

RAN organizes citizens to work on rainforest protection, and answers questions from the public. To anyone interested in local organizing it gives guidance and materials on setting up a Rainforest Action Group (RAG). As a result of its emphasis on outreach, there are now more than seventy RAGs across the United States and RAGs in other countries.

NUCLEAR ISSUES

CHRISTIC INSTITUTE
1324 North Capitol Street NW
Washington D.C. 20002
202-797-8106

The Christic Institute is best known for its prosecution of the Karen Silkwood case. It is also involved in litigation seeking to expose corrupt practices of the Nuclear Regulatory Commission, although its major project is on "Contragate." The institute builds coalitions and educates the public around its legal cases. In these efforts, it seeks help from local people.

THE NATURAL RIGHTS CENTER
P.O. Box 90
Summertown, Tennessee 38483
615-964-3992

A project of Plenty-USA, the center litigates on nuclear issues and other environmental concerns.

NUCLEAR INFORMATION AND RESOURCE SERVICE (NIRS)
1424 16th Street NW, Suite 601
Washington, D.C. 20036
202-328-0002

NIRS is a national clearinghouse and networking center for people concerned about nuclear power issues. Besides conducting its own research and publishing the biweekly *Nuclear Monitor* ($250), NIRS answers questions and helps groups obtain materials, if necessary by filing Freedom of Information Act requests. Members receive action alerts and the periodical *Groundswell,* and participate in a computer bulletin board, NIRSNET.

NUKEWATCH, THE PROGRESSIVE FOUNDATION
P.O. Box 2658, 1127 University Avenue
Madison, Wisconsin 53701
608-256-4146

Founded in 1979, Nukewatch in recent years has focused on creating national campaigns to stimulate greater resistance to militarism by calling attention to the nuclear weapons in our midst. Among these campaigns are a watch for H-bomb trucks and the dissemination of citizen action guides for major nuclear weapons laboratories and factories. Citizens are invited to join in the campaigns. For information on how to spot an H-bomb truck, for instance, contact the organization.

RADIOACTIVE WASTE CAMPAIGN
625 Broadway, 2nd Floor
New York, New York 10012
212-473-7390

This organization, which concentrates on nuclear waste issues, sells helpful materials including *Living without Landfills: Confronting the Low-Level Radioactive Waste Crisis* ($11 postpaid) and *Deadly Defense: Military Radioactive Landfills* ($15 postpaid).

RADIOACTIVE WASTE MANAGEMENT ASSOCIATES
306 West 38th Street, Room 1508
New York, New York 10018
212-629-5612

The associates work with citizens' groups confronting radioactive waste problems. A senior associate is Marvin Resnikoff, author of *Living without Landfills* and co-author of *Deadly Defense*.

UNION OF CONCERNED SCIENTISTS
26 Church Street
Cambridge, Massachusetts 02238
617-547-5552

UCS is an organization of scientists and other citizens focusing on nuclear power safety, national energy policy, and arms control. It carries on research, lobbying, and education. Occasionally it puts on televised programs, which the organization's sponsors across the nation publicize. Sponsors receive *Nucleus* quarterly and, if they wish, the bimonthly action newsletter "Catalyst." UCS has a major publishing program. The first five copies of its briefing papers are free.

PEACE

ACCESS
1730 M Street NW, Suite 605
Washington, D.C. 20036
202-785-6630

A non-advocacy security information service, ACCESS answers, or guides to the best sources of information, questioners seeking information on such subjects as arms control, regional conflicts, and the peace movement. ACCESS associates can freely use the Inquiry Service and a Speaker Referral Service, and receive all reports in the series Security Spectrum and Resource Briefs. (To become an associate costs an individual $30). ACCESS responds to occasional questions from people who are not associates as an introduction to the service and as a contribution to public education. The *ACCESS Resource Guide: An International Directory of Information on War, Peace, and Security* (Ballinger, 1988; $14.95) describes over six hundred organizations and institutions in sixty countries. *Search for Security* is a guide to foundations in peace, security, and international relations (2nd ed., 1990; $50).

ARMS CONTROL RESEARCH CENTER
Center for Peace and Progressive Politics
942 Market Street, Suite 202
San Francisco, California 94102

The center researches and publicizes the environmental impact of the military establishment and armed conflict.

CENTER FOR ECONOMIC CONVERSION
222C View Street
Mountain View, California 94041
415-968-8798

Founded in 1975, the center educates the public about the need for positive alternatives to excessive military spending and facilitates the process of converting to an economy responsive to human and environmental needs. It offers workshops across the country and assists communities in planning and effecting conversions. Its publications include the quarterlies *Positive Alternatives* (free to members) and *The Base Conversion News* (given in return for a donation).

JOBS WITH PEACE CAMPAIGN
76 Summer Street
Boston, Massachusetts 02110
617-338-5783

Jobs with Peace is a national effort to redirect federal funds from military spending to programs for people. Its key goals are providing viable examples of economic conversion of military facilities and encouraging local, state and federal conversion planning. Local Jobs with Peace Campaigns are active in Philadelphia and in Minnesota among other places.

NUCLEAR FREE AMERICA
325 East 25th Street
Baltimore, Maryland 21218-9944
301-235-3575

This Baltimore organization is an international clearinghouse and resource center for Nuclear Free Zones. It publishes the newsletter the "New Abolitionist" and maintains an online database of Department of Defense prime contracts for nuclear weapons from which it can print custom reports. Prices are available on request.

OAK RIDGE ENVIRONMENTAL PEACE ALLIANCE
P.O. Box 1101
Knoxville, Tennessee 37901
615-524-4771

Formed in 1988, the alliance illustrates the spread of opposition to nuclear weapons production that damages the environment as well as increases the likelihood of war. The alliance is committed to educating the public about issues of public and environmental health and safety at Oak Ridge. It also provides a public forum to raise questions about the need for nuclear weapons production in the post cold-war era.

RURAL SOUTHERN VOICE FOR PEACE (RSVP)
1898 Hannah Branch Road
Burnsville, North Carolina 28714
704-675-5933

RSVP offers education, training, and organizing assistance to activists in the Southeast. Representatives go to a community to assess a group's strengths and weaknesses and set up an appropriate program. Its Listening Project provides communications training that helps activists to influence previously hostile people. RSVP publishes a newsletter.

SANE/FREEZE
1819 H Street NW, Suite 640
Washington, D.C. 20006
202-862-9740

Formed by the merger of SANE and the Freeze Campaign in 1988, this association represents more than 150,000 members. Public education, political campaigning, and lobbying are main modes of action. It has numerous local chapters and produces factual brochures that activists can distribute. The SANE Education Fund in Philadelphia founded and produces the nation's only nationally syndicated radio program for peace and justice, Consider the Alternatives.

SKYGUARD/RAMA
2544 N. 47th Street
Milwaukee, Wisconsin 53210
414-871-2003

A program of the Rural Alliance for Military Accountability, Skyguard aims to stop overflights by low-flying and supersonic military aircraft. It has set up a hot line for the reporting of problems with military aircraft (800-SKYGUARD). The organization will funnel complaints to the appropriate government offices and use the data to help demonstrate the severity of the problem, eventually in testimony to Congress. It publishes a quarterly journal *Skyguard*.

PESTICIDES

BIO-INTEGRAL RESOURCE CENTER (BIRC)
P.O. Box 7414
Berkeley, California 94707
415-524-2567

The center compiles information on the least toxic pest control methods and publishes it in *The IPM Practitioner*, a survey of the field for professionals, and *Common Sense Pest Control Quarterly*, detailed articles for the general public on the control of specific pests. Members can obtain advice by telephone or mail. Allow time for the staff to gather information.

NATIONAL COALITION AGAINST THE MISUSE OF PESTICIDES
701 East Street SE, Suite 200
Washington, D.C. 20003
202-543-5450

NCAMP is a national, community-based network committed to pesticide safety and the adoption of alternative pest management strategies that reduce or eliminate toxic chemicals. It publishes a newsletter for members, "Pesticides and You," and a monthly, *NCAMP's Technical Report* ($20). It welcomes questions on pest control methods, but may have to ask that requesters agree to pay a couple of dollars on receipt of the information and wait a few weeks for it to arrive. NCAMP asks victims of pesticide poisoning to report their illness to the association.

NATIONAL PESTICIDE TELECOMMUNICATION NETWORK
Texas Tech., University Health Science Center, School of
    Medicine, Department of Preventive Medicine
4th Street and Indiana
Lubock, Texas 79430
800-858-7378

Sponsored by the U.S. Environmental Protection Agency, the network provides information to the public on pesticides.

UNITED FARM WORKERS
P.O. Box 62
Keene, California 93570
805-822-5571

Under the leadership of Cesar Chavez, the United Farm Workers is campaigning to make food safe to eat and to achieve safe working conditions for farm laborers. By means of a boycott, it is focusing on stopping the application of five dangerous pesticides to grapes.

POPULATION

CARRYING CAPACITY NETWORK
1325 G Street, NW, Suite #1003
Washington, D.C. 20005-3104
202-879-3044

The Network facilitates information exchange and cooperation among nonprofit organizations and activists on environmental, population, resource, and sustainability issues, and helps organizations and individuals concerned with carrying capacity to communicate with policy makers and with the public. Network participants receive the *Clearinghouse Bulletin*. The Network offers, by subscription, *Carrying Capacity News/Focus* ($20) and a *Fax Alert Service* ($25).

NEGATIVE POPULATION GROWTH
P.O. Box 1206, 210 The Plaza
Teaneck, New Jersey 07666-1206
201-837-3555

This organization, founded in 1972, believes that "a drastic reduction in total population size represents the only viable option consistent with human survival." It is educating the public to encourage the United States and other countries to establish national human population control programs. It advocates voluntary methods of lowering the birth rate, including tax incentives. Its publications include the *NPG Forum*.

ZERO POPULATION GROWTH
1400 Sixteenth Street NW
Washington, D.C. 20036
202-332-2200

A membership organization, Zero Population Growth works to achieve a sustainable balance between the world's human population and its environment. The organization's tools are educational programs for schools, media and public information campaigns, and citizen action efforts to build congressional support for key population issues.

SOCIAL/ENVIRONMENTAL QUESTIONS

ELMWOOD INSTITUTE
P.O. Box 5765
Berkeley, California 94705
415-845-4595

The Elmwood Institute was founded by Fritjof Capra to help facilitate the shift from a mechanistic and patriarchal world view to a holistic and ecological view. Through small gatherings, conferences, and publications, the institute hopes to cross-fertilize new ideas, develop ecological visions, and apply those visions to the solution of social, economic, environmental, and political problems. Members receive the "Elmwood Newsletter" quarterly. The institute welcomes help from volunteers for its projects.

ESALEN INSTITUTE
Big Sur, California 93920
408-667-3000

The institute is a center to explore those trends in the physical and behavioral sciences, education, religion, and philosophy that emphasize human potential. Its activities consist of seminars and workshops, residential programs, consulting, and research.

Weekend and five-day workshops introduce people to Esalen. Often they go on to seminars or enroll in a work/study program. When rooms are free, people can stay at Esalen without participating in a program. Accommodations are shared, and the rate is variable and subject to change. For information call 408-667-3005.

Garden tours are held twice a month from April to Sept. Cost is $10. Phone 408-667-3000 for information.

INSTITUTE FOR SOCIAL ECOLOGY
P.O. Box 89
Plainfield, Vermont 05667
802-454-8493

Since its creation in 1974, the institute has pioneered programs that focus, from a critical perspective, on the relationship of people to nature. Social ecology suggests that reharmonizing the relationship of people to one another will reharmonize their relationship to the natural world and thus make possible the creation of an alternative future. The approach is interdisciplinary and holistic. The institute therefore offers courses, workshops, and seminars, integrating theory and practice, in such areas as ecofeminism, bioregional agriculture, community technology, community and holistic health, and social theory. Students may obtain college credit for courses through their home institution or through Goddard College or Burlington College. Graduate students may earn a Master of Arts in Social Ecology from Goddard College.

The institute has begun publishing a series of monographs. The initial titles are *Social Ecology and Community Development, Reconstructive Anthropology, The Utopian Impulse,* and *Handbook on Composting.* For ordering information contact the office. It has also started a mail-order bookstore, for which a free catalog is available on request.

SPIRITUAL/ENVIRONMENTAL QUESTIONS

CENTER FOR REFLECTION ON THE SECOND LAW
8420 Camelia Drive
Raleigh, North Carolina 27612
919-847-5819

The center is one of the most radical theological think tanks in the country. In the summer of 1988 it hosted the international Fourth World Assembly.

CHINOOK LEARNING CENTER
Box 57
Clinton, Washington 98236
206-321-1884 or 467-0384

Located on Whidbey Island, Chinook was founded in 1972 as a contemplative learning center and dispersed covenant community. Basing its work on the link between the inner transformation of the individual and responsible action in society, Chinook was inspired by the sixth-century Celtic Christian monastic school on Iona, which combined the power of spiritual vision with creative action and service to the world. To carry out its purpose, it offers workshops, conferences and long-term programs.

INSTITUTE IN CULTURE AND CREATION SPIRITUALITY
Holy Names College
3500 Mountain Boulevard
Oakland, California 94619

In the words of Thomas Berry, the institute is "awakening Christian consciousness to its religious and moral responsibility for the fate of the earth." It offers a nine-month Master of Arts degree, a nine-month certificate, and a sabbatical program of approximately four months either fall or spring. Its three track options are Culture and Spirituality, Geo-justice and Spirituality, and Creation Spirituality and Psychology. Faculty include Matthew Fox, OP; Starhawk; and Brian Swimme.

TOXICS

CITIZEN'S CLEARINGHOUSE FOR HAZARDOUS WASTE (CCHW)
Center for Environmental Justice
P.O. Box 6806
Falls Church, Virginia 22040
703-237-2249

The clearinghouse characterizes itself as an environmental crisis center that focuses its work on grassroots environmental organizations across the nation. It offers an excellent information service and a wide range of publications, including the bimonthly *Everyone's Backyard*, which is sent to members.

GREEN LIBRARY
1918 Bonita Avenue
Berkeley, California 94704
415-841-9975

Green Library provides ecological literature to children, students, and environmental activists in Eastern Europe and the Third World. It solicits used or unsold books and periodicals on all topics relating to the environment and for all levels of readers, from preschool to postgraduate. The books go to educational institutions, public libraries, and health centers.

HIGHLANDER RESEARCH AND EDUCATION CENTER
Route 3, Box 370
New Market, Tennessee 37820
615-933-3443

The Highlander Center played an influential and courageous role in the Civil Rights movement. In 1989 it created Stop the Poisoning Schools, modeled on its earlier Citizenship Schools. The center makes its facilities available for workshops, and researches and publishes reports.

NATIONAL TOXICS CAMPAIGN FUND
1168 Commonwealth Avenue
Boston, Massachusetts 02134
617-232-0327

Arranges analyses of soil, water, air, and waste samples at well below commercial cost.

ROCKY MOUNTAIN STUDENT ENVIRONMENTAL HEALTH PROJECT
Department of Environmental Health
B127 Microbiology Building, Colorado State University
Fort Collins, Colorado 80523
303-491-7038

The project does soil and water testing for community groups at low cost.

SERVICE TRAINING FOR ENVIRONMENTAL PROGRESS (STEP)

c/o Center for Health Services
Station 17, Vanderbilt University
Nashville, Tennessee 37232
615-322-6278

Students offer technical assistance to community groups during the school year. In the summer they work in the field on environmental health projects.

VIRGINIA STUDENT ENVIRONMENTAL HEALTH PROJECT

Virginia Polytechnic Institute and State University
202 Architecture Annex
Blacksburg, Virginia 24061
703-231-6953

A program of the university's Center for Environmental and Hazardous Material Studies, the project provides technical resources for community groups confronting environmental contamination, including year-round laboratory service.

TRANSPORTATION

ALLIANCE FOR A PAVING MORATORIUM

c/o Fossil Fuels Action
P.O. Box 8558
Fredericksburg, Virginia 22404

The alliance works to achieve a national moratorium on paving new roads and parking lots. It circulates a petition, educates the public and officials by additional means, and conducts research on the ramifications of the nation's road building program and alternatives. At this writing, it was forming a road-fighting task force to assist communities seeking help. Jan Lundberg, executive director of the alliance, co-founded the *Lundberg Letter* for the oil industry in 1973.

BICYCLE NETWORK
P.O. Box 8194
Philadelphia, Pennsylvania 19101
215-222-1253

The network publishes *Network News*, a grassroots information service on bicycle transportation and human-powered transit technology, distributed quarterly to participants in more than twenty countries. Each issue consists of clippings on every aspect of human-powered transit.

NATIONAL ASSOCIATION OF TRANSIT CONSUMER ORGANIZATIONS (NATCO)
442 Summit Avenue, #2
Saint Paul, Minnesota 55102
612-227-5171

NATCO serves as a contact point for transit consumer organizations.

TRANSPORTATION ALTERNATIVES
494 Broadway
New York, New York 10012
212-941-4600

The activities of this New York-based organization headed by Charlie Komanoff include promoting legislative initiatives in Congress to reduce reliance on the automobile and develop a national system of alternatives. The organization's Auto-Free New York Committee (212-475-3394) developed a four-year plan for New York that would drastically improve metropolitan transit service; reduce auto travel in Manhattan by 20%, throughout the city by 5%; and introduce a network of auto-free streets. It works with city officials to realize these goals.

WASTE MANAGEMENT

INSTITUTE FOR LOCAL SELF-RELIANCE
2425 18th Street NW
Washington, D.C. 20009
202-232-4108

Through its research, publications, and technical assistance, the institute shows cities and neighborhoods how to benefit from the wealth they own by putting their assets to work and keeping the profits. At present it is emphasizing waste management. Among its publications is the Directory of Waste Utilization Technologies ($50). The institute searches its data base for a fee, but will send anyone who requests information articles and publications lists on solid waste management.

NATIONAL RECYCLING COALITION (NRC)
1101 30th Street NW, Suite 305
Washington, D.C. 20007
202-625-6406

The coalition brings together individuals, state and local governments, industry, and environmental groups to promote recycling. Members receive *Resource Recycling* magazine. The headquarters responds to questions about recycling.

NEW HAMPSHIRE RESOURCE RECOVERY ASSOCIATION
P.O. Box 721
Concord, New Hampshire 03301
603-224-6996

Founded in 1980 with a Board of Directors representing New Hampshire municipalities, the association acts primarily as a "broker" of recyclable materials for members. The staff seeks out long-term contracts with buyers of recyclables, so that they can guarantee the municipalities that belong to it long-term markets.

SOUTHEAST WASTE EXCHANGE
The University of North Carolina at Charlotte
Urban Institute
Charlotte, North Carolina 28223
704-547-2307

The Southeast Waste Exchange is a nonprofit information clearinghouse established to identify and bring together industrial waste generators with potential users, and companies seeking waste management services with those that can provide them. It furnishes information, research, and education services and publishes a bimonthly catalog, the Waste Watcher, listing materials available or wanted, and products and services available. The exchange was established in 1978 as a service for Mecklenberg County; in 1981 it expanded to cover all of North and South Carolina, and in 1986 to cover the whole Southeast. For additional information contact Maxie L. May at the exchange.

There are approximately fifteen regional waste exchanges, most of them nonprofit. By communicating with one another, they form a national network.

WORK ON WASTE (WOW)
82 Judson Avenue
Canton, New York 13617
315-379-9200

Under the leadership of Ellen and Paul Connett, WOW works with community organizations across the nation fighting incinerators and promoting recycling. Members receive *Waste Not: The Weekly Reporter for Rational Resource Management.*

WATER

CLEAN WATER ACTION PROJECT
317 Pennsylvania Avenue SE
Washington, D.C. 20003
202-547-1196

This national citizens' organization works for clean water and control of toxic chemicals. It provides strategies to local groups and local citizens beginning to organize themselves. It has a number of local and regional offices.

THE IZAAK WALTON LEAGUE OF AMERICA
1401 Wilson Boulevard, Level B
Arlington, Virginia 22209
703-528-1818

The league was founded in 1922 by prominent sportsmen and writers, and it continues to reflect the interests of hunters and fishermen. It founded the Save Our Streams program in which individuals or groups monitor sections of waterway. Publications include aids to monitoring water quality.

WILLIAM HOOVER CHEMICAL LABORATORY
264 High Street
Morgantown, West Virginia 26507

A program of West Virginia Mountain Stream Monitors and Appalachia-Science in the Public Interest, William Hoover tests water at minimal rates for consumer groups, environmental organizations, and concerned individuals. At present testing is for inorganic pollutants, conductivity, and pH.

General Index

Geographical Index

Sites mentioned in the book are divided by state below. Within each state, sites are listed by either the city in which they are located or by the geographical area within the state (northwest Alabama, for example). Sites that defy specific geographical placement (rivers, for example) are listed at the beginning of each state entry, by page number only.

ALABAMA
Dauphin Island: 141; Montgomery: 135; northwestern Alabama: 206; Tuskeegee: 14–15

ALASKA
308, 314, 323, 337; Anchorage: 155; Fairbanks: 326, 358, 388; Homer: 358; Palmer: 33; southcentral Alaska: 179

ARIZONA
8; Bisbee: 246; Hereford: 373; Mayer: 127; Mesa: 318; Oracle: 60; Page: 147; Phoenix: 195, 267, 268; Scottsdale: 16; southwestern Arizona: 170, 203; Tucson: 40, 60, 125, 272, 349, 352, 391

ARKANSAS
Clarksville: 167; Eureka Springs: 259, 284; Fayetteville: 348; Fox: 31; Jacksonville: 147; Perryville: 71

CALIFORNIA
217, 228, 336; Arcata: 84, 261, 351, 359, 383, 389; Berkeley: 85, 88, 89, 112, 130, 139, 389, 390; Beverly Hills: 256, 266; Bodie: 262; Brisbane: 274; Carmel: 19; Claremont: 55; Coarsegold: 240; Daggett and Kramer Junction: 63; Davis: 123, 339; Eureka: 349; Geyserville: 72: Harper Lake: 63; Hornbrook: 118; Klamath: 147; Lee Vining: 261; Lompoc: 134; Los Angeles: 45, 69, 100, 129, 149, 333, 346, 391; Martinez: 10–11; Middletown: 119; Monterey: 291, 333;

Moscone 53; Napa: 55; New Cuyama: 55; Norden: 372; northeastern California: 208; northern California: 183, 186; northwestern California: 170; Oakland: 292, 333; Ocean Beach: 391; Palo Alto: 340; Pasadena: 75; Petrolia: 285; Philo: 371; Riverside: 37; Rohnert Park: 67; Sacramento: 54, 63, 125; San Diego: 318, 333, 337; San Francisco: 45, 122, 149, 285, 303, 327, 333, 337, 360; San Jose: 333; San Luis Obispo: 125; San Mateo: 256; Santa Barbara: 67, 219, 291, 333; Santa Cruz: 37, 219, 333, 360, 382; Santa Monica: 352; Santa Rosa: 66; Sausalito: 35, 142; southern California: 188, 189, 234; Terminal Island: 276

COLORADO
Aurora: 64; Basalt: 35; Boulder: 339; Crested Butte: 255; Denver: 85, 124, 299; Durango-Silverton: 335; Gardner: 36; Mesa Verde: 47; northwestern Colorado: 186; Ouray: 73; Pueblo: 318; San Luis: 54; Silverton: 247; Snowmass: 59, 75; Snowmass Village: 152; Telluride: 36, 260; Valmont: 156; west central Colorado: 187

CONNECTICUT
Bridgeport: 354; Greenwich: 244; Hartford: 318, 345

FLORIDA
217; Cape Canaveral: 66; Gainesville:

ABOUT THE AUTHOR

Mary Davis is publisher and staff writer for the new environmental magazine *Wild Earth*. With a master's degree in library science from Simmons College and a doctorate in English from the University of Wisconsin, Madison, she has served as an academic librarian, taught college English, and edited the *Kentucky Review*, the Sierra Club's national *Energy Report*, and reports of Appalachia – Science in the Public Interest. Her publications include *The Military-Civilian Nuclear Link: A Guide to the French Nuclear Industry* (Westview, 1988), *The Green Guide to France* (Green Print, 1990), *Old Growth in the East: A Preliminary Overview* (Earth First! Journal, 1990) and numerous articles on nuclear and environmental issues. She currently divides her time between upstate New York; central Kentucky; and Lyon, France, where she is U.S. liaison and a board member for the Center for Documentation and Research on Peace and Conflicts.

Other Noble Press Books
When You Care...It's Noble

ECO-WARRIORS:
Understanding the Radical Environmental Movement
Rik Scarce

An in-depth and movingly eloquent look at the people, the actions, the history and the philosophies behind such groups as Earth First!, The Sea Shepherds, Greenpeace, and the Animal Liberation Front.

"...intriguing, if sometimes disturbing reading...a fine account for anyone looking for insight into the environmental movement." *New York Times Book Review*

"Warning! Potent ideas at work." *The Bloomsbury Review*

"[A] good and honest book that tells about an important social movement." *San Francisco Chronicle*

$12.95, paperback, 320 pages

EMBRACING THE EARTH:
Choices for Environmentally Sound Living
D. Mark Harris

A practical guide on how to turn every day into an Earth Day. Contains over 200 do-able projects to begin living more lightly on the Earth. Charmingly illustrated and gently persuasive. Directories.

"This book is not only a call to action, it is the guide you need to act." *East West*

"*Embracing the Earth* encourages us to live an environmentally sound lifestyle 365 days a year [and] Harris makes you want to." *South Carolina Wildlife*

$9.95, paperback, 164 pages

HANDLE WITH CARE:
A Guide to Responsible Travel in Developing Countries
Scott Graham

Practical guide on how to travel responsibly in such countries as India, Peru, and Mexico, among others. Based on Graham's extensive travels to Third World countries, *Handle With Care* shows the traveller how to help preserve the natural environment, observe local customs, support the local economy, and find responsible tour groups.

$7.95, paperback, 120 pages

POISONING OUR CHILDREN:
Surviving in a Toxic World
Nancy Sokol Green

Suggestions on how to rid your home of the deadly toxic chemicals that are a part of all our lives, by a woman suffering from Environmental Illness.

$12.95, paperback, 300 pages

A JUST AND LASTING PEACE:
The History of the U.S. Peace Movement from the Cold War to Desert Storm
Roger C. Peace III

A comprehensive history of how community, peace, and religious organizations have attempted to impact public opinion and U.S. policy on war, nuclear arms, and human rights. Photographs, maps, directories.

$14.95, paperback, 370 pages

LIVE THIS BOOK:
Abbie Hoffman's Philosophy for a Free and Green America
Theodore Becker and Anthony Dodson

An examination of the social and environmental philosophy expounded by one of America's most controversial and humorous political satirists.

$8.95, paperback, 120 pages

TERRORISM UNMASKED:
The Psychology, Tactics, and People Behind Worldwide Terrorism
Greg Petrakis

An in-depth look at worldwide terrorism, with specific reference to its threat to the United States. Also examined are terrorist ideologies, agendas, and methods.

$13.95, paperback, 350 pages

A FAR CRY FROM HOME:
Life in a Shelter for Homeless Women
Lisa Ferrill

The moving account of woman who worked side by side with homeless women as program director of a homeless shelter in New York City.

"A *very* important work." Jonathan Kozol

$10.95, paperback, 172 pages.

TENDER MERCIES:
Inside the World of a Child Abuse Investigator
Keith Richards

A harrowing first-person account of a Child Protection Service Worker whose job it is to investigate cases of child abuse. Co-published by the Child Welfare League of America.

$10.95, paperback, 192 pages

THE GOOD HEART BOOK:
A Guide to Volunteering
David E. Driver

A guide to becoming a volunteer, including a step-by-step plan for choosing the right volunteer job, overviews of areas of social concern, and profiles of human care organizations, professionals, and volunteers.

"One of the most significant books written about social change I have read in the last few years. Read it and share it." *St. Anthony's Messenger*

$9.95, paperback, 250 pages

ANCHORS FOR THE INNOCENT:
A Single Parent's Guide to Raising Children
Gail Christopher, D.N.

Strategies for single parents on how to raise healthy, happy, and emotionally balanced children. Topics include how to build support networks, meet financial needs, maintain a healthy diet, and build self esteem.

$11.95, paperback, 256 pages

JOYCE ANN BROWN:
Justice Denied
Joyce Ann Brown

The story of a black woman who served nine years in prison for a murder she did not commit. Her long nightmare was the focus of *Sixty Minutes* investigations, but the full story of the brutality, the tedium, the legal battles, and the long fight for freedom is documented here in this tragic instance of "justice denied."

"An autobiographical lament that serves as a compelling indictment of the U.S. judicial system. A frank, moving account." *Booklist*

"Readers get a crash course in life in a women's prison" *New York Times Book Review*

$11.95, paperback, 178 pages

PICTURE THIS!
A Guide to Over 300 Environmentally, Socially, and Politically Relevant Films and Videos
Sky Hiatt

Reviews of movies that address such subjects as racism, poverty, environmental destruction, political oppression, and animal cruelty, among others. Movies reviewed include *The Atomic Cafe, All Quiet on the Western Front, Mississippi Burning*, and *Drugstore Cowboy*.

$11.95, paperback, 288 pages

THE HUMAN SIDE OF DIABETES:
A Self-Help Guide for People with Diabetes and their Families
Mike Raymond

A guide to accepting, understanding, and coming to terms with diabetes, by a college professor who has had diabetes for nearly forty years. Contrasts problems people with diabetes face on daily basis with specific advice on how to handle them.

$12.95, paperback, 288 pages

TWENTY-SOMETHING, FLOUNDERING & OFF THE YUPPIE TRACK:
A Self-Help Guide to Making It Through Your Twenties
Steven Gibb

A practical but humorous look at how to make the most out of one of the most difficult periods in life, by a twentysomething psychologist. Chapters include Leaving the Beer Kegs Behind, Finding Meaningful Work, How to Survive on $14,000 a Year, Moving in With Mom and Dad—Again.

$9.95 paperback, 192 pages

TWISTED:
One Drug Addict's Desperate Struggle for Recovery
C. Adam Richmond

The powerful and shocking autobiographical account of an addict and his twenty-year battle with drugs. The book examines the life of an addict and the depths Richmond reaches before he finally seeks and is ready to receive help. A must read for addicts, their families and loved ones, and anyone wanting to understand the horrors of drug addiction.

$11.95, paperback, 224 pages

CHARLES VII AT THE HOMES OF HIS GREAT VASSALS
Alexandre Dumas

The first ever English translation of this play by Alexandre Dumas, which deals with issues of racism. The introduction by Dorothy Trench-Bonett brings to light the little known fact of Dumas' African heritage.

$10.95, paperback, 150 pages

All books are available from your local bookstore or directly from The Noble Press. Please add $1.50 for postage and handling for one book, $1.00 for each additional book.

The Noble Press
213 W. Institute Place, Suite 508
Chicago, IL 60610
1-800-486-7737